What people are sa, ⌄

The Flying Springbok

An absorbing account of a major international airline told against a background of pivotal historic, political, social and technical events. A fascinating and enlightening read.
Charles Kohlhase, Mission Design Manager, NASA's VOYAGER Spacecraft Interplanetary Mission, Jet Propulsion Laboratory (JPL) California.

This is a great story that includes world history wrapped in the aluminum skin of aviation. It contains extraordinary detail that burrows through wars, racism, determination, success, death and rebirth as South African Airways seeks new life after 2020. It is a wonderful read that should be mandatory for students of history and both civil and military service schools.
Brigadier General Bob Jordan, (retired), US Army

This is a fascinating tale that covers not only the development of air travel between Southern Africa and the rest of the world but also the too little-known evolution of the great, giant continent of Africa. The detailed aspects on aircraft and the amazingly courageous characters who flew the planes is spellbinding. This is a wonderful window on world history and is not to be missed.
Captain Stuart Bird-Wilson, (retired), British Special Air Services

This is a detailed and marvelous history of flying, commercial aviation and South Africa in general. It brought back many memories of my own career. The author has done an outstanding job of research and I highly recommend it to aviation aficionados, historians and general readers everywhere.
Lieutenant Colonel Ed Reynolds, (retired), US Air Force

Also by Lionel Friedberg

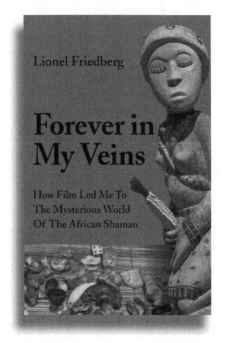

Lionel Friedberg

Forever in
My Veins

How Film Led Me To
The Mysterious World
Of The African Shaman

The Flying Springbok

A history of South African Airways
from its inception until the
post-apartheid era

The Flying Springbok

A history of South African Airways
from its inception until the
post-apartheid era

Lionel Friedberg

Winchester, UK
Washington, USA

JOHN HUNT PUBLISHING

First published by Chronos Books, 2021
Chronos Books is an imprint of John Hunt Publishing Ltd., No. 3 East St., Alresford,
Hampshire SO24 9EE, UK
office@jhpbooks.com
www.johnhuntpublishing.com
www.chronosbooks.com

For distributor details and how to order please visit the 'Ordering' section on our website.

Text copyright: Lionel Friedberg 2020

ISBN: 978 1 78904 646 5
978 1 78904 647 2 (ebook)
Library of Congress Control Number: 2020940133

A CIP catalogue record for this book is available from the British Library.

Design: Stuart Davies

UK: Printed and bound by CPI Group (UK) Ltd, Croydon, CR0 4YY
Printed in North America by CPI GPS partners

We operate a distinctive and ethical publishing philosophy in
all areas of our business, from our global network of authors to
production and worldwide distribution.

Contents

Dedicated to the memory of my beloved parents
Ann and Simon Friedberg

They taught me to look up in wonder... and in awe

Windhoek

Pietersburg

Kempton Park
Pretoria (Jan Smuts Airport)
Johannesburg
Germiston
(Rand Airport)
Palmietfontein *Vaal Dam*
SWAZILAND

Upington

Kimberley

Pietermaritzburg

Bloemfontein

Victoria West

Durban

Beaufort West

Umtata

Grahamstown

East London

Cape Town   George

Port Elizabeth

Mossel Bay

SOUTH AFRICA

(ALL PLACE NAMES REFER TO
PRE-1994 APARTHEID ERA)

GRAPHIC: SIMON FRIEDBERG

Introduction

The springbok (*Antidorcas marsupialis*) is a medium size antelope. It is the national animal of the Republic of South Africa. For more than six decades, a stylized rendering of the animal with sprouted wings was the symbol of the country's national carrier, South African Airways (SAA).

Pioneering air services throughout Africa and eventually flying to destinations on six continents, SAA became synonymous with expedient, safe and efficient air travel. Emboldened by a pioneering spirit, the airline could boast of many firsts. It also overcame what once seemed like insurmountable odds that threatened its very existence. Though colorful and fascinating, it is nevertheless a story not without controversy. Many saw SAA as the 'apartheid airline,' a state-owned agency of the white-controlled government that ruthlessly divided the country's racial groups.

The flying springbok logo emblazoned the tails of aircraft at many of the world's major international airports. This was crucial to South Africa's ruling National Party's imperative to maintain a 'presence' throughout the globe in the face of ever-increasing boycotts, criticism and isolationism due to its racist policies. Routes to some destinations did not even have to show a profit just so long as SAA aircraft could be seen pulling up at terminals abroad and proudly displaying the South African flag.

Today SAA has long-since shed its original logo. It was born anew in 1996 with a livery evocative of the post-apartheid era. But the years of the Flying Springbok were the richest, most progressive and internationally respected in the airline's 86-year history. This is an account of the era leading up to the rebranding and reincarnation of the airline, six years after Nelson Mandela was finally released from political imprisonment and two years after the African National Congress took over the reins of power when democracy and the end of racism finally came to South Africa.

Chapter 1

Taking Wing

Four separate territories once occupied the area that now constitute the Republic of South Africa. One of them was the British colony of Natal. It buffered the eastern coastline with the Indian Ocean and was favored by white immigrant settlers as a new home under the African sun. Among them was William John Houshold. With his wife Mary and their five children, they sailed from England and settled on a farm in the Karkloof area near the hamlet of Howick in 1864. But it was their youngest son John Goodman who really concerns us. He was to leave an indelible mark on the history of aviation in Africa and it is with him that our story begins.

For years farmers and innkeepers around Karkloof and the bustling town of Pietermaritzburg talked of the young John Goodman Houshold. It was rumored that he dabbled in the 'Godless vice' of attempting to fly. Tales described how, as early as 1871, Houshold nurtured a dream to soar like the birds that he so admired as they careened above the family farm. Coveting their ability, he is said to have obtained a large, firm dried-out hide from a slaughtered bull and attached a long leather thong to it. Climbing up a tree with it, he perched on a branch, maneuvered himself onto the flat hide, tossed the thong down to a handful of Zulu laborers waiting below, held on to either side of the hide and ordered the men to grab the thong and run. He hoped the hide would become a glider but his makeshift creation did not become airborne. The twenty-nine-year-old Houshold plummeted to the ground in a cloud of dust. Not to be outdone, over a period of weeks he carefully studied birds in flight, paying special attention to the ratio of their wingspan to their bodies. To understand something of aerodynamics, he shot a vulture, weighed it and measured the length of its wings. From this, he figured out the design for his next glider and showed it to a friend of the family, Bishop John Colenso in Pietermaritzburg. Colenso was a controversial figure in the Anglican Church who had landed himself in trouble for his outspoken liberal views on religion and race but he had excelled at mathematics during his years at Cambridge University. He fully supported Houshold's flying ambitions. Examining the young man's drawings, he pronounced them promising and encouraged him to construct his glider.

With his brother Archer's help, John set about cobbling together a glider made of wood and oiled paper or silk. Exactly what his invention may have looked like or where and how he procured the material remains a total mystery but that is perhaps part of the charm of the story. Belief has it that the glider was eventually constructed and then dragged to the edge of a thousand-feet high precipice of a hill on the farm. Pushed over the edge by his cheering brother, Houshold soared to a height of 65 feet for a distance of almost 3,300 feet. A second flight that same day ended in a sudden rapid descent in which the craft clipped a tree and crashed, fracturing one of Houshold's legs. When his mother was told of the reason for his injury, she begged her sons to abandon their flying aspirations. What she feared more than bodily harm to them was incurring the wrath of the Lord. She was convinced that her boys were defying Holy Scripture by attempting the sinful and unnatural act of human flight, thereby tempting the devil. The glider was subsequently packed away in a barn and eventually burned as trash. As no drawings or plans exist, we shall never know the truth behind this most alluring of tales. However, some people have taken it very seriously. In 1995, a plaque commemorating the flight was erected on the spot where the experiment is believed to have taken place. It reads:

First Glider Flight in South Africa
Between 1871 and 1875 John Goodman Houshold undertook
two flights in a self-constructed
glider from a ridge in this vicinity. One flight carried him
approximately 500 metres.
Erected by Lions River Heritage Society
Howick Museum
National Monuments Council
Mondi Forests
SAPPI (South African Pulp & Paper Industries) Forests, Natal
SAAF (South African Air Force) Association
RAF (Royal Air Force) Association
September 1995

If Houshold's flight really did occur, it is a remarkable accomplishment. Isolated as he was from mainstream scientific thinking and the many engineering experiments taking place in England and Europe at the time, he deserves every accolade for his achievement. After all, it was only a handful of years earlier that British engineer Sir George Cayley had constructed a glider and managed to get it airborne for a brief flight. In 1853, Cayley built a more elaborate device that flew a distance of about 885 feet (270 m) over Brompton Dale in the North York Moors. Did Houshold know of these experiments? If so, how had news about them have reached him in distant Natal in Africa? It is all very tantalizing, adding to the essence of this most beguiling of mysteries.

Apart from attempts at gliding, other forms of aerial transportation were not unknown in South Africa at that time. Between 1880 and 1902, Britain fought bitter wars against two self-proclaimed independent white-controlled republics that the Afrikaners or Boers—descendants of Dutch settlers—had established on the borders of the British colonies of Natal and the Cape. In their two republics the Boers lived outside British domination but animosities between the two sides constantly simmered, especially after diamonds and gold were discovered within the borders of the two Boer states. Based on experiments carried out by Royal Engineers with balloons in the territory of Bechuanaland (modern-day Botswana), Britain employed three military balloon units during the Second Boer War from 1899 to 1902. It was a complicated business. The balloons were finicky and could only be flown in favorable weather. Deploying them was extremely difficult and inflating them with hydrogen gas even more so. Apart from officers and enlisted men, each balloon unit required up to three ox wagons to transport supplies and its cargo of balloons, together with complex hydrogen-producing equipment. A balloon could carry one or two men aloft at a time. The primary task was to have someone in the basket suspended beneath the balloon to spy on the Boers and reconnoiter terrain. The balloons' functions were therefore limited, never ever used in combat but confined to an observation role. Together with field glasses, maps and notebooks, photographic equipment was also sent aloft. As a result, those early flights have left a rich legacy of early aerial wartime photographs. They provide a fascinating pictorial overview of the Boer War, a brutal affair in which approximately 22,000 British soldiers, 4,000 Boer forces and about 25,000 South African civilians—white and black—died.

But heavier-than-air powered flight is what drove the story of aviation forward in the southern skies of the African continent. In 1907, John Weston became the first South African to build a powered airplane. The event occurred at a very unlikely place—Kalkdam near Hopetown in the Northern Cape. This was farmland, relatively undeveloped and remote. Nevertheless Weston, a civil engineer who had studied and travelled abroad, was inspired by people like the Wright brothers and many others who were tinkering with the new tools and trappings of aviation. Weston based the design of his machine on the concepts of French airplane builders, Gabriel and Charles Voisin, as well as on the work of another French aviator, Henri Farman. Weston purchased and installed a thirty-horsepower four-cylinder Panhard water-cooled engine on his hybridized Voison-Farman craft but the little engine did not have enough power to get the airplane into the air. Undaunted, Weston dismantled the airframe, transported it via ox wagon to the coast and shipped it to France. There he reconstructed it, installed a fifty-horsepower Gnome rotary engine and the machine became airborne in 1910. Weston would later return to South Africa, establish his own aviation company, play a key role in establishing the Aeronautical Society of South Africa and give many demonstrations of flight to the general public.

John Weston in his biplane in 1912

Because his first home-built machine did not actually take to the air in South Africa itself, the distinction of flying the first heavier-than-air powered aircraft in the country goes to someone else—a suave, dashing, moustached 27-year-old French ice hockey player by the name of Albert Kimmerling.

Barely six years after the Wright brothers had made the world's first powered flight in North Carolina, the people of East London on the eastern seaboard of the Cape province heard the sputtering growl of Kimmerling's French-made Antoinette

V8 engine on a windswept grassy plain near Nahoon beach. The engine was installed in a flimsy biplane constructed by the Voisin brothers in Paris. It was dubbed 'The Flying Matchbox' because of its resemblance to the cubed wooden match containers popular among tobacco smokers at that time. Kimmerling had brought the craft from Europe after being lured away from his sporting activities at the invitation of the East London Town Council. Based on his love of ice hockey, fast cars and the infant field of aviation, he had a reputation for speed and daring. The council wanted him to show off his flying skills at the town's annual Christmas and New Year Gala as a promotional attraction. Historical sources differ as to the exact date but on either December 28, 1909 or on January 1, 1910, the young man took to the air in his fragile craft, attaining a speed of 30 miles per hour at a height of twenty feet above the city's Nahoon sand dunes. Two milestone events were inscribed in the history books that long-gone summer's day. It was one of the first powered heavier-than-air flights in the entire southern hemisphere and the very first time that the drone of an airplane engine had ever pierced the silent skies over the African continent.

Albert Kimmerling demonstrates his 'Flying Matchbox' at East London, December 1909 or January 1910. This was one of the first powered flights in the entire Southern Hemisphere and the very first in Africa

The event takes on even more dramatic proportions when it is remembered that Kimmerling's demonstration in East London took place only six months after Louis Bleriot had made his famed historic crossing of the English Channel from Calais to Dover in 1909. With confidence boosted by his crowd-pleasing performance in East London and enticed by the opportunity to make money by giving flying demonstrations to an even larger audience, Kimmerling dismantled his aircraft and had it transported by rail to Johannesburg. Those were optimistic times in the city that owed its origins to the discovery of gold. The public was more than ready for Kimmerling's flying demonstrations in the region known as the Witwatersrand, an Afrikaans word meaning 'Ridge of White Waters.' It was this enormous geologic feature on a plateau 6,500 feet above sea level that harboured some of the world's richest seams of gold. The city would eventually become the heartbeat of a thriving industrial complex, one of the most productive south of the equator.

When Kimmerling arrived in Johannesburg early in 1910, the mood was upbeat. The Boer War was finally over and Britain now ruled over all four territories of South Africa, namely the Cape, Natal, and the conquered Boer republics of the Transvaal and Orange Free State. Part of Britain's peace agreements with the Boers gave autonomy to the four regions which politically unified and became provinces of the new Union of South Africa on May 31, 1910. Although government was local under a Prime Minister and a cabinet, King Edward VII in England was head of state and the Union became another extension of the great British Empire. So it was into a very buoyant Johannesburg that Kimmerling arrived with his Flying Matchbox just a few months before unification took place. He reassembled his machine and after a few mishaps and minor accidents while testing it he made three flights in February 1910 at Sydenham Hill near Orange Grove in what was then an outlying suburb of Johannesburg. The public went crazy. Many clamoured for rides so, on March

19, 1910, Johannesburg businessman Thomas Thornton handed over the princely sum of £100 to Kimmerling, squeezed himself into the passenger seat of the Flying Matchbox and as the flimsy craft clamoured into the late summer air from the Sydenham horse race track he became the first paying aircraft passenger in South African history. Later that day local newspaper reporter Julia Stansfield gained the distinction of becoming the first female passenger in the country to become airborne.

Aviation rapidly came to be regarded as something more than just a way of thrilling crowds. Many began seeing it as a viable option for transportation with strong commercial possibilities. Some also saw it as an exciting sporting and recreational activity. One of them was wealthy Johannesburg timber merchant, Cecil Bredell. He commissioned French immigrant Alfred Louis Raison to build him an airplane. Raison was more than qualified for the task. He was a mechanic who had once run a small bicycle shop. Bredell's passion for flight was inspired by the success of Louis Bleriot's trans-Channel flight from Calais to Dover and the proven reliability of his French-built Bleriot monoplane. Raison had a brother who was an employee of Bleriot's company in France so he wrote to his brother and arranged to purchase a copy of the blueprints for Bleriot's aircraft design. As soon as the plans arrived, Raison set about constructing a modified version of the machine for Bredell in his Johannesburg workshop. With the exception of the wheels pilfered from a motorcycle and the British-made JAP V4 aero engine the entire craft was made from locally available components. The machine first took to the air from a grassy field in Highlands North on May 2, 1911, with Cecil Bredell at the controls.

Others now looked to the airplane as an expedient new way of delivering something else—the mail. One of them was Evelyn 'Bok' Frederick Driver. Born in Pietermaritzburg in 1881, he travelled to England and got a job with the Grahame-White Aviation Company at Hendon as a pilot-instructor. Driver was an excellent pilot and was invited to become one of four to fly the first airmail service in the United Kingdom. The Royal Mail Aerial Postal Service was inaugurated from Hendon airfield in North London to Windsor to mark the coronation of King George V. Driver piloted a Farman biplane as the service took to the air on September 9, 1911. He subsequently returned to South Africa with two flying buddies, pilots Guy Livingston and Cecil Compton-Paterson. Together they formed a company called the African Aviation Syndicate in Cape Town. Its purpose was to 'promote the science and practice of aviation in South Africa' by, among other things, teaching members of the public to fly.

Livingston was managing director of the company while Compton-Paterson and Driver took on the role of pilot and instructor. They brought two aircraft with them from Europe. One was a biplane designed and built by Compton-Paterson himself, and the other a Bleriot monoplane. In 1911, the Cape Town Publicity Association organized an 'Aviation Fortnight' to promote flying in the city. One of the highlights was the experimental delivery of the country's first airmail, covering the route from Kenilworth racecourse to the beach suburb of Muizenberg, a distance of eight-and-a-half miles. The flight captured the public's imagination and was eagerly anticipated. Flags were flown all over the city to alert people if weather conditions were favorable so that onlookers could catch a glimpse of the single-seat Bleriot XI monoplane. In the late afternoon of Tuesday, December 27, 1911, Driver took off from the Kenilworth racecourse carrying a bag of specially designed postcards that bore either a half-penny or one penny stamp, the former for local delivery and the latter for transportation by sea to destinations abroad. Driver landed at Oldham's field north of Muizenberg seven-and-a-half minutes later. On the return flight the winds were not as favourable and the Bleriot touched down at Kenilworth at 8.10 pm after a twelve-and-a-half-minute flight. The watching crowds were jubilant.

Evelyn 'Bok' Driver prepares to fly the first short experimental airmail flight in Cape Town, 1911

Many were watching these achievements with great interest. One of them was South Africa's Minister of Defense, General Jan Christiaan Smuts. He had been a brilliant Boer Commando during the Second Anglo Boer War, fighting against the British. After peace and the establishment of the Union he would become a prominent South African and British statesman, serving in both the South African and British Imperial War Cabinets and would twice serve as South Africa's prime minister. In time, Smuts would become a very close friend of the British royal family and would be one of Britain's staunchest allies during World War II. Smuts was most intrigued by the flights of Driver and Paterson. Visionary that he was he immediately foresaw the military possibilities of the airplane. In 1912, he sent his Commandant General of the South African Citizen Force, General Christiaan

Frederik Beyers, to Europe to observe British, Swiss, French and German military manoeuvres in which aircraft were participating. Smuts was anxious to know whether the airplane could be successfully integrated into military operations. Did Beyers think the airplane might serve as an instrument of war?

Beyers was enthusiastic about what he saw and encouraged Smuts as well as Prime Minister Louis Botha to establish a military Air Corps. Its primary purpose would be aerial observation and scouting, just in case any future hostilities involving the new Union should arise. The task presented numerous challenges, not least of which was the fact that no one in the government or the defense force knew anything about how to run an aviation school. Perhaps it was fortuitous that the syndicate between Paterson, Driver and Livingston in Cape Town had come to an end at the same time. A group of businessmen in Kimberley had bought the company's assets and Paterson was placed in charge of a flying school that the new owners set up with Edward Wallace Cheeseman as his co-instructor. An arrangement was made for the construction of a hangar at a dusty place called Alexandersfontein near Kimberley in the northern Cape and the Paterson Aviation Syndicate School of Flying opened for business there early in 1913. Paterson was soon approached by government officials to train civilian pilots for the proposed South African Aviation Corps (SAAC) so that it could become an active component of the Union Defense Force.

Successful candidates who met the criteria to join the new Aviation Corps were paid seventeen shillings and six pence by the government, plus an allowance of five shillings per student so that they could pay for the use of the school's aircraft. Pilot testing was supervised by the Aeronautical Society of South Africa, a regulatory body that had been formed by pioneering airman and aircraft builder John Weston in 1911 under the auspices of the Royal Aeronautical Society of Great Britain. Basic flying training courses commenced at the school in mid-1913 with ten students. The main aircraft in which they received instruction was the home-built Compton-Paterson biplane powered by a fifty-horsepower Gnome engine. The first pupils were John Clisdal, Gordon Shergold Creed, Edwin Cheere Emmett, Basil Hobson Turner, M. van Coller, Gerard Percy Wallace, Marthinus Steyn Williams, a young man with the last name of Hopkins, one whose last name was Solomon and a very bright 30-year-old from the town of Stellenbosch by the name of Kenneth Reid van der Spuy. Van der Spuy would later become a highly decorated airman and would go on to be tasked with the actual founding of the government-backed South African Aviation Corps. Three civilians also joined the class. One of them was Miss Anna Maria Bocciarelli. She was born in Kimberley in 1897, the daughter of wealthy Italian immigrant Achille Bocciarelli who owned the local brickworks. Miss Bocciarelli received her wings from the flying school in October 1913, thus becoming the first woman to be trained as a pilot in South Africa. Six of the male pilots qualified with such high grades that they were sent to the Central Flying School—part of Britain's Royal Flying Corps and predecessor of the Royal Air Force—in Upavon, England for further training.

Those were pioneering times but it was not all excitement and romance. Aviation was young and still plagued with numerous difficulties and dangers. Aircraft were fragile and unreliable. They were constructed mainly of wood and covered with stretched fabric. To say that they were easily susceptible to damage is an understatement. Engines were, at best, troublesome and untrustworthy. Most flying machines were capable of reaching speeds of no more than thirty or thirty-five miles per hour. They carried few flying aids, simple instrumentation, no radios and very basic equipment. Navigational instruments consisted of little more than a rudimentary compass. Airfields were usually makeshift affairs, either rough veldt, golf courses or horseracing tracks. Sometimes these landing areas concealed potholes, stones and other obstacles that punctured wheels and tore up undercarriages. General knowledge of the new science of aviation was still very much in its infancy. Rule books did not exist. It was more a matter of learning by doing. But all that was about to change.

When two gunshots shattered the mid-morning spring air in Sarajevo, capital of the Austro-Hungarian province of Bosnia in June 1914, snuffing out the lives of Austrian Archduke Franz Ferdinand and his wife Sophie, a series of cataclysmic events were triggered. A month later the first bullets and shells of World War I – the 'Great War,' the 'War to end all wars' – were fired. Europe was catapulted into a clash the likes of which had never been seen. It did not take long before all the world's great powers and many other nations were sucked into the conflict. The impact of all this on the airplane was dramatic.

Flying machines now became potent weapons of battle. Sputtering fire from machine guns as they engaged in savage aerial dogfights, they shot one another to smithereens. Manufacturers on both sides of the conflict did everything possible to improve their airplanes, making them faster, tougher and more easily maneuverable again. Bricks, nails, lethal dart-like weapons known as fléchettes and then grenades, bombs and other explosive devices were aimed by eye and lobbed by pilots from open cockpits onto targets such as troops, horses, cavalry, trenches, railroad tracks and cities before methods were developed for dropping bombs from mounts beneath the wings. Very early in the war the Germans employed dirigible airships to drop bombs on England. Clearly, there was an urgent need for lightweight fighters to metamorphose into fully fledged bombers and so airplane manufacturers in Germany, Britain, France, Russia, Italy and the Austro-Hungarian Empire scrambled to the task.

Those were the years of many awards and decorations

such as the prestigious Prussian order *Pour le Mérite*, or the Blue Max, and of famous pilots such as Germany's Manfred von Richthofen, the legendary 'Red Baron,' so-named because of the crimson color of his swift German-built Fokker single-engine triplane. It was the glory years of American ace, Eddie Rickenbacker, and of decorated British aces such as Frank McNamara, William Rhodes-Moorhouse, Albert Ball and fellow Royal Flying Corps pilot from South Africa, Andrew Beauchamp Proctor, who became one of the most decorated airmen during the war. Credited with an astonishing 54 victories in the air he was awarded the Distinguished Service Order (DSO), the Military Cross (MC), the Distinguished Flying Cross (DFC) and the Victoria Cross (VC), the highest military decoration for valor awarded to members of the armed forces in the British Empire.

The airplane had come into its own and went into battle as far away as German South West Africa (modern-day Namibia) and German East Africa (Burundi, Rwanda and Tanganyika or modern-day Tanzania). As an ally of Great Britain, South Africa despatched pilots from the newly-formed South African Aviation Corps as well as those flying with the Royal Flying Corps to support ground forces fighting there.

In Europe, one of the few heavy bombers that had been developed for the war came from the Vickers aviation company of Brooklands in England. It was called the Vickers Vimy. In 1917, three prototypes were ordered by the Royal Flying Corps.

They were fitted with engines from different manufacturers for testing. When the Royal Flying Corps became the Royal Air Force in 1918, a total of 776 Vickers Vimy machines with 360-horsepower Rolls Royce Eagle twelve-cylinder liquid-cooled engines were ordered. But before the aircraft could be delivered, let alone see combat, the war ended.

As peace returned to a solemn, battered and exhausted Europe in 1918, the existence of all those new Vimy airplanes opened up a host of new opportunities for intrepid airmen who wanted to break records, especially with regard to long-distance flight.

Two intrepid airmen — of whom we shall hear more later — in front of an RAF Vickers Vimy bomber

The Vickers Vimy was designed as a night-time bomber with a range of 870 miles. It was 43 ft seven inches long, had a wingspan of 68 ft one inch and was 15 ft eight inches high. Its empty weight was 7,104 lbs. It had a fully loaded maximum take-off weight of 10,884 lbs. It was a big, rigidly-built aircraft with a metal forward-section and a metal inner frame fuselage covered by stretched fabric. Powered by two Rolls Royce Eagle twelve-cylinder engines it flew at a height of nearly 9,800 ft and at a speed of 130 mph. It was intended to cross the English Channel or take off from France and reach deep into German territory where it could drop its 4,400 lb load of bombs.

On June 14, 1919, Captain John Alcock and Lieutenant Arthur Whitten Brown took off from St. John's, Newfoundland in a modified and improved version of the Vimy, the model IV. They landed the next day at Clifden, Ireland, after a non-stop flight of sixteen hours and twenty-seven minutes, making them the first to cross the Atlantic by air. It was an extraordinary accomplishment. Amazingly, there was still enough fuel left in the Vimy's tanks to take it another 807 miles. Their flight ignited the imagination of many others, including Australians Captain Ross Smith and his brother Keith. With Ross at the controls and Keith as navigator, accompanied by Sergeants J.M. Bennett and W.H. Shiers as mechanics, they departed Hounslow, England in a Vickers Vimy IV on November 12, 1919, landing in Port Darwin, Australia 28 days later. They had become the first to travel all the way from England via Asia to the Australian continent, a stunning distance of 10,500 miles, almost halfway around the world.

Britain had long wanted a quick and efficient means to connect with the outermost regions of its empire. The biggest problem was always distance. And nowhere did this present more challenges than in Africa. Much of the continent was still unknown and uncharted. It had always been the dream of one of the most successful and controversial industrialists, politicians, speculators, mining magnates and businessmen during the heydays of the British empire, Cecil John Rhodes, founder of the giant de Beers diamond mining company, to carve an unbroken trail of empire all the way up central and eastern Africa with a railway line linking Cape Town and Cairo. That aim was never fully realized, even though plans and intentions to achieve it would simmer for decades. More than anything else, Whitehall and the Colonial Office in London would have liked nothing better than a 'pink' map all the way up through Africa from south to north to signify British-held colonies. At that time all parts of the planet under British domination were colored pink on maps.

There were so many pink areas on globes of the world that it was said that the sun never set on the British empire. Somewhere on the earth, at any given time, a pink region under British control was always in daylight.

Just a few days after the Armistice ending World War I was signed in November 1918, terminating the most vicious conflict ever fought in recorded history, three military survey parties were despatched from Britain to Africa. Their mission was to search out sites for future African 'aerodromes' as airstrips or landing fields were commonly referred to by the British in those days. These places would hopefully become staging posts for aircraft that would accomplish what the eagerly anticipated railway line might also eventually do one day, forging a regular passenger and mail service between England and its African dominions by way of Cairo. But could airfields be built down the length of the African continent? Could landing fields be carved out of savannah grasslands, swamps, tropical forests, mountains and deserts? What were the logistic problems of bringing in supplies, fuel, spares, water and provisions? What were weather conditions like along the route? Were local inhabitants prepared to be trained for working at the airfields? Were tribal chiefs, headmen, elders and the population at large amenable to the idea? Because of the sheer scale of the venture the first of the three survey parties was responsible for exploring and developing the sector between Cairo and the Sudan, the second from Sudan to Northern Rhodesia (modern-day Zambia) and the third, under the command of Major Chaplin Court Treatt, for the leg from Northern Rhodesia all the way to Cape Town, primarily by following the routes of existing railway lines.

Establishing an air service as quickly as possible was of utmost importance to Britain. The survey teams worked quickly. Incredibly, just a year after setting out on this mammoth task they had examined vast tracts of land and established no less than twenty-three aerodromes as well as twenty-one additional places cleared as emergency landing sites. The job had been extremely demanding. Many workers had taken ill or had suffered injuries along the way. The teams had charted swamps, plateaus, jungles, rivers and grasslands that had never appeared on any previous maps and, together with paid or willing labourers recruited from local villages, they had hacked, chopped, cut and cleared patches that could accommodate aircraft as large as the Vickers Vimy. Thousands of trees had been felled. Stumps and roots had been removed and the holes filled in with soil. Tsetse flies frequently killed cattle and draft animals that were hauling trees, rocks and debris away so a lot of the work was done manually. Anthills had to be cleared, some as high as 33 feet. Depressions and dried riverbeds had to be filled in and made level. At one location alone 90,000 trees had to be removed. At another, a thousand wagonloads of rock had to be carted away. At Ndola in Northern Rhodesia, 700 local villagers had assisted in levelling over 25,000 tons of anthills. Airfields had to be constructed to a minimum size of 74 acres. All of them had to be marked with a large white circle so that they could be clearly seen from the air. Fuel had to be shipped in overland and storage drums had to be buried beneath ground to protect them from the searing sun. It was a superhuman task. But it was duly done.

Places chosen as primary airfields were Heliopolis (Cairo), Helwan, Assuit (Asyut) and Assouan (Aswan) in Egypt; Khartoum, Jebelain (Al Jabalayn), Eliri (South Kordofan), Atbara (Atbarah), Wady Halfa (Wadi Halfa) and Mongala in Sudan; Jinja on Lake Victoria in Uganda; Kisumu in Kenya; Tabora and Mwanza in Tanganyika (Tanzania); Abercorn (Mbala), Broken Hill (Kabwe), Ndola and Livingstone in Northern Rhodesia (Zambia); Palapye in Bechuanaland (Botswana) and then Pretoria, Johannesburg, Bloemfontein, Victoria West, Beaufort West and Cape Town in South Africa. The total distance from Cairo covered over 4,900 miles with the landing spaces roughly 124 miles apart.

The big question now was who would be the first to fly the route? Who would be brave or foolhardy enough to undertake such a perilous journey by air? Mechanical failure or getting lost along the way would almost certainly be fatal. Even if a crash did not kill the aviators, hostile tribes, wild animals and difficult terrain would severely impair any chances of survival. Locating wreckage by rescue parties would be virtually impossible. And yet the opportunities for undertaking such a venture would certainly stoke the spirits of any warm-blooded young adventurers willing to risk everything for accomplishing something never done before, especially on such an immense scale. In Britain the matter was discussed in parliament. Winston Churchill, then Secretary of State for War and Air, brought it up in the House of Commons. He proposed that there ought to be a substantial cash prize for the first person or persons to successfully complete a flight from London to Cape Town. Everything should be done to encourage that endeavor now that airfields had been established all the way down the spine of the African continent. The press picked up on the story and this piqued public interest. In fashionable West End gentlemen's clubs, ladies' tea parlors, village pubs and at social gatherings conversation often turned to who would accomplish the feat. Knowing how much publicity it would generate for the newspaper, the London-based *Daily Mail* came forward and offered a cash prize of £10,000, at that time a very handsome sum of money. Pulses quickened. Five entrants took up the offer, making them contestants in an exciting venture that the press and public rapidly dubbed the 'Great Air Race to the Cape.'

On January 24, 1920, the first plane in the competition took off from Brooklands in Surrey. It was a Vickers Vimy piloted by British airmen Stanley Cockerell and Frank Broome. The flight was sponsored by *The Times* newspaper. In his leather satchel Cockerell carried a letter from King George to the British

Governor General of South Africa, Lord Buxton. Unfortunately, the letter never reached its destination because the aircraft crashed on takeoff from Tabora, Tanganyika on February 27, slightly injuring the crew and putting *The Times* entrant out of the running. Three other participants in the race also crashed, bringing an end to their attempts to win the prize. One, a British-built Handley Page 0/400 converted bomber with 24-year-old Herbert George Brackley at the controls, aided by navigator Frederick Tymms and sponsored by the *Daily Telegraph,* crashed after leaving Assuan for Khartoum in Sudan on February 25. It sustained damage beyond repair. Another aircraft was a de Havilland DH 14A. It was a single-engine two-seater biplane piloted by its wealthy owner, Australian Frederick Sidney Cotton who, together with his engineer W.A. Townsend, began their flight from Hendon in February. But after numerous mishaps and problems along the way the craft was written off after crashing in Italy on July 24. Then there was an R.A.F. Vickers Vimy piloted by William Welsh and Robert Halley which crash-landed at Wadi Halfa on February 27. With the exception of Cotton's two-seater de Havilland, all the other aircraft carried a couple of passengers, most of them mechanics, and it is a miracle that no one suffered serious injury or death during their extraordinarily daring attempts.

But what about that fifth crew? By 1920, General Jan Smuts had become prime minister of South Africa. He desperately wanted South Africans to be the first to complete the entire length of the route, win the *Daily Mail* prize and generate international publicity and goodwill for the country. To achieve this he authorized the purchase of a military Vickers Vimy from the R.A.F. at Brooklands in England for £4,500. Marked with the official British aviation registration G-UABA on its wings and fuselage and spruced up in shiny aluminum paint the craft glinted magnificently in the sunlight and was appropriately named the *Silver Queen.* All she needed was a flying crew. But who would they be? General Smuts and his advisors scoured the rosters of the South African Aviation Corps. Two candidates were finally decided upon.

Helperus Andries 'Pierre' van Ryneveld was born in the little town of Senekal in the Orange Free State on May 2, 1891. After an initial education in the city of Bloemfontein he went on to gain a B.A. degree from the University of the Cape of Good Hope in Cape Town. He then sailed for England and obtained a B.Sc. degree from the University of London. Always fascinated by military matters he returned to South Africa and joined the recently formed Union Defense Force. This led to further studies at the Imperial Staff College in Britain. At the outbreak of the First World War he joined the Royal North Lancashire Regiment, seeing service in France and the Middle East. But he soon discovered that his real passion was for aviation and so from April 1915 he flew with the Royal Flying Corps. His brother John also became a pilot but was killed in action. Pierre van Ryneveld was an accomplished and courageous pilot. He accumulated an excellent flying record, earning the Distinguished Service Order (DSO) and the Military Cross. When the war ended, the twenty-nine-year-old returned to South Africa. And that was when General Smuts picked him for the *Silver Queen*. But there was need for a second crewmember.

Christopher Joseph 'Flossie' Quinton Brand was two years younger than van Ryneveld. He was born in Kimberley on May 25, 1893. Educated in Johannesburg he joined the Union Defense Force in 1913. During the first couple of years of World War I he served with the army in South Africa and then left for England in 1915. There he trained to become a pilot with the Royal Flying Corps. In 1916, he first saw service in the skies over France. His flying skills were second to none and he eventually became celebrated as the highest-scoring night fighter pilot with the Corps, earning himself the DSO and the Military Cross.

**'Pierre' van Ryneveld and Quinton Brand in front of their Vickers
Vimy, *Silver Queen*, 1920**

Pierre van Ryneveld and Quinton Brand were perfectly
matched. And Prime Minister Jan Smuts knew it. Together they
were offered the challenge of flying the *Silver Queen*, with van
Ryneveld as commander and Brand as co-pilot. Two others, a
Rolls Royce engine mechanic by the name of Sherratt and an
airframe engineer called Burton were engaged to accompany the
flight as passengers. On the cold, damp morning of February 14,
1920, to the cheers of military and civilian onlookers, the *Silver
Queen* took off from Brooklands, bound for its epic flight across
Europe and then down the length of Africa to Cape Town. On
board was a letter addressed from the British Prime Minister
David Lloyd George to General Jan Smuts. Dated February 3,
1920, from 10 Downing Street. It read:

My dear General,

I am told that two gallant South African officers, Colonel Van Ryneveld and Flight-Lieutenant Brand, are about to start on the pioneer flight to South Africa by the Cape to Cairo air route. I am glad to avail myself of this opportunity to send my best wishes to yourself and to South Africa by the first aerial mail. I do not suppose that Cecil Rhodes and other pioneers of the Cape to Cairo route ever dreamed that the first package to be carried along this route would travel by air and not by rail.

With best wishes,

Yours sincerely,

D. Lloyd George

Also on board the *Silver Queen* were 518 gallons of fuel, 30 gallons of lubricating oil, 32 gallons of fresh water, plus a variety of spares and tools. The Vimy behaved relatively well, flying across the English Channel and then, with periodic maintenance stops, breached the Alps, flew down Italy and then over the Mediterranean. Between Cairo and Khartoum near Wadi Halfa, disaster struck. A leaking radiator made the starboard engine overheat. The crew had no option but to shut it down. Having lost fifty per cent of its power the huge machine could not stay aloft, even in the cool evening air through which it was flying. The pilots spotted an open patch of sandy desert at a place called Korosko alongside the Nile and brought the aircraft down to a perfect landing. But in the dim evening light they did not see the crop of boulders that loomed before them. With an ear-splitting crash, the aircraft hurtled over it. There were no injuries but the wheels and wings of the *Silver Queen* were torn to shreds.

When news of the accident reached General Smuts in Pretoria, he immediately asked the Royal Air Force to place another Vickers Vimy at van Ryneveld and Brand's disposal. The RAF's response was swift and positive. An airplane that had been stripped of its engines was still undergoing routine maintenance at a base in Cairo and was quickly made ready. As the *Silver Queen's* own engines had not sustained damage in the crash, they were brought by Bedouins and local Arabs on carts pulled by donkeys and camels from the crash site to Wadi Halfa and then transported by rail to Cairo. On arrival the engines were fitted onto the replacement airframe and the machine was named *Silver Queen II.*

On February 22, 1920, the Vimy was airborne, bound for Bulawayo in Southern Rhodesia. After transiting the Sahara, the Great Rift Valley, skirting the eastern side of the Belgian Congo and crossing the Zambezi river with no major setbacks Bulawayo was reached on March 5, 1920. The aircraft touched down and came to a halt on the town's horse racing track. Van Ryneveld and Brand had flown further than any of their competitors and it looked like the goal and the prize were going to be theirs. They received a hero's welcome.

Crowds surround the *Silver Queen* after its arrival at Bulawayo, Southern Rhodesia, March 5, 1920

Revelry and celebrating took place in Bulawayo that night and early next morning, the revving Rolls Royce engines of *Silver Queen II* broke the stillness of the African bush. Van Ryneveld hoped that he would be able to reach Pretoria in South Africa without stopping to refuel. The distance between the two centers was 383 miles. To cover that amount of territory van Ryneveld decided to fill the Vimy's fuel tanks to maximum capacity. It was not a good idea. Bulawayo is 4,400 feet above sea level and at that altitude the air is not as dense as it is at coastal level, making it difficult for the engines to get enough 'bite.' At dawn on Saturday, March 6 the Vimy lifted off from the racetrack but it was too heavy and its engines struggled to keep it aloft. The craft barely cleared the bush and scrub at the end of the track. Van Ryneveld pushed the throttles all the way, desperately squeezing maximum power from the two laboring engines. Dirty oil made matters worse and the Vimy could not rise above fifty feet. Then, buffeted by a slight breeze the aircraft shook, lost height and with a deafening crash smashed into the ground. The crew was uninjured but *Silver Queen II* was a complete write-off.

Wreckage of the *Silver Queen*, Bulawayo, March 6, 1920

News of the disaster reached a very disappointed General Smuts in Pretoria. Mulling over the predicament of his two pilots he did not want the South African attempt to reach the Cape to end now. Smuts turned to resources within South Africa itself for a solution. Not long before the Bulawayo crash the British government had given South Africa 113 used World War I military aircraft to form the nucleus of its own internal air force.

Smuts immediately ordered one of them, a two-seater de Havilland DH9 with a six-cylinder 250-horsepower Siddeley Puma engine, to fly from Pretoria and be handed over to van Ryneveld and Brand in Bulawayo. Before departure the name

de Havilland DH9, one of 113 ex-RAF fighters given to South Africa as a gift by Britain at the conclusion of WWI

Voortrekker was painted on its nose. It was an appropriate name. It is an Afrikaans word meaning 'Pathfinder' and was used to describe the first Dutch farmers who packed up their wagons and left the Cape of Good Hope to escape British rule in the early 1800s to find freedom and pastures new deeper inland.

Anxious to complete what they had started almost a month earlier, Van Ryneveld and Brand left Bulawayo in *Voortrekker* on March 17. Stopping first at Serowe and then at Palapye (Phalatswe) in Bechuanaland (modern-day Botswana), they were anxious to meet Chief Khama III, leader of the Bamangwato people. Known as 'Khama the Great,' he was the eldest son of Chief Segkoma I who had befriended the great missionary and explorer David Livingstone when he visited the area in the early 1840s. Unlike many other European explorers Livingstone had become a legend among the indigenous people due to his efforts to liberate them from the curse of slavery. Because of this a generally well-disposed attitude towards the British existed among the descendants of Chief Segkoma. His son, Khama, had been especially helpful towards the survey parties who established aerodromes and landing fields in the territory in 1918 and van Ryneveld and Brand wanted to personally thank him for his cooperation.

After the meeting with Khama, the DH9 took off and droned onward to Pretoria, its first stop on actual South African soil. From there it flew to Johannesburg and a riotous welcome. After brief festivities the aircraft flew on to Bloemfontein and Beaufort West. Finally, on March 20 at 4p.m. *Voortrekker* touched down at Young's Field, Wynberg in Cape Town. The two aviators had achieved what many feared was the impossible. Fame was theirs. Their achievement made headlines throughout the world. Each of the two aviators received half of the *Daily Mail* prize money in recognition of their efforts and both were subsequently knighted by King George in London. They had traversed the entire African continent by air. A long-held dream had finally come true. At last a highway in the African sky had been opened.

While much of the media attention had been concentrated on the air race, additional events of importance had been taking place. At the end of 1919, there were others in South Africa who were already looking forward to starting a regular passenger and airmail service. The Handley-Page company of England took the initiative by forming a South African subsidiary, Handley-Page South African Transport Limited. The intention was to start a local mail and passenger service between the country's major cities and, ultimately, by using all those airfields that had been carved out of the African landscape to start a long-haul service between Cape Town and Cairo. In England two twin-engine biplane Handley-Page 0/400 bombers were converted to civilian use with accommodation for sixteen passengers and then shipped out to South Africa. Reassembled at Young's Field in Wynberg and bearing the registrations G-EANV and G-IAAI, they were the largest aircraft yet seen in the country. To keep the machines properly maintained and supplied with fuel— at that time they used the same type of gasoline that powered automobile engines—financial underwriting and support was sought from the business world. A willing sponsor soon came forward, a local Cape Town-based winery and distillery. Before long the wording *Commando Brandy* was emblazoned on the sides of the fuselage and beneath the wings of the two aircraft, ensuring a potent advertising message for the sponsor every time one of the craft flew overhead.

On Sunday, February 15, 1920, one of the big Handley-Pages named *Pioneer* with Major Henry 'Duke' Meintjes at the controls took off on an ambitious attempt to inaugurate the first passenger service between Cape Town and Johannesburg. There were nine passengers on board. Other crew members were co-pilot, Captain C.J. 'Boetie' Venter and a Flight Engineer by the name of Askew. The scheduled route was to be via Beaufort West, De Aar and Kimberley. Shortly after leaving Cape Town, heavy cloud was encountered over the surrounding Hex River mountains and after clearing this obstacle pilot Meintjes discovered that the aircraft's compass was faulty. It could not be relied upon so he decided to put down on a stretch of empty land near a farmhouse at an obscure little place called Brakkefontein to determine their position. Having ascertained exactly where they were Meintjies once again took off for Laingsburg, a small town on the main railway route. After an hour in the air, engineer Askew warned that *Pioneer* had a dangerously low fuel level. An immediate landing was necessary so the crew brought the aircraft down at a tiny farming hamlet called Blaauheuwel (Blue Hill). Careful inspection revealed that the reserve fuel tank had developed a leak. After sending a note via a farmer on horseback to Laingsburg, the crew and passengers had to wait on the ground for two days until a truck coughed its way along the dirt road carrying enough barrels of fuel to get *Pioneer* to Laingsburg. Once there, another delay awaited the exhausted passengers and crew. There wasn't enough fuel available locally to fill up the aircraft's tanks. More had to be sent by rail from Beaufort West. *Pioneer* eventually took off and landed at Beaufort West on Thursday morning, four days behind schedule. For the passengers, it would have been quicker to travel from Cape Town to Johannesburg by train. They would already have reached their destination but such was the allure of air travel in those days that they happily endured the delays and inconvenience. After all, weren't they making history? After lunch in town at Beaufort West, everyone boarded the aircraft for the next leg to De Aar. The Handley-Page took off and climbed to about 330 feet when suddenly an ominous cracking sound came from the rear. All at once the aircraft began to veer wildly from side to side. Struggling to keep the machine under control, Meintjes made an immediate and very violent forced landing at a little railway siding called Acacia. Although no one was hurt, the aircraft was damaged beyond repair. The problem turned out to be a broken port rudder post. The big ex-bombers simply weren't built rugged enough to withstand frequent take-offs and landings on gravel or uneven fields that subjected them to a lot of shaking.

The second Handley-Page with *Commando Brandy* painted on it did a few flights over the Cape Town area but nothing more came of the intended passenger service. The *Commando* logo was painted over and the surviving aircraft dismantled and shipped to Calcutta, India where it was sold. After the crash of *Pioneer*, the owners of Handley-Page South African Transport Limited decided that plans for an aerial service in Africa were way too premature and far too dangerous. In September 1920, the company ceased operations.

But other things were happening to nudge the development of aviation in the sub-continent forward. On February 1, 1920, the South African Air Force (SAAF) was formed out of the pre-existing South African Aviation Corps (SAAC). What made this possible was the gift of those 113 ex-RAF World War I aircraft from Britain, replete with spares, tools and all the necessary accoutrements to keep the machines in the air. A base with a permanent runway, hangars and all essential technical facilities was established at Swartkop just outside Pretoria. Pierre van

Ryneveld—not only a hero of the London-to-Cape Town air race but now a Colonel and decorated RAF and SAAC military pilot—was put in charge of operations. His second-in-command was Kenneth Reid van der Spuy, one of the first graduates of Cecil Compton-Patterson's flying school at Alexandersfontein in Kimberley almost a decade earlier.

Aviation was now a legitimate entity on the landscape of South African affairs. Keen weekend flyers and 'light aeroplane clubs' in towns and cities all over the Union began to proliferate. In 1923, Parliament passed what was known as the Union Air Act. This provided a legal operating structure for all aviation activities in the country as well as the necessary administrative mechanisms for granting aviation licenses to pilots, aircraft operators and aviation businesses. Airports—or aerodromes as they were still most often referred to—also came under the control and jurisdiction of the Act, as were ancillary services such as telegraphs, the infant field of wireless (radio) communication and even customs and immigration procedures. Enforcement of the Act was the responsibility of the Department of Posts and Telegraphs, with a Civil Air Board acting as an advisory body to the Minister of Posts and Telegraphs. One of the Civil Air Board's first recommendations to the Minister was to start an experimental airmail service.

Mail from sources abroad entered the country by sea through Cape Town which is over a thousand miles from Johannesburg. The agency responsible for bringing the mail from Britain was the revered Union Castle Mail Steamship Company. Their vessels were named with the suffix *Castle,* such as *Arundel Castle, Cape Town Castle, Edinburgh Castle, Winchester Castle, Pretoria* Castle and so on. They were easily identified by their distinctive lavender-colored hulls and red funnels topped in black. By the mid-twenties the voyage between Cape Town and Southampton took two full weeks, with the ships operating on a precise timetable. Every Thursday at 4 p.m. a Union-Castle Royal Mail ship would leave Southampton bound for Cape Town, arriving in the city on a Monday. It would then sail along the coast bound for Durban, calling at Port Elizabeth and East London en route. Meanwhile, another liner was underway on the return voyage to the United Kingdom. It would leave Cape Town bound for Southampton at 4 p.m. on a Friday. In 1925, the South African Air Force (SAAF) was given the task of flying an experimental airmail service to connect with the arrival and departure of the mail ship. At first, the flights did not serve the Johannesburg area directly but linked Cape Town with Durban and included intermediate stops at Oudtshoorn, East London, Port Elizabeth and Mossel Bay.

Eleven SAAF de Havilland DH9 aircraft equipped with 230-horsepower Armstrong Siddeley Puma engines were employed for the coastal mail run, with Captain H. 'Duke' Meintjies, Captain H.C. Daniel, Major 'Happy Jack' Holthouse, Lt. L. Tasker, Lt. H.P. Schoeman, Captain Hamman, Lt. Berger, Capt. C.W. Meredith, Lt. Joubert, Lt. L. Hiscock and Lt. Reinhard Ferdinand 'Caspar' Caspareuthus as pilots. Lt. Col. Kenneth van der Spuy headed up the administrative side of things with Pierre van Ryneveld in overall command.

Lt. Reinhard Caspareuthus loads mail bags aboard South African Air Force (SAAF) de Havilland DH9 experimental domestic airmail service, February 1925

Each DH9 carried a payload of 400 lbs. The mailbags were carried in an open cockpit normally reserved for a passenger. The seat had been removed to make space for the bags. It was crude but it worked. The aircraft operated four sectors in pairs. Mail flights left Durban on a Thursday afternoon and stopped overnight in East London. The next morning the two machines flew to Port Elizabeth where the mail was transferred to another pair of DH9s. Those flew the mail to Oudtshoorn, a small town that was the center of South Africa's thriving ostrich feather industry. There the mail was again transferred to another pair of DH9s and flown via Mossel Bay on the final leg to Cape Town. The cost of sending a letter domestically was three pence and to destinations abroad six pence. Flights began on February 23, 1925 and although the service was efficient and incident-free the public at large was reticent to pay the extra cost for sending mail by air. After only 32 flights in which 276 bags of mail were carried, the service was disbanded on June 27, 1925.

Forging air links between South Africa and the outside world was always the primary drive behind those wanting to fly the African skies. But further progress had to wait for the adventurous and for those willing to take unprecedented risks. One of them stood head and shoulders above the rest. British-born Alan John Cobham was a stickler for detail. Everything he did was planned down to the tiniest item. His war record with the Royal Flying Corps was second to none and he could not get enough of flying. As a test pilot for the young de Havilland aircraft company in Edgeware just outside London, he was highly optimistic about the future role of the airplane. The company knew that most aircraft built during World War I would soon need replacing so they turned their attention to developing new variants. Twenty-seven-year-old Cobham was hired to fly and publicize their latest offerings. In 1923, the company was particularly proud of its latest model, a single-engine biplane with accommodation for four passengers known as the DH.50. In August of that year,

Cobham flew the prototype to Gothenberg, Sweden where it was featured at the International Aeronautical Exhibition. In 1924 Cobham won Britain's prestigious King's Cup air race in the aircraft, flying it at an average speed of 107 mph. That same year, 1924, Imperial Airways—forerunner of the future British Overseas Airways Corporation (BOAC) and today's British Airways—came into being. Based at Croydon airport outside London, the fledgling airline was created to establish air links between Britain and the furthermost regions of her empire, especially India, Ceylon (Sri Lanka), Burma (Myanmar), Singapore, Hong Kong, Australia, New Zealand and South Africa. 'Route proving' became an imperative for the young airline. In order to establish permanent air links, the route first had to be repeatedly flown, tried and tested. Alan Cobham became involved in this ambitious endeavour. His first assignment was to fly from London to Rangoon, Burma (modern-day Yangon, Myanmar) to help determine the practicalities of the route that transited Europe, the Middle East and Asia. At about the same time the newest variant of the DH.50 aircraft was rolled out of the de Havilland factory. Designated the DH.50J, it featured slight airframe modifications and a more powerful 385-horsepower Armstrong Siddeley Jaguar engine. It was in this aircraft bearing registration number G-EBFO and christened *Youth of Britain* that Cobham took off on his most challenging flight. The date was November 16, 1925. Droning skywards from the de Havilland company's home base at Stag Lane Aerodrome in Edgeware, Cobham was bound for Cape Town. This was actually a route-proving flight on behalf of Imperial Airways but, unlike any flight before it, Cobham's intention was to return to the United Kingdom in the same aircraft. On board with him were flight engineer Arthur Elliott and Basil Emmott, a cinematographer and photographer. Ahead of them lay 8,115 miles of Europe, the Mediterranean and the vast sprawl of Africa itself. After making 26 stops along the way—mainly following the 'pink' airfield route established by the British military survey team of 1918/19, similar to that flown by Van Ryneveld and Brand five years earlier—they reached Cape Town 83 days later, on February 17, 1926. The trio received a tumultuous welcome and nine days afterwards, on February 26, they took to the air again for the return journey. It was the same day that the Union Castle Line mail steamer *RMS Windsor Castle* sailed out of Table Bay bound for Southampton. The intention was to see which one of the two modes of transport would reach their destination first. Cobham and the captain of the ship both carried signed letters from the Governor-General of South Africa, the Earl of Athlone, addressed to King George V. Although the Cobham flight experienced one or two delays and technical difficulties along the way, the trusty DH.50J touched down in London on March 13, two days before the *Windsor Castle* docked in Southampton. The footage that was shot by Basil Emmott on both sectors of the flight was edited into a feature film and released to cinemas throughout the world under the title *With Cobham to the Cape*. Audiences loved it and the appeal of air travel was considerably bolstered. Not long after his return flight from Cape Town, Cobham was in the air again, this time flying to Australia and back, for which he was knighted by King George V. Later, the now-Sir Alan Cobham organized a series of flying tours and aerial displays in Britain, Ireland and South Africa which were humorously termed 'Alan Cobham's Flying Circus.' These performances showcased some amazingly daring and skillful flying, furthering interest in aviation and helping to instill an even deeper awareness of flight among the general public.

By now a lot of people were trying their hand at opening air links between Europe and Africa. The first solo flight in a light aircraft from London to Cape Town—as opposed to a heavy commercial machine or a converted military airplane—was made between September 1 and 28, 1927, by 30-year-old British-born South African Aviation Corps Flight Lieutenant Richard Reid

'Dick' Bentley. He was piloting a de Havilland DH.60X Moth registered G-EBSO and named *Dorys*. The name was chosen in honor of Bentley's fiancé, Miss Dorys Oldfield. Bentley made another two return flights over the next two years, totalling a distance of 51,652 miles.

But it was not only the male of the species who was taking to the air during those exhilarating times. While women would not legally acquire the right to vote in the United Kingdom until the enactment of the Equal Franchise Act in 1928, it was that same year that the first female aviator took up the challenge of flying solo from South Africa to London. Thirty-two-year-old Irish-born Lady Mary Heath, the former Miss Sophie Eliot-Lynn, took off from Cape Town in an Avro Avian III monoplane registered G-EBUG on February 12 bound for London. In Uganda, she met up with Dick Bentley and his new wife as they were making their way northwards in *Dorys*. As Lady Mary was experiencing some immigration and legal trouble with the authorities, Bentley agreed to escort her from Uganda to Khartoum. She finally reached Croydon aerodrome near London more than three months later, on May 17. She had hoped her flight would take three weeks but, as so many had found out before and after her, flying across Africa was not for the faint of heart. Nevertheless, Lady Mary accomplished the task, joking that it was perfectly safe for a single woman to fly across Africa wearing a dainty frock from a French couturier and keeping her nose powdered provided she also carried half-a-dozen extra gowns, a fur stole, a tennis racket, a shotgun and a Bible, all of which she had indeed stowed in the baggage compartment of her aircraft. The British public reverently referred to her as 'Lady Lindy,' a play on the name of Charles Lindberg who had flown solo across the Atlantic the previous year. When Amelia Earhart arrived in London as a trans-Atlantic passenger, Lady Mary met her and invited her to take a flight in her Avro Avian. Miss Earhart was so impressed with the machine that she instantly bought it and had it shipped back to the United States for her own use. Speaking of the suffragette movement once again, it is interesting to note that women in the United States did not attain the right to vote until the 19th Amendment to the Constitution was ratified on August 18, 1920, only eight years before Lady Mary had traversed Africa alone by air.

Another feisty female pilot in the saga of opening up African airways was also Irish-born and of an aristocratic background. Thirty-seven-year-old Lady Mary Bailey, daughter of an Irish peer and wife of a South African mining magnate flew solo from Britain to South Africa in a de Havilland DH.60X Cirrus Moth registered G-EBSE. It was equipped with an extra fuel tank. She followed a route over the Sudan and Lake Victoria to Tanganyika. Leaving Croydon on March 9, 1928, she reached her destination three weeks later on March 30. In Khartoum she encountered Dick Bentley who was on another one of his flights. Being a single woman she was also experiencing difficulties with the local authorities and immigration officers so once again Dick Bentley rallied to the cause, escorting her out of the country before turning northwards again. It seemed that the British authorities and Muslim patriarchs in the Sudan were not entirely happy about single women flying hither and thither around the sky on their own. Nevertheless, Lady Bailey continued on her southward journey and then suffered an unfortunate crash in Tabora, Tanganyika. This necessitated the procurement of a replacement aircraft which her husband quickly arranged in Johannesburg. It was a new DH.60X Cirrus II Moth and was flown up to her. While Lady Bailey was thrilled with her African flying experience, she was not yet satisfied with the accomplishment of reaching Cape Town from London. She wanted more. Much more. In a very short while she was up in the air again on a return flight but this time following a more westerly route over the Belgian Congo (today's Democratic Republic of the Congo), the Sahara and Sudan. She left Cape

Town in September and landed back in England on January 16, 1929. Her total journey had covered 18,000 miles, making it not only the longest flight undertaken by a woman but also the longest solo flight accomplished by anyone up to that time.

Things were now buzzing in the skies. In March 1927, four British RAF Fairey IIID single engine reconnaissance biplanes flying in close formation made a return flight between Cairo and Cape Town. The first aerial trip from France to South Africa was flown by Captains Raymond Mauler and Maurice Baud in a single-engine French-built Caudron C128 in 1928. The journey took four months, leaving Le Bourget, Paris on March 2 and arriving in Cape Town on July 5. That same year Lieut. Patrick Murdoch of the SAAF left Croydon on July 29 for Cape Town in an Avro Avian III, registered G-EBVU, arriving at his destination fourteen days later. And then there was the young couple Stan Halse and his wife who departed the de Havilland factory on September 10 in a DH. 60G Gipsy Moth, also Cape Town-bound. In 1930, another remarkably brave woman took to the air. The 64-year-old Duchess of Bedford took off from Lympne Airfield in Kent on April 10 in her single-engine Dutch-built Fokker F.VII registered G-EBTS and named *The Spider*. With her was co-pilot Captain Charles Douglas Barnard. They reached Cape Town ten days later after having flown 9,000 miles, once again breaking the flying time record.

Shattering records was now all the rage. On Sunday, October 5, 1930, 31-year-old Rheinhold Ferdinand 'Caspar' Caspareuthus, one of the original SAAF pilots of the defunct experimental airmail service between Cape Town and Durban, took off from Croydon in a single-engine de Havilland Puss Moth registered ZS-ACD. The aircraft had been purchased by Reginald H. Marshall, a wealthy young Port Elizabeth aviation enthusiast, for his own use. Caspareuthus was only too happy to fly the machine from the manufacturers to South Africa on his behalf. When he landed at his destination he had set another record, beating the Duchess of Bedford's flying time by more than 20 hours.

With all these pioneering efforts paving the way, the wide blue domain above Africa beckoned ever more brightly. Clouds billowed, birds wheeled in lazy circles in the thermals while warm winds caressed the landscape. A new age was dawning for those whose frontier was the sky. The time was right. The next great chapter in the saga of African aviation was ready to be written. And one man was waiting in the wings to bring it to fruition. He, more than anyone else, would become the true doyen of commercial aviation in the southern skies of Africa.

Chapter 2

A Man Called Mac

Sandwiched between South Africa and neighboring Mozambique, lies the landlocked kingdom of Eswatini. Once known as Swaziland, it is roughly the size of the state of New Jersey. At the time of the British Empire, it was a Protectorate of the Crown. It was into this ruggedly beautiful and hilly land that an Englishman named Alexander Mitchell Miller came to settle. Born on board a ship in the Straits of Malacca near Singapore in 1865, he grew up in Britain, became a journalist with the *Liverpool Mercury*, married in London and then came to Africa to seek his fortune. After trying his hand at journalism for *The Argus* newspaper in Cape Town, he was lured northwards by a sense of adventure. On seeing Swaziland for the first time, he became enchanted by its promise and potential. Miller was a man of many talents, dabbling in agriculture and trade. He surveyed the land, created the first topographical map of Swaziland and laid out a water canal that would eventually nourish the little country's future sugar industry. But Miller was always a writer at heart. He was fascinated by local Swazi tribal lore and culture and wrote extensively about it, most of which was published in England. In 1897, he established the territory's first newspaper, the *Times of Swaziland*. As one of the first white men to put down roots in the kingdom, he became close friends with its ruler, Paramount Chief Umbandini. Their relationship was so cordial that in 1899, the royal Swazi court appointed Miller to become the king's personal secretary as well his representative in all dealings and negotiations with the British authorities and other white settlers. Miller and his wife Beatrice Mary produced seven children, the eldest of whom was the first white baby born in the kingdom. The birth took place at Schombeni on September 10th,

1892. The healthy little boy was christened Allister Macintosh Miller.

Little Macintosh Miller—who was sometimes called by the nickname 'Mac'—frolicked barefoot among the hills and grasslands with local Swazi children and was fluent in the vernacular language, Siswati. Horse and pony riding, swimming in the rivers, fishing, hunting, playing with *dolosse*—miniature oxen fashioned out of clay and dried in the sun—and other typical African boyhood activities were no doubt the key elements that made up an average day for him. A solid British-style education was impossible to come by in the isolated mountain kingdom so even though young Mac loved the adventurous outdoor lifestyle his parents sent him to Grahamstown in the Eastern Cape of South Africa. There he was enrolled at St. Aidan's School for Boys. It was an institution molded on the traditionally strict public schools of England where sport, fair play, discipline, religious observance and strong academic achievement went hand in hand. Other than serving as the school organist Miller turned out to be an average student but, in addition to his musical talent, he had a penchant for things mechanical. After completing high school, he was accepted as an engineering and chemistry student at the local Rhodes University College. This was another fine educational establishment based on the British model. In 1912, after a year at Rhodes, he was sent abroad to City and Guilds College at London University. When World War I broke out he volunteered for service with the Cavalry in the British Army, serving initially as a trooper in the Special Reserve of King Edward's Horse and then as a Second Lieutenant in the Royal Scots Greys. Miller was neither a large nor athletic man. His lanky frame was only five feet tall. But within this reserved figure beat a brave heart. He was imbued with an unusually sharp and alert mind. Mac Miller was game for anything. He had a friendly, outgoing disposition but was never overt or vociferous. He went about his duties with quiet alacrity, always gaining the confidence and trust of those around him. Those who knew him well not only trusted him but liked him enormously. As a result, Miller was extremely popular with his fellow soldiers.

Early in 1915, he was riding his horse when the animal was startled by a distant noise or gunfire. It reared up, slipped and fell on top of him, crushing one of his kidneys. During emergency surgery, it had to be removed. After recovering from his injury, Miller was deemed unfit to continue as a cavalry officer so he joined the Royal Flying Corps (RFC). This placed him on an irreversible path leading to events far beyond his imagining.

After qualifying as a pilot, Miller was posted to Number Three Squadron 'B' Flight in France. The squadron was operating French-built Morane-Saulnier aircraft along the Western Front. It was a Morane-Saulnier L single-engine, single-seat monoplane on which a fixed gun was first fired from an aircraft at the beginning of 1915. The weapon—a Hotchkiss 8mm M1914 machine gun—was mounted just behind the engine cowling and fired through the spinning propeller blades. As a firing system synchronized with the spinning blades had not yet been invented, the bullets were deflected off the wooden propeller by a sheathing of metal plates on each blade. It was crude but it worked. Later, a synchronous method was found that enabled pilots and gunners to fire directly through the spinning blades without hitting them. The Morane-Saulnier was the forerunner of many machine-gun-equipped fighters that followed, opening up the skies to the proverbial 'aerial dogfight.'

Miller took to the air as though he were born to it. While undertaking a series of observation flights over Delville Wood between July 15 and 20, 1916, he displayed remarkable bravery for which he was awarded a Distinguished Service Order (DSO.) The wording on the citation stated: "During operations when attacking troops on the ground under heavy fire on one occasion he flew close to the ground along a line of hostile machine guns, engaging them with his machine, drawing their fire and allowing the cavalry to advance. Again, when alone, he engaged five enemy machines, bringing one down and successfully bombing a troop train, coming down to 300 feet to make sure of hitting his target."

Shortly afterwards, Miller volunteered for an unusual mission. Some thought it a suicidal undertaking but he was determined to do it. Because of his prowess in the air, he was given the go-ahead. A man by the name of Hans Immelman—born in Dresden, Germany but brought up in Uitenhage, a town also in the Eastern Cape province of South Africa where Miller was educated—had been a German sympathizer when hostilities began. At the outbreak of the war, he travelled from South Africa to Europe and joined the German Air Force. Immelman rapidly became a renowned air ace with six kills to his name but in June, 1916, he was shot down and killed in his Albatross DIII aircraft by a Royal Flying Corps pilot. The pilot, George R. McCubbin flying a BE2c aircraft, was also from South Africa. Because of the strong South African connection behind the incident, Miller took off from France and, flying solo, made a dangerously low pass over the German airfield where Immelman had been stationed and dropped a wreath in his honor. Even though cruel and dreadful weapons such as mustard gas, grenades and barbed wire were used in the trenches during World War I, back in those days when the airplane first became an instrument of war chivalry, honor and tradition were virtues that defined the airman's code of conduct.

The British government and senior officers of the Royal Flying Corps were highly impressed by the caliber of their South African pilots. As the air war in Europe intensified, they realized that it was necessary to recruit more aviators for the RFC. When Miller's aircraft was shot down by enemy fire and he survived the crash, his commanding officers decided to temporarily take him out of battle and send him home to the Union of South Africa to recruit new pilots. In October, 1916, he returned to his homeland by sea in order to sign up 30 more young men. But his reputation preceded him and his arrival was met with such enthusiasm that far more potential candidates than anticipated lined up to join the Corps. Miller was allowed to sign up as many as 450 new recruits. Because of this success, when he returned to Britain, he was promoted to the rank of major. However, the war was intensifying and there was urgent need for even more pilots. There was little time to lose. All the countries that were either under British colonial rule or historically aligned with the United Kingdom did their part to send volunteers for the Flying Corps. Within weeks of his promotion, Miller was again dispatched to recruit additional candidates in the Union. This time he was given the use of two BE2e aircraft, an assistant pilot and two RFC mechanics. Britain itself could not spare any aircraft so they came from an unusual source. Miller's renown had spread so far and wide that the small British community in faraway Brazil had pooled their resources and donated the two aircraft for his African mission. About 3,500 BE2s in eight different variants were built for the war. Designed by the Royal Flying Corps, the machines were mass-produced at the Vickers, Bristol and other factories in England. The aircraft's wings and fuselage were made of light metal and wooden spars and ribs were covered with stretched Irish linen doped in varnish and pigment. Few pilots actually liked the biplane, primarily because the pilot's cockpit was situated quite far back in the fuselage. The forward seat was used by the gunner. It was a cramped, uncomfortable machine for its two-man crew but it was agile and highly maneuverable and gave excellent service as a fighter, bomber and reconnaissance aircraft. The two Brazilian machines were perfect for Miller's recruiting mission to South Africa.

Miller, his team and the crated BE2e components, arrived in Cape Town in October 1917. The aircraft were reassembled and test flown at Youngsfield in Wynberg, Cape Town. In recognition of their Brazilian-based donors they were named *Rio de Janeiro Briton No. 1* and *Rio de Janeiro Briton No. 2*. As soon as they were airworthy the recruiting campaign got underway, to the accompaniment of much pomp and fanfare. In November, Miller flew one of the craft to Port Elizabeth, a distance of 410 miles (660 kilometers,) setting a record for the first non-stop long-distance flight in South Africa. His popularity soared all over the country and the press loved him. Wherever he went he was treated like a hero. Apart from being a modest man with a very approachable disposition, Miller was also a good speaker. His audiences were captivated by his talks. More importantly, he was an outstanding pilot and role model. Making use of local racetracks, golf courses, open fields and clear stretches of road as airfields, he gave numerous flying displays, barrel rolling, looping the loop and recovering from purposely-induced stalls. The public was enthralled. Mayors, town councilors, welcoming parties, ladies and gentry bedecked in their fineries turned out to meet him wherever he landed. Lavish town hall banquets and dances were held in his honor. Schools, shops, banks and markets were closed to allow everyone to see the two flying machines and their pilots. Sporting clubs and public institutions issued commemorative brochures, special dinner menus, pamphlets, souvenir flags and ribbons to mark the events. Those occasions were invariably the first time many people in towns and rural areas had ever seen an airplane, let alone be treated to a thrilling flying display.

Crowds clustered around the BE2e's and had their photographs snapped with Miller and the pilot of the second machine, Lieutenant Jack Bagshaw. Enthusiastic young male candidates lined to sign up for the RFC. From all over the Union they came. On horseback, by ox wagon, buggy, train, in Model T's, on foot, in groups and on their own, English speakers and Afrikaners, the youth of South Africa scrambled for a place in the esteemed Royal Flying Corps. It is believed that a total of about eight thousand applicants turned up, many of them still

Crowds cluster around one of Miller's aircraft during his recruitment campaign in the Union for the Royal Flying Corps

in high school. Miller selected 2,000 of them for flying training in Britain, of which the vast majority were eventually accepted and became pilots. Those who did go on to join the RFC were dubbed 'Miller's Boys,' a distinctive label the budding young airmen were only too happy to carry.

During the tour Miller and his entourage also managed to collect £13,000 that was donated to the RFC hospital fund in England to help injured airmen. It was at this time that Miller, now 25 years old, married Marion Mercy Bagshaw, a young lady he met in Port Elizabeth. It remains uncertain whether she was related to Miller's co-pilot Jack Bagshaw but she was a year older than Miller and would faithfully remain at his side and support him in all his efforts for the next 34 years. The couple would go on to have three children, a son and two daughters.

By 1918, the Royal Flying Corps had officially become the Royal Air Force (RAF). When Miller returned to England in July of that year, he was immediately posted to France to command 45

Squadron, flying Sopwith F1 Camel biplanes out of Bettoncourt. While his fellow officers usually called him by his nickname, 'Mac,' Miller's outstanding reputation was such that not only those under his command but civilians and the press respectfully referred to him as the more formal 'Major Miller,' a name that would stick long after the war was over. Out of reverence, few outside his immediate circle of friends called him by his real first name or his nickname. To most, he was always 'Major Miller.' His commission commanding 45 Squadron lasted from October 1918 until February 1919 and in June he was summoned to Buckingham Palace in London and awarded the Order of the British Empire (OBE) for his dedicated and spirited wartime service.

Aviation was now well and truly embedded in Miller's blood. Above all else, he longed to create a passenger-carrying airline to serve South Africa. Immediately after being demobilised in June 1919, he formed a business. Registered in London, it was called the South African Aerial Navigation Company but, before returning to the Union, Miller merged the venture with the also-new South African Aerial Transport Company, an enterprise under the control of another ex-wartime pilot, Major A. Francis. Miller's role was Technical and Operations Manager. As the war had now ended, hundreds of surplus Avro 504 machines were available for sale so the company bought five Avro 504K versions of the aircraft, recruited additional staff and mechanics in England and in July 1919, they left for South Africa, lock, stock and barrel. Operations were set up at the new Baragwanath airfield on the western perimeter of Johannesburg. The Avro 504Ks' dual-seating arrangement made them perfect for pleasure flights or 'flips' as many aviation enthusiasts called them. They were also well suited as a glider tug for sportsmen or for towing advertising banners and even for American-style barnstorming and aerial displays. But to make the company pay for itself, Miller turned the craft into aerial 'taxis,' offering passenger services from Baragwanath to destinations near and far. The fare between Johannesburg and Pretoria—30 miles away—was ten guineas (£10.10.0). For five months things looked good. 2,000 passengers were flown a total of 29,800 miles before expenses exceeded income and the company failed. Not to be outdone, Miller moved to the city of Durban, turned to politics and ran for office with the predominantly English-speaking South African Party. In 1924, he became a Member of Parliament for the constituency of Point, a relatively well-to-do harbour, waterfront and industrial area of Durban.

But his sights were constantly set on the skies. A burning desire within him to bring a commercial air service to the country never faded. In February 1924, he visited Holland as a guest of Anthony Fokker, the famous designer and builder of military and civil aircraft. On that trip he was excited to witness the advances being made in modern aircraft design and construction. In 1925, the government of the Union of South Africa appointed Miller as a member the recently-formed Civil Air Board and in November 1926, he undertook a visit to aircraft manufacturers in the United States and Canada. In March, 1927, he brought the first de Havilland DH.60 Cirrus Moth aircraft to the country from Britain. With the formation of the Civil Air Board, all aircraft now had to be licensed and registered locally. According to arrangements with civilian aviation authorities around the world, every country was allocated its own prefix registration code. Before the formation of the Civil Air Board in South Africa, aircraft were registered with the British prefix G, followed by a U which stood for the Union of South Africa. An aircraft would be listed, for example, as G-UAAH or G-UABC and so on. But now South Africa had its own prefix, ZS. Miller's new Cirrus Moth was the very first airplane to be placed on the local register and was designated ZS-AAA. Delighted to have his airplane sport an official local registration, Miller went a step further and named it as well. As a nod to his political constituency, he called it *The Point*. Without wasting any time, he climbed into the machine, toured the country, landed at many small towns, encouraged interest in aviation and assisted in the formation of flying clubs for those who could afford to buy, co-own, rent or fly their own aircraft. By 1927, a total of 75 Moth variants had been registered to various owners in South Africa. Many of them were based at Baragwanath aerodrome in Johannesburg where the Johannesburg Light Plane Club was formed. This was soon followed by flying clubs in Cape Town, Port Elizabeth, East London, Durban and Kimberley.

Miller's passion to start an airline smouldered more strongly than ever. After many futile efforts asking the government to assist him to set up a company he began knocking on doors in the private sector, including mining houses and other big corporations. Almost at the point of despair, in 1929, Miller approached the South African office of oil and petroleum giant, the Atlantic Refining Company. To his surprise, they showed interest in the idea. Being associated with an airline would be a great way for them to market their products and, besides, airplanes needed fuel and oil. As far as Atlantic Refining was concerned, it was a win-win situation. To Miller's delight, an agreement was reached. He would get his airline. A company was duly registered with a capital of £5,000. One share was held by Dayton Clark, Managing Director of Atlantic Refining Company. His assistant manager, E.H. Lewis, held another share while Miller himself held all the rest.

The next challenge was to figure how to put the new airline together and make it profitable. Bubbling over with enthusiasm, Miller arranged a meeting with the Minister of Posts and Telegraphs in Pretoria, Henry W. Sampson. Miller knew that the government had set aside a paltry annual budget of £8,000 to subsidize any company willing to undertake a long-distance airmail delivery service on behalf of the Post Office. It was an absurdly small amount of money for the size of the task but Miller was determined to persuade the government to offer his new company the mail contract. He hoped that they would eventually allow him to start carrying fare-paying passengers as well as mail. At first, Sampson was reticent about the whole concept. What aircraft did Miller have at his disposal? How much mail could they carry? Were his planes reliable? How many pilots were in his employ? Where would his new company be based? The critical factor in the entire discussion was that any agency transporting the mails should have one primary objective in mind and that was to connect the country's major cities with the inbound and outbound overseas mail service of the Union Castle Line Royal Mail steamships in Cape Town. Flying the mail to and from Cape Town for the foreign mail service was of paramount importance. After much discussion, Miller agreed that he would procure a fleet of aircraft, use them to fly an exclusive mail-only service for the first year and thereafter offer them to carry passengers as well as mail. Would the Minister agree to that? Would that make the government happy? After some haggling behind closed doors with members of the Cabinet, Sampson eventually agreed to the operation, especially after Miller declared that in order to expedite the mail service he would base his company in a location that was a midway point between the furthermost principle cities of the Union and Cape Town itself. To that end, Port Elizabeth was chosen as the base of the operation. The city's location on the map made it the nodal point between Cape Town, East London and Durban and the inland cities of Johannesburg, Pretoria, Bloemfontein and Kimberley. The set-up was similar to modern-day airline hubs in the major cities of Europe, Asia and the United States, or like the role played by Memphis, Tennessee as the central point in the operation of today's giant FedEx Express freight service in the United States, whereby Memphis serves as the central distribution center for all incoming and outgoing freight regardless of their source or destination.

Allister Miller's first four de Havilland DH.60 Gipsy Moth biplanes that formed the nucleus of his new airline Union Airways for carrying airmail in 1929

One of Allister Miller's five de Havilland DH.60 Gipsy Moths in 1929

Major Allister Macintosh 'Mac' Miller tops up the fuel tanks of a de Havilland DH.60 Gipsy Moth for an airmail flight

Miller placed an order with the de Havilland company in Britain for four new twin-passenger DH.60 Gipsy Moth biplanes. An additional second-hand DH.60 was purchased from international racing champion Malcolm Campbell who had broken the world land speed record in his *Bluebird* racing car the year before in the United States. He had visited South Africa with a team of mechanics and a fast new car, intending to break his own record at a flat stretch of dry lake called Verneukpan in the northwest Cape province. As Campbell had been a fighter pilot during World War I, he owned his own aircraft and brought it with him to South Africa to commute between the dry lake and Cape Town and Johannesburg. Unfortunately, he failed to beat his land speed record in South Africa but he was more than willing to sell his Gipsy Moth to Miller.

The five Gipsy Moths in Miller's new company were registered ZS-ABH, ZS-ABI, ZS-ABJ, ZS-ABK, and ZS-ABL. Four pilots were engaged, Graham Wilmot Bellin, William Frost Davenport, Dennis Labistour and the renowned record-breaking aviator who had flown solo from London to Cape Town, Rheinhold 'Caspar' Caspareuthus.

A mechanical engineer by the name of Jock Robertson was hired to take charge of the maintenance side of the operation. His assistant was H.J.C. Klopper and there were four apprentices, Ron Madeley, Victor Smith, Jack Bagshaw and Fred Eggeling. In addition, three local Xhosa laborers joined the payroll. As Eggeling came highly recommended, he was recruited in the inland city of Germiston and relocated to Port Elizabeth. He would later pass his flying exams and become an outstanding pilot with the company. Victor Smith was originally from the coastal city of George. He too would go on to gain his wings and become an accomplished pilot, accumulating a total of 7,000 hours in the air over the next 46 years, which would include a trail-blazing solo flight in the 1930s from Cape Town to London via West Africa and a return journey following the eastern route.

With five aircraft, four experienced pilots, a team of mechanics, a technical base and an operations center at Fairview Aerodrome in Port Elizabeth, Miller set up his operations. At last he was a happy man. On July 24, 1929, his dreams were realized when the company called Union Airways formally came into being.

Major Allister Macintosh 'Mac' Miller

A government-issued Post Office Circular number 578 dated July 22, 1929, proudly announced that "All classes of mail matter except parcels can be sent by the aerial mail service, with a supplementary charge for conveying postal articles at four pence per ounce." *The Star* newspaper in Johannesburg gave the impending service much fanfare. It announced to its readership that "Five new aircraft are coming for delivering mail. Service delivery times will experience a saving of from 12 to 24 hours!" An excited public waited with bated breath.

At exactly 7.42 am on a chilly Monday morning on August 26, 1929, Miller took off in ZS-ABI from Brooklyn airfield, Cape Town with five bags of mail unloaded from the steamer from Southampton that had docked earlier that morning. He was bound for Port Elizabeth, initiating the official beginning of the airmail service. After a four-and-a-half hour flight, he landed at Port Elizabeth, taxied over to the Union Airways hangar and

Loading mail bags aboard a de Havilland DH.60 Gipsy Moth

handed the bags over to two waiting relay aircraft. The first one, ZS-ABJ, was bound for the coastal city of Durban. It was piloted by Rheinhold 'Caspar' Caspareuthus who arrived at his destination two hours ahead of schedule. The second aircraft, ZS-ABH, piloted by Graham Bellin, headed for Johannesburg by way of Bloemfontein. The weather was not in Bellin's favour and he arrived in Bloemfontein late in the afternoon, with insufficient time to make it to Johannesburg by nightfall. The mailbags were unloaded, rushed over to the railway station and taken to Johannesburg by overnight express steam train, just in time for postal delivery early the next morning.

All subsequent flights to Johannesburg landed at the new Germiston Aerodrome that had only been opened two days before the airmail service began. Consisting of little more than a grass-covered field and a single hangar, Germiston Aerodrome was situated to the southeast of Johannesburg, just a short distance from the center of the city. Germiston would soon become South Africa's premier domestic and international aerial gateway. The site had first been suggested by Miller himself as far back as 1917 when he was on his recruiting campaign to sign up pilots for the Royal Flying Corps. The aerodrome was better placed for the Johannesburg mail service than the older Baragwanath airfield further to the west, which would nevertheless remain functional for many more years as home to the ever-growing Johannesburg

Light Plane Club. The Germiston airfield was near what the locals called Victoria Lake. The large natural body of water into which effluent from surrounding gold mines was drained shimmered like a silver mirror and Miller said that would it make a perfect beacon, acting as he put it "like a guiding star to aviators by day as well as by night." A municipal golf course was on one side of the lake, right next to a vast open field where Miller said the aerodrome should be established. In February 1929, an agreement was signed between the Germiston Town Council, the nearby Elandsfontein Land and Estate Company and the Rand Refinery. The latter was the world's largest gold refining plant which processed ore from South Africa's many gold mines, turning them into the standard 400–troy-ounce pure gold bars for sale on the international bullion market. The three organizations became joint owners of what was initially called the Germiston Public Aerodrome or, in Afrikaans, Germiston *Vliegpark* (Flying Park). When the first Union Airways Gipsy Moth touched down on that grassy airfield with its load of mailbags, the aerodrome immediately became a vital cog in the country's communication and transportation system as well as an essential component in the mechanism that drove the South African economy.

On August 29, 1929, the first outgoing mail flight left the Germiston Aerodrome. At the same time a flight took off from Stamford Hill Aerodrome in Durban on the Natal coast. Both were bound for the Union Airways headquarters in Port Elizabeth. From there, Miller himself flew the combined cargo of mailbags to Cape Town, arriving there at 1.40 pm, two-and-a-half hours before the *Carnarvon Castle* mailship sailed for England. The South African airmail service had officially begun and was soon ticking like a precision Swiss chronometer. Miller was thrilled. As were his backers, the Atlantic Refining Company, and certainly also the Minister of Posts and Telegraphs in Pretoria, Henry W. Sampson and the entire staff of the South African Post Office, not to mention the public at large and the many mining, manufacturing and business interests who were going to benefit from the new, more expedient mail service to and from the United Kingdom, Europe and places beyond.

The mail service ran so smoothly that on January 29, 1930, Union Airways was given the go ahead to begin carrying passengers. To attract customers the company initiated an advertising campaign that proclaimed: "Travel by air in comfort and safety! Before and after every flight each plane is checked and overhauled by expert mechanics - an absolute guarantee of its airworthiness." The cost of a return ticket between, for example, Port Elizabeth and Cape Town was £18 but each of the Gipsy Moths could only carry one passenger. Miller believed that the travelling public was really keen to fly. Despite the fact that most people were actually terrified of going up into the sky in a noisy, bone-rattling machine of dubious reliability, Miller was of the opinion that a larger, more comfortable airplane would attract new customers. In 1929, just before he was granted his passenger-carrying license, he had placed an order for one of the latest commercial airliners of the day from the Fokker plant in Teterboro, New Jersey. The factory was a division of the Dutch-based Fokker company in Holland and was owned by General Motors in the United States who built the aircraft under license.

Fokker Model 8 Super Universal passenger aircraft

Major Allister Miller and his pride and joy, the Fokker Super Universal

The Fokker Model 8 Super Universal was a high wing monoplane with a single nine-cylinder Pratt & Whitney Wasp engine of 420-horsepower. It had accommodation for six passengers in an enclosed cabin. At a price of $22,000 it was at the cutting edge of technology and the latest word in comfort. It had a length of 37 ft, a height of nine ft and a wingspan of 51 ft. The wings were made of varnished wood with two main spars and light ribs covered in sheets of plywood. The nose containing the single engine was made of metal and the fuselage was constructed of steel tubes cross-braced with wires and covered in stretched cotton fabric. The floor and an internal bulkhead separating the cabin from the cockpit were made of wood. It carried 150 gallons of fuel, giving it a flying time of approximately six hours at a cruising speed of 100 mph. The Fokker had a service ceiling of 19,340 ft although it seldom flew at that height because those were the days before cabin pressurization. The thinner atmosphere at that height would have caused passengers considerable ear discomfort and made it difficult to breathe. But, if needed, the Fokker could briefly hop above low-lying clouds and adverse weather.

The fuselage of the Union Airways Fokker Model 8 Super Universal was painted in brilliant yellow with red trim lines. It was an eye-catching beauty and the airline's staff lovingly referred to it as the "red and yellow monster." Registered ZS-ABR, the Fokker took off from Port Elizabeth on its maiden paying flight with passengers on January 22, 1930. The man who bought the very first ticket was a local medical doctor, R.D. Laurie, who promptly became violently airsick as soon as the craft took off and turned towards its destination, Cape Town. The unfortunate incident was noted by a reporter named W. Gingell who was also on board. He unwittingly published the story in the Port Elizabeth newspaper, *Eastern Province Herald*. That kind of publicity did not exactly help to attract passengers to air travel. Quite the opposite. But Miller was unfazed. He loved the Fokker. It represented everything he had dreamed about and hoped for. The bright yellow machine with its powerful Wasp engine was his pride and joy. Later, when the Fokker began flying the Johannesburg route it became quite popular with the travelling public.

But, in actual fact, all was not well. The cost of running the airline and of maintaining the airmail service began to exceed income. Debts started mounting up. The Atlantic Refining company was becoming nervous about the future of the airline and its financial prospects. But Miller soldiered on, continually calling on them to inject additional funds into the operation.

Doing his best to keep it out of the headlines Miller had quietly found another form of financial assistance. General Motors South Africa Limited in Port Elizabeth—the same city where Union Airways was based—had a factory where vehicles such as Chevrolet, Oldsmobile, Pontiac and Buick were assembled from components shipped in from the United States. The plant was wholly owned by General Motors in the US which also owned the factory in New Jersey where the Super Universal airliner was built. When Miller decided to order the large Fokker airplane for his company, he held discussions with General Motors in Port Elizabeth and by signing a debenture agreement with them, he had managed to acquire the aircraft. Naturally, this left Union Airways with a considerable financial commitment to General Motors but Miller believed that ultimately all would be well and that his bond to the company would eventually be cleared.

What no one could foresee, however, was Black Tuesday on October 24, 1929, on Wall Street. The effects of the United States Stock Market crash rumbled violently around the globe. As the Dust Bowl and its ramifications swept through the financial corridors of the world, Miller's position became even more precarious. London-based Imperial Airways became aware of his woes and tried to capitalize on the situation. As Imperial was fostering its international route network to connect London with the outermost fringes of the British Empire executives believed that by investing in Union Airways, it would acquire an important foothold in the South African market. That would serve Imperial's interests, especially as the day would certainly come when the Imperial service from London would reach all the way to South Africa. In an overture to Miller, Imperial offered to buy Union Airways outright. But Miller would hear none of it. As far as he was concerned, Union Airways should remain a South African-owned and controlled enterprise. He even mentioned Imperial's offer to Oswald Pirow, the Minister of Defense and Transport. Pirow advised him not to accept it as the government also felt that Union Airways should retain its all-South African identity. Pirow went as far as promising that if Miller rejected the British offer the South African state coffers would provide him with financial support. The Prime Minister, General James Barry Hertzog, confirmed that promise. But, sadly, it never came. South Africa was reeling under the effects of the Great Depression and money was tight. Also, the state-owned railway system was reticent to see any opposition to its lucrative first-class rail travel revenues. A government levy had already been applied to air tickets which made them fifty per cent more expensive than rail travel for the same route.

By this time two de Havilland Puss Moths had joined the Union Airways fleet. The first one, named *Springbok* and registered ZS-ACD, was the same one that Rheinhold Caspareuthus had flown out from England for private buyer Reginald H. Marshall on his record-breaking flight. The second one, ZS-ACB, had been owned by a company called Aeros Pty. Limited and had been used by the de Havilland aircraft builders for demonstration and sales purposes to flying clubs and private buyers. The two Puss Moths had small enclosed cabins, were faster than the Gipsy Moths and could fly from Port Elizabeth to Cape Town in only four hours, nearly an hour quicker than the time taken by the Gipsy Moths. But faster flying times did not help much. Passenger loads were still not up to expectation. Nevertheless, Union Airways soldiered on.

And then the first accident occurred.

One of the original Gipsy Moths, ZS-ABK, was written off in a crash near Bedford in the Eastern Cape on August 4, 1930. According to the skimpy reports that exist about the incident the aircraft was on a Johannesburg-bound flight from Port Elizabeth. Fortunately, no one on board was injured but the accident put a deep dent into Union Airway's already-stretched finances. Miller turned his mind to thinking again about the Imperial Airways offer to buy the company. Would that not be the expedient thing to do at this time? He mulled over the prospects, then decided against it. It was an unwise decision on his part. The purchase would undoubtedly have bailed him out of his financial doldrums.

Despite the Wall Street crash, British-based Imperial Airways was on sound and solid footing. And it was growing from strength to strength. Its genesis lay in a long series of interesting historic events briefly worth exploring here. On December 20,

1918, Britain's Secretary of State for the Royal Air Force, Lord Weir of Eastwood, had visited the National Aircraft Factory, run by Crossley Motors Limited at Heaton Chapel in Manchester. World War I was over and the entire future of aviation stretched ahead in shrouded yet exciting mystery. During a pre-luncheon speech Lord Weir remarked: "Any adequate survey of the future of civilization must involve an enquiry into the future of transport, for transport is that which welds civilization together, and its function in human progress is extremely important. We have hitherto had transport by land and by water and today we have, in actual practice, transport by air. It may well be—but I am not here as a prophet—that the new mode of transport will one day rival and even surpass the other two."

How right he was.

In 1919, the British Secretary of State appointed an advisory committee on Civil Aviation under his chairmanship to plan air routes for the British Empire. The report recommended the establishment of services connecting all points of the empire, starting with a route to India, then to Australia and ultimately to South Africa. This was the catalyst behind the enormous undertaking by which airfields and landing strips had been etched onto all pink sectors of the map down the spine and along the eastern half of Africa, from Cairo to Cape Town. The air route to India was to pass through Cairo. Once established this would connect with the future service southwards to Cape Town. The scramble was on. Who would be the first to fly what would become known as the Empire Air Route in Africa?

The first private concern in Britain to plan a commercial air service in Africa was the Blackburn Aircraft Company, run by aircraft builder and businessman Robert Blackburn. His company was offered the cooperation of the governments of Sudan, Uganda and Kenya for the establishment of the route to Kisumu on the shores of Lake Victoria. The British Air Ministry was considering approving Blackburn's plans when Alan Cobham returned from his famous flight to Cape Town in 1926. Based on his experience of flying to and from Cape Town over long sectors of the continent, Cobham was enthusiastic about a commercial passenger air service but he insisted that any future airliner should have at least three robust and dependable engines. He went on to say that each aircraft should also have two experienced pilots on board and that one of them should be in possession of a navigator's certificate. In addition, he was adamant that any future passenger service should be backed by an efficient and reliable radio and weather reporting system. In 1927, Cobham registered his own aviation company and in November, he flew out to Africa on an extensive survey to plan its operations, returning to the United Kingdom in 1928. Shortly afterwards he merged his company with Blackburn Airlines, creating Cobham-Blackburn Airways. Anxious to begin flying passengers from London up and down the length of Africa, he submitted plans to the British government for a service from Alexandria to Mwanza in Tanganyika, hoping to eventually extend the service to Cape Town. The government of the Union of South Africa looked on all of this with great enthusiasm and even promised limited financial support for the venture.

Meanwhile, Imperial Airways had already come into existence in 1924 through the amalgamation of four independent British aviation companies; Instone Air Line, Daimler Airways, Handley Page Transport and the British Marine Air Navigation Company. After much deliberation the government of the United Kingdom decided to give Imperial Airways first option on routes throughout the empire. In doing so, they created the potential for a major a clash of interests regarding African routes between Imperial and Cobham-Blackburn Airlines. However, this little problem was quickly resolved when Imperial Airways absorbed Cobham-Blackburn for a tidy sum of £50,000. On June 6, 1929—just a month before Union Airways began its domestic operations in South Africa—Imperial Airways (Africa) Limited was registered as a sub-division of Imperial Airways. People have often thought that Imperial was a state-owned and operated airline. In the beginning, it was not. It was heavily subsidized by the British government but it was a fully independent commercial enterprise, one that proudly 'flew the flag,' giving the impression that it was nationally owned.

The British Air Ministry signed an agreement with the airline to operate a weekly service to Cape Town that connected with the proposed London to India service through Cairo. The contract was for an initial period of five years and provided Imperial with a subsidy of £940,000, of which the British government would pay £270,000, South Africa £400,000 and other colonial African Governments the remaining £230,000. A chain of radio transmitters was set up along the route down the length of Africa. These were low-power facilities with local operators manning each station and providing regional weather reports. With the aid of funds from Britain and the colonial governments, comfortable hotels, guest houses, rest stops, dining facilities and toilets were erected at the aerodromes and landing strips along the route.

On February 28, 1931, history was made. Imperial Airways introduced a weekly service from London as far south as Central Africa terminating at Mwanza on Lake Victoria. It took ten days to cover the 5,124-mile distance. It was an exotic experience for the passenger, filled with variety and uncertainty. Traveling through Africa was nothing short of high adventure, even though tea and cucumber sandwiches were never far away, often served punctually by waiters with black jackets, brass buttons and with white napkins draped over their left arms. Whenever passengers were on the ground, waiters hovered nearby to assure that multiple-course meals were made available with all due decorum and promptness. Of course, up in the air meal services were non-existent. Flying was an extraordinary blend of upper class imperial elegance but nevertheless a pretty precarious affair. Anything could happen. A million things could go awry. But it was thrilling and there was no shortage of passengers. There were many willing to exchange parasols for pith helmets under the blazing African sun. For the privileged few who could afford to take the risk it was fashionable to put oneself in harm's way while maintaining a stiff upper lip and display an attitude exuding a very British and suave aura of bravura.

The journey to Africa began at Croydon Airport using Armstrong Whitworth Argosy three-engine biplanes to Le Bourget in Paris. From there, passengers travelled on the luxury overnight Orient Express train to Athens. Short Calcutta three-engine biplane flying boats then flew them from Athens to Mirabella, Crete and on to Alexandria, Egypt. From there, they travelled to Cairo by train for another overnight stop. The sector between Cairo and Khartoum was operated by Armstrong Whitworth Argosy aircraft. These machines followed the course of the Nile for a thousand miles to Khartoum in the Sudan with stops at Asyut, Luxor, Aswan, Wadi Halfa and Kareima. That portion of the journey alone took two full days with an overnight stop at Aswan. From Khartoum to Mwanza the route was operated by Short Calcutta flying boats that landed on the Nile and other bodies of water at Kosti, Malakal, Shambe, Juba, Port Bell (Kampala) and Kisumu before reaching Mwanza. Once the service was operating to a reasonably efficient schedule, mail and passenger services were to be eventually extended all the way to South Africa using three-engine de Havilland DH.66 Hercules aircraft.

Well in advance of the beginning of the service and to establish technical facilities in South Africa to maintain those aircraft, Imperial Airways set up a permanent headquarters at the Germiston Aerodrome. Trained ground staff, mechanics, extra engines and spares were shipped out to South Africa by sea and then transferred by rail to the new base. To coincide with all this, the first radio stations dedicated to air traffic were installed at Victoria West and Cape Town. With the impending start of the Empire airmail and passenger service, the operators of the Germiston Aerodrome realized that the airfield needed major upgrading. As the owners could not afford the high cost of improving the field, a five-year partnership was entered into between the municipalities of Germiston and Johannesburg. The Germiston Town Council set aside £65,000 for constructing a spacious new terminal building. Made of brick and concrete, it was painted an elegant dull grey. A large ribbed metal hangar with all the necessary workshops and storage rooms was constructed. Floodlighting was installed and a number of small cottages built to house the Imperial Airways staff. The new facility was opened by the Governor General of South Africa, the Earl of Clarendon, on December 20, 1931, and was officially renamed Germiston Airport.

Before regular services began an Imperial Airways survey flight left Cairo on November 23, 1931, with Captain H.W.C. 'Jimmy' Alger in command of a DH.66 Hercules (G-AARY). That aircraft would be based in Germiston and would operate the Johannesburg to Cape Town sector of the London service. It

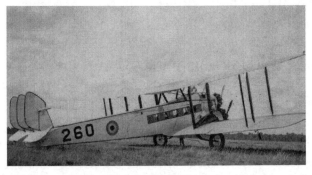

Imperial Airways de Havilland DH.66 Hercules. This one, originally registered G-AAJH and named City of Basra, was the aircraft that pioneered the route from London to South Africa in 1931. It was later sold to the South African Air Force.

arrived at Germiston Airport on Saturday, December 12, 1931. Ex-Union Airways pilot and record-breaker Captain Rheinhold 'Caspar' Caspareuthus was now in the employ of Imperial Airways and was stationed at the airport as one of the crew slated to fly sectors of the South African route. Another Imperial proving flight carrying only a consignment of Christmas mail left Croydon on December 9, 1931. The DH.66 Hercules (G-AAJH) *City of Basra*, under the command of Captain E.H. Attwood, arrived in time for the official airport opening on December 20, 1931.

The D.H.66 Hercules was a large biplane made of wood and plywood with steel struts connecting the two wings and a metal framework fuselage covered in stretched fabric. Its most distinctive feature was three upright rudder fins at the rear. Three Bristol Jupiter VI radial piston engines of 420-horsepower each powered the craft. One engine was mounted in the nose and one on each of the lower wings. It had a length of 56 ft, a wingspan of 79 ft 6 ins., a height of 18 ft 3 ins., an empty weight of 9,060lbs and a maximum take-off weight of 15,600 lbs. It could fly at a speed of 130 mph. With a crew of three and carrying seven passengers it had a service ceiling of 13,000 ft and could travel 525 miles between refuelling stops.

It had taken only twelve days for the mail to reach its destination from London via Mwanza. Regular passenger flights to Germiston and Cape Town began the following year. Germiston Airport was fully equipped to handle the ungainly but much-loved DH.66 Hercules machines. They landed on the airport's grassy field but in later years a paved runway would be laid down and a concrete apron constructed in front of the terminal area. A windsock atop a tall pole always fluttered to indicate wind direction. A visitors' viewing level was installed in the terminal building and the arrival and departures of the airplanes always attracted a large crowd. In those early days when it came to international air travel between South Africa and the outside world, Imperial Airways and Germiston Airport were totally synonymous.

In 1930, Imperial Airways had ordered more advanced aircraft for the southern sector of its African route. A total of eight Armstrong Whitworth Atalanta AW.15 four-engine machines were specially built for this purpose by the Armstrong Whitworth aircraft company in Coventry, England. The aircraft were primarily intended for the sector from Kisumu, Kenya to Germiston Airport and then on to Cape Town.

Imperial Airways Armstrong Whitworth Atalanta AW.15 at Germiston Airport

The Atalanta was a high wing monoplane made of steel, plywood and fabric. It had accommodation for nine passengers and three crew members. It was equipped with four 340-horsepower Armstrong Siddeley III ten-cylinder engines which gave it a cruising speed of 115 mph, a ceiling of 9,000 ft and a range of 400 miles. It was designed to fly safely on any three of its four engines, an essential requirement for long distances over Africa.

While all this was going on, Union Airways continued to operate, hiccupping its way from crisis to crisis in a struggle to be economically viable. And then another terrible disaster threw a wrench into the works. On Friday, November 13, 1931, Puss Moth ZS-ACD, under the control of experienced pilot William Davenport, broke up in the air over the Sir Lowry's Pass hills outside Cape Town. Davenport and his two male passengers, J.J.E.S. Pouradie-Dutail and J.C. Young were killed and the aircraft totally destroyed. It was another blow to the company. The South African public was now very wary of air travel. As a result, Union Airways aircraft often flew carrying only mail bags and no passengers at all. Even the 'red and yellow monster,' the big, comfortable Fokker, sometimes took to the air with no passengers on board. Nevertheless, Miller kept his eyes on the far horizons and remained optimistic. But then another catastrophe shattered the stability of the company.

Exactly one month after the Puss Moth crash, on New Year's Eve 1931, Miller and two of his employees took off in the late afternoon in the big Fokker Super Universal from Woodbrook Airfield, East London. They were heading for Port Elizabeth with 60 lbs of mail on board. Miller's co-pilot was Fred Eggeling who had originally joined the airline as a mechanical apprentice. The light was fading as they gained height and droned towards Kayser's Beach. With Eggeling at the controls, the aircraft suddenly encountered severe winds. Miller, seated in the passenger cabin behind the cockpit, shouted out asking what was wrong. Eggeling responded by yelling that he thought the weather was too bad and that they should turn back and land. And then buffeting began. It felt as though the airplane was going to be ripped apart. Miller tore himself out of his seat and rushed to the flight deck, seizing control from Eggeling. Grabbing the stick, he desperately tried to stabilize the aircraft but within seconds they were caught up in thunderclouds and lashing rain. Vision was negligible. The Fokker was being thrown around like a cork tossed about in an angry ocean. Miller yelled to Eggeling and the other passenger, pilot Denis Labistour. He commanded them both to move as far back as possible into the rear end of the fuselage in case the aircraft went into a nosedive and hit the ground. Suddenly there was a loud clap of thunder and a flash of lightning. The next thing Miller knew the controls were rendered useless. No matter how much he tugged at the stick or pumped the rudder pedals, the aircraft did not respond. He yelled again at the two men who were now crouching among the mail bags in the aft section of the aircraft, warning them that they were rapidly losing height and should brace for a crash landing. What followed was a bone-shaking jolt and a sickening crunch as the Fokker hit the beach, ploughing for what felt like an eternity through the wet sand before coming to a halt. Its fuselage was broken and the engine in ruin. Though badly shaken the men miraculously survived the crash because most of the impact had been absorbed by the engine, the metal casing of the nose and the port-side wing.

Fred Eggeling recalled the incident in later years: "We managed to get out of the aircraft, popping out of the broken fuselage like bursting popcorn. We scrambled away from the wreck as fast as we could because the main fuel tank had erupted and fuel was spewing everywhere. The engine was spitting and we were terrified of fire. Without checking for injuries all three of us suddenly realized to our horror that the mail bags were still on board. Major Miller rushed back into the plane, followed by the two of us. All three of us dived straight in to get those bags, colliding into each other as we scrambled around inside. It was sheer chaos." But the men retrieved the mail bags, the Fokker did not burst into flames, and the three aviators remained unharmed. Miller knew that another brutal blow had been dealt to his airline. Then providence intervened. A solution to Miller's dilemma lay in an unexpected source, far beyond the borders of South Africa.

At the top end of the Cape province, north of the Orange River where the Fish River meanders up towards the arid Kalahari Desert lies a vast and thinly populated land that was known at the time as South-West Africa. Today it is called Namibia, a name derived from the Namib Desert that stretches for hundreds of kilometres along the western coastline, with blisteringly hot sand dunes that cascade down into the frigid waters of the Atlantic. When Africa was divided up by European powers during the infamous Berlin Conference of 1884-1885, German Chancellor Otto van Bismark claimed East Africa and South-West Africa for Germany. As a member of the British Empire and out of loyalty to king and country South Africa declared war on its German neighbour during WWI. In 1915, a South African invasion force entered the territory and in July German forces who had been stationed there surrendered. At the end of the war the League of Nations – forerunner of the United Nations – placed South West Africa under a British mandate with administrative control of the territory entrusted to South Africa. Most German residents remained and Teutonic traditions gradually assimilated with indigenous culture. To provide the South-West African population with an air service in 1930 to help develop infrastructure and bridge the enormous distances between towns, as well as to connect people and mail with the impending Imperial Airways South African service, the government of the Union invited tenders for the establishment of an airline in the territory.

Coincidentally, that same year the Junkers Flugzeug und Motorenwerke (Aircraft and Motorworks) Company of Dessau in Germany formed a company called Junkers Sud Afrika with the intention of promoting and selling the company's products throughout the sub-Saharan continent. Junkers were famous for building sturdy, reliable metal-skinned aircraft during World War I. Now they were looking for new markets for their passenger aircraft. The company's representative, Friederich Hoepfner and engineer D. 'Kos' Koscielny, brought two demonstration models from the factory to Johannesburg for promotional and sales purposes. One was a Junkers F13 registered ZS-ABU and the other a Junkers A50 Junior registered ZS-ABV. Based at Germiston Airport, the company employed Captain Frederick Charles John 'Frikkie' Fry as chief pilot. On May 1, 1930, the F13 was flown to Maitland airfield, Cape Town on a promotional flight, with stops at Kimberly and Beaufort West. From Cape Town, it was flown to Windhoek via the drowsy South-West African town of Keetmanshoop. The arrival of the aircraft caused great excitement. Businesses and schools were closed for the day and almost the entire population came out to view the gleaming all-metal machine. Several more promotional flights were made to other small towns before the F13 returned to Johannesburg.

Pilot Frederick 'Frikkie' Fry relaxes on the wing of a Junkers F13

The A50 was also brought out and shown off. After making various flights around Johannesburg, including one to Lourenco Marques in the neighboring Portuguese colony of Mozambique on the east coast, pilot Frikkie Fry flew the A50 to Windhoek. A month's extensive survey of South-West Africa followed with

Fry and engineer Peter Falk urging towns and municipalities to build airfields for the revolution in transportation that the miraculous airplane would one day bring to the territory. Until then conditions were rough and primitive, to say the least. At the little town of Mariental, for example, the A50 simply buzzed the main street, clearing it of people, dogs, mules, cattle, horse carts and the few gasoline-powered vehicles that sputtered around, then landed and taxied up to the pumps at the only gasoline station for refuelling.

Frikkie Fry undertook many more promotional flights for Junkers. One of them was an ambitious promotional flight to Dar es Salaam in Tanganyika, far up the East African coast using the F13. The little machine had been fitted with extra fuel tanks to enable it to fly for 12 hours or a range of 1,200 miles. Hoepfner and Koscielny were also on board, their purpose to tout the aircraft's capabilities to all who came to ogle and wonder at it wherever it landed. The flight path to East Africa from Germiston Airport took the machine via Salisbury (modern-day Harare) in Southern Rhodesia (modern-day Zimbabwe). After arriving there, it undertook an emergency flight to the city of Bulawayo in the far west of the colony in order to pick up oxygen tanks for a desperately ill patient in a Salisbury hospital. With its mercy mission over, the aircraft continued on to Dar es Salaam via Mpika and Abercorn (Mbala) in Northern Rhodesia and then on to Dodoma and Tabora in Tanganyika. As Tanganyika had once been a German colony, the aircraft and especially German-speaking Friederich Hoepfner and 'Kos' Koscielny were welcomed with much fuss and flourish. The return flight to South Africa began on January 31, 1931, via Beira and Lourenco Marques in Portuguese Mozambique to Johannesburg. The entire trip had covered some 5,000 miles during which the F13 encountered torrential storms. One downpour had forced an emergency landing at Mpika where the crew had to wait for days for the grassy airfield to dry out before being able to take off. In Lourenco Marques, they not only had wait out another raging storm but for fuel to be brought in by rail from neighboring South Africa. It was with great relief that Hoepfner finally returned to the company's offices at Germiston Airport. The very first matter that he found himself needing to attend to was that alluring South African government invitation for tenders to form an airline in South-West Africa. Without delay he contacted his employers in Germany and persuaded them to offer a tender. With very little hesitation they heeded Hoepfner's recommendations, made an offer to the South Africans and won the bid. And so it was that in 1931, South West African Airways came into being. A contract worth £7,000 was entered into with the South African government for a period of five years for a regional service and for the carriage of passengers and mail between the South-West African city of Windhoek and the South African city of Kimberley. This allowed for connections to the Union Airways domestic air network and to the forthcoming Johannesburg to Cape Town Imperial Airways international service.

Another pilot, Ambrose Wright, was hired by Junkers and the two demonstration aircraft based at Germiston Airport were relocated to operate the new South West African Airways services. Friederich Hoepfner, engineer 'Kos' Koscielny and pilots Fry and Wright, arrived in Windhoek with the aircraft and set up their base in a hangar that had been built for them by the Windhoek town council. An airmail route was initiated, linking Windhoek with Keetmanshoop in South-West Africa and with Upington and Kimberly in the Union of South Africa.

In 1931, a further three Junkers A50's were bought by South West African Airways. Registered ZS-ACJ, ZS-ACK and ZS-ACL, they were unloaded at Walvis Bay on May 28 and sent by rail to Windhoek. Junkers engineer Erlich Wilhelm Gottlieb Pfeiffer was sent out from Dessau to assemble and maintain them. Frikkie Fry test flew them on June 9, 1931 and then they entered service. The first officially scheduled airmail flight in South-West Africa took place on August 1, 1931. Frikkie Fry and Gottlieb Pfeiffer flew the Junkers A50 ZS-ACJ from Windhoek to the towns of Grootfontein via Omaruru, Otjiwarongo and Tsumeb. Due to a minor engine problem, Fry had to make a forced landing 15 miles from Tsumeb and the mail was unloaded and sent onwards by road. But the aircraft was quickly repaired and continued on to Grootfontein the next morning. In those days a good engineer was worth more than his weight in gold. If an aircraft developed any kind of difficulties, the engineer who always accompanied it had to attend to matters with the minimum of spares and tools. If necessary, parts had to be invented or handmade from whatever material was available in order to get the airplane back into the air. With challenges like that, it was amazing how efficiently everything ran. It was a time when people had to be as resourceful and innovative as possible. Time and again, amazing skills were displayed in the face of great adversity. It had to be that way. Africa was as far away from the world's principle engineering and maintenance sites as it was possible to get.

Ambrose Wright was the pilot who operated the first scheduled airmail flight from Windhoek to Kimberley to connect with the new Imperial Airways overseas service. He left Windhoek on January 26,1932 and arrived in Kimberley the next day. Wright undertook the return flight seven days later, on February 2. Other pilots who flew the South West African airmail services were J. Koester, H.P. Schoeman, A.D. Knox-Perkins and Norman Richard Cook. In no time, the airmail service was running smoothly and South West African Airways became very popular with the traveling public.

When Friederich Hoepfner heard about Allister Miller's misfortune over the loss of the Union Airways' Fokker aircraft in the accident at Kayser's Beach near East London, he immediately made contact with him. Could he help? Could he offer assistance? Did Miller need money? Could some kind of a deal be struck between the two of them to help resuscitate Miller's struggling airline? Desperate to save his beloved company, Miller was only too happy to enter into negotiations. At the beginning of 1932, an agreement was reached in which he and Hoepfner would become joint managing directors of Union Airways and, in return, the Junkers aircraft company of Germany, owner of South West African Airways, would inject £85,000 into Miller's ailing company. This would not only be in cash but in the form of Junkers-built aircraft to expand the fleet. Junkers also took over the General Motors debenture of Union Airways for the original acquisition of the now-destroyed Fokker Super Universal. A public announcement was duly made on February 28, 1932, that an amalgamation had taken place between Union Airways and South West African Airways. But it was made clear that each airline would continue to operate under its own name. The effect was an immediate improvement in the public relations image of Union Airways. However, to all intents and purposes, the Junkers aircraft company had effectively taken over Miller's airline.

On January 5, 1932, pilot Frikkie Fry, accompanied by engineer Gottlieb Pfeiffer and a member of the South West African Legislative Assembly left for Cape Town to officially initiate cooperative activities between South West African Airways and Union Airways. En route a diversionary stop was made at Keetmanshoop. This was to enable Fry to marry his sweetheart, Kathleen Curtis, who was resident there. Everyone in the airline was very fond of Fry so formalities were happily dispensed with, to accommodate the ceremony. The following morning, with Frikkie Fry sporting a smile and now a happily married man, the group continued on to Cape Town. On January 11, 1932, Fry and Pfeiffer flew the mail from Cape Town to Durban as part of the new Union Airways deal. Thus began a two-and-a-half year professional partnership for the two men. Apart from mail, they flew many passengers as well as an impressive list of VIP's that included once and future Prime Minister Jan Christiaan Smuts, internationally renowned writer George Bernard Shaw and various members of parliament. Fry and Pfeiffer became very close friends with Fry helping Pfeiffer with his English and Pfeiffer helping hone Fry's German. This put Fry in very good stead in years to come when he went to Germany to take delivery of new Junkers aircraft.

Gottlieb Pfeiffer reflects on some of the adventures the two men had together. "Captain Frikkie Fry's enormous knowledge of flying by 'feel' — also known as flying by the seat of your pants — at a time when flight instruments were still very unsophisticated often came to the fore. One day we were forced down 35 minutes after taking off from Cape Town during an unusually heavy South-Easter wind and rain. It was just before eight o'clock in the morning. Conditions were terrible. Both of us had to grab hold of the controls after take-off to counteract the unbelievable turbulence on the wings and tail. We had four passengers in the cabin, all of them were very nervous as the plane was buffeted around. At 7,000 feet we were still in the clouds and suddenly found ourselves without a functioning compass. Frikkie was under heavy physical strain to keep the aircraft flying level. You could compare this to an acrobat's balancing act on a circus wire rope without a net or perhaps dancing on top of an active volcano. It was too unsafe and Frikkie decided to land. I watched the altimeter needle going down; 6,000, 5,000, 4,000, 2,900 feet. We were lucky that we did not hit Table Mountain because that is 3,000 feet high. And we were already lower than that. But where was the mountain? When the altimeter showed zero we should have been firmly on the ground but we were still soaring away, lost in the clouds. Then, way down below us, Frikkie saw a hole in the weather. And beyond that was a green surface. Showing no fear at all he nosedived through the hole and levelled out. And there, before us, was an unrecognizable grassy slope. Well, he put the machine down on that slope so smoothly I couldn't believe it. It was a masterpiece of a forced landing. We were surrounded by mist and had no idea where we were. When we got out to check the condition of the aircraft we saw that we were up to our axles in soft, soggy ground. Frikkie decided to calm his nerves with a cigarette. I was a non-smoker and just looked up at the clouds above us, wondering what to do next. The passengers were terrified and kept asking us where we were but neither Frikkie nor I knew so Frikkie simply said 'Oh, on the ground somewhere. Don't worry about a thing.' It was ridiculous. I don't know how it happened but a Cape Town newspaper got news of the incident, stopped their presses and ran a special edition that morning with headlines that said: JUNKERS CRASHED. But at around noon the weather cleared and the clouds thinned. As visibility improved a huge mountain loomed right in front us. Frikkie and I looked at each other in disbelief. We had landed somewhere on the slopes of Table Mountain itself! We grabbed the tail of the aircraft, turned it around so that the nose was pointing down the slope and away from the mountain, told everyone to hop on board and we started the engine and took off. We circled over Cape Town at the exact time that the newspaper vendors came out selling their papers with the headline: JUNKERS CRASHED. Well, of course, it hadn't. We had saved the day and were hailed as heroes."

Pfeiffer shared the cockpit with Frikkie Fry for more than 1,800 hours of flight in all types of conditions. Theirs was one of those magical professional relationships that brought out the best in men, regardless of circumstance or challenge.

Frikkie Fry was not the only pilot to be praised for his flying skills. Allister Miller had chosen carefully when he originally hired staff for his airline. Graham Wilmot Bellin, one of his original selections, was in command of a Junkers F13 flight from Johannesburg to Durban in March, 1933. This paraphrased account of the trip by one of the passengers, J. Graham Scott, appeared in the *South African Advertising Journal.* "I turned up at the airport for the Union Airways Durban flight with five other passengers. After the usual formalities which included getting the exact weight of each passenger by placing each one of us on a scale the pilot, Graham Bellin, took off at about 10.30. An engineer was also on board. After about an hour's flying heavy clouds began to form and the headwind increased. In another two hours the clouds were thick and formidable and stretched to the horizon on every side. Eventually Bellin decided that it was useless trying to fly over the clouds and said that he simply had to go directly through them. For nearly another half hour we flew through the thickest clouds imaginable, all the time Bellin hunting desperately for a hole to go lower. But the clouds just seemed to be descending beneath us. Eventually Bellin saw an opening, darted through it and we found ourselves flying low over the hilltops of the Mooi River basin in Natal. Bellin started making for a valley and we circled round and round looking for a safe place to land. But there did not seem to be the slightest hope of finding anything suitable. We zoomed up over a hill, through another cloud and then down low again and into another valley. We weren't sure if we'd ever find a landing spot. For another half hour Bellin circled the hills and valleys looking for a place to land his big 350-horsepower machine. Eventually he spotted a tiny flat spot and we swooped down, circling to see if the vegetation was alright and the area large enough. After flying in circles to make sure the place was safe Bellin decided to go for it. He circled once more, side-slipped over a low hill, straightened out, skilfully avoided a row of thick bushes and put his aeroplane down into that little valley with barely ten yards to spare. It was a wonderful example of an expert pilot at his best. It was also a real tribute to the toughness of the machines used by Union Airways. With a less experienced pilot or a flimsier machine the story might have had a different ending. After we stopped a very surprised farmer appeared out of nowhere and with his help we spent most of the afternoon clearing bushes and flattening mounds of earth in an endeavour to make it possible to take off from there again. As the weather did not improve we spent the night at a local trading store and returned to the aircraft at dawn the following morning. Bellin judged the distance very carefully and decided that we should be able to make it. The engine was started and all five of us passengers crowded as far forward of the machine as possible to enable Bellin to get her tail up quickly. We gathered speed, rushed down our improvised aerodrome, hit a mound with a bump, kangarooed up into the air, but managed to clear everything safely. It was a miracle. Again the skill of the pilot and the remarkable power of the machine were vividly illustrated. The remainder of the flight was uneventful. But, by golly, I was glad to get to Durban in one piece."

Junkers F13

The Junkers F13 was the world's first all-metal passenger transport aircraft. It was a single-engine cantilever-wing monoplane with accommodation for four passengers in a small but comfortable interior. At the beginning of the production run in Dessau, Germany, two versions were produced, one with a 160-horsepower Mercedes DIII engine and the other with a 185-horsepower BMW six-cylinder, four-stroke inline engine. The craft had a wingspan of 49 ft, a length of 31 ft, a weight of 2,097 lbs., a range of 870 miles and a cruising speed of just under 100 mph.

The slightly larger Junkers W34 was a direct descendant of the F13. It could accommodate six passengers and had a range of 560 miles and a top speed of 165 mph. It too had a single power source, a BMW radial piston engine, but more powerfully rated at 660-horsepower.

Junkers F13 flies past Signal Hill, Cape Town

Junkers W.34

Junkers W.34. Its single BMW radial engine can be clearly seen

The Junkers aircraft served Union Airways extremely well. Two W34s came to Union Airways through what was known as a 'purchase or return' credit option, placing the airline in debt to Junkers for an amount of £47,000. Allister Miller and Frikkie Fry travelled to Dessau, Germany, to take delivery of them. They were registered ZS-AEB and ZS-AEC. Acceptance and wireless (radio) tests were performed at Dessau before the machines were flown to South Africa, arriving in Port Elizabeth on June

2, 1933. Bringing a note of luxury and convenience to air travel, the aircraft were equipped with something radically new—an on-board toilet in the rear.

Meanwhile, in 1932, regular Imperial Airways service from London, Cairo and Central Africa to Germiston Airport had been extended all the way through to Cape Town. The first flight departed Croydon on April 27 and arrived in Cape Town ten days later. This opened up new opportunities for Union Airways, primarily as a carrier of mailbags to meet the Imperial machines. Mail brought in by Imperial were off-loaded during stops at Pietersburg (modern-day Polokwane), Johannesburg (Germiston Airport), Kimberley, Victoria West and Cape Town. Mail for Durban was off-loaded at Germiston Airport and then picked up there by Union Airways. Anything addressed to South-West Africa was off-loaded at Kimberley where it was picked up and flown to Windhoek by South West African Airways. It was a smooth symbiotic arrangement that worked very well.

By 1932 the airmail service was serving most of the country

The end of the post office's contract with Union Airways for carrying airmail was fast approaching and a public invitation for tenders was extended for its renewal. One of the tenders came from Imperial Airways, others from smaller new air carriers including the Aircraft Operating Company and Arrow Airlines, plus of course from Union Airways itself. Fortunately for Miller, in August 1932, the government renewed the contract with his company. It came with a subsidy of £10,000, became effective on January 2, 1933, but was for a period of one year only. However, in addition to the Cape Town coastal route, it now included flying three airmail services per week between Durban and Germiston Airport. The first of those flights was under the command of Graham Bellin in a Junkers F13. The flights left Durban on Mondays, Wednesdays and Fridays with return services leaving Germiston Airport on Tuesdays, Thursdays and Saturdays. The Wednesday flight connected with the arrival and departure of the Imperial Airways service to London. Despite the advances in air travel, mail from South Africa only reached London one day faster than mail carried by sea on the Union Castle steamships. As for local airmail, the overnight express train service between Durban and Johannesburg was barely slower than the airmail service. With the exception of bags intended to connect with the Wednesday Imperial Airways flight very little airmail was being carried. As far as the public was concerned, the service just did not warrant the higher postage fee. And although passengers were being transported between Johannesburg and Durban at a very reasonable fee of £6 for a one-way trip and £11 for a round-trip, customers were few and far between.

Optimist though he was it had become clear to Miller that his airline was in deep trouble. Even more painful was his suspicion that the government did not really have the finances or his interests at heart. He was convinced that they did not have much loyalty or respect for the airline that he had so painfully and carefully nurtured. What's more, the agreement between Union Airways and the German owned-Junkers Company had sparked negative comment in *The Times* of London. An editorial stated: "If Union Airways under the control of the Junkers Company were given a long contract then the development of aviation in South Africa will not be in local but in foreign hands. This has probably arisen out of the natural apathy of South Africans and the South African government towards aviation and lack of a full appreciation towards air travel."

By 1933, Union Airways had transported more than two thousand passengers and carried 34 tons of mail. 517,329 miles had been flown with an on-time departure rate of 98 percent. Of course, there had been mishaps. Nine forced landings had taken place and two passengers and one crew member had been killed. Despite the odds, things weren't all that bad. Or were they? Miller constantly vacillated between hope and despair. Whilst still burdened with heavy responsibilities and financial debt, he had enough lingering confidence in his company's future for him to place a huge order with the Junkers factory in Germany for three large brand new airliners. They were all-metal tri-motor monoplanes known as the Ju52/3m, wonderful machines at the very cusp of aviation technology at the time. But they came at a hefty price—£80,000. Junkers agreed to the sale on the strict understanding that they would be paid for in full upon delivery. It was their belief that payment would be guaranteed by the South African government, but they were unaware of the eroding relationship between the government and Miller. While the new aircraft were awaited, Union Airways maintained a busy flight schedule with its existing fleet. By now all aircraft had been kitted with radios, allowing for communication with ground stations as well as for receiving weather reports.

Because of shifting traffic demands and the growth of the passenger service between Germiston Airport and Durban, the company's operations and headquarters were transferred in their entirety from Port Elizabeth to Durban. Staff, pilots, mechanics, the airplane fleet and all ancillary equipment were now headquartered at Durban's Stamford Hill Airport. The airfield was located just north of the Durban downtown area and south of the Umgeni River, not far from where the waves of the Indian Ocean curled up on beaches and lapped at the tropical shoreline. Nearby, green fields of sugar cane quivered in humid breezes as flocks of Indian Myna birds—introduced into the area by immigrants in the late 1800s—twittered loudly in the coastal shrubbery. Stamford Hill Airport consisted of a concrete terminal building, a visitors' viewing gallery, a tiny tea room, a couple of hangars, a fire station and one or two small shacks plus, of course, the iconic wind sock atop a tall pole. Winds often changed directions so aircraft could land or take off in any direction from the all-grass field. It became a busy place. It was now the thriving nerve center of Union Airways' operations to inland cities as well as along the coastal route to Cape Town. Today, the very same location where Stamford Hill Airport once bustled is the home of the imposing 54,000-seat Moses Mabhida Stadium built as one of South Africa's many showcase venues for the 2010 FIFA World Cup soccer series.

Back in the early thirties, air travel was still viewed by most people as something risky and dangerous. Only the 'foolhardiest' of souls traveled by air. One of the passengers who flew on the Germiston to Durban service at that time was Johannesburg-based businessman Bill Slater who went down to the coast to spend the weekend with his fiancée. He recalled that everyone in his Johannesburg workplace looked upon him with sympathy and in shocked astonishment when he announced that he was going by air. But even more concerned were the members of his local church where he sang in the choir. On the Sunday before his departure, it was announced from the pulpit that the entire congregation would join in earnest prayer not only for his safe return but for his very survival. Needless to say, his round-trip flight on a Junkers W34 took place entirely without incident and his fiancée subsequently became his wife.

Union Airways flight arrives at Germiston Airport, 1933

Though still on rickety financial foundations, Union Airways remained fairly stable during 1933 but staff relations had deteriorated after the Junkers take-over. Miller's business partner, Friederich Hoepfner, was a retired World War I German U-boat captain. He could not fully reconcile himself with civilian life. According to many accounts, he still fancied himself as a senior naval officer and had a somewhat unfriendly and arrogant attitude toward others, especially those who could not speak German. Many Union Airways staff members including the aircrews resented his brusque manner. Things were not altogether happy at the company. It was difficult enough for Miller to keep his airline flying but this new internal conflict made things more awkward for him. It put him under tremendous strain and began affecting his health.

Pilot Fred Eggeling recalled how the overall stress of trying to balance finances, technical challenges, flight operations and human dynamics was beginning to take its toll. "We were all very fond of Major Miller and it was so painful to see what was happening to him. He was very hard-working but everything was beginning to take a lot out of him. He occasionally stayed overnight as a guest with my family in Germiston and it was obvious that he was absolutely exhausted much of the time. It was tragic to witness."

Rheinhold 'Caspar' Caspareuthus embellished on Eggeling's sentiments by adding: "Economic conditions at the time were at a low ebb. In addition, a very apathetic public resulted in poor support of the airline and this took a terrible toll on Major Miller. He was an outstanding pioneer of our aviation history and I have the highest regard for his efforts so it was really sad to see what was happening to him."

On December 14, 1933, more bad news exacerbated an already-worsening situation. One of the W34s crashed in bad weather whilst operating a passenger flight in bad weather from Durban to Johannesburg. The craft ploughed into the side of a hill on a sugarcane field on Oberle's farm near Eshowe, Natal. The pilot, F.H. Hiscock and radio operator W.M. Grobler and three passengers were killed. Miraculously, one passenger survived the accident, probably because he was sitting in a rearward-facing seat. The loss of life made it South Africa's worst aviation disaster at the time. The W34 accident and the upcoming payment due to the Junkers factory for the three new Ju52 machines that Miller had ordered were too much for the airline. The final blow had been dealt to its financial stability. Miller thought of selling the airline, even going so far as to consider approaching Imperial Airways in London or the Junkers company in Germany, but there really weren't any viable options available. No one was going to be interested in purchasing a struggling airline, let alone a bankrupt one. Perhaps the only answer lay in nationalization.

In January, 1934, Friedrich Hoepfner, in his capacity as Chief Financial Officer, negotiated the sale of Union Airways to the South African government. Miller must have been an absolutely heartbroken man, but there was nothing he could do. Discussions were short, brisk and matter-of-fact. The government had clearly seen that Union Airways was providing valuable service to the public and that despite its problems, it had become an important component in the national economy. It could not be allowed to simply disappear from the scene. It had to be rescued. It would become a state-owned carrier and the country's national airline. To that end, the government would take over its assets and its debts entirely, including the cost of the three new Junkers Ju52s awaited from the factory in Germany. This meant that it would also undergo a change in name, losing all identification with its existing incarnation.

On January 31, 1934, the last Union Airways flight was operated when Junkers W34, ZS-AEC, flew from Durban to Johannesburg. As soon as it landed at Germiston Airport and the engines were shut down Union Airways officially ceded into the pages of history. The next day, February 1, 1934, the sun rose on an all-new carrier.

South African Airways had been born.

Chapter Three

The Blue and Silver Way

With the birth of South African Airways (SAA) on February 1, 1934, a catchy image had to be created for the new airline. A logo was chosen to replace the one used by its predecessor, Union Airways. Thus was born the first incarnation of what would eventually become recognized around the world as the archetypal symbol of the carrier—a winged antelope, the so-called *Flying Springbok*. The emblem was a derivative of a stylized Springbok, an antelope native to southern and southwestern Africa, that for many years had been engraved on the windows and embossed on the varnished interior wood paneling of first and second class South African Railways carriages. But the springbok that now represented the airline had sprouted wings.

Original design of the Flying Springbok emblem (1934)

First version of the Flying Springbok logo painted on South African Airways aircraft (1934)

The logo was an image that would go through a number of subtle iterations over the years. It would grace the airline in one form or another for more than six decades. Now all aircraft would be painted in an appealing new color scheme. Engine nacelles, cowlings and wheel spats would get a coat of glossy blue while fuselages, wings and rudder fins would be painted silver. Within four years, all advertising campaigns would begin touting the slogan 'Fly the Blue and Silver Way.' With all these cosmetic changes the airline would look very different to what it was before.

After February 1934, SAA had ostensibly become an integral part of the government-owned and controlled South African Railways and Harbors system. With that came a somewhat staid and heavy-handed attitude as to how things should be done. The country's railway network was a component within the vast civil service with all its incumbent top-heavy bureaucracy. Nevertheless, Allister Macintosh Miller's airline had been pulled from the brink of extinction. With the resources of the state behind it, things were sure to grow and prosper. At least that is how Miller saw it from behind the desk of a new position that had been created for him within the airline. But things were bittersweet. With the formation of SAA, he had not only been dethroned as head of the airline but he was also grounded. His new bosses within the government saw fit not to allow him to continue flying as a pilot. Instead, both he and Friederich Hoepfner were offered desk jobs as Joint Airways Superintendents under the direct control of the government's Department of Railways and Harbors. No doubt achingly frustrating and boring as those roles may have been for them what choice did they have? At least they had not been entirely dropped from the airline. But flying was integral to Miller's life. It was in his blood. And the bug would bite again before too long. In the meantime, Miller took up his role at the airline's Durban headquarters before being transferred to the administration's offices in Johannesburg.

Stamford Hill airport in Durban now witnessed a vibrant surge of activity. The main terminal building received a fresh coat of paint, technical facilities were spruced up and new signs were erected. Brand new charts, paperwork and administrative documents appeared on desktops and workbenches. Reformatted timetables and maintenance schedules were pinned up on notice boards. Forty people had come to it from Union Airways but a great many more staff were now needed. Some were based in Durban with a few stationed at Germiston Airport or at other destinations served by the carrier. Initially, there were four pilots, Frederick Charles John 'Frikkie' Fry, Graham Wilmot Bellin, A. Murdoch and Robert Baillie Lovemore. Though records containing everybody's full names can no longer be traced the engineering staff included John (Jack) Robertson, H.J.C Klopper, the inimitable Gottlieb Pfeiffer, C. Buchwald, John (Jack) Bagshaw, A.E. Quinn and Ronald D. Madeley, assisted by apprentices P. Richmond, R. Brown, N.D. Batstone and Otto C. Schelin. Schelin would progress quickly and go on to become one of the airline's longest serving and most respected flight engineers. Air Commodore J.G. Hearson, Captain N.T.G Murray and C. Daverin were Station Superintendents. H.O. Summerton was Air Station Supervisor. C.F. Haywood was the ground-based wireless operator.

It was quickly realized that the Stamford Hill airport was way too small to accommodate the burgeoning operations taking place there. Jeff Scott was the airfield's young traffic clerk and in a 1982 interview for a television series about the history of SAA, he recalled how his cluttered workspace was jammed into a very tight corner of the main offices. Because of a severe shortage of space, the women in the office had to use his desk for making mid-morning and afternoon tea for the staff. The only way Scott could help them out was by having a false top made for his desk. This was attached to a system of pulleys hung from the roof. When tea-time came he would hoist the false desktop with all its files, pens, papers and bric-a-brac up to the ceiling to clear working space for the kettles, cups, sugar bowls and other accoutrements necessary for tea. Then, as now, all over the world wherever there was any semblance of English influence the tea break was one of the most important aspects of the work environment. Who could possibly get through the day without a couple of breaks for tea and cookies or — as the British and South Africans affectionately refer to them — biscuits?

As SAA's headquarters, Stamford Hill was bursting at the seams. Ex-Union Airways staff and new personnel stumbled over one another's feet as operations ratcheted up. Some of the many other names linked with those early days included bookkeeper, a Mr W. Burghardt. There were four shorthand typists; Mrs. A. Reissman, Miss G.E. Flint, Miss S. Robertson and Miss. E Kirby-Green. Two clerks, Miss A.M. Hiscock and L.G. Hearson took care of filing and general office duties which included the all-important tea breaks. The man in charge of stores and supplies was H.K. Girling and the driver was a Mr. R. Dawson. There was also a very busy carpenter, R. Lillie and one F.T. Gilson, who took up the duties of painter and sign writer. Seven other staff members included Arthur Kuwala and George Xaba and — typical of the way in which blacks were all too often treated back in those days — they were listed on the roster simply as 'Jack,' 'Simon,' 'Sam,' 'Philip' and 'Agungwana.' These were presumably members of the general cleaning and janitorial staff.

Other engineering members who joined the airline during those early days were William Britnel Scott, 'Ginger' Coates, Louis Trichardt and Ron Madeley, who later became a flight engineer and radio operator. Major John (Jack) Holthouse was loaned from the Air Force and served as technical adviser and liaison officer between the airline and T.H. Watermeyer, the General Manager of the South African Railways and Harbors administration in Johannesburg. Holthouse was a WWI Royal Flying Corps (RFC) pilot who had settled in South Africa after the war and was the man who flew the DH9 *Voortrekker* to Bulawayo so that Van Ryneveld and Brand could complete their historic flight from London to Cape Town in March 1920. In mid-1934, Holthouse summoned all the SAA pilots to the South African Air Force's (SAAF) base at Swartkop near Pretoria where they underwent a short but exhaustive course to hone their flying skills. His reasoning was double-pronged. He purposely leaked the story about their training to the press because he wanted to give the traveling public confidence in the new airline and he also wanted to assure potential passengers that they would be flying with only the best, safest and most competent air crews.

The hangar and facilities at Stamford Hill lacked much of what was needed to overhaul the six-cylinder Junkers L5 engines that powered the fleet of F13s. Help had to be sought from the outside. The engines had an overhaul life of 250 hours so two SAAF mechanical experts, Ovid Ottley and Jack Blamire, were sent from Air Force headquarters in Pretoria to Durban to assist in maintaining them. Technical assistance also came from the nearby railways workshops in Durban, where many mechanics and engineers worked on big steam locomotives and freight and passenger rolling stock. They became very adept at machining and milling small replacement parts for the airline as needed. Apprentices who helped service the aircraft had to learn how to crawl around inside the F13's wings, figuring out ways for fixing piping, tubing and cables. Enthusiasm ran high and everyone did their part to keep things in tip-top shape.

Apart from three Junkers F13s that were inherited from Union Airways, other aircraft included in the government takeover were a de Havilland DH.80 Puss Moth, a de Havilland Gipsy Moth, a Junkers W34, a Junkers A50 Junior, and another Junkers F13 which was leased from South West African Airways. The Junkers were immediately put into operation on the first mail and passenger flights. Three services per week linked Johannesburg and Durban and a weekly service was flown from

Durban to East London and Port Elizabeth with an occasional overnight stop in Uitenhage before continuing on to George, Mossel Bay and Cape Town. The Puss Moth was set aside for charter and meteorological flights and the Gipsy Moth used for charter and photographic work. Before long the Durban to Johannesburg sector was upgraded to a daily service and a new weekly operation commenced between Port Elizabeth, Bloemfontein and Johannesburg. For many years, flights into and out of Bloemfontein or anywhere in the skies above the Orange Free State province were strictly forbidden on Sundays. This was out of respect for the province's strict religious observances. Members of the Calvinistic Afrikaner church were very conservative. Sundays were set aside purely for worship. Until well into the twentieth century in the Orange Free State, no sport was played, no music performed, no movies shown and certainly no aircraft allowed to fly on the Sabbath. For the rest of the country things were somewhat less restrictive.

In mid-1934, the most eagerly anticipated event among the SAA staff, as well as the public at large, was the imminent arrival of the new Junkers Ju52s that had been ordered from Germany by Allister Miller during his Union Airways days. Now fully paid for by the South African government the machines were being readied for delivery at the Junkers factory in Dessau, Germany. In accordance with Miller's original order, a customized version of the basic Ju52 aircraft known as the Ju52/3mge variant was built for South Africa. It was powered by three American-designed Pratt & Whitney R-1690 Hornet engines made under license by BMW in Germany. Each engine incorporated a two-bladed fixed-pitch propeller. It is probably worth pointing out that variations in basic aircraft design have always been standard procedure in the aviation industry. Even today, factories offer many options to airlines and aircraft operators. Sometimes those differences are small but often they are very substantial and noticeable, including features such as longer or shorter fuselages, alternative engine types, customized interior configurations and even differences in wing flaps, ailerons and undercarriages. It should also be remembered that in most cases—unlike automobile manufacturers—the producers of aircraft airframes or 'hulls' are not necessarily the makers of the engines that power the airplanes. That is the highly specialized preserve of companies that focus primarily on producing propulsion systems. In today's world, the two major manufacturers of large, long-distance commercial airplanes, Boeing and Airbus, supply their products with engines made by US-based General Electric or Pratt & Whitney, UK-based Rolls Royce, the multinational International Aero Enginesa Group or the joint US-French-based CFM International. Neither aircraft manufacturer builds their own engines.

In September 1934, Captain 'Frikkie' Fry and his good friend and fellow professional, engineer Gottlieb Pfeiffer, left for Europe to take delivery of SAA's first Junkers Ju52. It had been registered ZS-AFA and was named *Jan van Riebeeck*. The title was given in honor of the first Dutch commander of the Cape of Good Hope who arrived in Table Bay in 1652, thereby founding the first European colony in South Africa. After an acceptance and test flight on October 20, 1934, Fry pronounced the aircraft fit for the long delivery flight to South Africa. It would not travel alone. The other two Ju52s that had been ordered were also ready

The first three Junkers Ju52 aircraft leaving Dessau, Germany, on their delivery flight to South Africa (1934)

to go. ZS-AFB was named *Lord Charles Somerset* after the first British Governor of the Cape of Good Hope who took office in 1814. ZS-AFC was named *Simon van der Stel* after another Dutch commander at the Cape who had assumed duties in 1679.

Together, the three aircraft would fly a route from Desseau to Budapest, then on to Athens, Cairo, Wadi Halfa, Khartoum, Juba, Kisumu, Dodoma, Mpika and Salisbury to Johannesburg. Their ultimate destination was Stamford Hill airport in Durban where they would be based. The journey from Dessau to Johannesburg would take eight days to complete. With Captain 'Frikkie' Fry and engineer Gottlieb Pfeiffer in charge of ZS-AFA, Junkers factory pilot Kapitan W. Neuenhofen assisted by SAA pilot Graham Bellin and an engineer by the name of Walther in ZS-AFB, and a Deutsche Lufthansa captain named Polte and flight engineer Willie Kunze on board ZS-AFC, the three planes fired up their engines and took off on October 29, 1934. Each craft also carried a radio operator. A doctor by the name of Von Sydow was on board ZS-AFA as flight manager. His responsibilities included handling cash to pay for fuel, food and accommodation along the way. After an incident-free flight from Dessau, all three machines landed safely at Germiston Airport on November 5. After incorporation into the fleet, the brand new ZS-AFA, *Jan van Riebeeck*, operated the first Durban to Cape Town service on November 15, 1934, completing the journey in a record time of five hours and 35 minutes.

Junkers Ju-52 ZS-AFA, *Jan van Riebeeck*, the first of the Ju-52s to join the SAA fleet

The arrival of the three aircraft ushered in a completely new dimension of air travel for the South African public. The Ju52 was an amazing aircraft for its time. It was faster, bigger and more sophisticated than anything else on the South African registry. It incorporated German engineering at its very best. Its ribbed all-metal skin made it a tough and hardy airplane. With a length of 62 ft, its interior cabin could accommodate 18 passengers. However, SAA reconfigured arrangements to seat 14, providing more space and comfort. Single leather-covered seats were placed on either side of the aisle. As the saying goes, there wasn't a bad seat in the house. Every passenger had a great view through the six large, square-shaped windows. One of them on either side of the cabin could be opened by turning a large knurled knob to allow in fresh air while the aircraft was on the ground or during flight. In the rear of the fuselage was a toilet. Behind that was a baggage compartment and beyond that a small area that held a gasoline-powered emergency electrical power generator. Of course, with three engines operating at full throttle and with no soundproofing, the passenger cabin was a noisy place. And it was not only mechanical sounds that contributed to the din. The flow of air brushing against the outside skin of the aircraft caused a constant roar. Passengers were offered cotton buds to stuff into their ears, not only for the noise but to alleviate some of the discomfort of travelling at high altitude.

Junkers Ju-52 undergoing minor maintenance before flight

The crew consisted of a captain, a first officer, an engineer and a radio operator. The radio operator had two additional functions on board. One was to slowly walk down the central aisle prior to take-off to check passengers' tickets, similar to the duties of a bus conductor or a train ticket collector. "All tickets, please. All tickets, please," he called as he smiled, ambling through the cabin examining tickets and tearing off stubs. His other job was to play steward or, in modern parlance, cabin attendant, pouring cups of hot tea, coffee or soup from a flask for passengers on long flights.

The Junkers Ju52/3mge had a wingspan of 95.92 ft, a height of 14.88 ft, an empty weight of 11,785 lbs and a fully loaded weight of 24,320 lbs. It could fly at a maximum altitude of 18,000 ft. Its three Hornet nine-cylinder air-cooled engines—one in the nose and one on either wing—each delivered 660 horsepower or 492 KW, giving the craft a maximum speed of 185 mph, a cruising speed of 160 mph and a range of 570 miles. Apart from its two main wheels early models had a skid at the rear. This dragged along the ground until sufficient speed was reached to allow the tail to rise during the take-off run.

The new SAA Junkers JU52/3mge aircraft were equipped with state-of-the-art extras including the latest radio equipment. This consisted of a Morse key transmitter and a headset-type receiver that sent and received long-waveband signals via a trailing wire aerial that was winched out of the tail by the radio operator and then retracted prior to landing. The aerial dangled out in mid-air far behind the airplane during flight. Of course, if it was not winched in prior to landing it could cause havoc on the ground. There are stories in the annals of the airline—some humorous but others rather more serious—that tell of aerials dragging across power cables and shorting out electrical supplies in urban areas, or across telephone lines, busy roadways, farms and open veldt inflicting a lot of damage and terrifying people, livestock and wildlife when radio operators had forgotten to winch in the cable before landing. As the Ju52 also carried a radio direction-finding system the trailing aerial served another purpose, to communicate with airports equipped with transmitters intended to help guide the machines to their destination. Over the years, one by one, airports in South Africa received directional navigation aids, making flying safer and more reliable. Prior to the implementation of these aids—primitive though they may have been by today's radar-assisted, GPS-guided and computer-operated standards—many air routes diligently followed the country's extensive network of railways. Large train depots and even the smallest railroad stations had their names painted on their roofs to help pilots identify exactly where they were. Charts and navigational maps at that time contained little detail of value to airmen. For many years, it was unabashedly admitted among SAA pilots that few of them ever flew without a railroad timetable stashed beneath their seat on the flight deck. This was so that they could get a precise fix on the time of day and thereby regulate their schedule based on the observation of passenger

Junkers Ju-52 at Germiston Airport

Interior of passenger cabin of Junkers Ju-52

and freight trains below. Captain Jan Marthinus 'Boet' Botes, who used to fly during those trailblazing days, once recalled that flight crews used to get bamboozled or downright angry if farmers had the temerity to cut down certain trees or drain a lake because SAA pilots relied on those geographic features to serve as identifiable landmarks.

Passenger being weighed before boarding flight on Junkers Ju-52

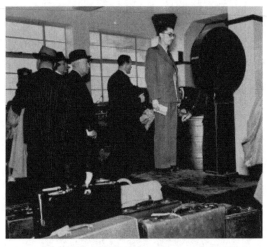

**Male passenger being weighed before boarding flight on
Junkers Ju-52**

Unlike modern airliners the Junkers Ju52s had no de-icing
equipment on the wings or fuselage. At certain altitudes—
especially when flying over high mountain ranges like the
Drakensberg—ice often accumulated on the leading edges
of the wings. This could prove lethal as it interfered with
aerodynamics and added to the weight of the aircraft. Even
worse, if ice built up on critical moving sections like flaps and
ailerons it could jeopardize the pilots' control of the aircraft's
flight surfaces. Flight engineer Otto Schelin recalled how air
crews sometimes struggled to get rid of ice on long trips to and
from Cape Town as the aircraft crossed mountain peaks. Fly too
high and the ice built up. Put the aircraft into a slow dive to
lower and warmer altitudes and the ice stubbornly increased
because of the additional flow of air across the wings. Sometimes
it was like playing with a yo-yo in the sky as crews struggled
to find the perfect height, perfect speed and the perfect mix
of aerodynamics and thermodynamics to deal with ice. Crews
literally had to write their own flying instructions and manuals
back in those days. Aviation was still a young science and there

was still so much to be learned, especially on routes far from where aircraft manufacturers were based and where aircraft had originally been designed and tested. Everyone—to some extent or another—was a pioneer.

Junkers Ju-52 flies past Signal Hill, Cape Town

The Junkers were not the only new additions to the fleet because three months after their arrival, on February 1, 1935, the South African government purchased South West African Airways (SWAA) for a sum of £7,000. Despite promising beginnings, that airline had not been doing well. Its most profitable route was the service between Windhoek in South-West Africa and Kimberley in the northern Cape province of South Africa where passengers and mail connected with the Imperial Airways London service that extended to Cape Town from Johannesburg. The takeover of SWAA meant that SAA inherited two more Junkers A50s and a Junkers F13 aircraft. With the addition of these three machines, SAA extended its route network to include all of South-West Africa, in addition to South African destinations.

Things really began to move quickly now. The speedy and spacious Ju52s allowed many more flights to be added to the schedule. However, Stamford Hill airport posed some unfortunate drawbacks to operations. As an all-grass airfield and because Durban has a tropical climate with frequent rainfall, things could sometimes get very wet and soggy. The heavy Ju52s could easily sink into the wet grass and mud while waiting for passengers or even during take-offs and landings, especially during the summer rainy season. Steve Grover, a ground engineer during that time, vividly remembered the gangs of local Zulu helpers who were always standing by to assist digging aircraft out of muddy patches after a summer thundershower. On more than one occasion, all three Ju52s were bogged down in Durban, causing chaos with flight schedules. Those same black work parties often had to assist ground engineers physically lift the rear end of the aircraft and turn the heavy machine into the wind after a shower. The wet ground and the relatively narrow wheelbase of the Ju52 made it very difficult for the pilot to manoeuvre the craft using its own power from a stationary position to one where its nose could be pointed into the wind for take-off. Eventually a permanent job position was created for the head of what colloquially became known as the 'debogging squad.' The first appointee was Bob Throssell who was originally the foreman mechanic of the local South African Railways' fleet of road vehicles in Durban. He eventually solved the problem of hauling airplanes out of mud and mire by using a combination of spades, crowbars, wheelbarrows, railroad ties, ropes, hooks and pulleys to lift them up onto large steel boiler plates. Every time an aircraft had to be dug out of the morass, the feverish activities attracted onlookers from near and far, especially as the Zulu-speaking gangs would loudly break into song as they toiled to get an airplane back onto firmer ground. As attested to by the rich legacy it has left on the world's modern musical scene, there is nothing quite like the magical sound of a chorus of rhythmic African male voices singing in unison. Gangs of workers on mines and farms often sang as they worked. It was a reflection of tribal culture where song, dance and music defined the warm-hearted spirit of African camaraderie. Many people in Durban welcomed the stranding of aircraft at Stamford Hill as it would herald the commencement of a wonderful musical concert that echoed far beyond the precincts of the airfield.

The all-grass runways at Stamford Hill Airport in Durban often caused aircraft to bog down after a rainfall

Despite the odd bogged down aircraft and interruptions to flight schedules things generally went well at SAA's Durban headquarters until increased traffic, passenger demands and an ever-expanding route network made it obvious that the Johannesburg area would be a far more practical hub than Durban. So, with government approval, on July 1, 1935, the entire operation was transferred from Stamford Hill to Germiston Airport, the airfield just a half-hour's drive from downtown Johannesburg. Amazingly, the move was made with minimum interruption to flight schedules. Germiston Airport now lay at the heart of the country's aviation activities. Not only was it Imperial Airways' gateway to South Africa for the international service between London and Cape Town but it also became home to the country's national airline. An extensive building program began there. All facilities were upgraded. This included extra hangars, workshops, a meteorological station, a brand new passenger terminal with a baggage handling hall, customs offices, a restaurant and medical center. One of the most attractive features of the new facility was a huge clock on the apron area in front of the terminal. Facing upwards, the clock with its oversized, whitewashed hands and numerals could be read by pilots flying 8,000 ft above the airport. Within a few years the airport would get one of its most essential new features, a paved runway with a length of 455 ft and a width of 50 ft, finally doing away with the need for airplanes to land and take off from a grass field. A change in name was deemed to be in order too so it was unanimously decided to call it Rand Airport, the word Rand being an abbreviation of the Afrikaans geographic term Witwatersrand which referred to the vast mining and industrial region that included Johannesburg and surrounding cities. With due pomp and circumstance, Rand Airport was officially declared open by the Governor General of South Africa, the Earl of Clarendon, on August 5, 1935.

Names associated with the airline's ground staff at that time include C.T.S. Capel who was Superintendent of Engineering. He had previously worked for Imperial Airways and joined SAA when it was relocated from Durban. S.W. Bailley was Chief Inspector. Ovid Ottley, who had originally been sent to Stamford Hill from SAAF headquarters at Swartkop to help service the early model Junkers aircraft, resigned from the Air Force to join the airline. Among other early technical staff members were B.P. 'Haas' Prinsloo, Steve Grover, James Copeland, James 'Jimmy' Lennard, Douggie Clegg, Leonard Smith, R.L. 'Collie' Clothier, Roland Gunn, Trevor Phillips, George Fuller and Norman Strudwick, soon to be followed by T.D. Kirkwood who joined as Technical Records Clerk. Ground engineers who came to the airline from Imperial Airways included A.C.M. Coates, Cameron Blake, C.W. Lippiatt and R. McKelvin. Three months after them A.P. Cowling and L. Smith joined the staff.

Original SAA flight crew, mechanics and ground staff once the airline had relocated to Rand Airport in Germiston, just outside Johannesburg in 1935

Gradual passenger confidence in air travel and demand for seats made it necessary for SAA to order more Junkers aircraft from Germany. This raised eyebrows in many quarters. The British press and English newspapers within South Africa itself did not look upon that decision with favour. Criticism was launched against the South African government for 'Germanizing' aviation in South Africa. After all, London was already viewing Berlin with grave suspicion. Adolf Hitler had become Chancellor in 1933 and by 1934, Germany was heavily re-arming itself. Rumours abounded, accompanied by nervous bouts of sabre-rattling, hinting at the prospect of war between Britain and her colonies with Germany. Many wanted to know why SAA was not buying British or American aircraft. Criticism became so vociferous that it made German-born Friederich Hoepfner feel uncomfortable and he eventually resigned from the airline and returned to Germany. But most of the unfavourable comments were levelled at SAA's head, South Africa's Minister of Railways and Harbors, Oswald Pirow. However, Pirow was unfazed. The son of German immigrants, his conservative political views were far to the right. He was a secret admirer of Adolf Hitler and had actually met him on a trip to Europe in 1933. Counteracting criticism about buying more German aircraft, he made public statements advocating the Ju52 as not only a highly reliable and trustworthy machine but one ideally suited to SAA's route network, all of which were solidly based on fact, of course. Dismissing any further questioning of his motives, Pirow placed additional orders with the Junkers factory for more Ju52s and, as a result, over the years SAA would operate no less than 15 of the type in different variants.

In 1935, ZS-AFD, the fourth machine, arrived from Germany. It was named *Sir Benjamin D'Urban*, after the British-appointed governor and commander-in-chief of the Cape who took office in 1834. It was he who went on to occupy the territory known as Natal and declare it a colony of the British Empire. The newly arrived aircraft was also a Junkers Ju52/3mge model but unlike the previous three aircraft, this one had been fitted with sleeping bunks and a mail compartment in the forward section of the cabin. It had originally belonged to Deutsche Lufthansa, the predecessor of today's Lufthansa airline. It completed the flight from Dessau to Rand Airport in a record time of 43 hours and 30 minutes. The crew was Commander H. von Mohl, assisted by Kapitan W. Neuenhofen, a flight engineer with the last name of Heinz, mechanic W. Theile, and wireless operator H. Nickel. Now SAA operated the four Junkers Ju52s and the single-engine aircraft that had come from Union Airways and South West African Airways. Eleven pilots formed part of a total staff of 57. By 1935, the public had enthusiastically taken to the air. 8,938 passengers were carried that year.

Eleven more Ju52s were to be ordered and delivered between 1935 and April 1938. They would come in different variants including models that replaced the tail skid with a steerable wheel at the rear end and some that would be supplied with American-designed Pratt & Whitney R-1340 Wasp engines driving three-bladed constant speed propellers. Other refinements would include the installation of two-way voice radio communication equipment that did away with the old cumbersome Morse code system used on the first few aircraft. With that improvement, radio operators in the air and on the ground could actually speak to one another instead of relying on mere dots and dashes to relay their messages.

The last models of the Junkers Ju-52 ordered by SAA were fitted with American-designed Pratt & Whitney three-bladed Wasp engines

One aircraft in particular among the new batch of Ju52s has an interesting sidebar to its history. In 1937, ZS-ALO, *Jan van Riebeeck*, was intended to replace the original aircraft with that same name that was delivered in 1934. The craft was completed at the Junkers works in Dessau but there was a shortage of Junkers pilots to fly it out to South Africa. Also, no SAA pilots were available to spend the necessary time travelling all the way from South Africa to Europe by sea to pick it up and then more time on its ferry flight to Rand Airport. So, what to do? The Junkers plant approached the Deutsche Lufthansa airline. Did they have any pilots they could spare to fly a new Ju52 to Johannesburg? The airline responded by saying that they had no pilots on their own roster that they could spare but they did know of a man who used to fly for them and who was now assigned to other duties. Perhaps he might be available. They would look into the matter.

The man they had in mind was 40-year-old Captain Johann Peter 'Hans' Baur. He was a brilliant pilot who had received his commercial license in 1921 and had flown for the German carriers Bavarian Luft-Lloyd and Junkers Luftverkehr, as well as Deutsche Lufthansa. Because of his outstanding safety record and flying skills, Baur was picked by Lufthansa for a special mission, to fly a 43-year-old firebrand of a politician around Germany on his campaign tour to become Chancellor. Thus it was that in March 1932, Hans Baur met Adolf Hitler. The two men hit it off immediately. Hitler was very nervous of flying but the airplane was the most expedient way for him to travel around the country and reach the widest spectrum of the German electorate. Baur quickly allayed all of Hitler's fears of flying as he transported him from city to town to tiny hamlet to village to deliver speeches during the intense campaign he conducted to become appointed as Germany's Chancellor by President Paul von Hindenburg. Once Hitler took power as Führer of the Third Reich in 1933, Baur returned to commercial flying. But not for long. Hitler had grown to like the man and to depend on him for safe and punctual travel, especially in the winter months when weather conditions could be treacherous. But, even more so, Hitler probably trusted Baur more than any anyone else. He felt comfortable with him. It is very likely that he felt closer to Baur than he did to most of the members of the inner circle of his Nationalsozialistische Deutsche Arbeiterpartei, or Nazi party. He felt so reliant on him that on January 30, 1933, Hitler appointed him as his personal pilot.

Theirs was a very special relationship that would evolve into a unique bond over the years. When Baur married his second wife Maria in 1935, Hitler was his Best Man. He held a wedding reception for the couple in his own apartment in Munich.

Whenever Baur flew Hitler to a speech, a meeting, a state occasion or across the German border to meet foreign political leaders such as Benito Mussolini in Italy, Hitler always made a point of making sure that Baur was nearby, going so far as ensuring that a place was set at his personal table for him during formal dinners. Baur was a very keen amateur cinematographer and wherever he went with Hitler he carried his 16mm movie camera with him and shot footage of any parades or welcoming receptions held in Hitler's honor. In 1937, his official duties as the Führer's personal pilot became somewhat less pressurized as Hitler spent more time on the ground hatching plans for the invasion of Poland and the conquest of territory for 'Lebensraum' or living space. Hitler adamantly felt that Germany had been hemmed in by the Treaty of Versailles following the end of World War I. He believed Germany needed room to expand. And so he spent much time behind closed doors planning the future invasion and conquest of neighboring countries. This freed up Baur. And the management of Deutsche Lufthansa knew it. When he was approached to take command of the delivery flight of a brand new Ju52 to South Africa, Baur was intrigued. He had never been to Africa. A mission like that was an ideal opportunity for him to take his wife on a once-in-a-lifetime vacation. At first Hitler was reticent to allow him to go but when Baur explained that the trip would be a great holiday for him and his wife Hitler finally agreed. The proviso was that he would return to Germany without delay after the flight.

With an all-German crew and his wife on board as a passenger, Baur took off from Dessau in the Ju52 on December 31, 1937, arriving at Rand Airport on January 13, 1938, after much adventure and excitement along the way. He and his wife met numerous interesting characters and visited tribal villages and wildlife areas during the course of the flight. His 16mm motion picture camera went with him and he filmed a detailed record of the trip. When they landed at Rand Airport, they were met by a large deputation from the Johannesburg, Pretoria and Witwatersrand German expatriate community. Baur was surprised at the fuss that was made of his arrival. He claimed that at no time prior to or during the flight did he make it known that he was Hitler's personal pilot and yet, when he arrived, the local German population knew all about him. They were anxious to learn about Germany's Chancellor and about the conditions 'back home.' As a guest of South African-based German industrial companies Baur, his wife and the delivery flight crew were taken on an underground visit to a gold mine and to the gold refinery in Germiston to witness the pouring of a gold bar. They were wined and dined like royalty. Baur also gave a talk to about 500 people at a gathering hosted by the German ambassador. When Baur asked how and why he was treated like a hero, the ambassador told him that he had received strict instructions from Ulrich Friedrich Wilhelm Joachim Von

Flight Captain and Lt. General Hans Baur, Adolf Hitler's personal pilot, photographed with Hitler in 1938. He flew Junkers Ju-52 ZS-ALO from the factory in Germany to Rand Airport in 1937. He signed this photograph and presented it to the author in 1983 after a television interview about the delivery flight

Television interview with Hans Baur at his home in Herrsching am Ammersee near Munich, Germany in 1983. The author is behind the camera

Ribbentrop, Germany's ambassador in Britain, telling him that Baur was to receive special treatment. The following year Von Ribbentrop became the German Reich's Minister of Foreign Affairs based in Berlin. It was then that Baur learnt that Von Ribbentrop had actually been acting on Adolf Hitler's personal orders. In accordance with the Führer's directive, no effort was to be spared to make a hero out of Baur during his visit to South Africa.

In a 1983 interview for a documentary TV series about the history of SAA, Baur openly admitted that he and Hitler always enjoyed a very special relationship. While entertaining this book's author and the TV crew with an excellent selection of schnapps, kirschwasser and Slivovitz at his quaint picture-book home in Herrsching am Ammersee near Munich after the interview Baur warmly praised Hitler for his kindness and consideration throughout the years, especially for his ongoing generosity towards his wife and his family. He explained that he was with Hitler in his underground bunker in Berlin on April 30, 1945, as the invading Russian army poured into the city. Hitler told Baur that the end had come and he thanked him for his years of loyal service. It was obvious, Hitler admitted, that Germany had lost the fight. Baur pleaded with Hitler to allow him to try and smuggle him and his wife Eva Braun out of the bunker and take them to an airfield where a few Luftwaffe transport aircraft were hidden and still intact. From there, Baur promised he could fly Hitler to safety, perhaps to Japan, South America or an Arab country. But Hitler refused. If Berlin was to fall, he would go down with it. However, Hitler begged Baur to fly his deputy Martin Bormann, also in the bunker, to Flensburg in northern Germany. There he could be united with Grand Admiral Karl Donitz whom Hitler had appointed as his successor. If Baur could get the two men together the Third Reich might still have a chance of surviving, even if not on German soil. Hitler was insistent that Baur leave the bunker before Russian troops got there. Baur did not want to leave his Führer but Hitler told him he that he intended to take his own life that night. Despite Baur's pleading, Hitler commanded him to evacuate the bunker immediately and flee to safety. Reluctantly, Baur obeyed. Together with Martin Bormann and a group of 15 others, Baur zigzagged on foot through the burning and rubble-strewn streets of Berlin. A day later he was shot in the chest and hands by invading Soviet troops, but his most severe injuries were to his legs. Bormann, Hitler's hope for rekindling the might of the Third Reich with Admiral Donitz, was ruined. Baur was captured and imprisoned by the Russians. During his incarceration his right leg was amputated and he was fitted with an artificial limb. Up to the time of Baur's release from prison in 1955, the Russians suspected that he knew that Hitler might have survived and that he was aware of his whereabouts. But Baur could tell them nothing. All he knew was that Hitler was dead. As history now has it, after taking his own life with a pistol shot to his head and after Eva Braun had swallowed poison, Hitler was cremated and the ashes buried near the bunker.

After the filmed interview was completed with Baur for the television documentary in 1983, he was proud to show the author his collection of photographs and other memorabilia. He described his long and happy association with Hitler. Although he no doubt had intimate knowledge about the inner thoughts and aspirations of his friend, commander and confidant Adolf Hitler as well as the most secret and innermost workings of the Third Reich—including the Holocaust—Baur professed to have been little more than a professional pilot caught up in the tumult of war and world conflict. During the war Von Ribbentrop—the man who issued the order that Baur be so well treated during his visit to South Africa in 1937—had become Hitler's Minister of Foreign Affairs. He was the first Nazi to be executed following the Nuremberg War Trails in October, 1946. Baur himself was never convicted of any wrongdoing. After release by the Soviets in 1955, he was detained by the French. They freed him in 1957 and he quietly retired to his home in Herrsching am Ammersee with his third wife, Crescentia. He died at the age of 95 in 1993.

But to return to the story of the Junkers Ju52 aircraft. On April 1, 1936, SAA had begun using them to fly a new route between Rand Airport and Cape Town via Kimberley. That year the South African government withdrew Imperial Airways' right to continue their London flights from Johannesburg to Cape Town route via Kimberley, giving that route solely to SAA. From then onwards Imperial Airways fights from London terminated at Rand Airport. All domestic flights in South Africa now became the exclusive preserve of SAA. On August 7, 1936, a new weekly service began between Rand Airport and Cape Town with two stops along the way, at Kimberley and Beaufort West. Refreshments were not offered to passengers on board the airplanes. People had to make use of small airport tearooms. Beaufort West did not have such a luxury so local attorney and businessman Johan Stroebel used to drive out to the airfield from town whenever an aircraft touched down, pitch a couple of large beach umbrellas for shade and serve tea and cake to the passengers and crew as they disembarked. There are even stories about members of the local ladies' sewing club preparing crumpets, scones and *koeksusters*—a sweet traditional Afrikaner confectionery made of deep-fried dough drenched in syrup— especially for Stroebel to take to meet the arriving flights.

When in-flight catering was gradually introduced on the Ju52s on some of the longer routes, it left much to be desired. The only items served on board were sandwiches wrapped in brown paper or a cup of soup poured from a vacuum flask. This was the job of the radio operator who doubled as flight attendant. Because of the change in altitude, the vacuum in the flask was affected by the difference in air pressure and often caused hot soup to be sprayed all over the passengers when it was opened. Those were the days when people dressed in their Sunday best for air travel. Ladies wore the latest fashions and men donned crisp business suits. Being drenched in hot chicken broth in those outfits was nobody's idea of fun. Nevertheless, most folks were only too glad for a cup of something hot to stave off the chill of flying at high altitude.

Whilst still observing the Orange Free State province's strict ban on Sunday flying, two additional services per week began from Rand Airport to Cape Town with stops at the province's capital, Bloemfontein. These continued onwards via Kimberley and Beaufort West. Another new route from Johannesburg went via Durban to East London, Port Elizabeth and Cape Town. On May 23, 1936, a new airport went into operation in Port Elizabeth, replacing the original one where Allister Miller had started it all. 1936 was a very busy year, particularly with regard to long-term planning. As Hitler's speeches began getting more vitriolic in Germany, the government decided to fold SAA into a component of the South African Defense Force. From then onwards, SAA was to be organized in such a way that, in time of war, it could aid in the defense of the country at very short notice. To achieve that the government's policy was not to buy expensive bombers for the Air Force—

which would be useless in peacetime—but to purchase civil aircraft for the operation of commercial air services but that could be rapidly converted into bombers if needed. That year all SAA pilots began military training for performing bombing runs and, together with the technical staff, were placed on the Defense Force Reserve list.

In 1936, orders were placed with the Junkers factory for 18 additional aircraft, but this time for the manufacturer's latest Ju86 twin-engine model. This was another big order for German-built airplanes even though the spectre of war with that country was looming large. To prepare for the worst, the order specified that the new machines should be able to be rapidly converted from passenger airliners to military transporters or bombers. We can only speculate on how this proviso was viewed at the Junkers plant in Dessau but, in actual fact, the factory was already producing quick-change passenger-to-bomber models for use by Germany itself. Clearly, expectations of war simmered with far greater alacrity in Germany than abroad. Hitler's speeches were becoming more belligerent each day. Racism and anti-Semitism were spreading like wildfire all over the Reich. Anti-British, anti-French and anti-American

The Junkers Ju86 was a smooth-skinned all-metal aircraft that had a crew of three. It could carry ten passengers in great comfort at a cruising speed of 150 mph for 932 miles. Its maximum speed was 205 mph. For the first time non-stop flights between cities as far apart as Johannesburg and Cape Town could be carried out. The Ju86's service ceiling was 23,293 ft. It had a fully retractable undercarriage which made for cleaner aerodynamics, thereby improving speed, cutting down on drag and substantially reducing fuel consumption.

feelings were running high. Even though the Summer Olympic Games were held in Berlin during August of 1936, the world was getting tense. War was inevitably coming. But Junkers Flugzeug und Motorenwerke AG in Dessau was a private company. At that point in time, it still operated independently of Third Reich and Nazi influence or control. It was only too happy to do business with foreign airlines wherever they may be, war clouds gathering on the horizon or not.

The first three Ju86 aircraft for SAA were fitted with British-made Rolls-Royce Kestrel XVI engines. The airplanes carried the designation Ju86 Z3. But it was soon discovered that the Kestrel engines did not perform as well as hoped so engines on the rest of the order were changed to American-designed Pratt & Whitney R-1690 Hornets. These airplanes were then designated as Ju86 Z7 models. The last machine in the batch had Pratt & Whitney Hornet S1E-G engines, built under license in Germany by BMW. This aircraft was called the Ju86K model. It was fitted out as a mail-only carrier but it too had the capability of being quickly converted into a bomber.

Junkers Ju-86 with Rolls-Royce Kestrel engines prepares for flight, Rand Airport, 1936

Junkers Ju-86 fitted with Pratt & Whitney Hornet engines in flight
near Johannesburg

Junkers Ju86 ZS-AGJ, *General David Baird*, in flight over the
Transvaal, 1938

The passenger model was nothing short of luxurious. The ones supplied to SAA had fully adjustable leather armchair seats, soundproofed cabin walls, interior heating and overhead interior strip lighting which made for an unprecedented passenger experience. To the relief of critics of the airline who had been accusing it of supporting only German industry, 1936 also saw the South African government placing an order for seven Airspeed Envoy III machines with the Airspeed Limited company in Portsmouth, England.

Airspeed Envoy

Four of the machines would be for service with SAA and three for the Air Force, but use of these aircraft would be interchangeable. Apart from the first one for SAA, ZS-AGA, which was flown out to South Africa by Captain Frank Elliott-Wilson and engineer W.E.B. Scott by way of Cairo, Juba and Nairobi to Rand Airport, and the second one under the command of the SAAF's Captain Donnelly, all the others were shipped out in crates and reassembled in Cape Town before being flown to Johannesburg. In the case of the SAAF aircraft, the airplanes went directly to Swartkop Air Force Base near Pretoria.

Airspeed Envoys had seating for six passengers. They were powered by two seven-cylinder Armstrong Siddeley Cheetah IX air-cooled radial engines delivering 335 HP/250 Kw of power. The aircraft were fast and versatile. They could fly at a cruising speed of 192 mph and a maximum speed of 210 mph at an altitude of 22,500 ft. Their non-stop range was 650 miles. They were constructed mainly of stressed plywood and fabric and had a retractable landing gear.

The Airspeeds began flying a weekly service between Johannesburg, Bloemfontein and Port Elizabeth on October 12, 1936 but, as things eventually turned out, they would not be popular with either pilots or passengers. During winter, the cockpit and passenger cabin were uncomfortably cold. Pilots curled up or sat cross-legged on theirs seats to keep warm and thick blankets would become standard issue to passengers. Like the Ju86s, the Envoys also had the capability to rapidly metamorphose from passenger carriers to military machines. The change could be made in a little less than 32 hours. The three military versions were designed to carry bombs and had a fixed forward-firing Vickers Mark V machine gun as well as a manually operated revolving turret fitted with a Lewis gun in the dorsal position.

With the introduction of Airspeed Envoy services on domestic routes, and while the new Junkers Ju86s were awaited from Germany, the trusty and dependable Ju52s soldiered on, forming the backbone of SAA's operations. They carved a much-loved historical niche for themselves into the airline's history. Although 1936 had been a banner year for aviation in Southern Africa, developments during 1937 would eclipse it. The Airspeed Envoys began augmenting Ju52 services by flying regular routes to many destinations in South-West Africa but, perhaps even more importantly, the little craft would also be the first to fledge the airline's wings in preparation for carrying the Flying Springbok motif to domains far beyond home turf.

To the north of the country lay the vast open spread of Africa. Far beyond the yellow-brown rocks and olive-colored bushveld scrub that clung to the Soutpansberg and the Waterberg mountain ranges, beyond the murky brown waters of the Limpopo river, beyond the giant baobab trees and the marula and mopane forests, far beyond the tribal lands of the Venda, Tswana, Sotho and Shangaan people, there was another emblematic presence on the landscape. Foreign flags fluttered everywhere in the African breeze. Across vast swathes of territory all the way to where the great landmass of Africa nudged against the Mediterranean, British, French, Italian, Spanish, Belgian and Portuguese flags proclaimed the rule of colonial power. In all those territories foreign masters held sway over the indigenous people and over one of the richest and most diverse continents on earth. For the businessman, the entrepreneur and the traveller the allure was magnetic. Endless possibilities and opportunities lay out there. The prospects for mining, agriculture, trade and tourism that could be conducted between the Union of South Africa and the rest of the continent appeared to be limitless. It was time to explore new routes for the Flying Springbok.

On a crisp autumn morning of May 29, 1937, Airspeed Envoy ZS-AGA departed Rand Airport under the command of Captain G.D.B. Williams with Captain 'Frikkie' Fry and Assistant Airways Manager Graham Stanley Leverton on board as passengers. After stopping at Pietersburg for refuelling, it crossed the Limpopo river, entering the airspace of the British colony of Southern Rhodesia. After a technical stop at Bulawayo, it flew northwards, crossed the Zambezi river and landed at Livingstone in the British territory of Northern Rhodesia. Then, onwards to the copper mining town of Broken Hill, then Mpika and across the divide between Northern Rhodesia and the British colony of Tanganyika to Mbeya before continuing on to Dodoma, Dar es Salaam and Moshi. Captain 'Frikkie' Fry left the flight at Dodoma where he journeyed overland to Tabora to meet a southbound delivery flight of a new Junkers Ju52 on its way from the factory in Germany. The Airspeed with passenger Leverton aboard then left Tanganyika and entered the airspace of the British colony of Kenya, landing at Nairobi and finally at Kisumu. Leverton, representing SAA and the South African government, held talks with officials of the various colonial authorities along the way as well as with board members of Rhodesia and Nyasaland Airways and Wilson Airways of Kenya. At these meetings they hashed out arrangements for SAA to begin an ambitious new service between Johannesburg and Kisumu.

Kisumu is situated on the northeast coast of the world's second largest body of fresh water, Lake Victoria. The huge lake sprawls for 26,828 square miles and is the source of the Nile river. It is skirted by modern-day Tanzania, Uganda and Kenya. In the thirties it was an important trading center and the inland railhead of the East African Railways system. Steamers plied the lake and in addition to trade, commerce and a lucrative fishing industry its shores and waters were always important tourist attractions for white travellers seeking adventure in the African hinterland.

Now the lake would take on another role. Reverting to the function it had once played at the beginning of the thirties when Imperial Airways first began flying through Africa, it would now become an important stopover in a brand new British aerial enterprise. Not long after the arrival of the SAA Airspeed Envoy with Leverton on board, a big new Imperial Airways Short Empire C-class flying boat named *Canopus*, registered G-ADHL, under the command of Captain E.H. Atwood took off from Southampton in England en route to South Africa. Proudly displaying the livery of Imperial Airways, it was the first of a fleet of large, comfortable, new flying machines to commence a regular service between Britain and South Africa, following a route that was dictated by Africa's great waterways and lakes. The executive management of Imperial Airways wanted to fly more passengers and larger mail and cargo loads on their flights from Britain. But Africa's notorious unpaved airfields imposed limitations on big, heavy aircraft. They could easily get stuck in sand or mud. More importantly, heavy airplanes needed distances longer than the length of existing airfields to become airborne or to accomplish a safe landing. So a decision was made to switch operations from land to water. That way aircraft would not get bogged down and ample take-off and landing runs would be assured. Early models of the flying boats, built by Short Brothers Limited, could carry 17 passengers. On-board facilities were the epitome of modern luxury. There were separate sitting, sleeping, dining and smoking sections on board. Each aircraft had five crew members and could carry up to 4,480 lbs of cargo. Four Bristol Pegasus radial engines developed 920 HP (690 kW) of power and could propel the craft at a speed of 200 mph. Flights originated at Southampton and terminated at Durban, landing at the city's harbor in the bay called Port Natal. From there, passengers could join SAA flights to other destinations in South Africa. It took seven days to complete the route from Britain, traveling from Southampton via St. Nazaire, Marseilles, Etang de Berre (Rome), Lake Bracciano (Brindisi), Athens, Crete, Alexandria, Cairo, Luxor, Wadi Halfa, Kareima, Khartoum, Malakal, Juba, Port Bell (a small quayside harbor at Kisumu on Lake Victoria), Naivasha, Mombasa, Dar es Salaam, Lindi, Lumo, Quelimane, Beira, Inhambane and Lourenco Marques to Durban. With the exception of the last sector through the Portuguese colony of Mozambique, all other stops in Africa were made in British-controlled territory, including Egypt and the Sudan. With the introduction of the new Imperial Airways flying boat service from London, all of its flights to Rand Airport came to an end. The last service from Johannesburg departed for London on June 7, 1937. Henceforth, the coastal city of Durban and its large bay would become the southernmost Imperial Airways terminal in Africa.

On June 9, 1937, as a direct result of negotiations conducted by SAA's Assistant Airways manager Graham Stanley Leverton on his Airspeed Envoy expeditionary flight, SAA began its first trans-border service to Central Africa. The route did not yet extend all the way to Kisumu but went from Rand Airport to Pietersburg, then to Bulawayo in Southern Rhodesia, continued on to Livingstone in Northern Rhodesia and then terminated in Lusaka. Those were important destinations. Livingstone was a small town near the Victoria Falls on the Zambezi River. The waterfall is one of the greatest natural spectacles on earth. To this day, they continue to be one of Africa's major attractions. The river is over a mile wide at this point. Water plunges over a gorge with a deafening roar. During the autumn months of April and May, two-and-a-half million gallons per second cascade over 300 feet into a churning cataract, creating a dazzling rainbow and sending up a cloud of spray visible 50 miles away. The falls are actually a magnificent geologic aberration in the meandering course of the mighty Zambezi which flows 1,700 miles eastwards from the heart of Central Africa to the Indian Ocean, bisecting the subcontinent like a life-sustaining artery. It was first described in 1855, by the celebrated Scottish missionary and explorer, Dr. David Livingstone. Though called *Mosi Oa Tunya* (The Smoke that Thunders) by the local Tonga and other tribes who lived in the verdant forests along the Zambezi's banks, Livingstone named the waterfall in honor of his queen. It says much about the remarkable life and character of that lonely and little-understood man that the waterfall he named and the town called after him still retain those names today. Conversely, the names of many early European explorers have been eradicated throughout much of the rest of Africa. Search the junkyards of cities in independent countries that were once colonies of European powers and you'll find heaps of statues of colonial heroes and explorers piled among the scrap metal or simply rotting among the weeds. But not so with David Livingstone. Carrying a bible and a compass, he was one of the first white men to cross Africa on foot from coast to coast and he, more than any other, helped rid Africa of one of its most ravaging scourges during the 19th century, the slave trade. More than the missionary and intrepid explorer that he was, Livingstone was, above all, an emancipator. After his death in the African tropics, his heart was buried beneath a tree but due to the incredible diligence and respect of his two closest African assistants, Susi and Chuma, his body was carried to the east coast and transported by sea to England. It is interred near the front entrance inside Westminster Abbey in London.

Lusaka, the terminal for the new SAA service in 1937, was the capital of the British-administered colony of Northern Rhodesia. It was a vital junction on the long railroad that ran all the way through Northern and Southern Rhodesia, Bechuanaland and then southwards to Cape Town. The glinting steel tracks linked South Africa with the Belgian Congo far to the north. The line was part of Cecil Rhodes' original dream of a Cape-to-Cairo railway but that ambition never materialized as far north as he had hoped. However, there was another man-made artery that ran right through the heart of Lusaka, the Great North Road. It stretched all the way from Cape Town to Cairo. Circuitous, treacherous and unpredictable though that route was, it was nevertheless possible to traverse the length of the African continent by road. But the word 'road' is perhaps something of a misnomer. It sometimes became little more than a dirt track or a barely recognizable rutted furrow in the ground. In places it was often closed due to flooding, rock falls, mudslides, fallen trees, downed bridges, shifting sand dunes, frequent border disputes and tribal clashes. In addition to the road northwards, Lusaka was also the starting point of what was known as the Great East Road that linked Central Africa with Nyasaland, Tanganyika and Mozambique to the east.

The new SAA air route would be operated exclusively by the venerable Junkers Ju52, with the first flight flown by ZS-AFC. Less than a month later, on July 4, 1937, SAA expanded the service all the way to Kisumu. That historic flight was inaugurated by ZS-AFB under the command of Captain Len Inggs, a pilot who would go on to have a long and distinguished career with the airline. The route went by way of Johannesburg, Pietersburg, Bulawayo, Livingstone, Lusaka, Broken Hill, Mpika, Mbeya, Dodoma, Moshi and Nairobi, terminating at Kisumu on the banks of Lake Victoria. It was to become an extremely popular service. Now UK-bound passengers from South Africa had the option of flying with Imperial Airways all the way from Durban to Southampton or with SAA from Johannesburg to Kisumu where they could connect with the Imperial Airways flying boat to Britain. Naturally, the new Kisumu route also attracted those seeking to open trade and business links between South and Central Africa as well as tourists, holidaymakers and members of the ever-popular trophy hunting fraternity. Wealthy 'big game' hunters flocked to Africa from the United States and Europe those days because wildlife was still aplenty. Hunting permits were never a problem and shooting licenses were cheap. It was a time when exclusive English gentlemen's clubs, the most stately European manor houses and many opulent plantation estate homes in the U.S. were not deemed complete without the heads of large dead African mammals like antelope, zebra, buffalo, elephant or lion mounted on the walls. With the advent of the new service, mailbags destined for London from Johannesburg were transferred from SAA flights to Imperial Airways at Kisumu. Southbound mail was off-loaded from the flying boats and placed on board the Ju52s. Getting the mail from the UK to Johannesburg was quicker on SAA rather than going all the way on Imperial Airways as the flying boats followed a longer, more easterly route to Mombasa and then southwards through Mozambique before reaching Durban. From Kisumu, mail reached Johannesburg a couple of days faster via the shorter Ju52 route.

Flights from Rand Airport to Kisumu took two-and-a-half days, of which a total of 37 hours were spent in the air. At first operated only on a weekly basis, flights departed Johannesburg at 8.00 a.m. on Sunday and arrived at 1.30 p.m. on Tuesday. The return flight left Kisumu on Wednesday at 1.30 p.m. and arrived in Johannesburg at 8.00 a.m. on Friday. Dodoma provided one of the most pleasant stops en route. There refreshments were served in a building resembling a plush English country club.

Waiters in white suits and gloves served tea and scones to passengers in a large, comfortable lounge where big fans slowly whirled overhead. Moshi was another popular stop-over. It was an airfield virtually in the shadow of Mount Kilimanjaro. A pleasant afternoon beer or gin and tonic could be enjoyed there before continuing on to Nairobi. The refuelling agent at Moshi, a Mr. Walker, was also the local mountaineering guide. For those who broke their journeys there, he was always only too happy to guide the more adventurous to the summit of Kilimanjaro. Overnight stops on the flight were spent at Broken Hill and Nairobi. Passengers were accommodated at local hotels and were wined and dined sumptuously, enjoying the best local cuisine. Chamber pots and mosquito nets were provided in the well-appointed hotel bedrooms. Many people recalled with fond memory the joy of waking up early in the morning to the aroma of brewing coffee and to hearing the three Junkers engines being started at the nearby airfield. It was a sound that broke the silence of the African dawn. Many claimed that there was nothing more pleasant than drifting off to sleep at night to the thumping of distant tribal drums mingling with the roar of a faraway lion or the trumpeting of an elephant in the surrounding bush. It was equalled only by the excitement of being woken up in the morning by the initial choking cough and then the reassuring guttural rumble of those three powerful Hornet nine-cylinder radial engines as they were warmed up for the flight, heralding the thrilling prospect of another day's low level flying over the African landscape.

Of course, flying over the hot terrain of veldt and scrub often meant that thermals and downdraughts would cause extremely bumpy rides. Air sickness bags were always carried for those who succumbed to nausea and vomiting. Flight crews often had to assist mothers with babies and young children or elderly passengers who were badly affected by bone-rattling vibration during the journey. In addition, at many of the airfields ground crew had to clear landing areas of wild animals and birds. Wildebeest, impala, warthogs, zebra and more than the occasional hippo, elephant, buffalo, rhino or lion wandered onto the airfield. Exciting though it was, flying in Africa was nevertheless a perilous business.

Refuelling the aircraft, topping up engines with oil and general technical inspections along the way were the responsibility of the flight engineer. Because of the long distances flown, sometimes minor repairs and maintenance had to be carried out at stops that were far from Rand Airport. To assist the flight engineer with such tasks a mechanic was eventually stationed at Broken Hill in Northern Rhodesia. It was his job to accompany the aircraft to Nairobi and Kisumu and then fly back with it to Broken Hill. Any minor repairs or maintenance that may have been necessary in those outlying areas could be performed before the airplane returned to Johannesburg. Jimmy Lennard was the first mechanical engineer stationed at Broken Hill, followed by Harry van Wyk. Their tours of duty were for two months at a time. The two men alternated with one another. Jeff Scott, once Traffic Manager at Stamford Hill in Durban, was eventually also stationed at Broken Hill as Traffic Manager. He too occasionally accompanied the Ju52s to Kisumu. Many tales from pilots and flight crews survive from those days. They speak of a remarkable time when flying was not only an adventure but downright fun.

The flight to Kisumu went directly over some of the most stunning scenery in Africa. This included the Great Rift Valley, the Serengeti Plain and the Ngorongoro Crater. Wildlife abounded in those regions. Elephants numbered in their tens of thousands. Migrating herds of buffalo, wildebeest, zebra and antelope spread across miles of East Africa's undulating grassy landscape and hills. Waterholes were crowded with giraffe and impala. Rhinos were plentiful. In those days Africa still evoked impressions of a primal Garden of Eden. It was a land that took people's breath away. The imprint of human activity had not yet left its mark.

Deforestation, large-scale lumber cutting, soil erosion, strip mining, river pollution, wildlife poaching, congested highways and scars caused by the international demand for Africa's rich natural resources still lay far in the future. In the mid-thirties, Africa was still pristine. But it had not always entirely been a bed of roses for the locals. Colonial masters subjugated indigenous populations wherever and whenever it suited them. Some places were worse than others, of course. Nowhere had it been more ruthless than in the Belgian Congo where slave-like servitude to King Leopold at the end of the 19th century often included barbarities such as the severing of hands and limbs of workers who did not meet their daily quotas of ivory or rubber collection. But for the most part by the 1930s rural Africa—at least *British* rural Africa—was a green, clean and relatively peaceful place. Grossly underpaid and overexploited laborers certainly toiled in fields under the midday sun while white folks sipped pink gins in the shade or played a bout of polo at the country club but aside from servitude to the local District Commissioner and the farm manager it was not all bad. Smoke from the fireplaces of a thousand rural villages wafted lazily across misty morning landscapes. Herd boys tended cattle and goats on the mountains while young girls walked in single-file along narrow paths with clay pots on their heads to collect water from streams and lakes. Sunlight cast long shadows of huts, trees and animals across the crimson grass in the late afternoon. Women pounded dry corn kernels with large mortars and pestles in the courtyards of settlements while elderly men sat huddled beneath trees smoking their pipes and pontificating on the social and political concerns of their communities. Wild animals were plentiful. This was Africa at that time. Being able to fly over it at low level was a joy and a privilege that no passenger ever forgot.

Many of the SAA pilots were enthusiastic photographers and knew exactly where to find large gatherings of wildlife, much to the delight of passengers. Sometimes the Ju52s would skim just a few hundred feet above the terrain, affording everyone amazing views. The pilots also knew many of the owners of farms and ranches along the way. Northbound flights on Sunday contained piles of Johannesburg's most popular weekly newspaper, the *Sunday Times*. As the aircraft flew over homesteads belonging to the captain and crews' friends pilots would buzz the place summoning their occupants outdoors. Then a rolled-up copy of the *Sunday Times* would be tossed out of an open window of the Ju52 to the folks below.

Now and again passengers were treated to something really special, an unscheduled stop at a large private estate in Northern Rhodesia called *Shiwa Ngandu*. Located northeast of Mpika on the way to Mbeya in Tanganyika, this was a place unlike any other in all Africa. Named after the nearby Lake Ishiba Ng'andu which in the local Bemba language meant 'Lake of the Royal Crocodile,' the estate was the property of a most unusual and eccentric character by the name of Lieutenant Colonel Sir Stewart Gore-Browne. Most of the Ju52 flight crews knew him and were only too happy to land on the lawns or grounds of his estate to pick up or drop off mail or small packages or items of cargo. The place was hundreds of miles from the nearest railway line and there were few reliable roads through the quagmire of swamps and rivers that separated it from civilization. Reaching it overland from Mpika was a treacherous journey that could take at least a week or more.

Gore-Brown was a British-born aristocrat who had gone to Africa in 1902 to work as a land surveyor in the colony of Natal. In 1911, he went to Northern Rhodesia to assist in defining the border between that colony and the Belgian Congo. He fell deeply in love with Africa but returned to the UK and served in the British Army during the First World War, attaining the rank of Lieutenant Colonel and winning the Distinguished Service Order (DSO). His aunt, Dame Ethel Locke King, owned a fine country estate at Weybridge and he began nurturing aspirations to own an estate too. Though independently wealthy, he simply could not afford the price of a country property in England so, when cheap land went on sale in Northern Rhodesia to encourage white immigration to the territory, he returned to Africa. Hacking his way through bush and forest with Bemba guides and porters, he found a vast tract of land that stole his heart near Lake Ishiba Ng'andu and bought it.

In 1920, he began constructing a mansion on the property. In the absence of roads and bridges everything had to be made on site, including bricks, mortar, woodwork and all the architectural trimmings. Metalwork and glass had to be carted in by ox wagon from sources far away. Hundreds of local people were recruited from surrounding villages to work on the project. Over the years Gore-Brown's dream of a country estate became a reality. Courtyards, colonnades, a library, a baronial-type dining room, a wine cellar, an imposing gatehouse, floral nurseries, tennis courts, gardens, pathways, stables, kennels and other structures came to exist in what can only be described as the wildest of wild Africa. Gore-Brown thrived there and eventually took it upon himself to become involved in politics, taking umbrage with Northern Rhodesia's white colonial masters and campaigning for equal rights for the territory's indigenous black population. In 1934, he was elected to Northern Rhodesia's Legislative Council. He eventually built a school, post office, sports fields, a trading store and hospital for his workers, all of whom were accommodated in comfortable brick cottages with cooking facilities and running water.

Shiwa Ngandu brought in an income from cattle, a few crops and the sale of citrus blossoms and other natural oils for the production of perfumes and toiletries. These were carted overland to the railhead hundreds of miles away and ultimately exported to Europe. In 1927, Gore-Browne married Miss Lorna Goldmann in England and, although she was 25 years his junior, they had two daughters. Despite the luxurious and comfortable nature of her home and a bevy of servants to attend to her every whim, Gore-Brown's wife was not as enamored with living in the African bush as her husband. From 1934, they began spending much of their time apart. They would divorce in 1950. Gore-Brown was always a very formal and disciplined man. He lived his life according to a strict code of conduct, dress and etiquette. He wore a monocle and sported a black tie and dinner jacket at mealtime every night. Dinners were sumptuous affairs and the table was always bedecked with the finest crockery, silverware and crystal, whether Gore-Brown dined alone or with the occasional guest. He was knighted by King George VI in 1945 for his political contributions to Northern Rhodesia. When he died in 1967, three years after Northern Rhodesia had become the independent Republic of Zambia, he was buried at *Shiwa Ngandu* in a state funeral attended by President Kenneth Kaunda, the only white man in Zambia ever to be so honored.

In 1937, *Shiwa Ngandu* was one of those rare treasures to be savored by SAA passengers who were lucky enough to be on a flight that landed there, if only for an hour or two to enjoy tea and refreshments on the lawn or on one of the verandas of the house. If the Ju52 captain felt that he could make up the time en route to Mbeya on a northbound flight or to Broken Hill on the flight southwards, he would allow his passengers and crew enough time to accompany Gore-Brown on a quick trip by truck or car to view a few of the many species of wildlife that inhabited the estate.

Around the time that the Central African services began, SAA experienced its first serious Junkers Ju52 accident. ZS-AKY was registered to the airline on June 12, 1937, after suffering minor damage to its propellers and landing gear during its delivery flight from Europe at Tabora, Tanganyika. After repairs were carried out, the aircraft was flown to Johannesburg and on the morning of June 14, it was preparing for its first passenger-carrying flight to Durban. The ever-popular 'Frikkie' Fry was in command, with co-pilot Gerwyn David Bowen Williams in the right hand seat. A German, W. Tornow, who had flown out with the aircraft on its delivery flight from Dessau was Acting Radio Operator. Newcomer to SAA, Leonard Smith was Flight Engineer. Eleven passengers were seated in the main cabin. The aircraft taxied to the south end of Rand Airport, turned around and began its take off run in a northerly direction against a strong wind. Suddenly, number three engine on the starboard wing began to lose power. Realizing that he would not be able to abort the take-off in the space available, Fry pushed the throttles of the other two engines all the way forward, desperately trying to clear the trees at the end of the runway. Struggling to remain airborne the Junkers headed towards a large yellow 'mine dump.' This was a man-made mountain of sand that was the remains of washed and strained crushed rock brought up from underground at the nearby Simmer and Jack gold mine. Catching Fry off guard, a sudden downdraught forced the aircraft towards the ground. Trying to keep his cool in the fast-moving and dire circumstances, Fry skilfully made for a small clearing, attempting to lower the aircraft's tail to reduce impact. But the right wing struck a tree which violently swung the aircraft around and it ploughed tail first into a railway embankment. The crash caused the fuel tanks to rupture on the starboard side and suddenly flames started licking at the fuselage. Tornow, the young German radio operator, rushed back into the cabin, smashing windows to evacuate passengers and then dashing back to the flight deck to assist the crew get out of the burning craft. Engineer Len Smith also displayed incredible bravery by helping passengers get away from the flames. One of the elderly passengers, a Mrs Highan, died of internal injuries a few days later. Sadly, she had become SAA's first passenger fatality. The two pilots suffered minor injuries. Thus ZS-AKY went down in the history books as having the shortest period of service of any aircraft in the airline's fleet—less than a week.

On June 11, 1937, the first Junkers Ju86 aircraft arrived from the factory in Germany. ZS-AGF, *Richard King*, was piloted by SAA captain Len Inggs. ZS-AGG, *Ryk Tulbagh*, was flown by Deutsche Lufthansa pilot Captain Erhard Rother. After landing at Rand Airport, Inggs pronounced the aircraft "a most excellent machine and wonderfully controllable." The next pair of Ju86s, ZS-AGH, *Sir Harry Smith* and ZS-AGI, *Sir John Cradock*, arrived on November 29, 1937. The pilots were Captains R. Illersperger and H. Topp.

The remainder of the Ju86s would be delivered at regular intervals well into 1939. Unfortunately, two of the Ju86s were wrecked on their delivery flights. On July 29, 1938, ZS-AJE ran out of fuel and crash-landed at Juba in the Sudan. On September 20, 1938, ZS-AND was severely damaged as it came in to land at Rand Airport. Pilot Piet Nell was in the captain's seat when the airplane clipped an electrical structure at the perimeter of the airfield. That tore off the left wing and engine. Miraculously, there were no serious injuries in either of those two accidents.

By 1938, the Ju86s allowed services to be increased and routes expanded. The new machines immediately became very popular with passengers. They were fast and comfortable. Flying times were reduced on all the sectors that they operated. Daily flights between Durban and Cape Town were introduced, with stops made at East London, Port Elizabeth and Mossel Bay. Weather permitting, stops were also made at Grahamstown and George depending on passenger demand. Flights from Durban to Cape Town on the Ju52s took seven hours and 45 minutes. The Ju86s slashed that time by more than an hour. In addition to expanding domestic services, three more flights per week were flown to Salisbury in Southern Rhodesia with stops made at the small towns of Gatooma, Que Que and Gwelo, all according to passengers' requests.

On November 4, 1938, the Ju86s began a new, faster route to South-West Africa from Johannesburg. ZS-ANA flew the first service across the Kalahari Desert from Rand Airport via Palapye Road and Maun in Bechuanaland to Windhoek. The Ju86 was sometimes operated by only a pilot and a co-pilot. If the co-pilot held a radio operator's license then he handled the radio as well. Long-serving SAA pilot Dennis Raubenheimer recalled that the first Ju86 flights across the Kalahari Desert carried no maps or proper flying charts as they simply weren't available. Crews had to rely on surveyors' maps. Flights had to be operated at very low altitude so that pilots could identify prominent hills and other terrain. Flying too high meant that landmarks might not be recognized and the pilots could easily become lost. Rivers marked on charts were invariably dry and easily blended into the surrounding landscape if crews weren't flying low enough to identify them. Sandstorms meant that the flight had to be aborted and the aircraft returned to its embarkation airport.

To give an idea of conditions at the time the following is an extract from an SAA promotional timetable dated November, 1938.

ANY TIME IS FLYING TIME ON THE
SOUTH AFRICAN AIRWAYS

All aeroplanes in use by South African Airways are modern multi-engined and of all-metal construction. The cruising speed of the various types of aircraft in use range from 150 to 200 miles per hour (241 to 322 kilometres per hour)

The crew carried on all South African Airways aircraft consists of a minimum number of three, two of who are qualified 'B' Licensed Pilots who are in possession of the International Navigation licence or its equivalent and the licence for

Wireless Telegraphy. All South African Airways aircraft are fitted with the latest wireless equipment, which includes Direction Finding apparatus and Homing Devices. A fully licensed Wireless Operator is carried on all aircraft. Passengers desiring to dispatch messages in the air may do so on payment of the appropriate charges, details of which can be obtained from the Wireless Operator.

Normally the loading of the aeroplane is completed five minutes before the scheduled time of departure and passengers are requested to be at the aerodrome 30 minutes before schedule time of departure to enable the loading formalities to be completed in order to allow the aircraft to leave on time. Should a passenger arrive too late for such formalities to be completed without delaying the departure of the aircraft, the passenger's ticket may be regarded as cancelled and no claim for the refund of the fare can be entertained. Refunds will only be made on unused tickets if the relative accommodation has been cancelled and if the administration has not been prejudiced thereby.

Where no direct connection is provided, all through fares include night stop hotel accommodation at the intervening stations, also regular meals or refreshments on the route. Children under three years of age, held in the arms, are carried free of charge. Children between the ages of three and ten years are charged half the adult fare and are allowed half of the luggage allowance.

At higher altitudes fountain pens have a tendency to leak. Passengers are advised to screw the cap down tightly.

Prevention of air sickness: Vasano, Peremesin and Coffeminal Comp are recommended for airsickness.

SOUTH AFRICAN AIRWAYS OFFER YOU

RELIABILITY	SECURITY
SPEED	ECONOMY
COMFORT	CLEANLINESS
SAFETY	FREQUENT SERVICES

In 1939, SAA began exploring the viability of operating a service to yet another over-border destination. On May 1 of that year, with Major J.D.T. Louw and Captain K.S.P. Jones at the controls, Junkers Ju86, ZS-ANA, took off on a survey and proving flight from Rand Airport bound for Luanda in the Portuguese territory of Angola on the west African coast. After a total flying time of 12 hours and ten minutes, travelling by way of Upington in the Northern Cape province, Windhoek and Ohopoho in South-West Africa, then Mossamedes and Lobito in Angola, the aircraft landed at Luanda four days later. On August 21, 1939, Junkers Ju86, ZS-AGH, *Sir Harry Smith* piloted by Captains K.S.P. Jones and Johannes Albertus 'Bert' Rademan began flying the first regular scheduled service to Luanda from Cape Town. Other flights using Ju52s and Ju86s were also operated from Johannesburg to Luanda. Under dictatorial Portuguese Prime Minister António de Oliveira Salazar in Lisbon, Portugal and its African colonies of Angola and Mozambique enjoyed a prosperous relationship with South Africa. Diamonds, timber, ivory, fish products, palm and peanut oil, cotton, cocoa beans, corn, tobacco and coffee were all commodities traded between the Union and Angola. In addition, there was a large expatriate Portuguese community residing in South Africa and the new air link provided a valuable service for them. Eventually, it was hoped that the Luanda service on the west coast might be directly linked with the Kisumu service at Lake Victoria on the eastern side of the continent. But war clouds were gathering ever more ominously in Europe, thwarting those plans. If conflict came it would affect all of Britain's colonies and her allies worldwide, including those in Africa.

In 1938, SAA had placed an order for two Junkers Ju90 aircraft with the factory in Dessau. They would have been the first four-engine all-metal single-wing monoplane to enter into service with the airline. Early in 1939, crews were sent to Dessau for conversion training to these large machines. Among them were Captains Len Inggs and Ron Madeley and ground engineer W.B. Scott. They were followed by the Minister of Railways and Harbors, Oswald Pirow, who travelled to Germany by sea with his family. It was planned that they would then return as passengers on the delivery flight of the new aircraft to South Africa. But Hitler's rhetoric and highly provocative speeches were intensifying. The Munich Agreement had already been signed in September 1938 guaranteeing "peace in our time" as British Prime Minister Neville Chamberlain had woefully and inaccurately predicted events. The Second World War was just around the corner. As the departure date of the two Junkers Ju90 for the delivery flight to Johannesburg approached, the Junkers Company — probably at the urging of Third Reich officials — began finding excuses to delay their release. On the eve of the war the Junkers management advised the South Africans to leave the country immediately or their safety might be jeopardized. Tickets were bought for them to exit Germany by rail without delay. In a recollection of the events the late Captain Len Inggs told what happened. "We were in Dessau where the aircraft were being built but we were informed by the factory that extra modifications became necessary and that the aircraft would not be ready for us for another three to four weeks. They told us to take a holiday anywhere in Germany at their expense. We stuck around in Berlin for a while and then saw that it was time to get out as the news was getting worse every day. War was imminent. Junkers was very good about it all and got us on to one of the last trains out of Berlin to the Baltic coast from where it was easy to get to neutral Stockholm. From there it was simple to get to Britain. Before we left on the train a Junkers official told us that if we had any difficulty getting out of Germany we were to return to Dessau where the factory would make one of its own aircraft available to fly us to a neutral country. I was most impressed with this gesture. From England we travelled by sea to Cape Town and, of course, to safety."

In the pre-dawn hours of September 1, 1939, Germany invaded Poland. At 11.15 a.m. on September 3, Britain's Prime Minister Neville Chamberlain announced on radio that, as Germany had refused to withdraw its troops from Poland, the United Kingdom was officially at war with Germany. Three days later, on September 6, Prime Minister Jan Smuts declared that South Africa was also at war with Germany. Needless to say, the Ju90s were never delivered.

But what of Allister Miller, the man whose vision had given life to aviation and had inspired all that had resulted from it in the sub-continent of Africa? What had become of him and his indomitable, ferociously independent spirit? Three years before the outbreak of the war he had still been pushing pen on paper behind a desk in an office in the Airways division of the South African Railways and Harbors administration building in Johannesburg. But he could not get flying out of his system. It gnawed at him like a mosquito sucking his blood. In 1936, the bug won. That year an air race had been arranged from the United Kingdom to South Africa and Miller was absolutely determined to participate in it. He applied for a short period of absence from his job and, to his surprise and delight, was given permission to take part in what was called the Empire Air Race. This ambitious event had been organized by the wealthy Johannesburg industrialist and business tycoon Isidore Schlesinger.

American-born Schlesinger had made his fortune in South Africa from insurance, real estate, citrus groves, theaters and film production. He was a very successful businessman and wanted to foster an entrepreneurial spirit to generate new economic opportunities in the country. The Empire Air Race was arranged to coincide with Johannesburg's Golden Jubilee in celebration of its founding as a goldmining encampment in 1886. The race started in Portsmouth, England and terminated at Rand Airport. It carried a total purse of £10,000 put up personally by Schlesinger. £4,000 was earmarked for the fastest overall entrant. Allister Miller could not resist. It was not the money that he was after but the sheer challenge and joy of flying once again. He procured and entered a fast, second-hand, single-seat, single-engine Percival P6 Mew Gull British racing aircraft with a six-cylinder de Havilland Gipsy engine. It was registered ZS-AHM, painted in gold and white and named *The Golden City*. It was a sleek, beautiful machine, throbbing with power. Miller had high hopes of winning the race with it. On the day the contest began in Portsmouth the aircraft was being refuelled but the mechanic mistakenly thought the Percival's tanks were full when in actual fact they were not. The result? Miller ran out of fuel in the skies above Yugoslavia. He had to make a forced landing in an empty field. By the time the aircraft was found and refuelled the weather had turned foul and the authorities refused him permission to take off. Deeply disappointed Miller opted out of the race, disposed of the aircraft and returned to Johannesburg a very bitter man. He had no recourse but to go back to his desk job.

At the start of the Second World War in 1939, Miller offered his services to the South African Air Force (SAAF) but, being past the age for active wartime service, he was posted as a Major with ground-based administrative duties with the SAAF in Nairobi, Kenya. A squadron had been formed there for the East and North African campaigns against German and Italian forces. Not long after arriving in Nairobi, Miller developed lung and heart problems and had to return to South Africa. After being discharged from hospital, he was posted to the SAAF's new Waterkloof Air Force base outside Pretoria for administrative duties. Shortly thereafter he was reassigned to the SAAF base at Alexandersfontein, Kimberley, the very same place where the first pilots for the original South African Aviation Corps head learnt to fly back in 1913. On April 28, 1941, he became Officer Commanding the SAAF's Number 70 Air School for the training of engine and airframe mechanics. He was subsequently promoted to the rank of Lieutenant Colonel and transferred as Officer Commanding to the Number 4 Air School located at Benoni, not too far from Johannesburg. The school was involved in elementary flying training for the war using de Havilland 82A Tiger Moth aircraft. It was a proud day indeed when Lieutenant Colonel Allister Macintosh Miller oversaw a passing out parade and pinned SAAF pilot wings on the chest of his twenty-year old son, also named Allister Macintosh Miller. A year later, on March 1, 1944, as a pilot on active duties in Europe, the younger Miller was shot down over Turin, Italy whilst flying a reconnaissance mission in a de Havilland Mosquito DH.98 for 80 Squadron. He was killed instantly.

Miller was devastated by his son's death. The ensuing depression further weakened his health. His last military command was at Number 47 Air Observer School in Queenstown in the Eastern Cape. The School operated Avro Avions and Airspeed Envoys but ceased operations as soon as the war ended in 1945. By that time Miller was a very sick man and was still grieving the tragic loss of his son. When his wife Marion passed away after a prolonged illness in 1950, he retired to his cottage, *Journeys End*, near Port Elizabeth. Although he still saw his two daughters regularly his zest for life had diminished. He became a somewhat lost and reclusive man and died on October 14, 1951. He was only 59 years old.

With Allister Macintosh Miller's passing a remarkable period of history came to an end. Without his singular tenacity and foresight it is hard to imagine how and when large-scale aviation would ever have found wings in the southern skies of Africa.

Chapter Four

Embattled Skies

Once again the world was embroiled in bitter battle.

As soon as South Africa declared war on Germany in September 1939, in alliance with Britain, all 18 of SAA's Junkers Ju86 aircraft were withdrawn from commercial service and placed under the command of the Air Force. This left only the trusty Ju52s for passenger flights. Aircraft operations were divided into two wings, one controlled by the South African Railways and Harbors Administration and one by the Department of Defense. Hastily pushed through the SAAF's hangars in Pretoria and at the airline's own workshops at Rand Airport, the Ju86s were converted into coastal patrol aircraft. The immediate fear was the presence of German U-boats and naval vessels in South African territorial waters. These could endanger Allied shipping and oil supplies as well as pose a direct threat to South African coastal cities and harbors. Requiring a crew of six, the Ju86s were fitted with external racks that could carry a bomb load of 1,160 lbs. They were also equipped with three machine guns. A fixed forward-facing .303 water-cooled gun was mounted in the nose for firing by the pilot and an open upper dorsal and a retractable lower ventral .303 machine gun were installed in the fuselage for firing by gunners. All these external protuberances created a lot of drag, reducing the aircraft's speed to 120 mph. To improve range a couple of additional steel fuel tanks were installed in the passenger cabin. Some of the Ju86s were also fitted with downward-facing large-format cameras for reconnaissance work. Durban received three of the aircraft, forming the nucleus of the SAAF's 13 Squadron. Port Elizabeth received another three, forming 14 Squadron, Cape Town three for 15 Squadron and Walvis Bay three more for 16 Squadron.

Action came earlier than expected. In fact, the very first major incident of World War Two involving an aircraft and a ship took place in the waters off the South African coast. On December 2, 1939, the German-registered Deutsche Ost-Afrika Linie (German East Africa Line) passenger and cargo vessel *Watussi* was spotted sailing sixty miles off Cape Agulhas, the most southerly tip of the African continent. It was heading towards South America. She was observed by a patrolling maritime reconnaissance Ju86 from 15 Squadron under the command of Captain Hennie Boshoff with Lieutenant T. Uys as co-pilot. The 952-ton liner with 43 officers and 155 passengers on board had quietly slipped out to sea from the port of Lourenco Marques in Mozambique on the night of November 22. She had been secretly sheltering there since the outbreak of hostilities after a voyage from Hamburg. Because Portugal maintained neutrality during the war, her colonies were also neutral. Mozambique, one of those colonies, was right on South Africa's north-eastern doorstep. And it was rapidly becoming a hotbed of espionage and counter-intelligence with spies from both sides of the conflict eavesdropping on one another.

Captain Stamer, the master of the *Watussi*, had ordered a bogus British Red Ensign flag to be flown from the ship's mast in order to fool anyone who saw her, but the *Watussi* was a familiar ship around the African coast. There was no mistaking her hull, profile and color scheme. But Boshoff and Uys could see nothing that revealed what she was carrying or what her mission and final destination might be. One thing, however, was known. The lethal 16,000-ton German pocket battleship *Admiral Graf Spee* was prowling the waters of the South Atlantic. Armed with 16 guns and eight torpedo tubes, her intention was to pick off and sink Allied shipping. Was the *Watussi* en route to rendezvous and resupply her? Or was she heading for Rio de Janeiro with some sort of unknown cargo on board? When Boshoff radioed South African maritime headquarters the mystery deepened. There was a complete absence of intelligence about the ship. No one knew what to make of her mission. All that was known was that she was a German-registered vessel and therefore an enemy. She had to be stopped.

Military headquarters instructed Boshoff to signal the *Watussi* and tell her to proceed to either Cape Town or the South African Naval base at Simonstown. Using a hand-held Aldis lamp as the Ju86 circled overhead, Boshoff flashed Morse-code messages to the *Watussi*. But to no avail. The ship ignored all efforts to communicate with her and stubbornly sailed on. There was no alternative but to use force to indicate that if the command was not obeyed the Ju86 would attack. Swooping in low, the aircraft's machine guns opened fire, strafing the water ahead of the *Watussi's* bow. Unperturbed, the ship proceeded on course. Gaining altitude Boshoff then dropped three bombs close to the vessel. Although she slowed down she did not stop. By now the airwaves were filled with radio chatter about the encounter. Cape Town, Pretoria, Berlin and London were all listening in as the saga unfolded. The Royal Navy immediately despatched two vessels that were hunting for the *Admiral Graf Spee* to the scene. Meanwhile, unbeknown to the British or the South Africans, Captain Stamer on the *Watussi* had ordered his crew to scuttle the ship. Honor-bound to prevent his vessel from falling into enemy hands he decided that it would be better to sink it. The ship's engines were stopped, fires were lit in the passenger reception areas, dining room and hallways and the shuttlecocks were opened. As water poured into the hull, flames spread rapidly through the upper decks, engulfing the ship.

All too soon their aircraft was running low on fuel so Boshoff and Uys in the Ju86 had to turn away from the scene and head back to Cape Town. But another Ju86, under the command of Major Jan Marthinus 'Boet' Botes, had been despatched from Cape Town. It soon began circling the crippled liner. This aircraft helped guide two Royal Naval vessels, the battlecruiser *H.M.S.*

Renown and the cruiser *H.M.S. Sussex*, to where the *Watussi* was now burning furiously and listing heavily. Her officers, crew and passengers had abandoned ship and were drifting aimlessly in lifeboats. *Renown* opened her 15-inch guns on the *Watussi* to make sure she sank so as not to pose a danger to other shipping. All the survivors were picked up by the two British cruisers and subsequently interred as POWs.

Perhaps the greatest irony of the whole affair was the fact that Germany's first loss at sea during the opening phase of the war was the direct result of an encounter between a German-built ship and a German-built aircraft. Both the vessel and the airplane were products of German engineering. But they represented opposite sides of a world at war. Due to the hasty process that had turned a passenger aircraft into a fighting machine, the Ju86 was embellished with the roundels of the South African Air Force but still sported the livery of South African Airways with the Flying Springbok emblem proudly displayed on either side of its nose.

By the end of 1939, twenty-two percent of SAA's personnel was directly under the command of the SAAF and the Department of Defense. Eleven Ju52s were retained by the Civil Administration for passenger flights but only 20 services per week were operated as against 70 at the start of the war. And then everything changed. On May 10, 1940, Germany invaded France, Holland, Belgium and Luxembourg. Clearly, this was not going to be a quick war. With these invasions the battleground widened. It was obvious that South Africa would have to become involved in the conflict far beyond its own borders. The Junkers Ju52 fleet continued to operate limited passenger services at home and to regional territories but 14 days later, on May 24, 1940, all commercial passenger flights ceased completely. SAA's entire fleet of aircraft was absorbed into the South African Defense Force for active wartime duties. It was placed under an operational wing called Bomber Transport Brigade. The commanding officer was Colonel Graham Stanley Leverton, the same man who had negotiated the rights to commence the first passenger air service from Johannesburg to Central Africa. Of all the dominions within the British Empire, South Africa was the only one to cease normal passenger traffic and to turn its entire national commercial airplane fleet over to the military. As if that were not enough, all private flying also stopped and every aircraft—small, large, private, club-owned or corporate—was placed at the disposal of the Defense Force.

SAA flight crew pose for formal photograph before commencing service with the South African Air Force (SAAF). Behind them is one of the later model Junkers Ju-52 aircraft equipped with Pratt & Whitney R-1340 Wasp engines with three-blade propellers

Interior fittings on some of the sequestered Ju52s were stripped and replaced with benches stretching lengthwise up the interior of the fuselage so that up to 21 people could be squeezed inside. The airplanes were immediately allotted to shuttling troops and freight to East Africa. These were needed for the build-up of Allied forces who were preparing to go into battle in North Africa against Italy. Mussolini had officially dragged Italy and its African colonies—Libya, Eritrea, Somalia and Abyssinia (Ethiopia)—into the war when it joined the Axis Forces on June 10, 1940. In addition to Germany and Italy, Japan was the third partner of the Axis. Between the three of them it was a formidable enemy. And now the war had spilled into Africa.

Initially, the Ju52s were operated by 50 Squadron under the control of 1 Bomber Transport Brigade, which later became 5 Wing. Their primary purpose was to ferry soldiers and supplies from military fields in South Africa to areas that most people simply referred to as 'up north.' In 1940, the North Africa Campaign got underway in earnest. It would continue for three years, especially when Hitler sent his crack Afrika Korps under the command of Panzer General Erwin Rommel into the desert sands in 1941 to bolster Italian efforts to hold on to territory. The biggest prize in North Africa was the Suez Canal. As a short-cut to Europe and sources of crude oil, it was a lifeline to whoever had control over it. With Egypt under British occupation, both Germany and Italy wanted to conquer it and prevent the Allies from using the canal. South Africa would go on to play a very decisive role in the North African theater of operations. Its troops would fight gallantly on the ground and, in addition to other aircraft flown by the SAAF, the Ju86s—many of them eventually diverted from coastal patrol work to bombing missions in the Western Desert—would carry out extensive operations against the Italians, helping to dramatically turn the tide of the conflict. Three Junkers Ju86s were lost fairly early in the opening phases of the North African campaign and another one—with Prime Minister Jan Christiaan Smuts as a VIP passenger on board—accompanied by a fighter escort of two Hurricanes was inadvertently attacked by friendly fire from two Hawker Fury aircraft near Archers Post in Kenya. The Prime Minister was on his way to inspect South African ground troops in Ethiopia and Egypt. Fortunately, the Ju86 landed safely, albeit slightly scarred from the attack. Two more Ju86s were lost not long after that incident.

SAA's Airspeed Envoys that had been sent to the Air Force were assigned to training and photographic operations. All the other single engine aircraft were used for either communications purposes or as transports for military commanding officers in the field. Included among the 400 members of the airline who had been placed under military command by 1940 was a roster of legendary pilots such as Japie Louw, Frederick Charles John 'Frikkie' Fry, Boet Botes, Bert Rademan, J.D. de Villiers Rademan, Ken Jones, Len Inggs, Ron Madeley, Piet Nel, Gerwyn David Bowen Williams, Dennis Raubenheimer, Ambrose Wright, A.D. Knox-Perkins, Doug Meaker, Bertie Leach, Charles Martin, Herman Beyers, I.J.M. Odendaal, Glynn Davies, Ferdie van Gass, C.D. McCrae, E. Newhorn, C.V. Sephton, A.J. Brink, Phil Kock, Ronnie Stewart, Hennie Q. Boshoff, Fred le Roux, 'Terrie' Terblanche, Otto van Ginkel, Dirkie Nel, Bertie Booysen, Harry Lauder, Peter Prophet, George Parsons and 'Ossie' Osborne. They would all serve valiantly with the South African Air Force in North Africa and Italy or be transferred for flying duties with the Royal Air Force over Europe during the coming dark and difficult days as the war intensified.

It would not be long before the SAAF would start flying airplanes as diverse as the Hawker Hartebeest, Gloster Gladiator, Bristol Beaufort, de Havilland Mosquito, Supermarine Spitfire, Hawker Hurricane, Douglas A-20 Havoc (Boston P-70), Douglas C-47, Martin Maryland, Martin Baltimore, Consolidated B-24 Liberator, Lockheed Ventura and many others types. By the time of Operation Overlord—'D-Day,' or the invasion of Normandy on June 6, 1944—SAAF operations in North Africa and Europe would consist of 35 squadrons flying 33 different types of aircraft. In Italy alone it would have four wings with more than 17,000 officers and men on active duty. In fact, as early as September 1941 the total number of military aircraft flying the roundels and colors of the SAAF already exceeded 1,700.

In 1940, the SAA Junkers Ju86s and Ju52s were carrying out critical missions for the war effort which meant that there were no airplanes to conduct any kind of passenger, cargo or VIP flights at home. Additional machines were desperately needed. With all of SAA's fleet now under the control of the SAAF, the government had no option but to acquire additional commercial equipment. This time—the first in SAA's history—an order was placed with an American airplane manufacturer. So, 29 new Lockheed Lodestars were purchased from the Lockheed Aircraft Corporation in Burbank, California.

Lockheed Lodestar

Lockheed's Lodestar was an excellent transcontinental passenger aircraft designed to fly non-stop from coast to coast across the United States. It was developed as a direct competitor to the Douglas Aircraft Company's enormously successful DC-3 'Dakota' airliner, the civilian version of the military C-47 'Gooney Bird.'

The Lockheed Lodestars bought by South African Airways were the L18-08 variant. Designed to seat 12 passengers in luxurious comfort it could be reconfigured to squeeze in 19 people. With a wingspan of 65.5 ft, a length of 49.86 ft, a height of 11.82 ft and a maximum take-off weight of 17,500 lbs, it normally carried a crew of three. Its service ceiling was higher than anything else on the South African registry at the time, up to 30,000 feet. It was equipped with two Pratt & Whitney R-1830 14-cylinder Wasp air-cooled engines. These propelled the craft at a maximum speed of 266 mph or a cruising speed of 200 mph. The aircraft had a range of 950 miles.

After coming off the assembly line in California, the Lodestars for SAA were flown across the United States to Floyd Bennett Airfield on Long Island near New York. There they were disassembled, packed into crates and shipped by sea to Cape Town where they were reassembled by 9 Air Depot based at Wingfield. Lockheed provided personnel and technical assistance for the reassembly process. After testing, the aircraft were flown to Rand Airport. Although sporting SAA livery the first three Lodestars to arrive, ZS-ASJ, ZS-ASK and ZS-ASL, were immediately transferred to the Royal Air Force for use in the Middle East. They would never see service with the airline.

The rest of the Lodestars also did not enter service with SAA right away. Instead, they were requisitioned by the SAAF for military duties. Most of them had their interiors gutted and reconfigured by Number 9 Air Depot. Passenger facilities and carpeting were removed and austere, heavy-duty seating installed. With very little delay the airplanes were assigned to the shuttle service flying 'up north' on operations between South Africa and Egypt, Kenya and Abyssinia. But there were exceptions. One Lodestar, ZS-AST, was set aside to operate limited, irregular passenger services as and when needed. Another, delivered on September 24, 1940 and registered ZS-ASO, was sent to the SAAF's 5 Wing on November 7, 1940. There it was allocated the military tail number of 234. This one became the personal VIP transport for Prime Minister Jan Smuts, operated by 28 Squadron based at Swartkop, Pretoria. Its pilot was Colonel Pieter Willem Adriaan Nel.

Two SAA Lockheed Lodestars at Rand Airport being prepared for wartime duties. Once transferred to the South African Air Force the rear aircraft, ZS-ASO, would become the personal VIP transport for Prime Minister Jan Christiaan Smuts

Few South African airmen put in more hours flying VIPs than Nel. He had joined the SAAF in 1926 and had a very distinguished flying career. Once Lodestar 234 was placed at Prime Minister Smuts' disposal, Nel was assigned the task of being his exclusive personal pilot. He was a likeable, friendly and thoroughly professional individual, widely known as a man who never took chances. An hour before take-off he was always seen prowling around his aircraft, keeping a scrupulous watch on what mechanics, service technicians and ground staff were doing. He always personally kicked the tires to determine whether their inflation pressure was sufficient or ran his hand along the fuselage or wiped a clean cloth around engine mountings to detect possible oil leaks. He never took off in inclement weather and always waited for ideal flying conditions, even when impatient top military brass or the Prime Minister himself insisted on going aloft as quickly as possible.

In an interview long after the war he recalled: "When war broke out in September 1939 I was sent to Alexander Bay. It was a dreary place and an absolutely boring beginning to the war. I little guessed what an intensely interesting time was in store for me in the next few years. In January 1940 I got the of job flying *Oubaas* (an affectionate Afrikaans word loosely meaning 'Big Boss' or 'The Old Man,' often used for Prime Minister Jan Smuts) and I flew him thousands of miles. It was only at the start of the war that *Oubaas* really warmed to flying. Before that he didn't know or care much about it. Eventually, a trip by air meant nothing to him. Breakfast in Pretoria and tea in Cape Town became routine. Eventually, lunch in Africa and dinner in Europe was commonplace. He could fly from North or South Africa to London with the minimum of fuss, hop out of the plane after a tiring, monotonous and sometimes gruelling journey, often over enemy territory, walk straight across to reporters and give a riveting speech that was quoted in newspapers around the world the next day. He always seemed as fresh as a daisy and was the wonder and admiration of men many years his junior. I often wished that all my passengers were like him. *Ouma* (Mrs. Smuts, or 'Granny') was also a good passenger, although the throbbing of the aircraft engines sometimes kept her awake. During the war years we had many VIPs as passengers on board but some of them spent half the flight ringing the steward for attention. But dear old *Oubaas* was always the perfect passenger.

He would board the aircraft, sit back, kick off his shoes and sleep soundly through it all."

Because of the need to maintain critical transportation and secure communications between the Union and neighboring countries limited passenger operations were briefly reintroduced on December 17, 1940, using one of the Lodestars. It was configured for twelve passengers and a four-man crew. The flights connected Johannesburg with Cape Town, Windhoek, Luanda, Bulawayo, Lusaka, Ndola, Dodoma, Mpika, Nairobi and Kisumu. In addition, a new service was introduced to Entebbe in Uganda and to Elisabethville, Irumu, Coquilhatville, Stanleyville and Leopoldville in the Belgian Congo. Although they were popular and well patronized, wartime demands eventually caused the flights to be cancelled. On May 31, 1942, the Lodestar was sent to the SAAF for military duties. Once again, South Africa was without a national carrier or any type of domestic aerial passenger service.

In contrast, flights to London continued to be operated by flying boats from Durban by the successor to Imperial Airways, the British Overseas Airways Corporation, or BOAC. Now fully government-owned by the British government, BOAC had been formed through an Act of Parliament in London on November 24, 1939, when Imperial Airways merged with British Airways Limited. As far as the British government was concerned air services to the outer reaches of the empire had to be maintained through thick and thin, wartime or not. That was the only way that Whitehall could exercise administration and control over Britain's overseas colonies and dominions and also remain in close contact with its allies. Large BOAC maintenance bases were established in Calcutta, Sydney and Durban to overhaul, service and repair aircraft operating long-haul routes from the U.K. In addition to the British carrier, Belgium's Sabena airlines introduced a fortnightly service between Elisabethville and Cape Town on January 23, 1942. No longer operational in

Belgium itself because of the German occupation there, Sabena nevertheless continued flying in and out of Belgium's African colony, the Congo. The Elisabethville – Cape Town service, using a Douglas DC3, immediately became very popular, creating another external lifeline between South Africa and the rest of the continent.

In early 1942, a potential Japanese invasion of the island of Madagascar became a very real threat. Strategically situated in the Mozambique Channel of the Indian Ocean 250 miles off the east coast of Africa, Madagascar is the world's fourth largest island. Over a thousand miles long and 350 miles wide it was then under the control of the Vichy government in France. If Germany or Japan wanted to do so Madagascar could become an ideal springboard for choking Allied shipping in the Mozambique Channel. It could even become a key element interrupting maritime traffic up and down the entire east coast of Africa, or the sea route to Australia and India. Not only that, it could make a lethal staging post for Axis forces to invade eastern, central and southern Africa. The RAF could not do anything to prevent this from happening as it was hard-pressed fighting the Nazis in Europe. The United States—now fully involved in the war following the Japanese attack on Pearl Harbor on December 7, 1941—was also concerned about a Japanese invasion of Madagascar. But it was too involved in preparing to strike Japanese forces in the Pacific. The onus would be on the SAAF to defend Madagascar. But it did not have enough bombers to carry out the task. Dipping into its available resources the SAAF earmarked 13 of the Lodestars for modification as bombers. Exhaustive tests were conducted on a number of them to determine what ordnance could be carried. Ideally, it was hoped that a bomb load of 2,200 lbs could be slung from racks beneath the wings but it was discovered that the maximum weight they could safely sustain was only 1,000 lbs. Try as they might, SAAF ground engineers and technicians could not wring enough performance or load-bearing capabilities out of the Lodestars, especially as they would also need extensive modifications to the airframe, luggage compartment and cabin, plus the additional weight of machine guns to defend themselves against possible enemy air attack. Their range was severely limited by all those changes so the plan was abandoned and the Lodestars returned to transport, cargo and shuttle services. Five of these overstrained workhorses were subsequently lost while flying for the SAAF but the rest continued to provide outstanding service throughout the war. Following many reconnaissance flights over Madagascar by other aircraft of the SAAF the defense of the island was ultimately left to British naval, land and Fleet Air Arm forces, assisted by South African ground troops in *Operation Ironclad*.

Whilst it is beyond the scope of this book to provide a detailed discussion of all the South Africans who flew with distinction during WWII, mention must be made of several individuals who rendered truly exemplary service. Marmaduke Thomas 'Tom' St. John Pattle (DFC) is widely held to be the most successful of all Allied fighter pilots during the entire war. Born in Butterworth in the Cape Province, he flew for the RAF and is credited with a whopping 41 enemy aircraft 'kills.' Another legendary name is that of Adolph Gysbert 'Sailor' Malan, (DSO, DFC.) Born in Wellington in the Western Cape, he flew with the RAF and brought down 35 enemy aircraft. There were many others, including Johannes Jacobus Le Roux (DFC), Petrus Hendrick 'Piet' Hugo (DSO, DFC), John Everitt Frost (DFC), Kenneth Weekes Driver (DFC), Malcolm Stephen Osler (DFC), Cornelius Arthur van Vliet (DFC), Servas van Breda Theron (DSO, DFC), E. J. Morris (DSO), Albert Gerald Lewis (DFC) and Robert Henry Talbot. With the exception of Albert Lewis who flew for the RAF, all the others flew with the SAAF. There were more, of course, far too numerous to list here. However, a tally of wartime pilots who later went on to have long airline careers with SAA when hostilities were over would not be complete without including the names of Bert Rademan, Doug Meaker, Bertie Leach, Denis Raubenheimer, Don Parker and Salomon 'Pi' Pienaar (DFC, AFC). Pienaar had many distinctions to his name, not the least of which is being credited as being the first Allied pilot to engage in direct conflict with one of Germany's most secret and potent new weapons.

Captain Salomon 'Pi' Pienaar, one of SAA's most distinguished pilots. This photograph was taken after WWII when he was in command of a Lockheed Constellation passenger aircraft

Born in Winburg in the Orange Free State in 1917, Pienaar joined the telegraph office of the South African Railways after leaving school in 1935. Always fascinated by things that flew, he undertook flying lessons as a hobby. When war broke out he joined the SAAF but was disappointed when he was sent to the Central Flying School in Bloemfontein to study to become an instructor instead of being posted to the front for active duty as a pilot. But it was an opportunity in disguise. The commission would serve him extremely well in later years. Constantly nagging his superiors to send him 'up north,' in 1943 his request was finally granted. With the rank of captain he was dispatched to Egypt and then to the SAAF's 60 Photographic and Reconnaissance Squadron under the direct command of the

Allied's Northwest African Photographic Reconnaissance Wing. Eventually he found himself stationed at an RAF base in San Severe, Italy, flying de Havilland Mosquitoes.

An all-wooden aircraft with two powerful Rolls-Royce Merlin engines the Mosquito was a light bomber-cum-fighter that was affectionately dubbed *The Wooden Wonder* by those who flew it. This was because of its light weight, speed and outstanding handling characteristics. With a service ceiling of up to 35,000 feet and a top speed of 450 mph, it was ideal for either low level or high altitude photographic reconnaissance work. Pienaar was teamed with navigator Archie Lockhart-Ross and together the two men in their agile Mosquito brought back invaluable photographic coverage of airfields, factories, military installations and surface activities throughout southern Germany, Austria, Italy and Yugoslavia. But one thing was especially intriguing to Allied military intelligence. Even in the early phases of the war they were aware that Germany was developing an all new type of military aircraft that was intended to be powered by a radically new power plant, the jet engine. But where was it? Did the Luftwaffe already have it? Was it operational? How fast could it fly? How high? How long could it remain in the air without refueling? What kind of punch could it pack? The list of questions was endless.

Both the British and the Germans, totally independent of one another, had been tinkering around with jet engines for many years before the war got underway. In England, Sir Frank Whittle had been granted a patent for a turbojet engine as early as 1930. In Germany, Dr. Hans von Ohain had registered a patent for a turbojet in 1936. Amazingly, neither men knew of the other's work. An aircraft using von Ohain's engine first flew in 1939. Whittle's jet took to the air in 1941. Aircraft manufacturers in both countries feverishly worked to incorporate the advanced new engine in a fighter but it was in Germany that Ernst Heinkel was the first to do it with the Heinkel He178 aircraft. It flew on

August 24, 1939. Taking the concept further, the brilliant engine designer Anselm Franz came up with a method for incorporating a jet into a fighter built by Willy Messerschmitt's company, the Bayerische Flugzeugwerke (BFW) (Bavarian Aircraft Works). Known as the Me262, this was the fighter that was supposed to win the war in the air. But it was very late in entering service. Its two jet engines guzzled a lot of fuel, giving it a short endurance period in the air. Then, as fuel supplies dwindled when Germany began losing the war, the Luftwaffe could only commence deploying the craft in limited quantities as late as April, 1944. In the summer of that year Allied military intelligence received a report that a squadron of Me262s was operating from a Luftwaffe base at Leipheim in the Black Forest near Munich. Was this true? Could pictures be obtained of these mysterious machines? There was only one way to find out.

Pi Pienaar and Archie Lockhart-Ross took off in their Mosquito from San Severe on a beautiful, clear early morning on August 9, 1944. Their mission was to photograph the Leipheim air base in Bavaria and hopefully acquire images of the enigmatic Me262 parked on the ground. At 30, 000 feet above Leipheim. Lockhart-Ross spotted an aircraft taking off at high speed from the main runway. Unconcerned because of the height at which they were flying, Pienaar turned on the cameras as they flew across the Luftwaffe base. He did not expect the aircraft they had just seen becoming airborne to reach him before they could turn back and head for home. But he was wrong. He had not foreseen the incredible speed of the jet. Suddenly in his rear view mirror he spotted an unidentifiable aircraft 400 yards behind them. It had two pods with air intakes beneath its wings. There were no propellers. And it was fast. *Very* fast. This was the very airplane that they had seen taking off. Pienaar estimated the craft to be traveling at a speed of around 500 mph. And then it dawned on him. This was none other than the mysterious new Messerschmitt Me262 jet fighter! No sooner had he realized what his adversary was when the Me262 opened fire.

de Havilland Mosquito fighter-bomber configured for reconnaissance work. (Note camera pod in nose.) It was an aircraft like this that was flown by Captain 'Pi' Pienaar and Navigator Archie Lockhart-Ross when they encountered one of the first German jet fighters over Bavaria in August, 1944

German Messerschmitt Me 262, the world's first jet fighter. It was one like this that engaged Captain 'Pi' Pienaar in a dogfight in 1944

Shells from the fast jet's cannons ripped through the wooden Mosquito, tearing off the port aileron. Pushing both throttles forward. Pienaar heard his two Merlin engines screaming at full power as he made a tight starboard turn, trying to throw off the jet. But he could not shake it off. More cannon shells tore into the

Mosquito, shattering the port elevator and damaging the main wing spar. With no port control the aircraft began to spiral down towards the ground. Struggling to maintain control, Pienaar eased the control column forward and applied full opposite rudder. Nothing doing. The Mosquito continued plunging earthwards. Throttling back on the engines to reduce power the sickening spiral slowed and Pienaar was able to recover from the dive. In only seconds they had fallen from 30,000 feet to 19,000 feet. By now the enemy jet had disappeared into the clouds above them but it was not as maneuverable as Pienaar feared it might be and he was able to turn his airplane back towards Italy. And then he heard Archie Lockhart-Ross yelling.

"Watch out! He's coming back!"

At a distance of 600 yards, the Me262 swooped out of the clouds and was heading straight towards them. But Pienaar was without weapons. He could not protect his aircraft as all its guns had been removed to save weight to allow for the heavy photographic gear that it carried. Remembering to turn on the forward-facing cameras before swerving to port, Pienaar watched as the Messerschmitt streaked by, narrowly missing them.

Not knowing what else to do, Pienaar brought his aircraft down to a little more than 9,000 feet before leveling out. But the German jet kept up the assault, opening fire another twelve times before heading back to base, presumably because it was running low on fuel. Fortunately, none of those attacks inflicted any more damage. But the Mosquito was in very bad shape. It vibrated badly because of its severely damaged control surfaces and Pienaar could not fly it at more than 180 mph for fear of shearing off more pieces of the aircraft. He had to keep the stick jammed to the right to maintain straight and level flight. As precious photographs had been taken of the elusive new Me262, the importance of getting back to base was now absolutely crucial. The pictures would tell analysts a great deal about the

Luftwaffe's new 'secret weapon.' But could Pienaar make it back home? The turn and bank indicator, the altimeter and the airspeed indicator of the Mosquito had ceased functioning. Pienaar was desperately squeezing all he could out of his critically damaged machine.

Guided by Lockhart-Ross, Pienaar coaxed the plane over the Alps with very little airspace separating it from the craggy mountain peaks below. Oil lines were now leaking and fuel was trickling from a ruptured tank. Struggling like the 'little engine that could' in the classic children's story the Mosquito coughed and spluttered its way through the clouds, breaking into open sky above Udine, one of the most heavily-defended enemy airfields in Italy. Pienaar warned Lockhart-Ross to brace for possible impact with the ground if they were to be hit by flak or any more gunfire but, surprisingly, they managed to limp past the airfield without being detected. The Mosquito eventually reached the RAF's San Severe air base but now another problem reared its ugly head. The hydraulic oil lines had been ruptured. It was impossible to lower the undercarriage for landing. The emergency system was also inoperative. Pienaar struggled to crank the wheels down mechanically but the entire system was jammed.

"Brace yourself, Archie!" Pienaar called out to his navigator. "I'm going to have to do a belly landing."

Landing with wheels undescended is one of the nightmares that haunts every pilot. Pienaar was no exception. He was going to have to land the aircraft on its fragile underbelly. There was nothing to cushion the landing and nothing to help stop the aircraft once it was on the ground. Pulling back on the throttle so that the stricken Mosquito was barely above stalling speed, he coasted it towards the runway like a glider. What made things especially difficult was the fact that he had no port elevator or aileron for adjusting yaw, pitch or direction. Seconds before touchdown he cut all electrical switches, stopping the fuel pumps. There was a deafening crunch as the Mosquito hit the tarmac. Without an undercarriage the aircraft had a low profile and the propeller blades buckled or were torn off as they spun into the ground. Sliding halfway down the runway the Mosquito barely managed to remain intact before it came to a grinding stop. Pienaar and Lockhart-Ross tumbled out as quickly as they could. Emergency vehicles soon arrived and the first priority was the retrieval of the exposed film containing the images of the Messerschmitt Me262. Fortunately, no fire broke out. Both Pienaar and Lockhart-Ross were badly shaken up but unscathed. When asked about the experience many years later Pienaar merely shrugged it off, broke into a broad smile and confessed, "I have to admit that it was the only time in my entire career in the cockpit that I was really scared. But if you've got a job to do you just get on with it. In aviation there's no point in panicking."

Pi Pienaar would eventually qualify to fly a total of 39 different types of aircraft, from the swiftest military machines to the biggest commercial passenger jets in the sky. His career lasted 45 years and was without comparison. After the war ended he joined SAA as a pilot and rose rapidly within its echelons. He was promoted from First Officer to Captain in 1948, and then to Chief Flight Instructor in 1953. His pleasant, outgoing personality and unique professional experience made him extremely popular with all of SAA's pilots. It was then that his early training at the Central Flying School in Bloemfontein paid off handsomely. He was given the task to train his colleagues to fly all the big commercial passenger aircraft in service with the airline. In 1969, he became Chief Pilot and in 1975, he was appointed to the highest of all positions, becoming SAA's Chief Executive Officer, answerable directly to the Minister of Transport. During his period as a pilot Pienaar was responsible for delivering more new types of aircraft to the airline from factories abroad than any of his colleagues. His reputation spread far beyond the borders of his homeland. Over the years he received commendations and praise from airplane manufacturing companies the world over, including Lockheed, Douglas and Boeing in the United States. In fact in 1975, the year that he was promoted to the position of Chief Executive Officer, he was also offered a job as a senior test pilot with the Boeing Commercial Airplane Company in Seattle, Washington. That was how much the world's largest and most successful maker of big commercial jet aircraft thought of his flying skills. It was an enticing offer. Pienaar loved the big jets, especially the widebody 747derivatives built by that company. But as a very loyal and patriotic South African, he opted to stay at home and helm his country's airline instead, retiring in 1982, at the age of 65.

By late 1944, the writing was on the wall for Germany. It was obvious to Hitler, Churchill and Roosevelt that it would only be a matter of time before the Third Reich would relinquish the fight and give up. Japan was still another matter, of course. The Pacific war would only end once two United States Army Air Corps Boeing B-29 Superfortresses unleashed their atomic bomb loads on Hiroshima and Nagasaki in August of 1945. But the end of the conflict in Europe was already in sight. As far as the South African government and SAA were concerned, the war was winding down. Plans had to be made for the resumption of passenger air services within the Union. As early as January 1944, Colonel Graham Stanley Leverton was asked to resume activities as Acting Manager for SAA. During the ensuing year arrangements were made for the recalling of some of the airline's staff from military duties, including pilots and ground engineers. As part of the Allied war effort that year the SAAF had received a number of Douglas C 47 (Dakota) aircraft, thereby releasing six of the surviving thirteen Lockheed Lodestars from ferry, freight and transportation duties. These were returned from the war zone to South Africa to begin limited domestic and regional services.

And so, battle-scarred and war-weary, the six Lodestars descended from the blue skies of the north and landed at Rand Airport, there to be spruced up, serviced, repaired and reconfigured for passenger services with SAA. Fortunately, large contingents of mechanical and engineering staff had already been dismissed from military service to re-join the airline. And so, on November 30, 1944, Captain 'Frikkie' Fry seated himself behind the controls of Lodestar ZS-ATE, took off from Rand Airport and flew the aircraft on what is known as a 'positioning flight' to Cape Town. Next morning, with ten passengers on board, Fry piloted the first scheduled new service from Cape Town via Kimberley to Johannesburg. Later that same day, December 1, Captain Graham Wilmot Bellin flew a Lodestar from Rand Airport to Durban. Once again, the Flying Springbok had taken wing.

Lockheed Lodestar at Stamford Hill Airport, Durban after the recommencement of domestic passenger services during the last phases of the war, 1945

At first the passenger schedule was limited to a daily service between Rand Airport and Durban, three services a week from Johannesburg to Cape Town via Durban, East London and Port Elizabeth, two services to Cape Town with stops at either Kimberley or Bloemfontein and a weekly service from Johannesburg to Salisbury via Bulawayo, making a total of 26 services a week. In early 1945, four more Lodestars were released from military duties and returned to SAA, making it possible to increase services to 50 flights per week. The additional flights commenced on February 1 of that year.

Without exception, the members of SAA who were attached to military forces during WWII served with distinction, often being decorated for their efforts. Far too many paid the ultimate price, either being killed in action, in accidents or as a result of illnesses contracted whilst stationed in the various theaters of conflict. Some of the SAA officers and men who gave their lives were D.N. Campbell, P.D. Hahn, A.D. Knox-Perkins, F.W. le Roux, A.A. Louw, Charles Martin, J. Ninis, J.W. Shelly, J.G. van der Westhuizen, A.P. van Wyk and O.A.K. Wright. Major I.J.M. Odendaal perished when his B-24 Liberator bomber was shot down on a supply mission to Warsaw. Lieutenant A.T. Farr died during an attack on a German tanker intended to resupply Rommel's tank corps off the North African coast. Ronnie J. Stewart died in his Martin Maryland while serving with 21 Squadron. The surviving pre-war pilots who returned to SAA at Rand Airport became known as the 'Royal Family' by their successors. This was a mark of respect not only for their participation in the war but due to their accumulation of experience and their ability to fly almost any type of aircraft under the most trying and difficult of circumstances. Three grades of pilots were formed. In accordance with international tradition captains wore three gold stripes on the cuffs of their blue uniforms, junior captains two-and-a-half stripes and first officers two.

As the dust of war began to settle the men and women of SAA regrouped and looked to the future with renewed confidence. The time had come for the airline to spread its wings both at home and to areas much farther afield.

Chapter 5

The Springbok Service

Despite the fury of it all, there were always those who foresaw that the war would not last forever. In 1943, two full years before military hostilities ended, a handful of visionary members of the government were instrumental in setting up a committee under the auspices of the South African Railways and Harbors (SAR & H) administration—the authority responsible for running South African Airways during peacetime—to consider the country's commercial aviation future. This was optimistic thinking. A lot of people had no idea what sort of world would be left after the war. But the committee members firmly believed that the restless surge of economic progress would one day take SAA's Flying Springbok logo and the South African flag far beyond the country's borders to destinations abroad. A number of important topics were investigated. One of them was the need for improved and upgraded airports. Paved runways were few and far between. Rand Airport was the only major aerial gateway with adequate technical and passenger-handling facilities to deal with a large volume of traffic. But room to grow was limited. The airport was surrounded by roads, a railroad track, a lake, a golf course and the mountains of yellow soil brought up from nearby gold mines. Besides, the undulating topography of the terrain around the airport's location made expansion impossible. Surely, it was thought, the time would come when a bigger airport with longer and wider runways would be needed. The size and performance of the big bombers that were used during the war gave a hint at what was to come in the commercial market. Large, long-range airliners would inevitably follow. And the country had to be ready to accommodate them, not to mention the increased passenger and freight traffic they would bring. So, members of the departmental planning committee began looking around for an alternative site for an airport to serve the Johannesburg metropolitan area and to handle anticipated international flights. It wasn't long before they found something suitable.

Witkoppies (White Hills) was a vast farm bordering the small town of Kempton Park about 20 miles to the northeast of Johannesburg. A few vegetable patches, cornfields and a herd of cows were on the farm but most of the land consisted of scrub, bush and fragrant eucalyptus or 'Blue Gum' trees, an exotic species originally imported from Australia that had become ubiquitous all over the country. The sleepy little town of Kempton Park next to the farm was on the main rail link between Johannesburg and Pretoria. It could easily expand to include new housing estates, shopping areas and public facilities. The place was perfect for developing an airport. As soon as the farmland was purchased by the SAR & H the title *Witkoppies* was changed to *Highveld*, the intended name for the great new international airport that would rise there.

At the same time, plots of land were also purchased at Reunion flats nine miles from Durban and at a spot 12 miles outside Cape Town for the construction of new airports to serve those cities. All in all, a sum of £9 million was set aside for the development and construction of these new facilities, £6 million for the Johannesburg site alone. It was a considerable amount of money at the time, but considered well worth it by the planning committee. The three new airports would bring the country into line with the best and latest civil aviation airports abroad. The biggest and busiest airports in the United States at that time were Washington Airport in the nation's capital and La Guardia in New York City. In England, Hurn Bournemouth and Croydon were still London's main airports. The new Heathrow airport was still under construction. Because Johannesburg is located 5,559 feet above sea level, it fell into the category of a 'hot and high airfield.' This means that the atmosphere is less dense at that altitude than it is at sea level and so heavy aircraft would need longer runways and higher speeds to become airborne. Highveld's main runway would be 10,500 feet in length, far longer than those in New York, Washington or London. Or anywhere else in the world for that matter. The task of building Highveld would be arduous. Thousands of eucalyptus trees had to be felled. Rocks, mounds and hillocks had to be bulldozed and carted away. Tens of thousands of tons of concrete had to be poured to create runways, three in all. The runways had to be designed to withstand the loads of the heaviest aircraft in service or on the drawing boards of the day. The project would take years to complete. In the meantime, the war was winding down and new developments could not be held back. Things began moving fast.

In March 1945, delegates from the aviation and transport industries of the United Kingdom, East Africa, Northern and Southern Rhodesia, the British Protectorates of Bechuanaland, Swaziland and Basutoland and the Union of South Africa met in Cape Town to discuss the establishment of a new air link between South Africa and the United Kingdom. The conference, under the leadership of Sir Evelyn Baring, the British High Commissioner for South Africa and Field Marshall Jan Christiaan Smuts, Prime Minister of South Africa, laid down guidelines for the new overseas service. It stipulated the routes that would be followed and the type of aircraft that would be used for flights to be jointly operated as a 'pool partnership' between SAA and BOAC. In layman's parlance that meant that the two airlines would equally share routes, passenger reservation systems, costs and revenue. In order to identify the planned new regular flights between the United Kingdom and South Africa, the operation would officially become known as the Springbok Service.

The equipment selected for use between Johannesburg and London was the British-built Avro York, a passenger aircraft derived from the famed World War II Lancaster heavy bomber. It was a squadron of RAF Lancasters under the leadership of Wing Commander Guy Gibson that had carried out night bombing raids on dams of the industrialized Ruhr Valley region of Germany in an operation that became immortalized in the motion picture, *The Dam Busters*.

Avro York, 1945

The Avro York was powered by four Rolls-Royce Merlin 24 liquid-cooled V12 engines developing 1,280 HP or 955 kW each. The York was a high wing monoplane with a length of 78 ft 6 ins, a wingspan of 102 ft, a height of 16 ft 6 ins and an empty weight of 40,000 lbs. It could carry a payload of 20,000 lbs at a maximum service ceiling of 23,000 feet. It had a top speed of 298 mph and a very impressive range of 3,000 miles.

The Avro York model selected for the joint BOAC/SAA service was equipped with fourteen seats and was intended to provide passengers with maximum comfort. To reduce noise and vibration a 'synchroscope' was fitted to ensure the smooth synchronization of all four propellers and, as the publicity material of the day described it, 'the cabin has been sound-proofed in such a manner that normal conversation will be possible during flight.' Interior appointments were luxurious. Seats provided armchair luxury.

They were wide, deeply cushioned and as comfortable as those found on many first-class seats today. Carpets were plush. Neat little drapes hung on either side of the large, circular windows. Naturally, the York never flew with any passengers at its maximum height of 23,000 feet. Air pressure, oxygen levels and temperatures at that height were too low and could be lethal. Most cruising—as with all non-pressurized aircraft—took place at an average height of between 5,000 and 8,000 feet. The York carried a crew of six, comprising two pilots, a flight engineer, a navigator, a radio operator and a cabin steward. The layout of later models used by SAA could accommodate between 12 and 16 passengers. The York was based on the Lancaster bomber but its fuselage was wider and more box-like. The awkward aerodynamics of the craft made it necessary for an additional central rudder to be added to the tailplane, giving it three upright stabilizers in comparison to only two on the Lancaster. Nevertheless, the airplane represented the latest and best on offer by the British aviation industry at the time. In due course, SAA would lease nine of the aircraft, not from the Avro company but directly from BOAC.

For SAA there was one major problem with the York. It was too big, too heavy and too slow to use Rand Airport. And Highveld, the new airport at Kempton Park, was still years away from being ready. The government and the SAR & H frantically looked around for a solution. The answer was found in the form of a large Air Force facility to the south of the town of Alberton along the main road and railroad track linking Johannesburg with the coal-mining complex of Vereeniging. Called Palmietfontein (Bulrushes Fountain), it was a perfect interim airport to replace Rand Airport until Highveld was finished. Without wasting any time a hardened and extended runway was laid down. Hastily cobbled-together structures for handling passengers, immigration control, customs and baggage were erected. Hangars were built, large fuel storage tanks were brought in, taxiway and runway lighting was installed, a public parking area was created and, within months, Palmietfontein was ready for use. Management was placed under the watchful care of Major Harry Campbell, a Johannesburg-born aviator who had served with distinction with the RAF and the SAAF Transport Command during the war. Initially designed to handle one international flight per week, Palmietfontein's capacity would rapidly be increased to serve 12 weekly flights.

Avro York at Palmietfontein Airport

After aircrews and ground staff had been sent to the Avro factory in Bristol in England for familiarization training on the York and to the Rolls Royce plant in Derby for learning about its engines, the first of the new aircraft to be used on the Springbok Service arrived on September 28, 1945. It was under the command of captains 'Frikkie' Fry and Doug Meaker. Additional aircrew training on the plane took place at Palmietfontein and at Kimberley before the machine was officially taken into service. Still bearing its British registration number the aircraft performed a final test on November 7, 1945, and was then reregistered ZS-ATP and named *Springbok*. Freshly painted in SAA livery and embossed with the Flying Springbok logo on its fuselage it was this aircraft that droned into the summer dawn at 5.00 a.m. on November 10, 1945 to inaugurate the Springbok Service to London. At the controls once again was captain 'Frikkie' Fry. His co-pilot was captain Len Inggs, with Malcolm McKendrick as flight engineer, Jack Bagley as radio officer and Mick Makin as navigator. Taking his place in the rear was a brand new member of SAA crews, a cabin attendant. This was the first time a dedicated cabin crew member was part of the flight crew. His name was F.D. van der Vyfer. He had been a dining car steward on the state-run railway service. In accordance with SAR & H policy van der Vyfer had been recruited from existing staff. Both railways and airways were under the jurisdiction of the SAR & H. Depending on which service they worked for staff merely referred to their employer as 'Railways' or 'Airways.' The bureaucratic mindset was that if someone was good at being a waiter or a steward in a railroad dining car they should be good at attending to passengers aboard an aircraft. It was all part of the prevailing civil service mentality. Mr. van der Vyfer's duties on the York were minimal. Only sandwiches, tea and coffee were served on board. Main meals were all taken during refueling stopovers or with overnight breaks on the ground. However, after a few weeks of training his primary function was not only to serve meals or take care of the creature comforts of the passengers but to look after their safety. Though few contemporary passengers flying on board modern jetliners are aware of it that is still the principal function of cabin crews today. They happen to serve coffee or cocktails and hand out bags of peanuts or potato chips—at least on those flights that still serve them—but their primary role is to oversee passengers' safety in times of emergency.

The first passenger-carrying journey of the York to London was completed in 69 hours of which just under 34 hours were actually spent in the air. Flying took place mainly during the day. At night, passengers were accommodated at hotels in Nairobi, Cairo and Tripoli. The one-way fare was £167 and a round-trip ticket cost £301. According to the logbook of flight engineer Malcolm McKendrick, the sector from Palmietfontein to Nairobi took eight hours 50 minutes. Nairobi to Khartoum was flown in six hours, Khartoum to Cairo in four hours 50 minutes, Cairo to Castel Benito (Tripoli, Libya) in five hours 50 minutes and the final leg from there to Hurn, England in eight hours 20 minutes.

Passenger cabin of Avro York during a Springbok Service flight from Johannesburg to London

As the heavy York touched down at Hurn Airport in Bournemouth, it was the first time the Flying Springbok logo had ever been seen at an overseas airfield. It was also the first time the South African flag appeared on the tail of a civilian airliner outside the African continent. It was an historic occasion. It also heralded the beginning of a long history that would lead to the opening up of the skies by SAA to many destinations abroad in the years to come. SAA now began to take its place among the major air carriers of the world. In fact, when the International Air Transport Association (IATA)—the regulatory body of the world's commercial air traffic—was created at a meeting in Havana, Cuba on April 19, 1945, SAA was one of the organization's 44 founding members.

With the advent of the Springbok Service in 1945, the BOAC flying boat service that had terminated in Durban after a lengthy flight down Africa following the continent's rivers, tributaries and lakes came to an end. Because BOAC was in pool partnership with SAA, it now operated from Palmietfontein with its own Avro Yorks. Six flights per week were initially flown, three operated by BOAC and three by SAA. The service was immediately popular with the traveling public. Instead of a two-week sea voyage to the United Kingdom, London was now only three days away by air from Johannesburg. Businessmen were only too eager to patronize the service. Admittedly, some discomforts came with the speed and expediency of air travel. Very early morning departures were necessary all along the way. Climate and weather dictated that. Bumpy and uncomfortable conditions invariably developed following afternoon thunderstorms along the route or when the fierce African sun baked the ground causing turbulent air to rise. And, unlike modern day high-flying jets, the York always flew beneath or within the weather. Looking back on those days with humor during a filmed television interview in 1983, Flight Engineer Malcolm Mackendrick related the story of a southbound flight from Khartoum to Nairobi where the aircraft was flying at a level of 6,000 feet when it got caught up in a fierce tropical thunderstorm.

"As crew members we were used to that sort of thing," Mackendrick recalled. "Turbulence and bad weather didn't bother us one bit. But for the passengers it was another story. Most of them didn't like it at all. I clearly remember the captain asking me to leave the flight deck one afternoon as we were being buffeted around while flying through a deluge of rain and to go to the passenger cabin and investigate an incident reported by a very worried cabin steward. As I entered the cabin I spotted the problem. Huddled all on his own in the second last row was a smallish, timid, well-dressed English gentleman in a dark pin-striped Saville Row suit, a look of anguish all over his face, his eyes pinched shut and his hands tightly clutching a bowler hat on his lap. The air vent above him was wide open and a torrent of rainwater was gushing out of it, drenching him from head to foot. He seemed surprised as I gently tapped him on the shoulder. 'What's wrong?' he asked politely. I didn't want to embarrass him by bursting into laughter so I simply reached up, closed the air vent, and asked the steward to bring a towel. The gentle little man simply looked up at me, shrugged his shoulders and smiled a thank you. Clearly, as far as he was concerned, that was the way things were supposed to be. When you flew down Central Africa and it rained you got wet. Far too British, reserved and polite to display any emotion he never thought of questioning the situation."

Within a few months of the commencement of the service, Castel Benito in Libya was replaced by Malta as an overnight stop-over. In Cairo, two Avro Yorks occasionally met as one arrived from South Africa and the other came in from the United Kingdom. The event often received much publicity in the local Cairo English press which always published a list of passengers on board the flights. On arrival at Hurn Airport in Bournemouth, which consisted of a motley collection of converted ex-RAF wartime buildings, passengers still faced the prospect of a two-hour train journey to London. But there was no shortage of customers for the Springbok Service. However, not all aircrew liked the York. As it was not originally conceived of nor designed as a passenger aircraft but a derivation of the Lancaster bomber it had its faults. One of them was power. As it was too heavy and cumbersome even its beautifully engineered Rolls Royce Merlin engines—beloved by aircrews, mechanics and engineers the world over—were not sufficient to give it the speed and power it needed. Flight engineer Don Smith flew on dozens of Avro York flights. When asked about those days his eyes twinkled and a smile crossed his face as he recalled: "Oh, the York. Some of us loved it but most did not. It was hopelessly underpowered. In fact, many of us on the flight deck were convinced that the only reason it ever got off the ground was not due to its take-off power but purely because of the natural curvature of the earth."

Among other idiosyncrasies about the York was the lumbering

nature of its manoeuvrability in the air. It did not respond easily or quickly to commands. After all, it was really little more than a fattened, over-bloated military machine in civilian guise. Some crews were even unhappy with the configuration of the controls in the cockpit. Unlike most passenger airliners the throttles were located on the ceiling above the pilots' heads instead of extruding from a column on the floor or placed between their seats. One particularly short pilot complained bitterly that he had trouble stretching up to reach the controls, especially when he was bouncing around in his seat while flying through tropical thunderstorms. His arms simply weren't long enough for him to grab hold of the throttles.

When asked about flying the Yorks, Captain Dennis Raubenheimer offered a number of interesting anecdotes. "We were accustomed to the Junkers family of aircraft with their American-made Pratt and Whitney engines and with the Lockheed Lodestars. They were low wing monoplanes. And then along came the Avro York, a high-wing four engine aircraft with those marvellous in-line liquid-cooled Rolls-Royce Merlin engines but with characteristics very different to what we were accustomed to. The Merlins might have been fine in the Lancaster but this new, makeshift, heavy passenger design was too heavy for them. My first impression of the cockpit was of roominess with very soft comfortable seats but these were later to prove a handicap in times of severe turbulence. Because of the springiness of the seats this made it extremely difficult to sit still and reach the controls or read the flying instruments while your eyeballs were rattling around in your head. Many of us had operated new American equipment towards the end of the war and we loved them. As a result, we weren't enamored with the York's instrumentation, controls, radio equipment and handling characteristics. During those early morning Palmietfontein departures from a field altitude of nearly 6,000 feet the climb-out was really labored. I must confess to a certain fiendish pre-dawn sense of humor as we skimmed low over Hillbrow Ridge in Johannesburg because we awakened hundreds of citizens at that early hour with the ear-splitting noise of our four Rolls-Royce engines roaring at full power. Of course, most of us had experience of flying over Africa during the war or in the Ju52s so the first part of the journey was old hat to us but unless you had served with the RAF many of us were new to flying over Europe with its totally different weather patterns and busy air traffic. On the other hand, BOAC crews told us that they were more apprehensive about the southerly route over Africa with its lack of navigational aids, fewer emergency airfields and the ever-present thunderstorms. There were nevertheless wonderful compensations for aircrews on those lengthy flights. We often exchanged crews with BOAC at the stopover airports. The flights were spaced days apart so we frequently got a nice break when we stopped. As the Springbok Service was shared with BOAC we SAA crews members would operate some of their sectors and they in turn would operate some of ours. The stopover places were very pleasant. At Nairobi, Cairo and Tripoli there were good hotels with well-stocked bars, swimming pools, access to British-style clubs, golf courses, wildlife viewing trips, sightseeing, shopping, bazaars and local entertainment. It was also a pleasure to have the opportunity to get to know many of our passengers who stopped over with us. Not everyone undertook the entire flight all at once. Some people broke their journey along the way. Many lasting friendships originated this way and indeed there was the same kind of rapport with local townsfolk. We got to know the people along the way and we were often invited into their homes. Those really were the long-gone, wonderful, leisurely days of flying, unlike the frenzy of modern air travel nowadays."

Flight engineer Don Smith had these recollections to add. "Take-off time from Johannesburg for England was at 5 o'clock in the morning and I used to motor out to Palmietfontein at 2 a.m. in the morning with my standby flight engineer. We prayed that we'd make it because my car wasn't terribly reliable. If all went well and it didn't break down we'd get to Palmietfontein where there usually wasn't a soul in sight, not even a policeman or a security guard. We'd open up the hangar, turn on the lights, hitch a tractor to the aeroplane and tow it outside, locate the battery cart, connect the battery to the engines, start them up, run them for a while and then change spark plugs or fix whatever we found faulty in the run-up. Then when everything was all warmed up and running smoothly we'd switch off the engines, tow the aeroplane out to the departure area which was in front of the single main building. Then, eventually the traffic clerk would show up. There was only one traffic clerk on duty those days. Then some other folks would arrive to handle ticketing and baggage and that sort of thing and, finally, the passengers would start arriving. We only carried 12 passengers in the early versions of the York. Once the rest of the crew had arrived we'd do our final checks and, after fueling up, we'd board the passengers, restart the engines and head out on the first leg of our flight towards Nairobi. We always carried a navigator as there were no navigational aids along the route those days. We also had a radio operator on board. Beyond South Africa's borders most of the radio work was done with the Morse key system and not via voice transmission. We would fly to Nairobi where we would night stop and, if we were scheduled to fly the next sector, early the next morning we'd take off for Khartoum. Ultimately, depending on the flying roster, you'd reach London. Finding your way along the route was a very difficult business because there were no navigational aids at all. It was all done by a very smart, capable and hard-working navigator on board. If you flew in the dark then navigation was by astro-navigation—by the stars—and during the day by dead reckoning and visual navigation. Accurate charts, maps and compasses were essential. At first we used to land at Hurn in Bournemouth as there was no Heathrow yet. They were still building it. To get into Hurn we had to have very clear visibility because of the lack of radio or electronic aids. Eventually, when the runway at Heathrow was finished we used to land and drop off passengers there and then fly to Hurn for maintenance. At Heathrow there were no buildings or maintenance facilities at all. So, we used to land at Heathrow, disembark our passengers at the end of the runway and the poor folks would have to walk through mud, mist and rain to big marquee tents which served as customs offices, immigration and passport control, reception halls and everything else. A little later they had Quonset huts that took the place of the tents but at first conditions at the new London airport were very primitive. Eventually, ground approach control or G.C.A. was introduced at Heathrow and with that the man in the control tower used radar to talk you down through the clouds and fog. Just as you were nearing the ground he would shout: 'Look up now! You should be able to see the runway!' And if you were lucky the runway was straight ahead. If not, you'd have to go around again. Later, there was another system called BABS, which stood for Beam Approach Beacon Signal, though most of us referred to it as the Rebecca system. This produced a blip that you saw on a little screen. We would tune our Rebecca receiver to a ground station that was transmitting a signal to produce the blip. It roughly gave you an indication of where you were. Once, we were on our way from London airport to Hurn which was really just a short hop away and our navigator decided to use this new-fangled Rebecca contraption. Then we were told over the radio that the weather at Hurn had turned really bad. When the blip on the Rebecca system indicated that we were somewhere in the vicinity of Hurn we started to let down. As we broke through the clouds we saw an aerodrome beneath us. But it wasn't Hurn. It was a grass airfield, filled with gliders. But we had no choice. The weather was so foul that we had to land. Our captain, Dirkie Nel, put us down on the grass and applied the pneumatic braking system but even though the wheels stopped turning the York just kept on going because the grass was so wet and slippery. We slid along until we almost hit a fence at the end of the airfield before the aeroplane came to halt. Then we slowly taxied to the only building in sight and switched off. There wasn't a soul to be seen anywhere. We got out and went to look for people but couldn't find anybody until a guard or a security person appeared out of the rain. He ran inside the building to phone his superior, informing him that an aeroplane had just landed. When the man arrived a half-hour or so later we learned that we had landed at a place called Netheravon, an ex-RAF base. He was the Station Commander and he was absolutely fuming because we had dug up the whole runway and they had been carefully nursing the airfield for some kind of major air show and glider competition the following weekend. Anyway, we calmed him down, bought him a beer at a nearby pub and stayed at a local hotel that night. The following morning, having enough fuel on board, we took off for Hurn. There was an enquiry about our error and it turned out that the radio frequency of the BABS system for Netheravon was exactly the same as that for Hurn. So, the blunder wasn't exactly our fault. It was still very early days in the development of navigational aids and there were obviously still a great many teething problems and glitches to iron out, not the least of which was to ensure that different airports transmit different radio identification signals."

As 1945 drew to a close, it had become obvious that better, faster, larger, more efficient aircraft were needed to supplement the SAA Avro Yorks flying the Springbok Service from Palmietfontein and the stalwart Lockheed Lodestars flying domestic and regional routes from Rand Airport. A decision was made at SAR & H headquarters that led to SAA placing an order for three Douglas DC-4 Skymasters from the Douglas Aircraft Company in Santa Monica, California. Designed prior to the outbreak of the war the four-engined airliner was re-designated as the military C-54 transporter as soon as Japanese bombs fell on Pearl Harbor, drawing the United States into the war. From 1942 to 1945, over 1,200 C-54s were built, serving all branches of the United States military. Later, between 1948 and 1949, they would go on to form the backbone of the Berlin Airlift when the Soviet Union blocked Allied access to West Berlin. South Africa was a very active member of that operation with the SAAF flying many of the 200,000 cargo flights that brought food relief, first aid and other essentials to the embargoed people of Berlin. When the war ended in 1945, the Douglas plant ceased producing the military version of the C-54 and began turning out the by-now familiar passenger variant, the DC-4. Less than a year after SAA placed its initial order it doubled its requirement to three more and then went on to order a seventh aircraft. The DC-4 — or simply the 'Skymaster' as the traveling public referred to it — was eagerly anticipated while the Yorks and the Lodestars continued plying the skies, carrying the full brunt of the airline's ever-growing workload. They were the only types of aircraft now in service. Although a few of the old Ju52s and Ju86s had survived the war they were now deemed obsolete. Besides, spare parts were hard to come by for them and so, after languishing in hangars, on dusty patches of ground or on the perimeters of airfields, in 1947 they were all scrapped. Sadly, none of them were preserved for posterity.

On March 30, 1946, the first Douglas DC-4 Skymaster, registered ZS-AUA and named *Tafelberg* (Table Mountain, the name of the iconic geographic feature that looms behind Cape Town), touched down at Palmietfontein after a long flight from the factory at Clover Field in Santa Monica, Los Angeles, California. The aircraft was under the command of Douglas Aircraft Company captain Bert Fould with SAA captains Jacob Daniel, Theron Louw and Phillipus Rudolf Kok flying as co-pilots .After a two-hour 45-minute acceptance test flight by

SAA Captain Bert Rademan on March 24 in Santa Monica, the aircraft was officially handed over to SAA on March 25. Taking 44 hours and 30 minutes to complete its delivery flight it had flown by way of Los Angeles to West Palm Beach, Florida, then on to Trinidad, to Port Natal in Brazil, to Ascension Island in the South Atlantic and finally to Johannesburg.

Douglas DC-4 'Skymaster.' Publicity shot from the Douglas Aircraft Corporation in California before the aircraft was delivered to South Africa

The Douglas DC-4 'Skymaster' was powered by four Pratt & Whitney R-2000 D5 14-cylinder air-cooled radial engines driving Hamilton Standard three-blade propellers. Each power plant developed 1,450 HP (1,081 kW.) The aircraft could fly at a maximum ceiling of 22,600 feet at a speed of 227 mph for 3,500 miles. Its maximum speed was 280 mph. It had a length of 94.9 ft, a wingspan of 117.5 ft and a height of 27.6 ft. The DC-4's empty weight was 43,300 lbs and its fully loaded weight 63,500 lbs. It had an excellent payload capability and could carry up to 46 passengers in refined comfort and style.

Passenger cabin of Douglas DC-4. The photograph depicts the interior of the first of these aircraft delivered to SAA, ZS-AUA, Tafelberg

Although earlier models had flown before WWII, the post-war Douglas DC-4 represented the very pinnacle in passenger aircraft. Its seats were luxurious. Legroom was more than generous. The flight deck could seat five crew members, a captain, co-pilot, flight engineer, navigator and radio operator. Although cabin attendants had not yet been introduced on the DC-4 there was a modest but well-equipped galley behind the cockpit where food could be heated up. A small refrigerator could provide ice for a bar service that would eventually become available once cabin crew were appointed. Two toilets with hand basins and running water in the rear of the fuselage doubled as ladies' powder rooms. The DC-4 really had everything to cater to the whims and needs of the most discerning passengers. It embodied something else that was totally new to the SAA fleet—a tricycle undercarriage. This was the first of SAA's airliners that did not have a tail wheel dragging along on the ground. Instead, there was a fully steerable nose wheel that neatly folded up into a wheel well under the nose when the main undercarriage beneath the wings was retracted during flight. The Skymaster was a beautiful machine and was destined to become very popular with the traveling public.

On May 1, 1946, DC-4s began flying a regular Johannesburg to Cape Town service, taking three hours and 45 minutes to complete the trip. Once Heathrow airport outside London had been completed SAA introduced the DC-4s on the Springbok Service. In addition to the Avro Yorks the DC-4s were responsible for three flights a month from Palmietfontein. These were gradually increased in frequency once all seven of the DC-4s had been delivered. With the DC-4, the total elapsed flying time to London was reduced to 36 hours.

Douglas DC-4 in its original SAA livery or color scheme. Note the old South African flag on the tail. This particular aircraft was the very last one to come off the Douglas Aircraft Corporation's production line in Santa Monica, California, making it the last of 1,242 of the type ever built

Douglas DC-4 in flight over Johannesburg, 1946

Everyone loved the Skymaster; air crews, ground staff, engineers, mechanics, baggage handlers, despatchers, travel agents, executive at airways headquarters and, not least, passengers. Everybody sang its praises. It quickly took its place as a dependable and highly efficient flying machine. Even residents underneath its flight path near airports were not overly bothered by the drone of its four Pratt & Whitney radial engines, in comparison to the loud roar of the York's Merlins. By August 1946, Salisbury, Southern Rhodesia was added as a stopover to and from London. The last DC-4 to join the SAA fleet was originally built as a C-54 military aircraft by the Douglas Aircraft Company. At the end of the war, it was purchased from the United States Navy by Pacific Overseas Airlines and reconfigured as a DC-4. In September 1947, it was sold to SAA. Registered ZS-BWN with the name *Swartberg*, it was delivered on December 11, 1947. The penultimate DC-4 to join the fleet arrived from the Douglas factory on August 9, 1947 after a 50-hour 35-minute delivery flight from Santa Monica via Chicago, Gander (Newfoundland), London, Amsterdam, Castel Benito, Khartoum, Kisumu and Nairobi. Registered ZS-BMH, it was named *Lebombo,* after a mountain range that bisects South Africa from neighboring Swaziland and Mozambique. It was flown out under the command of SAA captain Gerwyn David Bowen 'Bill' Williams with Douglas Aircraft Company assistant chief pilot William J. Morrisey as first officer, J.F. van Aswegen as radio operator and Emile Adolf 'Bill' Maré as flight engineer. This was the very last DC-4 to come off the Douglas Aircraft Company's production line, making it the last one ever built. Still airworthy today, more than seven decades after its delivery, *Lebombo* no longer flies for SAA but has been transferred to the South African Airways Museum Society and operates charter flights with independent operator Skyclass Aviation. With a sister ship, ZS-AUB *Outeniqua,* these are the only two airworthy DC-4s anywhere in the world. Both are still flying. Seeing them next to one other in the late afternoon sunlight they look every bit as striking and as imposing as they did when they first touched down on South African soil over seventy years ago. They are a lasting reminder of the legacy of these great airliners and also a testament to the dedicated men and women who restored, service and operate them.

Back in 1947, passenger demand was soaring on domestic routes which were being flown by a mix of DC-4s and the ever-faithful fleet of Lockheed Lodestars. Pressed for more carrying capacity SAA had little option but to purchase two ex-military twin-engine Douglas C-47 aircraft from the SAAF. These were converted into the passenger version of the type, thereby transforming them into DC-3s. They were immediately absorbed into the fleet and began flying internal routes. Within months, four more C-47s were acquired from the SAAF. Three were transformed into DC-3s but one of them, ZS-DJX, remained in the freight configuration and spent much of its time ferrying karakul sheep pelts to the Union from remote farms in South-West Africa.

SAA's Douglas DC-3s were equipped with two Pratt & Whitney R-1830 S1C3G air-cooled radial engines driving three-blade constant speed Hamilton Standard propellers. The aircraft could fly at a cruising speed of 207 mph at a maximum altitude of 23,200 feet for 2,125 miles. The craft was 63 ft long, had a wingspan of 95 ft 6 ins, an empty weight of 16,865 lbs and a fully loaded weight of 25,200 lbs. The DC-3 carried a crew of two pilots. If needed on long-haul flights beyond the regular domestic route network it could also accommodate a radio officer.

The first scheduled DC-3 service was on May 8, 1946 when ZS-AVJ, piloted by Captain Peter Prophet and First Officer Ian

Cribbens, flew a full load of 21 passengers from Johannesburg to Durban, operating a return service later that day. It is a tribute to SAA's innovative engineering staff that the interiors of the DC-3s were turned into comfortable, well-appointed airliners replete with carpets, soundproofing, plush seating and overhead storage racks for the stowage of carry-on baggage, purses, coats and hats, in comparison to the bare-bones nature of their previous incarnations as transporters for infantrymen or for carrying cargo.

Douglas DC-3 (Originally built as a C-47 military transporter but converted into a civilian version by SAA technical staff after the war)

The military version C-47 was designed to drop paratroopers far behind enemy lines, to deliver soldiers to the front and to tow troop-carrying gliders deep into enemy territory such as during the D-Day invasion of Normandy. It ferried arms, ammunition, supplies, food and even trucks into battle. Extra-large cargo doors in the rear of certain models made the loading and off-loading of either people or equipment a quick, no-nonsense procedure. Often severely damaged by enemy gunfire far beyond where most other airplanes could remain airborne, the venerable C-47 took it all in its stride and simply kept on going, sometimes limping home on only one engine or with its flying surfaces and rudder shot to pieces. Its strength and resilience often defied expectation or understanding. General Dwight D. Eisenhower,

Allied Supreme Commander in Europe during WWII and later President of the United States, once said that other than the human factor in the form of soldiers, sailors, airmen and marines, three critical things were responsible for winning the war against the Nazis. They were the seaborne landing craft, the Jeep and the C-47 airplane. Few experts would argue with that.

Douglas's amazing creation was called the 'Skytrain' by most US servicemen, the 'Dakota' or 'Dak' by the British and the 'Gooney Bird' by many troops in Europe. Between 1934, when production on the first model began and 1945, when the last aircraft came off the assembly line over 16,000 variants, both civil and military, had been built. That is an astonishing number of airplanes. Many were made under license including 2,000 built in Russia during the war. Indicative of the Dak's phenomenal endurance is the fact that today—nearly nine decades since its first flight in 1934—between 300 and 400 of these extraordinary airplanes still remain in active commercial and private service worldwide. From the steamy jungles of Papua-New Guinea to the windswept steppes of Central Asia or the tundra of South America, there is not a place on the planet where the drone of a DC-3 is not a familiar sound. No other aircraft in history can claim anything even close to its remarkable record.

Another Douglas C-47 that was converted into a DC-3 for SAA

SAA Technical Instructor Len Meerholz recalls some of his experiences with the airplane. "As the airline grew, more technical staff were needed and so people were recruited from the ranks of those who served with the SAAF during the war. For the first ten years of SAA's post-war existence 95-percent of the technical staff were former wartime Air Force members. I believe that played a very important part in the airline's development. Those were men who had experienced at least five years of intense wartime service with all the discipline and training that goes with it. They carried those qualities with them into civilian life. Because of it they became a tightly-knit, well organized and formidable work force. By their example they instilled the same sort of spirit and work ethic into those who joined the airline later on. After the war SAA also employed a few young men straight out of school as trainee ground engineers. Because there was no officially recognized trade such as an 'aviation technician' in those days the youngsters were not subject to any formal apprenticeship contract or training program. But the airline was intent on providing these fellows with the best practical experience that was later required by the DCA for licensed ground engineers. Their total training period was five years and, without exception, they all rose to the challenge and became fine mechanics and engineers."

Ground engineer Willie Louw was one of the first inductees into the program. He shared some of his many memories. "97 of us, all teenagers, were selected to undergo training in aviation engineering, covering everything to do with mechanical, electrical, radio and instrumentation. Palmietfontein was the service and maintenance base for all our aircraft except the Lockheed Lodestars, which were still serviced at Rand Airport. The main SAA workshops and overhaul base were located at Rand Airport as were the administrative offices and, most important of all, the pay office. A lot of time was wasted with everything split up between two airports. We desperately needed to consolidate engineering and operations at only one place, instead of two. The engineering staff that worked at Palmietfontein was bussed in on a daily basis from Rand Airport. But by 'buses' I mean old, canvas-topped, olive-colored Ford ex-Army three-ton trucks repainted blue. They were continually shuttling backwards and forwards between the two airports. We were given the option of travelling to and from work on those noisy, uncomfortable trucks or on a slow, noisy, smoky steam train popularly called the 'Palmiet Express' or the 'Coffee Grinder' which left from Germiston railway station. Road transport took about 25 minutes to make the trip whereas the 'Palmiet Express' took at least an hour. To give an idea of how awkward things were we juniors were required to attend morning lectures every Tuesday and Wednesday at Rand Airport. But we had to show up for work first at Palmietfontein in order to clock in. That meant that as soon as we arrived there we would immediately board road transport to go to back to Rand Airport for lectures. Although Palmietfontein was the only international airport in the country at the time it was relatively small. We young engineers used to refer to it as 'The Farm' because it was so far out of town. Although more were built later at first it consisted of only two hangars, one for British-made aircraft and one for those made in America. That was because all the tools, spanners, socket sizes, seals, gaskets and couplings were different. The British and American aeroplanes also used different types of oils, lubricants and greases. To complicate matters, British aircraft had pneumatic systems whereas the Americans favoured hydraulics. International commercial aviation was not yet standardised. To find part numbers, references and information in the different servicing manuals was a nightmare. And then there were the language differences to add to the confusion. One manual referred to a spanner whereas another called the same tool a wrench. As far as I was concerned the Douglas DC-4 was the preferred aircraft to maintain. Its engines and airframe were more accessible and much cleaner and easier to work on. Lodestars that landed at Palmietfontein had to be ferried to Rand Airport for night servicing after unloading their passengers and baggage. That sometimes gave us an opportunity to catch a ride home. What fun it was to chat up the captain for a flip to Rand. As there were no passengers aboard we were allowed to stand in the open doorway of the cockpit and watch with excitement as all those gauges and instrumentation came to life that we personally worked on. It was such a treat. The flight from 'The Farm' to Rand was a mere ten minutes or so, flying at an altitude of about a thousand feet. After landing at Rand Airport we would catch a local bus into town or cycle home to our hostels or boarding houses in Germiston. What a wonderful way of travelling to and from work; by bicycle, train, truck, airliner and then finish the day on a bicycle again!"

Technicians at work in the engine overhaul shop at Rand Airport

Mechanics work on maintenance of a Lockheed Lodestar at Rand Airport

Ground engineer Willie Louw continued his recollections. "Test flights after periodic maintenance schedules were par for the course back in those days. We ground technicians were required to accompany those flights after an engine change or a major overhaul that we had worked on. During the flight it was a requirement that any replaced engine be 'feathered' (stopped) and then restarted in the air. It was during one of those tests that my admiration for the DC-4 as an extremely safe aircraft was firmly established. I remember that we were flying somewhere over the East Rand at 9,000 feet one day when the number one engine was stopped, followed by number four and then number two. Because of the hydraulics system that relied on it for power only number three was kept going at METO (maximum except take off) power. It was a spine-tingling experience to look out of the left side of the aircraft and see both engines feathered. With only one engine running the DC-4 became very quiet inside and, I must add, so did the twenty-odd young ground staff on board. We continued on for about five minutes with only one engine operating as the airplane made a slow descent. The DC-4 was a marvellous machine, except for one thing. One or two of them occasionally developed leaking fuel tanks. The underside of the wings sometimes showed ugly green Avgas 100-octane fuel stains. Leaking fuel tanks could only be sealed by first draining all the fuel from them and evacuating all the gasses. We gained access to the tanks through manhole panels on the underside of the wing. Face masks connected to an air pump had to be worn whenever we were working in an empty fuel tank. This terrible and dangerous procedure of sealing tanks with a zinc chromate slushing compound was the most revolting and sickening task one could ever experience. If you weren't in the foreman's good books you were assigned to tank sealing. But they were terrific days and I consider myself most fortunate to have started my career on 'The Farm' at Palmietfontein. It was a great training ground."

Uniform of the first batch of 'Air Hostesses'

On September 1, 1946, the airline made history — and nationwide headlines — when a young brunette in a neatly coutured pale blue skirt, jacket, pillbox hat, white blouse and highly polished black flat shoes boarded a DC-4 for a flight from Palmietfontein to Cape Town. She was Miss Pat Hardy and she was the very first of the airline's 'air hostesses' to serve on board a domestic flight. Among the required qualities of an airhostess — as prescribed by the airline — were 'charm, poise, personality, dignity and intelligence.' There was a height and weight restriction and, preferably, she should be single. Needless to say, at that time in South Africa's troubled political history, she also had to be white. Once a specially appointed selection committee at SAR & H headquarters had chosen a hostess, she had to undergo an arduous two-month training course to prepare her for her career. The first eight women chosen for the role were Pat Hardy, Rosa Jurcich, 'Willie' Oates-Williams, Gwen Preston, Joyce Clarke, Cathy King, Irene Visagie and Jean Warrand. Long-retired ex-cabin crew attendant Joey Peenz sketched the early intake of hostesses into the airline. "Dozens of candidates applied for the job but only twelve finalists were selected. We were aged between 22 and 25. We came from all corners of the country; Pretoria, Johannesburg, Uitenhage, Worcester, Humansdorp, Bloemfontein, Germiston. I came from Harrismith in Natal. We had responded to a nationwide recruitment campaign that included notices in most English and Afrikaans language newspapers. We were so excited to even be considered for the job and were only too happy to give up our many occupations to become part of this adventurous new avenue open to women. The girls came from all walks of life.

Air hostess welcomes passenger aboard aircraft. Palmietfontein Airport, 1946

"Some were qualified civilian or military nursing sisters, army radiographers, stewardesses who had worked on trains, teachers, a pharmacist and even an architectural tracer. Before embarking on our intensive two-month training course in Johannesburg, Pretoria and at Rand Airport our instructress, Miss Melba Smit, had to determine whether we were physically and emotionally fit to stand up to the rigors of the job. The first and most trying test that I recall took place at Lyttelton outside Pretoria where we were put inside the Air Force's decompression chamber to ascertain our reaction to high altitude flying. Aeroplanes of that time all flew below the weather but we sometimes reached altitudes of 6,000 feet or higher. The air is very thin up there. In those days of unpressurized aircraft we were required to check that passengers were not suffering from lack of oxygen and we had to administer emergency oxygen if necessary. After decompression and high altitude exposure came aptitude tests but the part I loved most of all was the actual flying at Rand Airport to see if we were able to withstand airsickness. They took us up and threw us around in the air quite a bit to simulate turbulence in bad weather. Some of us got really scared and those that did were automatically eliminated from the course. It was after those flights that our group was reduced to the eight that finally qualified.

Hostess assists passengers with baby on board a Douglas DC-4 'Skymaster'

"More training followed, including physical fitness, learning how to care for all types of passengers, ensuring that we were proficient in both official languages—English and Afrikaans—and that we had a thorough knowledge of first-aid and home nursing. We were especially prepared to handle cases of air sickness. We were shown how to set a splint and dress a wound and even how to play midwife in case one of our pregnant female passengers went into labor. Our training included an extensive introduction to etiquette, manners and diplomacy. The Railways Catering Department was another port of call. There we were initiated into all aspects of catering including the preparation and garnishing of dishes, the handling of trays and the correct manner to wait on people. A lot was focused on how to serve passengers on tray tables while in the air. We had to learn how to pour beverages without spilling, especially in bumpy conditions. That was no easy task. Tea or coffee was served in heavy crockery on silver trays. There was no plastic in those days. Everything was glass or porcelain or silver. We also gained a thorough knowledge of travel conditions in the Union by going through an intensive course in the Railways Publicity and Travel Department. There we were exposed to large doses of travel data such as routes, scenic attractions, rail and air tariffs and hotel costs. On the job a lot of time was spent chatting to passengers as we didn't provide too much catering those days. We used to hand out neatly wrapped little wads of cotton floss for passengers to stuff into their ears to help them deal with changes in air pressure and, just before take-off and landing, we'd pass around little bowls of sweets or mints for people to suck on. This helped ease blocked and painful ears. During the flight, especially on long distance routes, the captain would send back hand-written notes from the cockpit informing passengers about the height, speed and position of the aircraft. We would pass these around and answer any queries people might have. It was all quite wonderful, really."

With post-war fuel prices on the rise the Lockheed Lodestars that flew the internal and regional route network were now proving to be less economical than what could be achieved with more modern commercial equipment on the market.

So, grieved by many, the Lodestars were retired. But the type was not destined to entirely disappear. Lockheed Lodestar 18-08 Lodestar, ZS-ASN, *Andries Pretorius* arrived in South Africa on

December 3, 1940. On April 22, 1955, it was sold to the British-owned aerial survey firm, Aircraft Operating Company. It survived an accident in September 1957 but by 1972, its air service days were over. ZS-ASN was then parked rather ignominiously in an open storage area at the private airport, Grand Central, north of Johannesburg for a year. After having flown a total 14,911 hours, its airworthiness certificate was cancelled on February 14, 1973. At that time there was talk of SAA setting up a museum so the airplane was hauled by road to Jan Smuts Airport on December 3, 1973. After restoration and repainting in vintage 1940s SAA livery by apprentices at SAA's technical workshops, it was moved to the Swartkop Air Force Base near Pretoria where it languished for many years. With the formation of the South African Airways Museum Society, it was moved to its final resting place in a static aircraft display park at Rand Airport, where it remains to this day.

The Vickers Viking was the aircraft that replaced the Lodestars for service with SAA. Coming from the Vickers Armstrongs stable its pedigree was excellent. Like the York that was based on the Lancaster bomber the Viking was a derivative of the classic Wellington bomber that provided such sterling service during WWII. In 1947, eight Vikings were ordered by SAA. The first one to be delivered, ZS-BNE named *Simonsberg* (Simon's Mountain), arrived at Rand Airport from the Vickers plant at Wisley, England on August 5, 1947 under the command of decorated WWII pilot Captain Salomon 'Pi' Pienaar with first officer Otto Greder as co-pilot. The aircraft made the journey from London via Bourdeaux (France), Castel Benito, El Adem (Tobruk, Libya), Khartoum, Nairobi and Ndola in a flying time of 28 hours 10 minutes.

The Vickers Viking 1B was deemed to be an ideal aircraft to take over the domestic and regional service from the Lodestars. Three days after its arrival from the factory the first of the Vikings entered service on the domestic route network. Subsequent arrivals saw the beginning of Viking flights to Windhoek in South-West Africa, to Bulawayo and Salisbury in Southern Rhodesia, Lusaka and Ndola in Northern Rhodesia, Tabora in Tanganyika and Nairobi, Kenya.

Vickers Viking

The Viking was originally designed to have a tricycle undercarriage with a nose wheel like the Douglas DC-4 Skymaster. But the Vickers Armstrong company was lured into a compromise. Because the British Ministry of Aviation's large fleet of surplus post-war bombers all had tail wheels these readily-available wheel assemblies were offered to the company at very low cost. As a result, Vickers made a last minute design change to the Viking, turning it into a tail-dragger. Unfortunately, this made the aircraft nose heavy. That did not affect its airworthiness or flying characteristics but on the ground it did present an ungainly problem. If there were no passengers or baggage on board ballast always had to be loaded into the rear baggage compartment whenever the aircraft was on the ground. If not, the airplane had an embarrassing habit of tipping down onto its nose if four or more persons were in the cockpit. The result was a dented nose, a broken radio aerial and badly bent propeller blades.

The Vickers Viking 1B was equipped with two Bristol Hercules 14-cylinder sleeve-valve radial air-cooled piston engines. Each one delivered 1,690 HP (1,261 kW) driving a four-blade variable pitch propeller. The Viking had a cruising speed of 210 mph and a maximum speed of 263 mph. It could fly at a height of 25,000 feet for 1,700 miles. With a length of 62 ft 9 ins, a wingspan of 89.25 ft, an empty weight of 23,000 lbs and a fully loaded weight of 34,000 lbs, it could carry between 24 and 27 passengers, depending on seating configuration. Its crew consisted of a pilot, co-pilot, flight engineer and radio operator.

The Vikings remained in service with SAA for only four years. Their Bristol Hercules engines were troublesome in the hot and high regions of the airline's route structure. Dust and heat were too much for them to handle. Although the Vikings were good money earners, their engines spent too much time in the workshops and so they were eventually sold to British European Airways (BEA.) An interesting sideline here is the story of Vickers Viking V498/1A, registered ZS-DKH. It never flew for SAA but it has a fascinating history. It first took to the air on August 30, 1946, registered as G-AHOT with British European Airways and was used in the 1948 Berlin Airlift. On September 26, 1954, it was sold to the small South African-based private airline, Trek Airways, and was registered ZS-DKH. Operated in the colors of Protea Airways, a subsidiary carrier of Trek Airways, for many years it transported hundreds of passengers on leisurely and scenic flights between South Africa and Europe. After nearly 14,000 flying hours ZS-DKH was retired and flown from Rand Airport to the old Baragwanath Airfield near Johannesburg. There it was disassembled and transported by road to Armadale south of Johannesburg, where, in January 1963, it was perched atop the roof of a Caltex gasoline station owned by Victor Edward de Villiers. The gas station became known as Vic's Viking Garage and the airplane became a famous landmark. On March 5, 1987, the Viking was replaced by an Avro Shackleton 1723 maritime patrol aircraft once used by the SAAF. The Viking was removed from its rooftop perch and donated to the South African Airways Museum Society.

Another short-haul airliner that came into service with the airline in 1947 was the de Havilland Dove. SAA purchased two of these small aircraft that were built at the de Havilland plant in Hatfield, England for use on low density routes such as Palmietfontein to Upington in the Northern Cape and to Karasburg, Keetmanshoop and Windhoek in South-West Africa. Other routes flown were from Lourenco Marques in Mozambique to Durban and Palmietfontein. The Dove seated eight passengers and had a crew of two. In addition to passenger services, they were also used for crew training, airfield inspection and non-scheduled flights, as well as for occasional VIP flights and as expedient transport for SAA executives and senior officials.

de Havilland Dove

Both the Viking and the Dove had a limited service period with the airline of about four years before being sold to Northern Rhodesia Air Services. But, like the Lockheed Lodestar, the Dove

The de Havilland Dove was equipped with two de Havilland Gipsy Queen 70-3 inverted six-cylinder air-cooled in-line engines driving de Havilland Hydromatic three-blade variable pitch propellers. Each engine delivered 330 HP (246 kW) of power. The aircraft had a wingspan of 57 ft, a length of 39 ft 3 ins and a height of 13 ft 4 ins. Its empty weight was 5,650 lbs. Fully loaded it could weigh up to 8,500 lbs. The Dove had a maximum ceiling of 20,000 feet, a top speed of 201 mph, a cruising speed of 165 mph and a range of 1,000 miles.

was not to disappear completely. Almost three decades after the type was retired a rusting hulk of one of them, ZS-BCC, was found in England. After years of flying for various operators in South Africa in 1968, it was exported to Fairey Surveys, an aerial survey company, based at White Waltham airfield near Maidenhead, Berkshire. Registered G-AWFM, it continued flying until the end of its service life when it was bought by a small charter company, Fairflight, based at Biggin Hill, for use as a source of spares. Eventually the British Hawker Siddeley company purchased what was left of the craft for £500 and it was disassembled and moved to Salisbury Hall, the home of the famed WWII Mosquito Museum, north of London. The idea was to store it there until it could be refurbished and put on public display. And that is when Johann Prozesky of SAA's engineering division heard about it. Realizing the historic importance of the aircraft, Prozesky arranged for funding to be made available and the Dove was purchased, crated and returned to Johannesburg in the cargo hold of an SAA Boeing 747. After arrival at Jan Smuts Airport, it was handed over to the SAA Apprentice School and, as a form of instruction and a labor of love, over the next few years, it was restored to pristine condition. In 1986, it became part of the collection of the South African Airways Museum Society. When the museum got its permanent home at Rand Airport in 2004, the Dove took its place in the static display area where it can still be seen.

In 1946, regular services to destinations in the Union had been introduced by Central African Airways (CAA), the airline formed by the colonial governments of Northern Rhodesia, Southern Rhodesia and Nyasaland. By 1947, SAA and BOAC weren't the only carriers providing services to Europe from South Africa. On August 29 of that year, Belgium's Sabena introduced a DC-4 service linking Brussels via Leopoldville in the Congo with Johannesburg. Competition on routes to Europe was now ramping up. One of SAA's answers was to introduce yet another first in its history. After a trial period in May 1948, on board a DC-4 Skymaster service between Johannesburg and Cape Town, a 'cinema in the sky' was introduced on most DC-4 flights of the Springbok Service. Following coffee and liqueurs after the main meal, cabin attendants closed all the window blinds, rigged up a collapsible screen in the front of the cabin, perched a 16mm Bell & Howell projector on a fold-up table at the rear end near the toilets and screened recently-released full length feature films to passengers. It was an instant success. Passengers loved the 'bioscope flights' to and from London. 'Bioscope' was the brand name of one of the earliest cinema projectors imported to South Africa at the end of the 19th century. Its use in small town farming communities made the name synonymous with the cinema and so, even until recent times, the word bioscope in South Africa really meant going to the movies. Radio technician P.P. van den Berg remembered how the system worked. "Each passenger seat was fitted with a volume control and a headphone socket. Before the show began every passenger was issued with a heavy S.G. Brown headphone. Some of the women didn't like it because it messed up their hair-do. On quite a few occasions the aircraft would arrive at Palmietfontein with most of the film lying unwound on the cabin floor. That usually happened when the weather was rough and passengers got airsick. In those cases the hostess just abandoned the projector and let the film unspool onto the floor."

Flight Engineer Don Smith remembered a cabin attendant who had been so enthralled with the movie that she failed to notice that at the start of the show the film had broken and was not winding onto the take-up reel of the projector. It was simply unspooling onto the floor. The distressed young lady came running to Smith on the flight deck in tears, pleading for help. On leaving his post to assist her, he discovered that the film had not only unravelled but had also torn. As he carefully wound up the celluloid mess, he counted fifty-nine breaks. The cinema in the sky project was not a great success and was abandoned within 18 months. Nevertheless, those trailblazing shows took place decades before regular inflight entertainment and movies became commonplace on other carriers around the world.

More foreign airlines were waiting in the wings to begin serving Johannesburg but most had to wait until the new Highveld international airport was ready at Kempton Park. It would be years before the airport was capable of accommodating them. However, on December 3, 1947, led by a group of siren-screaming police motorcycles, a fleet of black Rolls Royce sedans, Rileys and Packards carrying government representatives and VIPs paraded through Kempton Park from Pretoria, turned off at a dirt intersection deep in the surrounding veldt, stopped in the middle of nowhere where a lonely but tall and imposing three-pillared white concrete archway had been erected. To the accompaniment of a military brass band, the archway was officially christened by visiting British dignitary Field Marshal Viscount Montgomery of Alamein, G.C.B., D.S.O. 'Monty,'as he was affectionately known because of his spectacular defeat of Rommel's crack Afrika Korps during the desert campaign of WWII, announced that the archway would serve as the main entryway to the new international airport that was being constructed nearby.

Archway to the new Jan Smuts International Airport stands in an empty field 16 east of Johannesburg while the airport is still under construction. Chairs await VIPs for the archway's dedication, 1947

Soldiers line up for the dedication ceremony

Field Marshal Viscount Montgomery arrives to dedicate the new archway, December 3, 1947

The half-built airport buildings were still not visible because the clearing of eucalyptus trees and bush was still incomplete and the archway looked as though it was a portal to little more than virgin wilderness. Nevertheless, Monty assured the accompanying contingent of VIPs, press corps and newsreel cameras that the airport would soon begin operating. It would not be named Highveld as originally planned, but in honor of the country's esteemed and much-admired prime minister, General Jan Christiaan Smuts. And so, in the midst of the veldt on a breezy summer afternoon, the name Jan Smuts Airport took its place in the consciousness of South African society and in the lexicon of the international aviation industry. It would only be a matter of time before the terrain would be cleared and the bright new yellow brick buildings and metal hangars revealed to become the focus of the country's air travel industry. Meanwhile, its long runways lay like silent ribbons stretched across the landscape waiting and shimmering in the intense summer heat.

'Monty' was a welcome guest in South Africa. Because of their wartime experiences, he and Prime Minister Smuts were on excellent terms. But his wasn't the most important high-profile British statesman's visit to the country in 1947. Earlier that year another visit had eclipsed anything ever before or, indeed, since. Between February 17 and April 24, King George VI, Queen Elizabeth and their daughters, the princesses Elizabeth and Margaret, had undertaken an extensive tour of the Union and the neighboring British colony of Southern Rhodesia. Traveling in gleaming black Daimler limousines, by air (in RAF Vikings of the King's Flight) and in a specially-built South African Railways eight-carriage luxury train painted ivory white, the royal family charmed all in the country, including many Afrikaners who had been bitterly opposed to South Africa taking Britain's side during the war. This was because of the crushing defeat suffered by their ancestors during the Anglo-Boer War at the beginning of the twentieth century. But it was because of South Africa's support for Britain as an ally during WWII that the royal family came out to acquaint themselves with the country, to say thank you and to cement closer ties between the two nations.

The royal family, His Majesty King George VI, Her Majesty Queen Elizabeth and Princess Elizabeth and Princess Margaret, photographed during their official visit to South Africa in 1947

King George VI walks with Prime Minister Jan Smuts during the Royal Tour to South Africa, 1947

The royal family arrives for a visit to a rural Zulu community in Natal, South Africa, 1947

The king presided over the opening of parliament in Cape Town, delivering a speech from a magnificent gold throne specially made for the occasion. Princess Elizabeth celebrated her 21st birthday on April 21, delivering a heartfelt speech to the nation and to the entire British Empire on the BBC external radio service from the Cape Town City Hall. It was in every way a rich, festive and joyous tour. By the time the royal family departed Cape Town for Portsmouth on the battleship *HMS Vanguard* on April 24, the two countries could not be closer.

Chapter Six

Changing Times

By 1948, SAA was firmly established as a regular carrier between Johannesburg and London. Flights were so popular that travel agencies often found it difficult to book seats for their clients on the Springbok Service. Things were good on the domestic front too. A network of scheduled regional and internal flights were not only moving people, mail and freight around but contributing to the nation's dramatic post-war growth. In keeping with the changing times, the familiar Flying Springbok logo got a make-over, replacing the original design with something more flashy and up-to-date.

The Flying Springbok logo gets a more modern make-over, 1948

On January 1, 1948, the cumbersome business of operating two separate airports in the Johannesburg area came to an end.

On that date all SAA facilities, fleet, staff and operations were transferred from Rand Airport to Palmietfontein, the interim airport that served both local and overseas flights until the new Jan Smuts Airport came into operation. This brought to an end the long association that SAA had with Rand Airport in Germiston. There were many who lamented the termination of the airline's activities there. Many a traveller, airman and engineer had a strong nostalgic attachment to the place. As the country's principal international aerial gateway and the home of SAA for the past 13 years, Rand Airport would now be turned over to smaller independent air carriers, charter operators and private aviation. Because Palmietfontein Airport was located quite a distance away from the Johannesburg metropolitan area, the SAR & H invested in a fleet of 26 British-made Commer Commando buses to transport passengers to and from the city. These blue and white coaches sported a large Flying Springbok on their sides and could seat 20. They had a cavernous cargo hold beneath the rear half of the coach for baggage, ostensibly transforming them into a double-decker.

Part of the fleet of 26 Commer Commando coaches for transporting passengers to the temporary international airport, Palmietfontein, outside Johannesburg, 1948

Because SAA and BOAC had a working partnership, some of the coaches also carried the gold 'Speedbird' logo of BOAC and the full name, 'British Overseas Airways Corporation,' on their sides. A handful of them were also sent to Durban and Cape Town for ferrying SAA passengers to and from airports in those cities. Another significant step had been taken the previous year when SAA withdrew the much-maligned Avro Yorks from the Springbok Service, leaving the faster and more efficient Douglas DC-4s to operate the route to London. Things were well. SAA was thriving. But other things were happening too.

For South Africa, 1948 was a watershed year.

To understand why we need to step back in time for a moment. The end of the Anglo-Boer War in 1902 left Britain the winner and the two Afrikaner-controlled Boer republics the losers in a bitter conflict that had lasted four years. This resulted in a unification of the country's four territories; or provinces; with self-rule under the British crown. That gave Britain and English-speaking South Africans the upper hand in the country's economic and political affairs. Once the Union of South Africa came into being in 1910, the Afrikaans population was largely relegated to a position of economic subjugation. Diamond and gold mining companies and a multitude of manufacturing industries were all firmly under English-speaking control. Afrikaners were employed in secondary positions in these industries or were engaged in lower-tiered and relatively underpaid positions in the civil service. Their only alternative to substantially better their lot was to return to the land and till the soil as their forefathers had done before them. Or they could try to climb the political ladder and carve out a niche in the economic structure of the country, a goal that posed enormous challenges. Naturally, aspirations like that created considerable dissent between English-speaking and Afrikaans-speaking communities. Afrikaners dreamed of the day when they could wrest control of the country and its economy from their English-speaking counterparts. But English and Afrikaans-speaking whites were not the only players on the stage. There were many others. As the population of two-

and-a-half million whites fought their wars and defined the political and economic spectrum of the country, nearly eleven million blacks were relegated to the shadows, mere onlookers, a presence and a concern kept out of sight and out of mind.

Black South Africans were seldom regarded with any degree of respect or recognition by either of the country's dominant white language groups, even under British jurisdiction. In fact, after the Union was formed blacks were denied the vote and totally removed from the electoral rolls. They had no say whatever in governing their own affairs. The Mines and Works Act of 1911 prescribed that only whites could hold skilled jobs in the mining industry. The Natives Land Act of 1913 prohibited blacks from owning any land other than a paltry 13 percent of the country that was set aside for their exclusive use, primarily in traditional tribal areas and mostly in backwater regions. Laws like these ensured that blacks had no alternative but to seek jobs from white employers in white-owned areas. And without the right to vote they could do nothing to change laws that excluded them from the political process and which kept them trapped on the bottom rung of the economic ladder. An inferior education system also ensured that they would have little skills to compete with whites.

The animosities and competition generated between white Afrikaners struggling under the yoke of English dominance and the repressed black population that was trampled underfoot by both white groups caused the Afrikaner to constantly look over his shoulder at the black man shuffling along behind him, viewing him as an adversarial competitor, while they both groped for the limited economic opportunities grudgingly handed down to them by white English-speaking bosses and employers. As time went by some Afrikaans-speaking individuals managed to rise to positions of political prominence. One of them was Prime Minister Jan Christiaan Smuts. But when he decided to throw South Africa's weight behind Britain during the Second World

War many Afrikaners voiced their opposition to him and to his reconciliatory policies towards the British. The entire political ambience was a brittle, sensitive one.

The Royal Tour of 1947 certainly smoothed things over between all things English and the larger Afrikaans community but beneath the surface pervasive animosities perpetually seethed. To aggravate an already difficult situation, the black community that outnumbered the whites by a ratio of five-to-one was all too often perceived as an overwhelming threat to the whites. Fear was the primary reason. Like so much about Africa, whites were scared of what they could not control. But to many whites, especially the unskilled Afrikaners who were lured from their farms to the cities, blacks were perceived as competition in the workplace. As a result, from the 1920s to the 1940s, a virulent Afrikaner nationalist movement grew in popularity all over the country.

1948 was more than just another year in the calendar. It was an election year. It was a decisive year. It was a year in which the status quo could change. Things were therefore primed for a tough political stand-off between Englishman and Afrikaner. And so a vigorous election campaign got underway while the black community stood by on the side, voiceless and voteless. But there were other players in this social drama. There was close to a million people classified as 'Coloreds' who were descendants of predominantly Muslim slaves brought to the Cape from the islands of the Dutch East Indies in the 17th century. Others who fell under this broad yet vague classification included those who were the offspring of multi-racial parents, usually an indigenous black African and a white Caucasian. And then there were about half-a-million 'Asians,' descendants of Hindu indentured laborers who were brought from India to work on the sugar cane plantations in British Natal during the mid-nineteenth century, as well as immigrant or 'Passenger Indians' — mainly Muslim traders — who followed them. Depending on their economic status and on where they lived, some of the Coloreds and Asians were initially allowed to vote but it would not be long before these two racial groups were also stripped of their electoral rights. Pared down to its fundamentals, the 1948 general election campaign was waged between white English-speaker and white Afrikaans-speaker for power and domination. And so, on May 26, 1948, the whites went to the polls.

The result was a shocker for everyone. The conservative Afrikaner vote won. Prime Minister Jan Smuts was unseated from office and the English-led United Party—which had been in charge of the government since 1933—lost its majority in parliament. The Afrikaner-supported National Party now came to power. Its leader was a Dutch Reformed church cleric, Dr. Daniel Francois Malan. He became the country's new prime minister. With these developments a new word edged its way into the lingo of the day and slowly became etched into the headlines of the world—'apartheid.' Seizing on the fact that the Afrikaners wanted blacks removed from a path of competitive economic development and also because many whites, both English and Afrikaans, felt threatened by black political aspirations, the Afrikaner Nationalists quickly formulated a harsh, all-embracing system of social organization and named it apartheid. It was a newly invented Afrikaans term that loosely translated into English as 'apartness' or 'separation.'

Apartheid would define the very essence of South Africa in the years and decades to come. It would be the underpinning of much of the legislation passed down by parliament and in the way life was lived on the streets and on all levels of society. By acts of parliament, apartheid would lay down strict rules of separation between people of all racial groups from the schoolyard to the sports field, from housing to hospitals, from beaches to banks, from the cinema to the church, from parks to the post office. It would decide where you lived, how you lived, who you could marry, how your children would be educated, what jobs you could hold, even where you were allowed to be buried. As far as relations between blacks and whites were concerned the twain would not and could not meet. To transgress apartheid's laws was a criminal offence. But it was enshrined in the statute books and from 1948, it would be clinically infused into society like a pharmaceutical drip seeping into the veins of a patient, drop by drop, law by law, act by parliamentary act.

SAA, being a government owned and controlled entity, would now fall under the dominance of this tyrannical system. But local and regional services continued to grow and the Springbok Service to London prospered.

Despite the election results and the dawn of officially sanctioned racism, in 1948 relations between Britain and South Africa remained strong. Britain was by far South Africa's largest trading partner and British companies had a huge stake in the South African economy. From children's candies to motor vehicles to soap powders, much of what South Africans bought and used were made by companies with strong ties to Britain. This fact was evident everywhere. For every Packard, Buick, Chevrolet, Renault, Citroen, Mercedes Benz or Alfa Romeo on the road that came from American or European automobile manufacturers, there were twice as many Austins, Hillmans or Vauxhalls that came from British factories. The two country's economic ties were immutably strong.

As BOAC was a pool partner of SAA, it decided to withdraw its Avro York flights from the Springbok Service, in line with SAA's decision to replace them with the much faster and more comfortable Douglas DC-4 Skymasters. A decision was made in London to replace BOAC's Yorks with something equally as fast as the DC-4, as reliable and with a large seating capacity. As there were no land planes—as opposed to flying boats—coming out of the many British airplane manufacturing facilities at that time which could match the American-made Douglas DC-4s, BOAC introduced flying boats once again. But these were the latest generation Solent airplanes that superseded anything else in the air at that time for sheer luxury. Developed by British airplane builder, Short Brothers, the Solent was based on wartime Seaford and Sunderland military flying boats. The Mark III version of the Solent—the one used on the South African route—could accommodate 34 passengers. Even though it operated the Springbok Service only during daylight hours, the aircraft boasted large, comfortable armchair-style seats and sleeping berths in sumptuous compartments on two levels connected by a spiral staircase. It offered a lounge, a smoking area, a ladies' powder room, panoramic windows and a well-equipped galley and bar, plus a very spacious freight and baggage hold. The Solent carried a crew of seven, including three cabin attendants. Unlike previous BOAC flying boat services to South Africa the Solents bypassed Durban. Flights now terminated near Johannesburg. Because the city has no lake or river the big flying boats landed at Vaal Dam, a large body of water formed by an artificial barrage built across the Vaal River on the border between the provinces of Transvaal and the Orange Free State, 88 miles south of Johannesburg.

The Short Solent III was powered by four Bristol Hercules supercharged 14-cylinder radial sleeve piston engines developing 1,600 HP (1,176 kW) driving de Havilland four-blade variable pitch oropellers. The craft had a maximum airspeed of 273 mph, a cruising speed of 220 mph and a range of 2,100 miles. It had a wingspan of 112 ft 9 ins, a length of 87 ft 8 ins and a height of 37 ft 7 ins. Its empty weight was 47,760 lbs and a fully loaded weight of 76,000 lbs. Its service ceiling was 17,000 feet but it normally flew at a more comfortable altitude of between 6,000 and 8,000 feet.

On March 10, 1948, BOAC undertook the first route-proving Solent flight to Vaal Dam and on May 4 the service was officially introduced with fare-paying passengers. The flight followed a course from Southampton to Augusta (Sicily,) Cairo, Luxor, Khartoum, Port Bell (Kampala, Uganda), Victoria Falls and Vaal Dam. Taking four-and-a-half days to complete the route frequencies were initially operated three times per week in each direction.

BOAC Short Solent flying boat, *City of Cardiff*, landing at Vaal Dam outside Johannesburg, 1949

With Palmietfontein airport functioning at peak efficiency under its very capable supervisor, Major Harry Campbell, other international airlines began operating services to Johannesburg. In addition to Belgium's Sabena, on April 24, 1948, KLM Royal Dutch Airlines introduced a twice-weekly service between Amsterdam and Johannesburg using the latest generation Douglas DC-6B aircraft. DETA airlines, which had begun operations from Lourenco Marques in neighboring Portuguese-controlled Mozambique in 1946, increased its services to Johannesburg. Southern Rhodesia-based Central African Airways ramped up its services to Johannesburg from Salisbury, Bulawayo, Lusaka and Ndola. In every way, air travel was bustling.

Meanwhile, things were progressing well at Kempton Park where the new Jan Smuts International Airport was still under construction. Big yellow Caterpillar bulldozers and graders were clearing the area of all remaining trees and shrubs around the newly-built runways.

Digging the foundations for one of the main runways at the new Jan Smuts Airport, 1948

Working on laying down one of the runways at Jan Smuts Airport, 1948

The domestic and international arrivals and departure terminals were nearing completion. When ready, the main terminal would include large public lounges and waiting areas, passenger check–in counters, a restaurant, a bar, a book and magazine store, a customs and immigration hall in a basement level and an extensive exterior visitors' viewing gallery on the upper floor. Not far away a building to house the Division of Civil Aviation

(DCA) and a control tower, built of brick with white concrete accents, was nearing completion. Outside the main terminal a large rose garden was laid out. It separated the car park from the terminal building by a network of neatly designed bricked footpaths. The wide two-lane access road to the car park went directly through the archway that had been opened the previous year by Viscount Montgomery. To the west of the car park, a series of hangars had either been constructed or were nearing completion. Between them a large concrete apron was being readied to receive aircraft that would one day be parked in the open before being wheeled into the hangars for maintenance. With the absence of surrounding fences, residents of the neighboring little town of Kempton Park spent weekends taking leisurely drives on the many dirt service roads that skirted the runways, or by parking in front of the rose garden on weekdays to watch all the feverish construction work going on nearby. On Sundays all worked ceased, of course. The country was now under strict Calvinistic rule as demanded by the Dutch Reformed church, the predominant religion of the Afrikaner and the ruling National Party. Sunday was the Sabbath. You went to church or you stayed home or you picnicked quietly on a river bank. But there was no work, no entertainment, no music, no sport. On weekday afternoons schoolboys cycled in the cleared fields of the vast airport-to-be and sometimes even dared to compete in races down the pristine new runways, much to the consternation of construction workers. The place was buzzing with expectation. Everyone knew that exciting things would soon be happening there.

On February 2, 1949, Nairobi replaced Kisumu on the DC-4 Springbok Service to London. Even though the 'cinema in the sky' in-flight cabin service was no longer offered flights were consistently full. Unlike the BOAC flying boats, the DC-4 did not stop overnight along the way. Operating from Palmietfontein on Tuesdays, Thursdays and Sundays, the schedule was:

Depart Johannesburg: 02.00	Arrive Nairobi: 11.40
Depart Nairobi: 13.10	Arrive Khartoum: 18.10
Depart Khartoum: 19.40	Arrive Castel Benito or Malta: 3.25
Depart Castel Benito or Malta: 04.55	Arrive London: 11.40

With the popularity of the service a need grew for a larger, faster airplane to fly the route. It so happened that at the Lockheed Aircraft Company in faraway Burbank in California, the perfect product was now available to fulfil that requirement. And so, early in 1949, an order was placed for four Lockheed L-749A 'Gold Plate' airliners for delivery during May, June, July and August the following year. The Constellation with its graceful lines and distinctive upswept triple stabilizers was a magnificent-looking aircraft. But apart from its handsome profile, the big new machine offered something special that would literally take it to new heights when it came to passenger comfort. It was pressurized. The sealed interior cabin air pressure could be increased to allow it to fly higher than any commercial airliner currently in service with SAA. No longer would passengers have to suffer the buffeting and discomfort of flying beneath the clouds. Pressurization made breathable air available inside the cabin at greater heights and also made painful eardrums a thing of the past. Most inclement weather conditions were now well below the aircraft's cruising altitude. When flying at a height of 20,000 feet, the internal air pressure was equivalent to an altitude of only 6,000 feet. The airplane was deemed so luxurious and with such efficient air-conditioning and soundproofing that it was given the suffix 'Gold Plate.'

Colloquially referred to as the 'Connie,' the Constellation L-749A model that was ordered by SAA was the last word in comfort and safety. The latest generation Sperry 'Zero Reader' instrumentation system provided pilots with accurate information for approaches to airports. This was a vast improvement over older navigation aids. The 'Zero Reader' picked up a signal from the destination airport and displayed the aircraft's direction—or 'vector' or 'track'—to the pilot in the form of a needle in a circular glass-covered instrument. If the needle remained centered or 'zeroed,' the pilot was flying what was called the 'center line' directly to the airfield. This was a great help, especially in bad weather when visibility was poor.

Lockheed Constellation

Passengers boarding Lockheed Constellation at Palmietfontein Airport

The Lockheed Constellation L-749A could seat 42 'standard' class or 58 'tourist' class passengers. It had a flight crew of five and could accommodate up to four cabin attendants., although many flights carried only two. It had four Wright Cyclone R3350 BD1 18-cylinder radial engines, each one delivering 2,500 horsepower (1,864 kW) and driving three-blade Hamilton Standard Hydromatic propellers, although these were later changed to three-blade Curtis Wright electric variable pitch airscrews. The power plants gave the aircraft a cruising speed of 327 mph or a top speed of 358 mph. The Constellation had a length of 95.17 ft, a wingspan of 123 ft and a height of 23.66 ft. Its empty weight was 58,970 lbs and fully loaded it weighed 107,000 lbs. Its maximum ceiling was 25,000 feet and it had a range of 1,760 miles when carrying a load of 16,300 lbs or a range of 3,580 miles with a load of 7,800 lbs.

The first of the new Connies, ZS-DBR, was delivered by crew members Captain 'Frikkie' Fry and Captain 'Pi' Pienaar as pilots, with flight engineers Malcolm McKendrick and Otto Stumke. According to the log book of Stumke, the flight departed the Lockheed plant in Burbank on May 2, 1950. Flying from Los Angeles to Idlewild Airport in New York City in 8 hours 15 minutes, the Connie then departed for Gander, Newfoundland on May 4, completing the leg in 4 hours 20 minutes. On May 5, it travelled from Gander across the Atlantic to London in 9 hours 15 minutes. The next sector to Castel Benito in Libya was flown on May 7 in 5 hours 15 minutes and then on the same day to Nairobi, completing that sector in 10 hours 15 minutes. The final leg from Nairobi to Palmietfontein was flown on May 8 in 6 hours 50 minutes. On May 19, 1950, the aircraft was flown to Wingfield Airport, Cape Town where a public christening ceremony took place. Mrs. Maria Malan, wife of Prime Minister Dr. D.F. Malan, watched as a bottle of imported French champagne was popped open, then she said a few words and named the airplane *Cape Town*. That name was painted on one side of the nose while on the other side the Afrikaans equivalent *Kaapstad* was added. As had been the case with all SAA aircraft since the 1930s, the full name of the airline was always painted in bilingual versions on either side of the fuselage. On one side—sometimes the port and sometimes the starboard—the wording 'South African Airways' was emblazoned above the window cheat line. On the other side was the Afrikaans equivalent, 'Suid-Afrikaanse Lugdiens.' Once all four of the Lockheed Constellations had been delivered, they

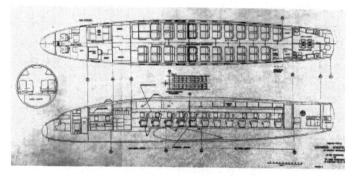

Seating plan of Lockheed Constellation

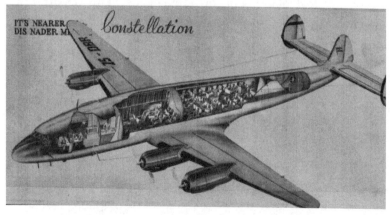

Cutaway view of Lockheed Constellation interior

Interior of all-Tourist Class passenger cabin version of Lockheed
Constellation

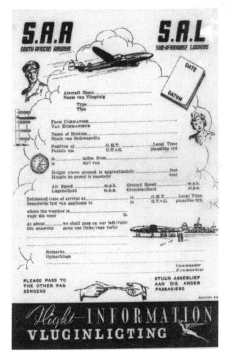

Passenger information sheet passed out from Captain on flight deck
to passengers during the 1950s to point out highlights of the flight
and route. This one was used on the Constellations

were incorporated into the flight schedule on the Springbok Service, commencing on August 26, 1950. The other three Connies were named after the cities of Johannesburg, Durban and Pretoria. In the years to come the four airliners would provide outstanding service to SAA, flying a total of 92,261 passengers 18 million miles.

Fortunately for aviation enthusiasts everywhere, a later version of one of these airliners has been assigned a spot in the static display park of the South African Airways Museum Society at Rand Airport. Lockheed L1649A Starliner, ZS-DVJ, was the final development of the basic Constellation design and first flew on October 11, 1956. Only 44 of the type were built. They were the last piston-engine airliners constructed by Lockheed. Lufthansa was the original operator of this aircraft when it flew with the German registration, D-ALOL. It was delivered to that airline on January 17, 1958, operating Transatlantic flights between Europe and North America. From October 1962 to February 1964, it was leased to World Airways, operating under the registration number N45520. On April 24, 1964, the aircraft was sold to the privately owned South African-based airline Trek Airways (Trek Lugdiens) and reassigned the registration ZS-DVJ. From May to September 1965, ZS-DVJ was leased to SAA to operate its regular services between Johannesburg and Perth. It was also chartered to operate services between Johannesburg and Cape Town during the peak holiday seasons of 1967 and 1968. Sporting basic Trek livery, it also carried the wording South African Airways and Suid-Afrikaanse Lugdiens on opposite sides of the fuselage.

In 1966, ZS-DVJ scored two firsts in South African aviation history. It flew the first non-stop commercial crossing of the South Atlantic by a South African operator when it touched down at Rio de Janeiro shortly after midday on February 15, having left Luanda, Angola at 10.30 p.m. the previous night. On July 5, 1966, it operated the first service from Johannesburg to Tokyo. After flying for Johannesburg-based Safari Travel

Limited, it was leased to low cost international carrier, Luxair, on May 18, 1967, with registration LX-LGX. In June 1968, it was returned to Trek Airways as ZS-DVJ. When Trek Airways moved into the jet age the airline no longer required the services of the Starliners so they were made redundant. ZS-DVJ was retired in April 1969 and stored at Johannesburg. The airliner had a sister ship, ZS-FAB, which was sold to a Germiston scrap metal dealer for R5,000 (South African rand). When the dealer realized that he could not sell it for a profit, it was broken up at Jan Smuts Airport. ZS-DVJ was the lucky one. On July 27, 1971, it was purchased for a puny R2,000 by W.J. Pelser, the owner of a vacation and pleasure resort, Klein Kariba (Little Kariba) outside the city of Warmbaths (modern-day Bela Bela) in the Waterberg Mountains of what was then known as the Transvaal province. On October 9, 1971, the noble old Starliner undertook its last flight. Former Trek Airways pilots Laurie Giani and Piet Retief landed the airplane on a specially prepared dirt air strip at Klein Kariba. As it languished there over the years as a tourist attraction, it was slowly robbed of its dignity as well as various bits and pieces of outer and inner trimmings. But that was not to be its final fate. In May 1979, ZS-DVJ was donated to SAA for the airline's planned future museum. A bevy of engineers and apprentices traveled up to Klein Kariba and dismantled it. The fuselage, engines, wings, undercarriage and other parts were taken by road to Jan Smuts Airport and painstakingly reassembled. Full restoration began in February 1984 and was completed in April 1988. When completed, ZS-DVJ once again wore the elegant livery of Trek Airways and is now a stunning example of what a dedicated group of aviation enthusiasts—all members of the South African Airways Museum Society—can do to restore a neglected and dilapidated old aircraft into something beautiful once again. ZS-DVJ is one of only four of the type that survive anywhere in the world. Many old Constellations and Starliners were sold to smaller airlines but with the arrival of more modern equipment, those regal and graceful ladies of the skies were either demolished under the breaker's hammer or simply allowed to rot or die parked out of sight and out of mind on some remote airfield.

On February 20, 1950, SAA introduced a weekly DC-4 service from Johannesburg to Lydda Airport, Tel Aviv, Israel, flying via Nairobi and Khartoum. It was a short-lived operation, discontinued just over a year later when the faster Constellations were assigned to all the northern routes. The Connies reduced the flying time to London to 28 hours. On November 7, 1950, Rome was included as a port of call on the Springbok Service. When that happened the DC-4 fleet was transferred to domestic and regional flights. In January 1950, a new service from the United States to South Africa began when Pan American Airways started a regular service between New York and Johannesburg, also using Lockheed Constellations. A weekly flight was routed from Idlewild Airport, New York City via Santa Maria island in the Azores to Lisbon, Dakar (Senegal), Monrovia (Liberia), Accra (Ghana) and Leopoldville (Belgian Congo) to Palmietfontein. In November 1950, BOAC replaced its Solent flying-boat service with faster, fully pressurized airliners, the Handley Page Hermes IV.

The introduction of the Hermes brought to an end the use of flying boats on the Springbok Service, a fact bewailed by many. Gone forever was the thrill of landing on the Zambezi River or Lake Victoria or the Nile. Gone were the flocks of pink flamingos taking wing in graceful waves as the flying boat skimmed low over Kenyan waters. Gone were the overnight stays in luxurious houseboats or at exotic hotels and guest houses overlooking waterways or valleys teeming with wildlife. Gone were leisurely after-dinner evenings sipping cocktails over a game of cards while getting to know fellow travelers before turning in for a night under the protective canopy of a mosquito net as the sounds of tropical Africa murmured outside the window.

BOAC Handley Page Hermes IV arriving at Palmietfontein Airport

The Handley Page Hermes IV had four Bristol Hercules 763 radial engines developing 2,100 horsepower (1,566 kW) each. The aircraft had a maximum speed of 350 mph and a cruising speed of 270 mph. With an empty weight of 55,350 lbs and an all-up weight of 86,000 lbs, it had a range of 2,000 miles. Its service ceiling was 24,500 feet. Being pressurized it could fly well above the weather. With a length of 96 ft 10 ins, a wingspan of 113 ft and a height of 30 ft, it could carry between 40 and 80 passengers and had a crew of seven.

The British-made Handley Page Hermes IV was a fine aircraft. It was similar in appearance to the Douglas DC-4 and was a perfect complement to the Constellation on the Springbok Service. Initially, three services a week were operated from London via Tripoli (Libya), Kano (Nigeria), Brazzaville (French Equatorial Africa) and Livingstone (Northern Rhodesia) to Johannesburg. This meant that the Springbok Service was now operating on two distinct routes down Africa, namely the 'West Route' flown by BOAC and the 'East Route' operated by SAA.

On October 15, 1951, SAA experienced its first fatal crash since the end of the war. Douglas DC-3 Dakota ZS-

AVJ *Paardeberg* slammed into high ground near the town of Kokstad in southern Natal province, killing all 17 persons on board. The aircraft crashed near the summit of the mist-covered Ingeli Mountain which is 7,442 feet high. The wreckage was strewn over a wide area. Most of it was charred in the ensuing fire. The DC-3 had left Port Elizabeth's St Albans airfield at 3.00 pm that afternoon and set a course for Stamford Hill Airport in Durban. The scheduled flight would normally have stopped at the coastal city of East London but the runway there was under repair. A Board of Enquiry investigation followed the accident. During the ensuing deliberations, the meteorological officer at Durban Airport stated that his office was under the impression that the aircraft was to fly from Port Elizabeth directly to Durban following the normal coastal route and not inland, as it had done. He admitted that because of this all the weather forecasts issued to the aircraft were for the coastal area only. In addition to this error, the high frequency radio direction-finding equipment at East London was not operating and to exacerbate an already-serious situation, the beacon at the coastal resort town of Port St. Johns along the route was also not working. Furthermore, the board found that the DC-3 crew had failed to maintain a safe altitude above the highest obstacle on the aircraft's flight path. This was a recipe for disaster in poor visibility. The South African Airways Pilots Association (SAALPA) chipped in with their own grievances stating that poor meteorological facilities and inadequate high frequency direction-finding coverage in South Africa together with insufficient navigational equipment fitted on board the Dakota were all contributory factors to the accident. The crash had spillover effects encompassing the overall state of affairs of civil aviation in the entire country. Much criticism of obsolete and inoperative navigational aids and even reports of a lack of staff to maintain the Instrument

Landing System (ILS) at Palmietfontein Airport were dredged up by the press and aviation journals. The result was an overall shake-up and upgrading of all of these systems in the following months.

Meanwhile, as all this was going on in South Africa, something remarkable was taking place in England. The location was the de Havilland Aircraft Company Limited's plant at Hatfield in Hertfordshire, a place deeply rooted in British aviation history. Under the leadership of the company's founder, Geoffrey de Havilland, a prototype jet fighter, the Vampire, had taken to the air from there as far back as September 20, 1943. A year later it had reached a speed of 500 mph using an engine also made by de Havilland. However, the Germans had beaten the British in the race to get jet fighters into the air during WWII with the Messerschmitt ME262—the type encountered by Captain 'Pi' Pienaar over the Alps in 1944—but the Vampire gave the de Havilland company an enormous edge in the science of developing future commercial passenger jet aircraft. de Havilland was a company with an impeccable track record, reaching back to September 1920 when it was first formed. During the war years it produced the inimitable Mosquito bomber and reconnaissance aircraft, the type flown by 'Pi' Pienaar during his historic encounter with the ME262.

Even though WWII would drag on for almost another three years, as early as December 1942 the British War Office and the RAF believed that the tide against the Nazis was slowly turning in the Allies' favor so, under the direction of Prime Minister Winston Churchill, a special committee was set up to try to foresee the nature and needs of commercial air travel once the war ended. Their aim was to plan for that eventuality so that British aviation would not be lagging when peacetime returned. The chairman of the committee was Lord Tara of Brabazon, a respected member of many previous British military and civilian air commissions. The committee named itself after him. It was primarily because of suggestions by the Brabazon Committee that airliners such as the Avro York, Vickers Viking and Short Solent came into being. They were all based on military aircraft and made extensive use of existing production plants, components and tools left over from the war. Geoffrey de Havilland was one of the members of the Brabazon Committee. Man of vision that he was, he firmly focused on where Britain's commercial aviation potential might lie. Backed by the talents of his chief designer Ronald Eric Bishop and his brilliant engine designer Major Frank Halford, he implicitly believed in the future of the jet-powered airliner. And so it was that, under great secrecy, the de Havilland company hatched plans to build such a machine, code-named the DH.106.

When the company finally announced its intentions to the world, BOAC immediately placed an order for eight of the DH.106s. Production began at Hatfield in 1947. As development progressed and in accordance with tradition the DH.106 was eventually given a name: the Comet. It would be a sleek, fully pressurized, all-metal, jet-powered aircraft that would fly at a speed of between 400 and 500 mph. There was no question in anyone's mind that it would revolutionize air travel. And it would be way ahead of anything on the production lines of the great American airplane manufacturers on the other side of the Atlantic at that time. The Comet would be a much-needed feather in the cap of a sagging and depressed British aviation industry that was struggling to recover in the post-war years. The first Comet was powered by four of de Havilland's own Ghost 50 gas turbine engines. With a thrust of only 5,000 lbs. (22 kN) at 10,250 rpm each, the Ghosts were considerably underpowered and the aircraft barely met the speed, payload and range required by BOAC and the many other airlines that were clamoring to place orders for it. But that wasn't deterring anyone. Excitement about the jetliner was rife. In any case, Rolls Royce was working on a more powerful engine, the Avon, that would eventually replace the Ghost engines. But it would not be ready in time for the prototype or the first production models of the Comet to come off the assembly line. To accommodate the shortfalls of the Ghost engine, de Havilland resorted to lightening the weight of the Comet by using thinner gauge aluminum metals and by developing a new technique for sheet metal bonding. This did away with the need for many rivets on the airframe. Fewer rivets had two advantages: the aircraft was not only lighter but its smoother skin was aerodynamically better, giving it greater speed by lessening drag and also reducing fuel burn. The prototype of the Comet flew on July 27, 1949. And it exceeded expectations in every way.

Even its aesthetics were beyond comparison. Never in the annals of aviation was there a more beautiful aircraft. The engines were 'buried' in the root of the swept-back wings, close to the fuselage. Other than the subtly visible elongated air intakes imbedded in the leading edge of the wing, there was no sign that the engines even existed. The Comet was a thing of unrivalled beauty. It was clean, uncluttered, elegant. When airborne, it gave the appearance of a sculpted silver swallow in flight. Its swept-back wings made it look swift and serene. It is perhaps no exaggeration to say that it was breathtaking to behold, an embodiment of poetry in engineering. In 1951, BOAC took delivery of its first aircraft, the Mk. 1 version. Although the fuselage and many components of the wings continued to be made of lighter materials employing the same manufacturing techniques used for the prototype, later production models would be equipped with the more powerful Rolls Royce Avon engines, giving the airplane even better performance.

The passenger cabin of the DH.106 Comet Mk. 1 and Mk. 1A embodied the latest in luxurious appointments and amenities. Seats had finger-touch adjustments for selecting reclining angles. Every row—two seats on either side of a 17-inch wide aisle—had a large square picture window, allowing for unimpeded vision.

The D.H.106 Comet Mk.1 and Mk.1A had a wingspan of 115 ft, a length of 93 ft and a height of 28.3 ft. The Mk.1 had a maximum weight of 105,000 lbs and the Mk.1A 115,000 lbs. Equipped with four de Havilland Ghost single stage centrifugal flow gas turbine engines fueled by kerosene, both variants had a cruising speed of 450 mph. The Mk.1 had a ceiling of 35,000 feet and the Mk.1A 40,000 feet. With a full payload the Mk.1 had a maximum range of 1,500 miles while the Mk.1A could fly 1,770 miles. The Mk.1 could carry 36 passengers and the Mk.1A 44. Both models carried a crew of five.

In the forward section of the fuselage was a private area that had two rows of seats facing each other with a fold-away table in-between. It was the perfect spot for a sit-down dinner with a white tablecloth and place settings for eight passengers. Two separate 'dressing rooms' with toilets in the rear of the cabin — one for gents and one for ladies — had hot and cold running water. A large hat and coat closet or 'wardrobe' and a deep overhead luggage rack swallowed up passengers' accessories and carry-ons. A very adequate galley allowed cabin crew to prepare and serve hot meals and mix chilled drinks. There was nothing else in the sky like this revolutionary new airplane. Reporters who flew on demonstration flights could not stop talking about the smoothness of the ride and the fact that the cabin was completely free of vibration. On the outside, however, the Comet was a noisy machine. The extremely high-pitched whine of the jets and the thunderous roar of their exhausts could be heard for miles around, but the sleek new airliner sailed through the sky at close to the speed of sound and at twice the height of any aircraft before it.

Fully loaded the Comet did not yet have the range to

accomplish a non-stop crossing of the Atlantic so, until the Rolls Royce Avon engines and extra fuel tanks became available, BOAC committed to using their rapid new airplanes on the Springbok Service between London and Johannesburg. Because BOAC was in pool partnership with SAA, an agreement was reached between the two airlines whereby SAA would lease two of the Comets from BOAC. In addition, all Comet flights operated by both airlines would have interchangeable flight crews. This decision would put SAA alongside BOAC in the forefront of international commercial air travel. But before that could come about extensive crew training had to be carried out at the de Havilland works in England. So, behind closed doors at SAR & H headquarters flight crews were selected and detailed plans were drawn up for converting pilots, flight engineers, radio operators, navigators, ground engineers and mechanics from piston engine aircraft to the brave new world of the jet.

Pre-production BOAC de Havilland DH.106 Comet 1 G-ALZK arrives at Palmietfontein Airport, Johannesburg, on July 18, 1951, after its route-proving flight from London. It would spend a week here undergoing trials and tests before returning to the UK.

Pre-production BOAC de Havilland DH. 106 Comet 1 at
Palmietfontein. Note single wheel on each main undercarriage strut.
Production models of the aircraft would have a four-wheel bogie on
each main strut.

The beautifully sleek and clean lines of the Comet. The Rolls Royce
jet engines are subtly concealed within the wings close to the
fuselage

On July 17, 1951, the second prototype Comet, registered G-ALZK,
painted in full BOAC livery, took off from London Airport for a
route-proving flight to South Africa. In command were Captains
A. M. Majendie and R. Alabaster who took it in turns to occupy
the left seat of the cockpit—the captain's seat—during the flight.
Flying via Cairo and Entebbe G-ALZK landed at Palmietfontein
at 1.03 pm on July 18 after covering the 6,212-mile distance in
17 hours 33 minutes, with an actual flying time of only 14 hours

22 minutes. It was an astonishing record. After spending a week in Johannesburg where it undertook a series of touch-and-go take-offs and landings at Palmietfontein, the Comet returned to Britain by way of Lusaka, Livingstone, Entebbe, Khartoum and Cairo, landing at London Airport on July 29. Satisfied that all the African airports could safely handle its new jet, BOAC began planning for the Springbok Service once it began receiving its first production aircraft. In the meantime, in an effort to make the Comet one of the safest airliners ever built, the de Havilland Aircraft Company continued with the most exhaustive testing program that any commercial airliner had ever been subjected to.

By 1952, most domestic airports within South Africa had been overhauled and upgraded. On June 8, 1951, Captain K.S. Hayward had landed the first DC-4 Skymaster carrying 35 passengers and six crew members at the new airport in Reunion, south of Durban. In December 1951, it was officially opened and named Louis Botha Airport, after the first Prime Minister of the Union of South Africa. And that great stretch of land outside Kempton Park with its still-incomplete hangars and buildings where earth-moving equipment had rumbled for years was now cleared of trees, rocks and brush and ready to receive its first aircraft. While little else was finished the runways were good to go so all was ready for the first landing to take place at Jan Smuts Airport.

Everyone—government members, the Department of Transport, executives from the South African Railways and Harbors administration, SAA officials, Johannesburg city council members, Kempton Park municipality members, Pretoria city councillors, the state-run South African Broadcasting Corporation (SABC), the press and the public—threw their full weight into celebrating the event. After all, this was no ordinary airport. When complete it would be the most modern in all Africa and perhaps even in the entire southern hemisphere. It would have every navigational aid available. It would have long-distance radio equipment capable of voice communications with SAA aircraft anywhere on earth. It would have temperature-controlled, dust-free workshops for maintaining, repairing and overhauling complex aircraft parts thousands of miles from where they had originally been manufactured. The airport's price tag had soared to more than £6.2 million and it was still climbing. But it would have every bell and whistle essential to maintaining and servicing an ever-growing African aviation industry. What really distinguished it was the fact that because it was located at an altitude of 6,000 feet above sea level and because summer temperatures could often exceed 84ºF (29ºC) it had the longest non-military runway in the world, all 10,500 feet of it. If needed, in future years the runway could be extended even further.

On the sunny autumn morning of April 17, 1952, the South African flag was raised on a mast situated at the perimeter of the concrete apron outside the airport's new technical area and half-built hangars. School children were bussed in from nearby Kempton Park, a military brass band took its place near the flag, a set of mobile passenger stairs was wheeled onto the apron, photographers and newsreel cameramen took their places, a crowd of 200 poured into a large roped-off public viewing area and everyone waited and searched the skies. Then, silhouetted against the sun at 11.00 a.m., a Douglas DC-4 Skymaster droned high overhead. The brass band struck up playing a series of military marches while the crowds and schoolchildren started cheering as the aircraft began circling above. At precisely 11.37 a.m., the DC-4 descended from the sky and gently touched down on runway 03L/21R. It was the first time that an aircraft's rubber tires had met the clean asphalt surface of the runway. And so SAA Douglas DC-4 Skymaster ZS-AUA *Tafelberg* teased the crowds by slowly taxiing towards the concrete apron where everyone enthusiastically awaited it. As it approached an airport marshaller in neatly starched crème-colored overalls snappily strode onto the apron and shot a green flare into the air as a sign of welcome. Then, waving his orange-colored 'wands' he flagged the airplane to a halt. The engines were turned off and the four propellers slowly spun down. At the controls of the Skymaster was veteran SAA pilot Captain Piet Nel, the man who had been Prime Minister Jan Christiaan Smuts' personal pilot throughout the war years.

Douglas DC-4 ZS-AUA *Tafelberg* prepares for take-off from Palmietfontein for the short flight to the new Jan Smuts Airport. The aircraft has not yet been embellished with the new version of the Flying Springbok emblem

Tafelberg and its load of VIPs after arrival at Jan Smuts Airport, April 17, 1952. The occasion marked the first flight to land at the new airport, initiating Jan Smuts as South Africa's premiere international airport and the future home base of SAA. The photograph was taken at a small apron adjoining the new technical area, hangars and workshops, not visible here

Tafelberg had taken off from Palmietfontein Airport at 10.27 a.m. that morning and had flown a triangular course over the Vaal Dam, the little town of Parys on the banks of the Vaal River and the Hartebeespoort Dam to the west of the capital city of Pretoria before heading towards the airport. A number of VIPs were included in the 45 passengers on board. Among them were Mr. Paul Oliver Sauer, Minister of Transport, General C.J. Venter, Chief Manager of SAA, and the mayors and mayoresses of Johannesburg, Pretoria and Kempton Park. As the mobile stairs were wheeled over and nudged up against the highly polished fuselage of the stationary aircraft, the front passenger door opened and the Minister of Transport, wearing a light grey suit, stepped onto the upper platform of the staircase. Grinning from ear to ear, he waved his hat at the crowd. A roar went up from everyone and the brass band played ever louder. It was an historic moment. The VIPs alighted, taking their seats in a row of chairs that had been positioned near the flag at the edge of the apron. A small highly polished teak desk had been erected in front of them. The Minister of Transport stood behind it and delivered a short speech declaring Jan Smuts Airport unofficially open but, he emphasized, the actual official opening would take place in September the following year after international flights had begun and once the new Comet jet was operating the Springbok Service between South Africa and Britain. With that the band heartily struck up with the country's two national anthems, first *God Save the Queen* in English and then *Die Stem (The Voice)* in Afrikaans.

Fifteen days later, on May 2, 1952, international aviation history was made when a bevy of press photographers and newsreel cameramen converged on London Airport under an overcast spring sky to photograph BOAC's first production Comet, G-ALYP, prepare for take-off for Johannesburg.

A unique moment in aviation history. BOAC de Havilland DH. 106 Comet 1, G-ALYP, departs London Airport for Johannesburg, initiating the world's first pure jet passenger service. May 2, 1952

This was the world's very first fare-paying passenger jet flight, a fact about to be lauded in the international press. Passengers had paid £175 for a one-way ticket to Johannesburg and £315 for a round trip. Under the watchful eyes of Sir Geoffrey de Havilland, his chief designer Ronald Eric Bishop, engine designer Frank Halford, members of BOAC's senior management, representatives from the Foreign Office and other dignitaries standing on the apron outside the terminal building, Captain A. M. Majendie taxied the sleek, gleaming aircraft out to runway number five. The Comet's four Ghost engines emitted an ear-splitting shrill that completely drowned out the sound of every propeller-driven airplane in sight. On board was a full load of 36 passengers. Majendie and his flight crew plus a steward and stewardess in the main cabin would take the Comet to Rome and then Beirut, where a 'slip-crew' would take over for the leg to Khartoum and then another 'slip-crew' would fly the machine to Entebbe, Livingstone and on to Johannesburg. At precisely

3.00 pm, Majendie thrust the throttles forward and the Comet took to the air with a deafening roar, beginning its 23 hour 38 minute journey to Johannesburg. As it thundered into the low clouds and disappeared from view one undeniable fact was on everyone's minds—the world of aviation would never be the same again. Jet travel would change everything.

But no one could foresee the catastrophic events that lay ahead.

Chapter 7

A Sound Like Thunder

When the world's first passenger-carrying BOAC de Havilland Comet jet aircraft touched down at Palmietfontein airport near Johannesburg at 3.35 p.m. on Saturday, May 3, 1952, an entirely new chapter in the long story of international transportation was opened. Covering the distance of 6,724 miles from London at a height of seven miles above the surface of the earth at the incredible speed of eight miles a minute, this was the flight that catapulted commercial aviation to an all-new level. People from every walk of life gasped at what the Comet had accomplished. It had shrunk the planet in half. It had compressed the very meaning of time itself. The gas turbine engine would affect the travel industry, commerce and communications in unimaginable ways. Speed was the essence of the jet, and speed would change the way the world went about its business. On the Comet's trip out to South Africa, the Chairman of BOAC, Sir Miles Thomas, joined the flight at Livingstone in Northern Rhodesia. Exuding pride, he was the first to step off the aircraft when it landed in Johannesburg. Surrounded by journalists and reporters, he proudly announced that the new British airliner was bound to bring about a new epoch in air travel. The sense of excitement and an anticipation of things to come were overwhelmingly palpable.

The return Comet flight from South Africa to Britain took off on May 5, 1952, arriving in London the next day. Although the inbound flight from London had landed at Palmietfontein the outbound flight had to take off from the still-incomplete Jan Smuts Airport. Because of the airfield's high altitude the 6,000 feet runway at Palmietfontein was just too short for a loaded, fully-fueled Comet to become airborne so, after being cleaned and serviced at Palmietfontein, the empty aircraft was flown on a short 'positioning' flight to Jan Smuts where it awaited its passengers and their baggage plus 30 bags of mail that it would carry to London. Passengers checked in for their flight at Palmietfontein where they cleared immigration and customs. Then, accompanied by an immigration official, they boarded two luxury coaches and the doors were locked before the vehicles drove off for Jan Smuts Airport, about an hour away. As the passengers were now officially cleared for departure they were tantamount to being in a state of 'no-man's land' and were not allowed to alight from the buses until they arrived at Jan Smuts. Because the terminal buildings there were still unfinished, the coaches drove right up to the awaiting Comet, the doors were unlocked, and the passengers directly boarded the aircraft. Once the jet had been refueled and all baggage, freight and mailbags stowed in the hold, the Comet took off using most of Jan Smuts Airport's longest runway. Captain Robert Clifford Alabaster was in command. The awkward arrangement of using two airfields for Comet flights continued for almost a year until Jan Smuts Airport came into full operation on September 1, 1953. Less than a month later, accompanied by much pomp and fanfare, the bigger airport was officially opened by the Minister of Transport, Paul Oliver Sauer.

Flight Engineer Don Smith recalls the event. "I vividly remember the opening ceremony. All four of our Lockheed Constellations were lined up on the tarmac outside the terminal building, each of them with their propellers at exactly the same angle. The aeroplanes looked very beautiful, almost like soldiers neatly smartened up and waiting in line for inspection. The pilots and we flight engineers were aboard at our respective stations. It was a bit nerve-wracking because our job was to start our engines in all four aeroplanes at exactly the same time after the official speeches had been made. Eventually we got a signal to start our number three engine. All four Connies had to turn over at precisely the same moment. I was terrified that my engine wouldn't start but there were no problems. Everything worked out fine. All four of the aircrafts' number three engines turned over at precisely the same time. Then we started the rest of our engines, numbers one, two and four, and then all the Connies taxied out and took off, one after the other. We got into formation and flew over the airport to conclude the opening ceremonies. It was a marvellous and truly exciting day. I'll never forget it. But I wish I could have been on the ground to hear those sixteen engines roaring overhead."

Two of the all-metal hangars at Palmietfontein had been dismantled and reassembled alongside the other new hangars at Jan Smuts. After the transition to the new airport all flights—domestic, regional and international, whether flown by SAA or by any foreign carrier—plus all of SAA's technical services, maintenance and flight operations were transferred from Palmietfontein to Jan Smuts, leaving Palmietfontein an abandoned and deserted place until it was converted into a motor racing circuit for the 1956 Rand Grand Prix. After that it fell victim to the government's iniquitous Group Areas Act which kept the races apart and was given over to the construction of Thokoza African Township. This was an area set aside for black residents as prescribed by apartheid laws. However, a hint of Palmietfontein Airport still lingers even now. Although covered with houses, shops and buildings, the outline of the main runway is still faintly visible from the air.

In April 1953, the control and ownership of all of South Africa's main airports were transferred from the South African Railways and Harbors Administration (SAR & H) to the Department of Transport. This did away with SAA's responsibility for running the airports from which it had operated. Now, with the opening of Jan Smuts, it had a brand new, state-of-the-art home. At this time, Constellation flights on the Springbok Service to London included Frankfurt and Athens as stopovers. In addition, a sales office had been opened on the prestigious Via Barberini in Rome. BOAC Comet flights on the Springbok Service were proving to be extremely popular and Cairo had now been substituted as a stopover in place of Beirut. In September 1952, the first scheduled flight from Sydney, Australia had arrived in South Africa. Operated by Qantas Empire Airways, the Lockheed Super Constellation VH-EAD *Charles Kingsford Smith* had flown to Johannesburg by way of Australia's west coast city of Perth and then via the Cocos Islands and Mauritius in the Indian Ocean, taking three days to complete the flight. The service was dubbed the *Wallaby Route.*

But it was the Comet that was all the rage at that time. Following her glittering coronation at Westminster Abbey in London on June 2, 1953, Queen Elizabeth II together with Queen Elizabeth the Queen Mother and Princess Margaret were treated to a flight aboard the Comet in the skies above the United Kingdom on June 30, hosted by the head of the de Havilland Aircraft Company, Sir Geoffrey de Havilland and his wife Lady de Havilland.

1953 was also the year when administrators at the Department of Transport in South Africa had to decide who among SAA's personnel would be sent to Britain for training on the Comets that had been leased for SAA from BOAC. Delivery was about to be taken of the airliners and SAA aircrews and ground staff had to be fully acquainted with all aspects of the machine before it could enter regular service. Initially, thirteen pilots and flight engineers were sent to Hatfield in England, later followed by additional groups of pilots, navigators and ground staff. One of them was Flight Engineer Don Smith who remembers the experience. "We had to undergo a very long and difficult course. The flight engineers spent most of their time at Hatfield. de Havilland expected us to know every single bolt, nook, cranny, switch and circuit breaker on the aeroplane and the British Air Registration Board was very strict with us. Some of us found it difficult at times because the Afrikaners among us felt that BOAC wasn't too keen on South African *plaasjapies* (farm boys) flying their wonderful new jet. But it was all in a good spirit of fun and everybody got along fine. We were using the Brits' aeroplanes and that was quite a responsibility. We did a great deal of classroom work first and then the actual training which was initially done in a flight simulator. It was one of the very first flight simulators ever made and was actually quite primitive. After that we did the rest of our training on the actual aeroplane. Once we passed our written and verbal exams we flew along with BOAC crews on actual scheduled flights. I did my first supernumerary flight to Bahrain. After that we did a few short flights from London to Rome and back. It was a tremendous challenge for us because the time taken between places was half the duration taken by the Constellations. It was a real eye-opener and very exciting but, I must admit, at first a little nerve-wracking. We were always in awe of that mighty new beast, the Comet, and we certainly deserved to be. It was an amazing aircraft."

Captain Bert Rademan, one of the longest-serving pilots with the airline, recalled that the training period on the Comet with the de Havilland company constituted some of the happiest moments in his entire career. Pilots were especially intrigued with the jet. Because of its speed its handling characteristics were different to anything previously flown by them. Aircrews had to think fast. Decisions had to be made quickly. They needed to be acutely aware of what was going on at all times and had to train to be sharply attuned to the nuances and behavior of the jet. After all, everything was now happening more than twice as fast as it did on propeller-driven aircraft. But, without exception, the pilots loved the Comet.

On October 4, 1953, a brand new Comet jetliner registered G-ANAV stood on the apron outside the main terminal building at London Airport. Emblazoned in the livery of BOAC, it also carried a Flying Springbok logo and the wording 'South African

Airways' on one side of the forward fuselage and 'Suid-Afrikaanse Lugdiens' on the other side. On its tail a Flying Springbok logo and a South African flag appeared below BOAC's 'Speedbird' emblem and the aircraft's registration number. Other than the fact that the aircraft was leased from BOAC and carried a British registration number to all other intents and purposes it was entirely an SAA flight.

de Havilland DH.106 Comet 1 jetliner in BOAC and SAA livery in flight, 1953

SAA's Flying Springbok emblem proudly displayed on the nose of the Comet

This was SAA's first scheduled Comet flight, making the airline the second in the world to offer a jet passenger service. It was an accomplishment to be proud of. Here was a relatively small airline that had its base at the bottom end of the African continent offering a pure jet international service that was, apart from BOAC, way ahead of any other operators in the world. In command of G-ANAV was Captain Dennis Raubenheimer. He would be responsible for the first sector of the flight and Captain Jan Marthinus 'Boet' Botes would be in command of the final leg into Jan Smuts Airport, Johannesburg. The other Comet that had been chartered from BOAC was registered G-ALYY. It too proudly carried the SAA logo and identity on its brightly painted, smooth-skinned fuselage and soon entered the Springbok Service. Each of the jets carried forty 'standard class' passengers—tantamount to today's Business Class—in four-abreast seating.

According to the logbooks of many SAA aircrew, all the Comets in the BOAC fleet were also operated by SAA pilots who took it in turns with their BOAC counterparts to fly one another's airplanes and to participate in 'crew-slipping' along the route. SAA Comets departed from Johannesburg at 10:00 am on Tuesdays and Fridays. The routing was from Johannesburg to Livingstone, Entebbe, Khartoum, Cairo, Rome and London. Return flights departed London at 2:45 p.m. on Sundays and Wednesdays.

In addition to the jets, three tourist-class Lockheed Constellation flights per week were also maintained on the overseas network, serving destinations in Israel and Europe as well as London. Because of the strong German ties that existed with the large German community in South-West Africa, as from Wednesday October 7, 1953, one SAA Constellation flight per week was operated via Windhoek. The flight routed through Frankfurt to London. The Constellations were configured to carry 58 five-abreast passengers. Because of the world's enthusiasm to embrace the jet, it wasn't long before BOAC and SAA were no longer the only operators of the radically new aircraft. Air France and the independent French airline Union

Aeromaritime de Transport (UAT) were next to introduce the Comet. On November 4, 1953, UAT began a fortnightly Comet service from Paris to Johannesburg, with stops at Tripoli (Libya), Kano (Nigeria) and Brazzaville (French Equatorial Africa).

Many foreign carriers were eager to buy the Comet but some perceived it as having too short a range, as well as being too limited in passenger-carrying capacity. de Havilland were hard at work at the drawing board designing a slightly larger version of the aircraft which would be equipped with the more powerful Rolls Royce Avon engines. An even more sophisticated version, the Comet 3, was also in the design stage. Orders for these aircraft—still unbuilt but solidly founded on the excellent reputation and operational record of the Mk 1 and 1A versions—were ordered by Air India, Japan Airlines, British Commonwealth Pacific Airlines, Linea Aeropostal Venezolana and Panair do Brasil. In the United States, Pan American, National and Capital ordered the longer-range Comet 3 for their transatlantic services. Also waiting in the wings for the bigger aircraft was Qantas Empire Airways who were anxious to use the jet for flights linking London with Sydney, Melbourne and Canberra. In the meantime, BOAC's fleet of Comet 1s were now flying on other routes from London as well as to South Africa, revolutionizing air travel to places as far afield as India, Ceylon and Japan. The Comet had made its mark and all was going well. Its future looked promising indeed.

Until the evening of January 10, 1954.

On that date, BOAC Comet G-ALYP—the first production aircraft to come off the assembly line—was operating the final leg of Flight BA 781 from Singapore to London. Twenty minutes after taking off from Rome's Ciampino Airport following a refuelling stop the jet was climbing to its cruising altitude over the Mediterranean when, at 10.51 p.m. GMT, it suddenly disintegrated in mid-air and plunged into the sea near the Italian island of Elba. All 35 persons on board died. There were no witnesses. The only report came from an elderly fisherman repairing nets in his cottage on the island of Elba who said he had heard "something far away that sounded like a clap of loud thunder in the sky."

All Comet flights were immediately voluntarily grounded by BOAC and SAA. The de Havilland factory and its team of engineers were at a complete loss as to what had happened. Even sabotage was suspected but no proof could be found of foul play. Besides, who would do such a thing? What motives could they have had? Recommendations were made for 60 minor modifications to the Comet's airframe and flying surfaces, just in case something mechanical was at fault. Meanwhile, the Royal Navy began to search for pieces of wreckage. The search would go on until September 1954, by which time most of the wings, fuselage and engines were retrieved and sent to the de Havilland factory for study. But long before then, on March 23, 1954, the Comets were reintroduced to passenger service.

On April 8, 1954, SAA Comet G-ALYY was operating flight SA 201 from London to Johannesburg with 14 passengers and seven crew members on board. Flight Engineer Don Smith was stationed at Entebbe, Uganda, awaiting its arrival on the leg from Cairo and Khartoum. Together with Captain Frank Edward Wood, he was part of the 'slip crew' that was to take over the flight for the final sector to Livingstone and Johannesburg. The flight was due to arrive early in the morning but, for whatever reason, it was overdue. Captain Wood checked with the Entebbe control tower but all they could learn was that the flight had taken off from Rome's Ciampino Airport on time and had set a normal course for Cairo. Then, without warning, all radio communications with it had ceased. A few hours later the full story of what had happened came through. The Comet had taken off from Rome and was climbing to its cruising altitude when it suddenly exploded, cascading into the sea near Naples. Engineer Don Smith emotionally recalled the events. "I was on the crew that was waiting for that Comet at Entebbe. We were ready to take over for the final sector to Johannesburg when the terrible news came through that 'Yoke Yoke' had suffered a similar fate to 'Yoke Peter' three months earlier."

Air crew always referred to aircraft by quoting the last two letters of its registration number, thus G-ALYP was called 'Yoke Peter' and G-ALYY was 'Yoke Yoke.'

Smith continued with his memories. "It was a terrible blow to all of us. Every one of us knew the crew members on board Yoke Yoke and in one way or another the disaster touched us all on a very personal level. I had actually been rostered to serve on that sector of Flight 201 out of Rome but my good friend Steve Lagesen had asked me to swap with him because he wanted to put in some extra time to build up his hours so that he could take some leave to go away with his wife for a few days. Of course, I said yes. And look what happened. My life was spared. His was not."

Fate played a hand with some of the other members of the crew too. Captain Bert Rademan was supposed to have been on the flight deck on that sector but his colleague and friend Captain Wilhelm Karel 'Mossie' Mostert asked him to switch because he wanted to attend a family get-together and the change in the roster would suit his plans. Rademan agreed. And lived. Mostert perished. Other crew members killed were First Officer B.J. Grove, Navigator Albert E. Sissing, Radio Officer B.E. Webbstock, Senior Flight Steward J.B. Kok and Air Hostess Pam L. Reitz. The catastrophe even touched the lives of people in the little town of Kempton Park next to Jan Smuts airport. Many SAA crew members and cabin staff lived there. As it was a small-knit community they were known to local shopkeepers and traders. Some stores draped their display windows in black cloth surrounding photographs of the SAA crew members and cabin staff who had died. The town was in mourning and flags at schools and on government and municipal buildings flew at half mast for a week.

The entire Comet fleet was immediately grounded once again. An investigation board was formed under the auspices of the Royal Aircraft Establishment at Farnborough in England. British Prime Minister Winston Churchill instructed the Royal Navy to do whatever they could to retrieve wreckage from the crash. Before the Comets could fly again the causes of the two accidents had to be determined. Clearly, they had something in common. There had to be some kind of telltale sign buried somewhere in the wreckage. Those were long before the days of 'black box' flight recorders so the only hint at what might have happened would have been in actual steel and metal fragments. But what to look for? How would the cause even be recognized? For months the Royal Navy dredged the waters around Naples where G-ALYY had come down but little of the aircraft was ever found. The water around Naples was too deep. However, more pieces of G-ALYP—the previous aircraft that crashed—were found on the sea bed near Elba. Careful inspection revealed that the aircraft may have suffered a catastrophic break-up due to what is known as 'metal fatigue.' It looked like the aircraft had literally torn itself apart. But why?

All Comets had now been fully withdrawn from service and grounded. With little delay, one of the most intensive accident investigations in history got underway. As metal fatigue was now the most suspected culprit of the disasters, BOAC's Comet G-ALYU was pulled from the grounded fleet and entirely immersed in a specially-built giant water tank that could accommodate the length of the fuselage at the Royal Aircraft Establishment's research center at Farnborough. The purpose was to test the integrity of the fuselage or 'hull' during repeated pressurization and depressurization cycles to replicate events that actually occurred when the aircraft was in use.

It is almost impossible to conceive of the tremendous strains exerted on the metal structure of an airframe when internal atmospheric pressure is repeatedly increased and decreased during flight operations. It is like a balloon being continually blown up and then deflated. But an aircraft's skin is not made of rubber or plastic or nylon. Being made of steel it is not that pliable. Yet, that steel is stressed and stretched, sometimes up to a dozen or more times per day. Is this what caused the airplane to tear apart? Was the lighter gauge steel used to reduce the weight of the Comet at fault? Or did the reduction of rivets weaken the hull? Finally, on June 24, 1954, the answer came. After 3,057 'flight cycles'—equal to repeated pressurization of the cabin after take-off and then depressurization before landing—the fuselage of G-ALYU that was submerged in the water tank at Farnborough blew itself open. On close examination it was found that an explosion had occurred at one of the cabin windows. It wasn't the glass or Perspex of the window itself that failed but the metal join at the corner. What gave passengers on board the spectacular views that they enjoyed was also a lethal design error. One of the sharp-edged corners of the big square-shaped windows suffered fatigue, resulting in a tiny crack that became a tear that quickly spread to the surrounding sheet metal and ripped open the fuselage, somewhat like a tin can exploding under extreme pressure. The square design was a major flaw. The corners could not withstand the pressurization process and made the windows the weakest spots on the airframe.

The result of this dramatic finding was that never again would a sharp-edged corner on a window design ever appear on a pressurized airliner. Rounded corners, yes. But sharp corners, absolutely not. A valuable lesson had been learnt. The findings were made known to every single aircraft manufacturer the world over. Many lives had been lost but, because of the discovery, a great many future lives would be saved. Companies who took special note of the findings were American manufacturers Convair, Lockheed, Boeing and Douglas, all of whom had been watching de Havilland with eagle eyes since the introduction of the Comet and were now working on designing jetliners of their own.

SAA's brief romance with the beautiful de Havilland Comet came to an abrupt and permanent end. Needless to say, the de Havilland Aircraft Company remedied the design flaw in all future incarnations of the Comet and, beginning in 1958, 77 aircraft of the Mk 4 series would provide decades of incident-free service flying with dozens of the world's major international airlines. As for SAA, following the disasters over the Mediterranean, the airline had to come up with an immediate plan to allow it to continue providing services to Europe. Once again the Lockheed Constellations were called in to maintain the Springbok Service while BOAC resorted to replacing their Comets with Canadair DC-4M North Star aircraft that BOAC called the Argonaut. Very similar to the American-built Douglas DC-4 in many ways, the Argonaut was built in Canada and was equipped with Rolls-Royce Merlin engines. Neither the Constellations nor the Argonauts were jets and they certainly didn't embody the prestige and charisma of the Comet but at least the Springbok Service between London and Johannesburg continued uninterrupted, albeit at a considerably slower speed once more. But the travelling public was unfazed. Flights remained full. Business was as good as ever. As for the French carrier, UAT, their weekly Paris to Johannesburg Comet service was replaced by a Douglas DC-6.

From July 1954, SAA operated an all-tourist class Constellation flight departing from Johannesburg every Tuesday at 7.00 a.m. for Livingstone, Nairobi, Khartoum, Cairo, Athens, Rome and London, arriving at Heathrow Airport at 3.30 p.m. on Wednesday. Another Connie was also all-tourist class, departing Johannesburg every Wednesday at 07.00 a.m. for Livingstone, Nairobi, Khartoum, Cairo, Athens, Rome, Frankfurt and London, arriving at Heathrow on Thursday at 5.30 p.m. A third flight was configured as a purely first class service, departing Johannesburg every Friday at 10.00 a.m. for Nairobi, Khartoum, Cairo, Rome and London, arriving at Heathrow at 3.00 p.m. on Saturday. A fourth flight, also tourist class, departed Johannesburg every Saturday at 07.00 a.m. bound for Lusaka, Nairobi, Khartoum, Cairo, Athens, Rome and London, arriving on Sunday at 3.10 p.m. Return flights departed London on the day after their arrival.

However, contrary to what many pundits thought, the era of the jets was by no means over. The lessons of the Comet had been carefully monitored by airplane manufacturers in the United States. They had not merely sat back and watched the Comet saga unfold. They had gleaned invaluable information about jet aircraft design and operation by observing every facet of the de Havilland DH.106 Comet 1's birth, short lifespan and demise. Now, as they saw things, it would be the turn of the United States to take up the task of reintroducing mass travel by jet-powered airplanes to an eagerly awaiting public and much wider world. In factories in Los Angeles, San Diego and Seattle, exciting things were already underway as new incarnations of the commercial passenger jet began to take shape.

Chapter 8

Last of the Propliners

The Comet tragedies were a bitter blow, not only to SAA but to all the operators of the jet, especially SAA's long-time pool partner, BOAC. But in the aviation and travel industries nothing can be allowed to thwart the smooth continuity of operations that move people, mail and packages around the planet. Echoing the perennial motto of those in the entertainment industry, 'the show must go on.' So it did. SAA wasted no time and switched back to the exclusive use of Lockheed Constellations on the Springbok Service. BOAC began using Canadian-built Argonaut DC-4M aircraft. These piston-engine airplanes certainly saved the day by ensuring that the Springbok Service remained uninterrupted but, in many ways, it was a step backwards. The flying time from Johannesburg to London was increased once again. After all, in the case of SAA, the Constellations flew at half the speed of the jets. There was only one option. Once again it was time to re-equip. It was time to go shopping.

This time SAA went back to the Douglas Aircraft Company in Santa Monica, California. The company had recently come out with a suave, slick, completely reinvented line of its popular piston-engine aircraft, the DC-7 series. The latest model was called the DC-7B. This was by far the fastest piston engine airliner ever built. Its DA4 engines were derived from the Wright R-3350BD engines fitted to the Constellation, but with far more oomph and guts. Extra power was obtained from three turbines driven by the engine's exhaust gases. The turbines were connected to the crankshaft and were known as 'power recovery turbines.' Each aircraft was equipped with a Wright Turbo Compound air-cooled radial engine delivering 3,250 HP (2,423 kW) driving four-bladed propellers. SAA was the first airline outside the United States to operate these brand new, exceptionally powerful aircraft. The purchase price was a whopping £3 million for three aircraft. But they were the latest and fastest generation of passenger aircraft available anywhere in the Western world at the time. The order was placed in August 1954, with a delivery date set for early 1956.

SAA's DC-7Bs were initially configured to carry 18 first class and 43 tourist class passengers plus four sleeper berths enclosed with privacy curtains in a separate cabin. This arrangement was later changed to 12 first class and 54 tourist class seats plus the four sleeper berths. The crew consisted of five on the flight deck and two cabin attendants.

Douglas DC-7B. This was the fastest piston-engine airliner ever built. 1956

Douglas DC-7B landing at Jan Smuts Airport

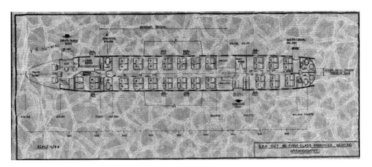

Douglas DC-7B in all-First Class cabin configuration

The Douglas DC-7B had a wingspan of 117.5 ft, a length of 109 ft and a height of 28.6 ft. Its empty weight was 67,995 lbs and its fully loaded weight 126,000 lbs. Its cruising speed was 360 mph, exceptionally fast for a piston engine airplane. It had four Wright Cyclone R3350-DA4 engines that were each rated at 3,250 horsepower (2,424 kW). Its service ceiling was 28,000 feet and it was fully pressurized. With a maximum load of fuel, it had a range of 4,920 miles. When fully loaded with passengers and cargo, the range dropped down to 3,280 miles which was still an extremely good distance for an aircraft of its size and weight. What made that extra capability possible were additional small fuel tanks built into the top of the four engine nacelles, each one holding 220 US gallons of fuel.

The first Douglas DC-7B for SAA, ZS-DKD, arrived at Jan Smuts Airport on February 29, 1956. It was named *Dromedaris* after one of three sailing vessels used by Jan van Riebeeck who had been sent to the Cape of Good Hope in 1652 to establish a replenishment station for ships of the Dutch East India Company plying the trade route between Europe and Asia. Details of the delivery flight of ZS-DKD are recorded in the logbooks of crew members

Owen Richard Mackin, Malcolm McKendrick and Salomon 'Pi' Pienaar. The commander was American pilot, Captain Bill Carr, who undertook a lot of delivery flights for the Douglas company. The flight departed Santa Monica, California at 3.10 p.m. on February 26, 1956 for Montreal, arriving there at 10.30 p.m. local time after a journey of seven hours and 20 minutes. It took off at 1.20 a.m. on February 27, arriving in London nine hours and 50 minutes later at 11.09 a.m. local time. From London, it flew to Rome in three hours five minutes on February 28 and then, on the same day, it proceeded on its longest leg to Nairobi, arriving there 11 hours and five minutes later at 5.11 a.m. the following morning. The final sector—from Nairobi to Johannesburg— was accomplished in six hours 10 minutes, touching down at Jan Smuts Airport at 12.55 p.m. The total flying time from Santa Monica to Johannesburg was 37 hours 55 minutes.

By the end of March, the other two DC-7Bs had arrived from the manufacturer. ZS-DKE was named *Reiger* (*Heron*) and ZS-DKF *Goede Hoop* (*Good Hope*), both also names of sailing ships in Jan van Riebeeck's original fleet from Holland. Two years later, a fourth DC-7B was purchased. ZS-DKG was called *Chapman*, the name of a ship that had landed a large contingent of British immigrants on South African shores at Algoa Bay (Port Elizabeth) in 1820.

Early in 1956, a new terminal was opened at the Port Elizabeth Airport and was named after the country's Prime Minister at the time, Dr. Hendrik Frensch Verwoerd, a Dutch immigrant who came to South Africa as a small child and rose to become Minister of Bantu (indigenous black African) Affairs in 1950. He subsequently became Prime Minister in 1958. It was under his leadership that the most stringent apartheid laws of the country went into effect, causing the first mutterings of intended international sanctions and embargoes against the country to be whispered in the hallowed halls of Washington, Whitehall, the United Nations and elsewhere. The world—and especially member countries of the British Commonwealth of Nations, to which South Africa belonged—were becoming extremely irate with the country's racist policies. Nevertheless, South Africa was booming. Tall new skyscrapers loomed above the ever-changing skylines of Johannesburg, Durban, Pretoria and other large cities. White immigration to the country from Europe was gaining in popularity. New highways and freeways criss-crossed the landscape. Electrified railroads connected far-flung ports, mining towns and inland cities with Johannesburg and the greater Witwatersrand metropolitan complex. On April 3, 1956, Italian airline Alitalia began flying a weekly service between Rome and Johannesburg. SAA opened more offices abroad as well as in neighboring Southern Rhodesia.

On April 21, 1956, the DC-7Bs took over the Springbok Service to Europe, cutting flying time down to just 21 hours. In July of that year the Federation of Rhodesia and Nyasaland's Central African Airways (CAA) joined the ten-year-old SAA-BOAC alliance. SAA added more services to destinations in Southern and Northern Rhodesia, using Constellations and DC-4s to operate the flights. Because of the speed of the DC-7B and low traffic demand for the route through Egypt, Cairo was dropped from the main Springbok Service to Europe. Agreeing to help promote local businesses every now and again SAA participated in innovative and novel publicity events. In 1956, the first ever fashion show held aloft was staged on board an SAA DC-4 flying between Johannesburg and Kimberley. Models paraded up and down the aisle wearing a new line of clothing from a local manufacturer of ladies' dresses and children's school uniforms.

A Lockheed Constellation and a Douglas DC-7B on the apron at Jan Smuts Airport in preparation for international flights

As route networks abroad expanded additional SAA sales offices were opened in Frankfurt and Amsterdam. Zurich soon followed. Because BOAC had now replaced its Argonauts with fast British-made Bristol Britannia 102 turboprop airliners on the Springbok Service, SAA switched one of its services from the easterly route to a more direct westerly route over Africa to Europe, flying DC-7Bs from Johannesburg via Leopoldville, Kano and Amsterdam to London. This reduced the flying time from Jan Smuts to Heathrow by 15 minutes less than the BOAC Bristol Britannia service. But another appealing prize was now in sight. Flights operated by Qantas airways from Australia were proving popular so, on November 5, 1957, an SAA route-proving flight to Australia was undertaken by Douglas DC-7B ZS-DKD under the command of Captains 'Pi' Pienaar and Boet Botes. The route went from Johannesburg to Mauritius, the Cocos Islands, Perth and Melbourne to Sydney. The return flight arrived back at Jan Smuts Airport on November 11. Two weeks later a regular Australian service was introduced, beginning on November 25, 1957. The first flight was operated by DC-7B ZS-DKE under the command of Captain de Villiers Rademan. Flights departed from Johannesburg at 9.00 a.m. on Mondays and returned from Perth at 9.30 a.m. on Wednesdays. Most of the long over-water sectors of the journey took place at night so that crews could keep a close check on their direction—or 'vectoring'—by astral navigation. In the absence of computers, GPS systems and automated navigational technologies, in those days the most reliable method to find your way across vast stretches of ocean was to navigate by the stars, just as intrepid explorers had done for centuries while travelling under sail at sea. To accomplish this in an aircraft one of the flight crew used a sextant through which he sighted the heavens through a clear plexiglass dome that was built into the roof of the airliner, just behind the cockpit.

Known as the Wallaby Service, the Australian flights were operated in pool partnership—sharing costs, revenue and passenger reservations systems—with Qantas. In the early years of operations SAA flights terminated in Perth, with Qantas then taking over and ferrying passengers onwards to destinations throughout Australia and New Zealand. Qantas operated the Wallaby Route with Lockheed L749A Constellation aircraft and, later, Lockheed L1049 Super Constellations. An interesting fact about the Australian service is that SAA was the first foreign carrier to ever operate a flight from abroad into the western Australian city of Perth. Because both SAA and Qantas operated services to their home bases from London, this gave passengers a novel option to reach Australia. Instead of flying the faster route from London to Australia by way of India, Asia or Singapore, passengers sometimes could see a little of Africa by flying from London to Johannesburg on the Springbok Service and then crossing the Indian Ocean to Australia on the Wallaby Service.

The departure of an SAA Douglas DC-7B aircraft to Australia was a frenzied time for ground crew who saw the aircraft off from Jan Smuts Airport. Here is an account from Ground Engineer John Hart. "We called the DC-7B the 'Hot-Rod of the Fleet.' It was the world's fastest piston-engine airliner. Those engines were really complex pieces of machinery. We ground engineers had to make sure they operated at maximum performance over the Indian Ocean as most of the flight took place in darkness so that the crew could perform their astral navigation. On the day of a departure from Jan Smuts Airport we started very early. The morning shift commenced at five a.m. and heaven help any individual who overslept or arrived late for work. Ground crews were small and carefully selected. Each person had a very specific role to play but the team had to operate as a seamless, well-oiled machine. Those who did not shape up were soon told to pack it up and leave. To assist in the arduous task of arriving at the airport on time we all made various modifications to our household alarm clocks at home. I myself used an electric time switch that was connected to a loud electric bell that could wake the dead. It also turned on my bedside reading light. In case of an electrical failure I had a conventional wind-up alarm clock placed inside an empty biscuit (cookie) tin that was kept near my bed but difficult enough to reach. You had to get up to turn it off. None of us had any excuse for being late for work. The first task when we got to the technical area at the airport was to start up and run the engines. This early morning ground run was essential to prove that the aircraft power plants and all related systems operated at peak efficiency and that the engines delivered the required take-off power. Running the aircraft also served to warm up the engines prior to flight, particularly in the cold winter months, saving time later. In the case of the DC-7B this task was allocated to a specialist trouble-shooting supervisor who was assisted by members of the departure staff. Witnessing the run-up of the powerful Wright Cyclone R3350-DA4 engines was an awesome sight. In the dark hours of early morning the engine exhaust stacks and the power recovery turbines glowed a bright cherry red when they were running because the metal got so hot. It was marvellous to see. If all was well then the aircraft was towed to the departure area outside the passenger terminal. The scheduled time of departure was 09h00 and there was always still so much work to be done. Everyone worked at peak efficiency, aided by lots of good, strong, black coffee. A detailed pre-flight inspection was then carried out by the engineering staff and only then was the aircraft fuelled. Depending on the aircraft's all-up weight the final fuel requirement would invariably be for full tanks. And that meant absolutely one-hundred-per cent *full* tanks and not *almost* full. To achieve this the fuel bowser would be brought alongside and we would fill the tanks and then wait for the aircraft to settle on the oleo shock absorbers of its landing gear, usually aided by a couple of us doing a little jumping on the wings to make sure that the fuel trickled down and settled completely inside every nook and cranny of the tanks. And then we'd top-off the tanks again. And then repeat the process until not another single drop could be added. The Indian Ocean is a big body of water. You didn't want your aeroplane running out of fuel between islands and airports! Then the flight engineer would go aboard and perform his pre-flight inspection, followed by another inspection by the first officer and then one by the captain. Finally, the ground engineer would do a last minute walk around the aircraft, checking everything and scrutinizing the tiniest detail. By now the passengers were boarding and getting settled in. At precisely 09h00 it was 'doors closed.' Then landing gear ground locks were removed and clearance would be given for 'engine start.' The DA-4 engine had a fuel injection system and a warm engine would start easily and without emitting too much smoke. Passengers and onlookers on the visitors' gallery were always alarmed by seeing smoke belching out of the engines on start-up. But that was normal and nothing to worry about. The aircraft could not start on its own. It needed a ground power unit or 'GPU' to provide enough electrical charge to fire up the engines. Once all engines were running smoothly the GPU was detached, moved out of the way, and then the airplane's wheel chocks were taken away. At idle power brakes were released and the DC-7B would smoothly taxi away. After a quick check of reverse power by the flight engineer the taxi continued. At that time the flight engineer had his work cut out for him. He was extremely busy using the on-board Sperry engine analyser to check whether every single one of the 144 spark plugs fitted to the 72 cylinders of the four big engines were firing correctly. Any defective ignition pattern or oil-fouled spark plug would show up on his oscilloscope. If that happened the engine power had to be increased in an attempt to clear the plug of oil. If that didn't do the job the aircraft would have to go into RTR (Return to Ramp) mode so that ground engineers could take whatever corrective maintenance action was necessary. That was a nightmare for the ground engineers because it meant having to work on an extremely hot engine to replace the spark plug, the high-tension ignition lead and the ignition coil. All three of those components had to be replaced. Of course, there was no time to let the engine cool down. It was like working on a red hot stove. If the flight did not depart within its planned time a lot of the flying would not be able to take place during dark hours so a 24-hour delay would be automatically enforced. The primary reason for this was that the Cocos Islands were just a tiny a speck in the Indian Ocean and astral navigation was essential to finding it. Arrival there had to be made before daylight while things were still dark, otherwise the crew wouldn't be able to see the runway lights.

"After the required maintenance and a quick check by ground and flight crew at Jan Smuts the aircraft attempted to depart once again. If all was well it proceeded to its allocated runway, stopping on the white painted line at the very threshold of it in order to get the maximum runway length for take-off. The DC-7B was heavy, full of fuel and fully loaded with passengers and freight. She needed all the length of runway she could get. The four DA-4 engines were opened up and, with a great roar, the aircraft accelerated down the runway. Seeing her become airborne and the undercarriage raised and tucked up inside her was a beautiful sight but, to be honest, for us departure boys it

Passengers disembark from a Douglas DC-7B after a flight from Australia

was just another job well done. Then we'd return to the departure building to log our aircraft's take-off time, grab another cup of coffee, gulp down a doughnut or a sandwich and then wait for the next inbound aeroplane which was due at precisely 09h45."

As much as the flight and ground crews loved them, the DC-7B's powerful Wright DA4 engines were complex, intricate pieces of machinery that often proved troublesome. Many a time a Douglas DC-4 Skymaster had to ferry out a replacement engine to a DC-7B that was grounded at some or other remote airfield because of mechanical—meaning engine—problems. Some of the engineers even joked that, even though it had four engines, the DC-7B was actually 'the best and fastest three-engine aircraft in the fleet.'

Crew members of a Douglas DC-7B

Captain stands below one of the troublesome Wright Cyclone engines of a Douglas DC-7B

Captain on the flight deck of a Douglas DC-7B

Air hostess greets passengers aboard a Douglas DC-7B

Air hostess aboard a Douglas DC-7B

No freight was too large or cumbersome for the Douglas DC-7B!

Stories abound about the Douglas DC-7B, some of them serious, some of them less so. Captain Dennis Raubenheimer recalls an incident that occurred aboard ZS-DKE on one of his flights. "This is probably the most hilarious experience in my long years of flying. From the very beginning of passenger-carrying aircraft there were always problems concerning the removal of odours emanating from the galley and the toilet areas. Various venting systems were tried and I recall that the Douglas DC-4 Skymaster employed a little tubular affair which sucked air out of the toilet cubicle in flight and vented it outside. The Constellation L749A was more advanced because it was pressurized so that system meant air had to be forcefully expelled from a vent far more efficiently. Then came the Douglas DC-7B with shiny new facilities and brand new toilet appointments, but therein hangs a tale. On May 4, 1958 I set off on flight SA 220 with 53 passengers from Jan Smuts Airport to Kano in Nigeria. My first Officer was Johan 'Lampies' Lamprecht and the flight engineer was Hugo Duckworth. Also on board was Captain J.A. Bert Rademan who was travelling with us as supernumerary so that he could take over the flight onwards from Kano to London. All went well during the climb-out but as we neared cruising height Bert suddenly appeared in the cockpit with a very earnest expression.

When I asked him what was wrong he rather embarrassedly announced that a lady in tourist class was screaming because she was stuck on a lavatory seat in one of the restrooms and the hostess could not free her. We flight crew were always inventing stories like that to amuse each other but when Bert told us that I said that I thought the joke was in rather poor taste and I made some derogatory comment to dismiss it. However, my reaction merely served to change Bert's already serious expression to one of extreme alarm at my light-heartedness. This in turn made me realise that something was really amiss. An elderly lady passenger had indeed become stuck on the toilet seat. How did this happen? And what could be done to free her? It was clear that for some odd reason the pressurization system inside the airplane was forcing the poor woman tightly down onto the toilet seat. Something had to be done quickly. Emergency depressurisation of the aircraft at our altitude of 18,000 feet was not feasible so we decided to try lowering the cabin pressure very slowly to reduce the differential pressure between the inside and outside of the toilet bowl. But this action proved far too slow to be of any effect. At our altitude there was a pressure differential of about five pounds per square inch of cabin atmosphere. Over a total approximate area of 80 square inches pressing down at the top of the toilet bowl it meant that the poor woman was being sucked down by an equivalent weight of about 400 pounds, in addition to her own weight. It was terrible. This was serious business. She desperately needed help.

"Our air hostess, Louise Hoorn, together with a helpful young lady passenger from tourist class tried to pull the stuck woman off the toilet but they couldn't budge her. Meanwhile our flight engineer, Hugo Duckworth, a quick-thinking and practical man, proposed making tiny holes in the top of the toilet bowl using the sharp point of the emergency axe. This would allow pressurized air to flow into the bowl, minimizing the suction effect and perhaps facilitate her release. But I quickly dismissed the idea as being much too dramatic. Just picture the poor woman stuck on the toilet with a uniformed man suddenly appearing in front of her brandishing a fearsome-looking axe. She would have had a heart attack. It was then that first officer Lampies Lamprecht volunteered to go and see what he could do.

"Always the gentleman, Lampies gently knocked on the toilet door, squeezed inside, excused himself for the rude intrusion, ignored the frantic woman's on-going screams, braced one of his legs against the compartment wall behind her, grabbed her tightly around her waist, pulled her towards him and then heftily rocked her back and forth about two dozen times as she howled and wept. Suddenly there was a loud plop and then a sucking whoosh as cabin air rushed beneath her buttocks into the toilet bowl, equalizing the pressure and setting her free.

"The cause of the trouble was that the poor dear, a Mrs. Huston, a retired nursing sister of 75 years of age with arthritic wrists, had lifted the toilet seat—a function specifically intended for male passengers in need of emptying their bladders—and had sat down directly on the smooth, cold metal opening of the toilet bowl itself, completely sealing it. While internal cabin air pressure increased as the aircraft climbed to cruising altitude there was no way to equalize the vacuum building up in the bowl. Hence Mrs. Huston's terrifying and unfortunate plight. After being plied off the bowl she was none the worse for the experience, other than a temporary deep red round bloodshot ring-shaped indentation on her behind. When she got over her ordeal she apologized profusely to the crew and her fellow passengers for what had happened. She also sheepishly admitted that her greatest fear was being sucked right out of the aircraft and expelled outside. 'And I wasn't even wearing a parachute,' she exclaimed. 'What would have happened to me then?'"

There was a great lesson to be learnt from that experience. From then onwards all aircraft manufacturers the world over made certain that their toilet bowls had small air-bleeds near the top, just in case some unsuspecting and unwise passenger ever tried repeating Mrs. Huston's mistake. The saga in the DC-7B restroom led to a cute if not slightly risqué poem that was written by SAA ground engineer Taffy Evans after the aircraft returned from London for maintenance, and it is repeated here for posterity.

Plight in flight

Picture the scene a flight serene
Sweet music from every tappet
Despite duff gen a DC seven
Can fly like a magic carpet.

Passengers snoozed or read or boozed
According to their bent
All unaware a bottom bare
Was in a sad predicament.

A piercing scream made men blaspheme
Women went pale with fright
A hostess tore at the toilet door
As if she was alight.

She went inside no doubt to chide
The squealer for her squealing
But when she saw those buttocks raw
She nearly hit the ceiling.

The poor old lady was full of fear
I'm stuck she cried in pain
The brave girl tugged then turned and shrugged
I think I'll need a crane.

She reported to the flying crew
While shuffling embarrassed feet
The poor old duck is firmly stuck
To the blasted toilet seat.

With laughter bent the skipper sent
His pal to check the story
But when he knew that it was true
He cursed her rump to glory.

It sure ain't paint he bellowed quaint
It's this ere pressurisation
Let's have a crack at getting her back
To a state of tranquilization.

All sweaty-browed they duly ploughed
Through a pressure differential
They went berserk over tricky work
Like a bottom circumferential.

Then in despair with courage rare
Up jumps a volunteer
I'm off says he to set her free
They sped him with a cheer.

When he arrived he strained and strived
Ignoring her yelp so clamorous
With fingers laced around her waist
He wished she was more glamorous.

But now his grin was nearing thin
For she stuck there like a limpet
He placed his feet against the seat
And shook her like a whippet.

With a squelchy suck she came unstuck
Amid screams of wild hysteria
She wore a mark like the bite of a shark
Upon her plump posterior.

She turned and vowed to the gaping crowd
I'm tired of being a snag
I shall refrain from using that drain again
And make do with a paper bag.

Aerodynamics and thermodynamics are integral to the science of air travel. They are two branches of physics that make flight possible. Because the airport at Johannesburg is located at such high altitude—6,000 feet above sea level—it has often been used to test the performance of new aircraft in 'hot and high' conditions. The world's first and only supersonic airliner, the European-made Concorde, underwent its hot and high trials at Jan Smuts Airport during the 1970s and, a decade earlier, the British Aircraft Corporation's BAC-1-11 medium range airliner also underwent hot and high trials there. But they were not the first. On September 29, 1955, a British-made Vickers Viscount 700 turboprop airliner arrived for six weeks of tests. In October of that year, it undertook a brief goodwill flight to Cape Town for the opening of that city's new airport near Bellville. Named after the country's first Nationalist Prime Minister in 1948, the new airport was named D.F. Malan. The opening ceremonies were performed by the Minister of Transport, Benjamin J. Schoeman. After the ceremonies were over the Viscount returned to Johannesburg to complete its testing program. The aircraft was also demonstrated to flight crews of SAA and to members of the SAR & H. Everyone was so impressed with it that in 1956 an order was placed with the manufacturer for seven aircraft, with deliveries to begin in 1958.

In the meantime, a lot of other developments had been taking place. Zurich was now included as a stop-over on the west coast route to London. The fast service between Johannesburg and London was altered to add Amsterdam to the Kano route, allowing uncut gemstones from the rich diamond fields of Nigeria to be flown directly to Amsterdam, at that time the diamond-cutting center of the world. Other routes on the Springbok Service included stopovers between Leopoldville and Rome. By April 1958, SAA included Paris on one of its DC-7B services routed via Salisbury, Nairobi, Khartoum, Athens and Rome, terminating in London. By now frequencies had been stepped up to five European services per week. In June 1958, SAA's Springbok Services' crews were decentralized with some now stationed in London. Six captains, six first officers, six flight engineers, three navigators and three radio officers now called London home. Flight crews operating out of the Union on the western route to London would now only fly as far as Kano while those flying the eastern route would only go as far as Rome. Crews based in London took over from those two cities. Although the pool partnership between SAA and BOAC continued, crew-slipping—or 'sharing'—between the two airlines were slowly phased out as each airline operated its own aircraft with its own crews.

Efficient and interruption-free communication between SAA's home base at Jan Smuts Airport and its aircraft that were flying domestic, regional and international routes now began to receive top priority. Located at Jan Smuts Airport, Radio ZUR—the letters ZUR standing for the station's call sign—was established on June 28, 1956. After initial teething problems, ZUR slowly had its transmitters and receivers upgraded and a forest of stationary and fully steerable antennas installed to provide direct continuous communication with SAA aircraft throughout its entire route structure. This was initially only by telegraphic Morse code but later upgraded for direct voice communications. Right from the start the system was unique in the civil aviation world and SAA gained international recognition for its efforts. It had little choice in the matter. Situated so far away from aircraft and engine manufacturers in Europe and the United States and with a route network so vast and developing so quickly, it was essential that the engineering and technical divisions of the airline have immediate contact with all flight crews and aircraft. With major advances in the field of radio technology, by 1960 the radio station acquired single side-band (SSB) equipment, making SAA the first airline in the world to use this revolutionary method of radio communication. Under the watchful eyes of SAA's senior communications officer George Gribb, initial transmission tests were carried out between June 21 and July 31, 1961. From 1962, ZUR had 24-hour, non-stop voice communication with all its aircraft throughout its entire worldwide route system. ZUR served many purposes. It was a direct connection between the technical and engineering workshops at Jan Smuts Airport and the aircraft; it provided essential technical updates to flight crews; it could help flight crews work through technical issues in aircraft on the ground and in the air; it was an informational lifeline for topics that covered navigation, maintenance, meteorological conditions and anything to do with the electronic and mechanical aspect of the airline's fleet. But, perhaps most importantly, it was a discreet channel between home base and SAA aircraft in a world that was gradually becoming more hostile towards South Africa, especially as colonial countries in Africa began gaining their independence from their European overlords. White-ruled South Africa with its racist apartheid policies was becoming something of a pariah, most notably in Africa. Contingencies had to be in place at all times in case a foreign country turned belligerent and threatened the welfare and safety of an SAA aircraft and its passengers. And it would not be long before just such an event would come to pass but, for the time being, all was well.

The only real problem was that the airline was not operating at a profit during the late fifties. Even though it was state-run and not a for-profit corporation it would have been nice if its income met or exceeded its operating expenses. But that was not the case. Some of its overseas services were functioning despite heavy financial losses. Some of those routes were operating purely to 'show the flag;' to give South African-registered aircraft a presence abroad. Even a few of the domestic routes were costing the government money by not paying for themselves. This state of affairs was a foreshadowing of things to come. It was a situation that would plague the airline again many years in the future.

In August 1958, aircrew and engineering staff were sent to the Vickers factory at Hurn in England to study the new Viscount aircraft that had been ordered. Later, they went to the Rolls-Royce plant at Derby to learn all about the Dart turboprop engines that powered these new planes. On October 29, 1958, the first of the new aircraft arrived in Johannesburg from the factory. Dennis du Plooy of SAA's Flight Performance and Operations Section provides his impressions of the delivery flight. "ZS-CDT *Blesbok* and ZS-CDU *Bosbok* looked positively gleaming and resplendent in their new SAA livery as they came out of the hangar at the Vickers' delivery centre at Bournemouth on that chilly October morning in 1958. The long, elegant nacelles housing the Rolls-Royce Dart Mark 525 engines were conspicuously beautiful. These were the first two of the original seven Viscount 813 aircraft purchased to replace the Douglas DC-4s on SAA's domestic and regional networks. Lou Trichardt, SAA's technical representative, was there to co-ordinate the departure from the factory. He had been at Vickers' Weybridge facility to oversee the manufacturing process and to sign off all the acceptance paper work. The first leg of the delivery flight was a relatively leisurely track across France and Italy, arriving at Rome in the early afternoon. The pilots were the two Rademan brothers, de Villiers and Bert. They had command of the two aircraft. Both planes departed within the minimum separation time allowed by ATC (air traffic control,) leaving at 11.00 a.m. and arriving at Rome without incident. After completing the usual immigration and customs facilities the crews checked into the Hotel Quirinal and had a few hours to do some sightseeing in the late afternoon and early evening before enjoying dinner and then an early turn-in. The next leg of the flight was more demanding and consisted of a full day's flying from Rome to Nairobi, with stops at Benina and Benghazi on the North African Coast, and then at Wadi Halfa and Khartoum in the Sudan. Departure from Rome was at first light. After rising with the sparrows and then being picked up at the hotel we were taken to the airport. The flight across the Mediterranean was very smooth in the grey light of early morning. On arrival at Benina the crews enjoyed a hearty breakfast while the aircraft were being refuelled and departure checks completed by the accompanying Vickers aircraft maintenance engineers.

"The flight across the Sahara Desert in daylight was utterly spectacular and very smooth, with the pilots maintaining 730°c TGT (turbine gas temperature). Propeller synchronisation was impeccably controlled and both aircraft behaved flawlessly. As the flight progressed it became evident that meteorological conditions were very favorable to us so just abeam of Wadi Halfa on the Nile it was decided that there was sufficient fuel on board to continue on to Khartoum. There are probably many hotter places on earth than Khartoum at 1.00 p.m. in the afternoon but I have yet to experience them. On leaving the aircraft the impression was of entering a blast furnace. There was little respite on entering the terminal building where ceiling fans were turning at maximum RPM but to no avail whatsoever. Everything melted, even the jelly and custard we had for dessert after lunch. It was a relief to board the aircraft again and experience a cooler environment as soon as we took off and began to climb.

"We arrived at Nairobi in the late afternoon and were met

by the South African High Commissioner. Later that evening the crews were his guests at the new Stanley Hotel for a superb dinner, after which we all retired early for a well-earned rest. The last leg of the delivery flight was completed after taking off from Nairobi, calling in at Salisbury for fuel and touching down at Jan Smuts Airport in the afternoon of the third day. The Viscounts gave excellent service to SAA over the years and were generally very reliable. Passengers were able to experience the comfort of a smooth, vibrationless flight with the introduction of these turbine-engine aircraft. But whether they lived up to the manufacturer's sales pitch of 'a new sound in the sky and a new sound in the cash register' is, however, somewhat debatable. Ground crews and mechanics were not always enchanted with them because some components of the airframe were extremely difficult to reach during servicing and maintenance."

SAA's Vickers Viscount 813 was a streamlined, handsome machine with beautifully engineered Rolls Royce Dart engines that combined a gas turbine jet engine connected to exterior propellers. When running at top throttle, those engines emitted a very pleasant and unique sound, something akin to a very high-pitched buzzing hornet's nest. It was a magical audio imprint

---

The Vickers Viscount 813 had a wingspan of 93 ft 11 ins, a length of 85 ft 8 ins and a height of 26 ft 9 ins. Its empty weight was 43,200 lbs and its maximum take-off weight 72,500 lbs. Its ceiling was 27,000 feet and its maximum speed 365 mph. Cruising speed was 351 mph. Maximum payload range was 1,275 miles and maximum fuel range 1,350 miles. The Viscount 813 was equipped with four Rolls-Royce RDa 7/1 Mk.525 Dart turboprop engines developing 1,990 HP (1,483 kW) each driving four-blade Dowty-Rotol propellers.

that echoed pleasantly over the folds and valleys of the African countryside for many years. The Viscounts carried 52 'normal' class or 58 'coach' class passengers and had a crew of three or four, depending on the route. All of the Viscounts were built according to SAA specification with the exception of ZS-CVA which was originally owned by Cubana Airlines (Compania Cubana de Aviacion) of Cuba. That aircraft was purchased in 1962, after the initial batch had been delivered.

Vickers Viscount on flight line at Jan Smuts Airport

The Flying Springbok on the nose section of the Vickers Viscount

Vickers Viscount ZS-CDU operated the first proving flight on November 24, 1958, when it flew from Johannesburg to Salisbury. Full-scale domestic and regional services began operating on

January 1, 1959. Within a year they had made a difference to SAA's dwindling domestic finances. The turboprops were so much more efficient, expedient and economical than the earlier piston-engine machines. Of equal importance was the Viscount's exceptional popularity with the travelling public. Its large oval windows, 19 by 26 inches in size – the largest ever used in a passenger airliner—gave passengers unprecedented views. Also, compared to the thumping of their piston-engine predecessors, a very quiet, comfortable, vibration-free ride was enjoyed by all in these fine machines. In order to train more crews, an £80,000 Viscount flight simulator was purchased and installed in the SAA Flight Operations building at Jan Smuts Airport. This facility was now state-of-the-art and the envy of many other airlines. In fact, carriers from some African countries and other areas abroad were now beginning to send their pilots there for training.

On February 1, 1959, SAA celebrated its 25th anniversary with a brief but boisterous flurry of champagne, parties and travel promotions. At this point many Douglas DC-4 and all Lockheed Constellation flights were phased out, although some of the DC-4s would soon be put to good use again operating a schedule of low-cost domestic flights that were dubbed the Skycoach Service. These flights, connecting Johannesburg with Durban, Cape Town, Port Elizabeth, Bloemfontein and Kimberley, commenced on March 25, 1959. Travellers could save up to a third of the standard class fare by flying Skycoach. The budget flights immediately caught on, putting air travel well within the reach of many people who would otherwise not have flown. With apartheid laws in force, SAA's domestic air travel was unfortunately not yet available to black passengers. However, on December 4, 1959, Douglas DC-3 Dakotas began flying domestic services exclusively for the use of black customers. It was a small step forward but, nevertheless, under the draconian laws of the country at that time a giant leap forward in bringing air travel to all South Africans, regardless of color, creed or racial classification. The service would be withdrawn in May 1961, after which all races would be allowed to travel on any flight.

On December 4, 1959, BOAC rewrote the rule book all over again. It was then that they introduced an all-new pure-jet airliner to the Springbok Service. The de Havilland Comet 4 was a dramatic new incarnation of the original ill-fated Comet DH.106 Mk 1 of 1952. Bigger, faster, more comfortable and safer than its earlier predecessor, the Comet 4 was an altogether new, redesigned and reengineered airplane. Magnificently refined, it embodied the very best that British aeronautical engineering could produce. With accommodation for between 56 and 81 passengers in a first class and tourist class configuration, it could fly non-stop for up to 3,225 miles at a speed of 520 mph, reducing the flying time between Johannesburg and London to just over 15 hours.

Then, on February 15, 1960, Belgium's Sabena Airlines introduced another brand new jet airliner to South Africa. But this one was not British-made. Flying between Brussels, Leopoldville and Johannesburg, the radically new Boeing 707 was the ambassador of the best that the United States aerospace industry could create.

The jet was back. Big time. But SAA did not have it. At least not yet. Within months all that would change.

Chapter 9

Return of the Jets

As the sixties began SAA proudly announced that it had carried 2,408,243 passengers during the preceding decade. There were now 24 aircraft in its fleet, made up of five Vickers Viscounts, six Douglas DC-3 Dakotas, five Douglas DC-4 Skymasters, four Douglas DC-7Bs and four Lockheed Constellations. These machines served the airline's expanding route network very reliably. But times were rapidly changing. The world was becoming a different place.

The Cold War between West and East was in full swing. In 1957, the Soviet Union had launched *Sputnik,* the world's first artificial satellite into orbit around the earth, triggering the Space Race with the United States. In 1959, the microchip was invented, paving the way for the future computer age. In 1960, President Dwight Eisenhower dealt the first official death knell to racism in the United States by signing the American Civil Rights Act into law. But, perhaps of more immediate pertinence to our story, after the de Havilland Comet DH-106 Mk 1 disasters, the jets had made a comeback. Though still very much secluded by the Iron Curtain, as early as 1955 the Russian national airline, Aeroflot, had begun regular passenger services on its domestic route network using twin-engine turbojet medium range Tupolev Tu-104 'Camel' aircraft.

Based on the design and airframe of the Tupolev Tu-16 'Badger' military bomber, the Tu-104 did not serve any of Aeroflot's international routes but it caused considerable surprise to everyone in the aviation industry outside the USSR. Work began on the aircraft in the spring of 1953, just a year after the de Havilland Comet 1 had entered commercial service. With Captain Y.I. Alashayev at the controls the prototype Tu-104 made its first flight on June 17, 1955. Fully pressurized and carrying 50 passengers—far more than the early Comets—the first versions of the airplane were powered by two Mikulin AM-3 turbojets producing 14,880 lbs. of thrust each. They were extremely powerful machines and helped reduce travel times across vast stretches of the Soviet Union to less than half of what they used to be. The Tu-104 was operated by a crew of five, comprising a pilot, copilot, radio operator, flight engineer, and navigator. Not since the Comet had there been anything like it.

Like many others around the world, the Russians had paid very careful attention when the Comet swept the skies with the world's first scheduled commercial passenger jet service between London and Johannesburg in 1952. In addition to observant engineers in the Soviet Union, on the Pacific coast of the United States scientists, entrepreneurs and dreamers also watched and wondered as the Comet soared into history, planning for the day when their own airplane manufacturing industry could take a place in the brave new frontier of jet travel. Perhaps nowhere else was this more evident than in the city of Seattle in the northwest state of Washington.

Seattle was, and still is, the primary development and manufacturing base of what was then known as the Boeing Airplane Company. Jet aircraft were certainly not new to Boeing. Its huge six-engine B-47 stratojet long-range bomber first flew in 1947, entering service with the United States Strategic Air Command (SAC) in 1951. Their primary aim was to carry nuclear weapons and to penetrate Soviet airspace. But at that time Boeing had no experience whatever with commercial passenger jets. When Britain's de Havilland Aircraft Company was developing the Comet Mk. 1, Boeing's president William (Bill) Allen had led a deputation from his company to the Farnborough Air Show in 1950 to see a demonstration of the Comet as well as to visit the de Havilland plant at Hatfield to observe testing and construction of the jet. The Comet fascinated Allen and his team. Although it had swept-back wings similar to the design of the big Boeing B-47 bomber its engines were buried inside its wings, unlike the B-47 where the engines were slung beneath the wings in pods. Allen believed that the podded design was superior to the Comet's engine configuration and, even though he and his principal designers were extremely impressed with the Comet, they felt that they could come up with an airplane that was larger than the British machine, that could carry a greater payload, that would have longer range and that was more convenient for maintenance and servicing.

Returning to Seattle that year, 1950, Allen and his designers drew up specifications for a jetliner that was given the model number 473-60C. Doing their best to try to sell the concept to U.S. airlines, Boeing's sales and marketing teams could not convince anyone to buy the airplane. American and foreign carriers were more than happy with the familiar piston-engine commercial airliners built by Boeing, Douglas and Lockheed that they were flying and saw little need for an expensive, untested, untried, new-fangled jet. But Boeing's board was determined. They believed that if airlines doubted the viability or need for a jet the only way to pique their interest was to build one and show them what it could do. Needless to say, this would require a large capital investment with no guarantee of financial recuperation if the airlines remained skeptical. Tossing $16 million at the project and going back to the drawing boards, the designers wanted to come up with something that would give the new jet a unique identity of its own, separating it from all the company's previous aircraft models. As earlier Boeing products carried the series prefix numbers 300, 400, 500 and 600, it was decided to assign the new aircraft the designation 700. After tweaks and alterations were made to the initial concept the aircraft that would become the first production model of the 700 series was allocated the number 707. However, to keep the project secret from the prying eyes of spies engaged in industrial espionage and because work was already in progress on developing an aerial refueling tanker for the U.S. Air Force, most people did not refer to the new jet as the 707 but simply as the 367-80 or, in short, the 'Dash Eighty.' And that is the name that has now been enshrined in the history books.

Hopes were initially centered on an anticipated order by the U.S. Air Force for a jet to replace its fleet of Boeing KB-50 piston-engine tankers that were used for refueling fighters and bombers in mid-air, so the prototype of the 707 jet—or the Dash Eighty—was built as a tanker, not as a passenger aircraft. It had no interior fittings, no ceiling, seats or wall panels and also no windows. The airplane made its first flight from Boeing's Renton plant outside Seattle on July 15, 1954. The Air Force was so impressed by the performance and characteristics of the new machine that they immediately placed an order for 29 tanker versions, under the designation 717. As for the 707 commercial version, there was no demonstration model and still no takers.

In the meantime, the Douglas Aircraft Company in Santa Monica had begun working on its own turbojet project. The Douglas DC-8 was being developed in direct competition to the Boeing 707. The race was on. Which one of the two aircraft manufacturing giants would be the first to secure an order from a major airline for a passenger version of its new aircraft? Frustrated at the lack of interest in a commercial jetliner, Boeing's William Allen invited members of the aviation industry to watch a demonstration flight of the Dash Eighty during the Seattle Gold Cup Hydroplane Races on Lake Washington on August 6, 1955. Without telling his boss of his intentions Boeing's chief test pilot, Alvin 'Tex' Johnston, strapped himself into the left-hand seat of the Dash Eighty's cockpit and decided to pull out all the stops by thrilling the crowd in a way that no one would ever expect. As the big jet swooped in low over the lake for its anticipated stately flyover, Johnson suddenly flipped the aircraft upside down like a fighter jet and performed two breathtaking 360-degree barrel rolls, utterly stunning everyone from airline executives to the general public to William Allen himself. Big airplanes—especially airliners—are not meant to do barrel rolls. The next day a furious and very shaken Allen summoned Johnston to his office and demanded an explanation.

"What did you *think* you were *doing* out there yesterday, Tex?" Allen demanded.

Totally unmoved and not in the least bit intimidated Johnston coolly looked Allen straight in the eye and replied, "Oh, just sellin' airplanes."

And sell them he did.

On October 13, 1955, Juan Trippe, president of Pan American World Airways, placed a firm order for 20 Boeing 707s. But—in the true spirit of American competitive enterprise—at the same time that Trippe ordered the 707s he also bought 25 DC-8s from the Douglas company. Now, both Boeing and Douglas were firmly committed to the passenger jetliner industry. They started up production lines and began making airliners. On October 26, 1958, Pan American began a daily jet service between New York and Paris and on December 10, National Airlines inaugurated a daily domestic jet service between New York and Miami. The public loved the planes. The press and the media touted them. The passenger jets were here to stay.

Competition between the two aircraft manufacturers intensified and orders began flowing in. Airlines such as Trans World Airlines (TWA), Continental, Braniff, Air France, Qantas and Sabena ordered 707s. On the other hand, Eastern, KLM and Scandinavian Airways System (SAS) purchased Douglas

DC-8s. Other carriers would soon follow but in the meantime Boeing and Douglas were not alone in this incredible new enterprise to dramatically alter the way humans moved about their world.

There was another player vying for attention and for possible jetliner orders. In San Diego, at the southernmost tip of the state of California, the Convair division of General Dynamics was hard at work preparing its own prototype of a machine it called the Convair Coronado. Its first flight took place on January 27, 1959. Produced in two variants—the 880 and the 990—the Convair jet would never be as popular or as successful as either the Boeing 707 or the Douglas DC-8 but, nevertheless, it was a fine aircraft. Because it had a slightly narrower fuselage and was a little shorter in length, it flew faster than either of its competitors. But during its three short years of production only 65 would be built.

As far as SAA is concerned, the story of the new American jets is centered on the legendary Boeing 707. It, above all others, would go on to play a significant role in the saga of the airline. Following a public announcement in 1958, by the Minister of Transport, Benjamin J. Schoeman, on February 22 of that year six men dressed in dark business suits met in the office of Mr. D.H.C. du Plessis, General Manager of South African Railways & Harbors Administration (SAR & H)—the government agency in charge of SAA—in Johannesburg. In addition to du Plessis, the group was made up of representatives from SAA as well as from the Boeing Airplane Company. Pleasantries and handshakes were exchanged, fancy fountain pens were pulled from breast pockets and a sizeable stack of documents that had been printed on crisp white cotton bond paper were signed, committing SAA to the purchase of three Boeing 707-320 'Stratoliner' jets. Their scheduled delivery was slated for 1960. Within months of SAA signing the order a small group of ground engineers and their families, headed by Algernon

'Algie' Laxton, relocated from South Africa to Seattle to spend the next couple of years learning all about the technical aspects of the new jetliners and to monitor their construction. The price tag for each aircraft was $4.3 million, making a total cost of almost $13 million. It was the largest single order ever placed by the airline at that time for new equipment.

The new jets now being offered by the three West Coast-based aircraft manufacturers in the United States would have a profound affect that even the most visionary of business analyst, politician or poet could not foresee. Capable of carrying up to 170 passengers in some models, nothing like them had ever taken to the skies. Never before were more people capable of being accommodated in pressurized metal tubes that could whisk them at greater speeds over longer distances than was now possible with the Boeing 707, the Douglas DC-8 and the Convair Coronado. The mass-produced jets would change the way humans travelled in the same way as the Model T Ford revolutionized road transportation when it replaced the horse and buggy. Attractive airfares and other incentives put long distance journeys well within the reach of the most unseasoned of travelers. As more of the new airplanes came off the assembly lines and as additional airlines began flying them the world yielded to their impact.

Within just a few years, in the most remote and inaccessible of places, hotels and vacation resorts started springing up to cater to an exploding tourism industry. Faraway cities, ancient cobblestoned town squares, out-of-the-way hamlets, islands, snow-clad mountains, national parks and tropical beaches on all inhabited continents began bustling with amenities to cater to surging crowds of holiday-makers. But with the jet airliner also came an end to traditions that triggered a deep sense of nostalgia that would linger in the hearts and minds of older generations. Railroad companies and long-distance passenger travel by rail diminished in many places. Small towns, especially across the United States, lost their traditional links with the world beyond their local main streets, gas stations and Dairy Queens as express sleeper trains stopped coming. Farther afield on the high seas even more dramatic things were happening. Ocean liners could not compete with the jets and were emptied of passengers. Iconic shipping lines gobbled up one another in a desperate attempt to survive or simply ceased operations. Unless people were taking a leisurely vacation cruise, no one travelled by sea any more. By the time the seventies arrived, people who wanted to get from point 'a' to point 'b' just about anywhere on the map now went by air. It was quicker, more convenient and a lot cheaper than going by sea. And it was primarily the Boeing 707 that led the way.

The very first Boeing 707 to land at Johannesburg was on January 26, 1960, when a Belgian Sabena airlines 707-320 registered OO-SJB arrived from Brussels via Leopoldville. Crowds thronged the visitors' viewing gallery at Jan Smuts Airport to see the jet. People gaped in wonder at its sheer size. Some were simply enthralled by the enormous number of windows that sparkled along its fuselage. It was a magnificent-looking machine that in every way lived up to the media reports and commercial advertising that preceded its arrival. Sadly, OO-SJB was the ill-fated aircraft that operated Sabena flight 548 from New York to Brussels on February 15 the following year when it suffered a stall while trying to avoid a light aircraft that had not cleared the runway at Brussels airport. The ensuing crash killed all on board including the entire U.S. figure skating team on its way to the World Figure Skating Championships in Prague. But the traveling public were unperturbed. Everybody wanted to fly the 707, so much so that during the 22 years that it remained in production in different variants 1,010 of them would come off the assembly line at Boeing's Renton facilities in Seattle.

SAA Boeing 707-344A, 1960. Note the new 'boomerang' style emblem on the rudder (rear tail fin). Together with the ubiquitous Flying Springbok this was superimposed over an orange background. An orange tail would become synonymous with the livery of all SAA aircraft for the next 36 years

The first of SAA's Boeing's, the model 707-344A, had a wingspan of 142 ft 5 ins, a length of 152 ft 11 ins and a height of 41 ft 7 ins. Its empty weight was 135,000 lbs and its maximum all-up weight 312,000 lbs. Its highest operating altitude was 42,000 feet and its maximum speed 623 mph. Its longest range was 4,630 miles. The aircraft was equipped with four under-wing pod-mounted Pratt & Whitney JT4A-12 twin spool compressor turbojet engines. Early models of Pratt & Whitney's turbojet had a novel exhaust outlet that resembled an organ pipe cluster, unlike the cleaner design that would follow in later years. Their purpose was to reduce noise. But nevertheless they were very noisy engines and they emitted considerable smoke trails. All the same, they were extremely powerful, developing a phenomenal 17,500 lbs of thrust. On the flight deck were three or four crew members, depending on the route to be flown. In addition to a captain, a first officer and navigator, some flights also carried a radio operator but, in time, that position would be phased out.

At 10.05 a.m. on July 15, 1960, SAA's first Boeing 707, ZS-CKC named *Johannesburg* touched down at Jan Smuts Airport after flying 11,445 miles on its delivery flight from Seattle in only 21 hours 35 minutes. That was halfway around the world, yet it covered the distance in less time than it took to fly the fastest piston-engine aircraft from Johannesburg to London, a route that was half the distance. At the controls of the brand new Boeing were Captains Salomon 'Pi' Pienaar and Jan Marthinus 'Boet' Botes. Also on board was Boeing Airplane Company pilot, Ed Hartz. The flight engineer was Malcolm 'Mack' McKendrick and the navigators Owen 'Mick' Richard Makin and J. F. 'Koos' Van Aswegan. The aircraft had departed Boeing Field in Seattle on July 12, 1960, flying via Goose Bay, London, Milan and Nairobi to Johannesburg. Before landing in Johannesburg, Captain Pienaar performed a low fly-past over the terminal buildings and technical areas at the airport to loud cheers by an enthusiastic crowd of SAA personnel.

The second Boeing 707, ZS-CKD *Cape Town*, arrived on August 26, 1960. Just a week later, on September 4, aided by a cooperative tailwind, it established a stunning record for a flight from Cape Town to Johannesburg, covering the 800 miles in just one hour, 15 minutes and 10 seconds. The third 707, ZS-CKE, *Durban*, was the first of its type produced with leading edge wing flaps. Before

Boeing 707-344A. Note distinctive daisy-shaped exhaust pipe on early models of the Pratt & Whitney JT3 engines

Disembarkation from Boeing 707 after international flight at Jan
Smuts Airport, 1961

being handed over to SAA by Boeing, it was used for testing
and certification purposes, resulting in a delivery on February
10, 1961, six months later than the first two aircraft. The leading
edge flaps allowed for slower take-offs and landings and gave
the airplane a higher coefficient of lift, important for mid-day
operations at hot and high airports like Jan Smuts.

Alas, ZS-CKD was the second of the new Boeings to be
subjected to a spate of unfortunate incidents during their early
phase of operations with the airline. (The first incident will be
discussed later in this chapter.) During a take-off from Athens
on the night of August 1, 1961, it sustained minor damage when
it struck a grove of olive trees and a stone wall located at the
far end of the runway. Unbeknown to the crew, the bottom half
of the ventral fin at the rear of the aircraft was torn off by the
wall. Captain Dirkie Nel, First Officer Matthew MacFarlane
and Flight Engineer Harry Joynt were only aware of clipping
the olive trees and believed that the aircraft was safe enough
to continue onwards to Nairobi. When it landed there, they
were shocked to find branches of olive trees still firmly lodged
in the undercarriage but they were totally horrified to discover
the damage to the tailplane. A replacement aircraft was sent
up from Johannesburg to pick up the passengers and their

luggage and ZS-CKD was taken out of commission for a couple of weeks while the ventral fin was repaired. Because it had not interfered with the airworthiness of the aircraft, the damage to the tailplane spoke eloquently of the remarkable strength and airframe integrity that Boeing were building into their jet-powered passenger products.

Apart from the fact that the new Boeing 707s were fast and looked like nothing before them, something else made them stand out from all previous aircraft in the SAA fleet. Up until their arrival in 1960, the rudders and tail fins of all SAA aircraft were painted white, with a neat blue horizontal line just below the tip and a South African flag and Flying Springbok logo superimposed over the white area. But with the Boeings came something very different. SAA, its parent organization SAR & H and probably even a few senior members of the South African government had decided that the aircraft should have a new look and be painted exclusively in the colors of the South African flag. These were orange, white and blue. No doubt more astute or cynical observers also saw in this an attempt to convey the colors of the National Party, the ruling political party at the time. Its colors were also a combination of orange, white and blue. The tall rudder fin of the new Boeings was now entirely painted orange, with a slick blue and white boomerang-like flash on the side nearest the leading edge. Superimposed over the flash was the ubiquitous Flying Springbok, painted blue. It was certainly an eye-catching design, if not perhaps a little garish when it first appeared. Bill Poyser, once SAA Station Manager at Heathrow Airport, recalled that administrative personnel and both SAA and BOAC ground staff at the airport were quite shocked when they first saw the new livery as ZS-CKC touched down in London on its delivery flight from the United States. At first, a lot of people openly proclaimed the color scheme downright vulgar. But that attitude mellowed in time. People got used to it. In fact, during the almost four decades that it was featured on SAA aircraft the livery became a favourite of airplane junkies, spotters, photographers and enthusiasts around the world.

Another typically South African flair was featured in the interior cabin design of the Boeings. Panelling surrounding the windows along the entire length of the cabin featured very subtle light brown motifs of South African wild animals and flowers, including the national flower, the protea. These were depicted against a tasteful crème-colored background. The combination created a restful and very attractive ambience immediately evocative of South Africa, making passengers feel as though they were setting foot in the country as soon as they boarded the airplane.

Interior of SAA's first few Boeing 707 aircraft featured specially commissioned artwork reminiscent of South African flora and fauna on walls and bulkheads

Boeing 707 interior. Specially designed South African motifs were featured on walls and bulkheads in both First and Economy class cabins

Cabins of the Boeings were configured with a first class and coach (tourist) class section, carrying a total of 139 passengers. On September 14, 1960, ZS-CKD operated flight SA 220 in place of a DC-7B on a route proving flight to London. Later that month three DC-7B services to London were replaced by Boeing 707 airliners for route training and evaluation purposes and then, on October 1, the Boeings took over the Springbok Service from the Douglas DC-7Bs. Their introduction slashed actual flying time down to only 13 hours from Jan Smuts to Heathrow.

One of the more unfortunate aspects of the arrival of the jet age was the phasing out of the position of Radio Officer. At the beginning of Boeing 707 operations, the Radio Officer was given the new title of Flight Traffic officer. Although he was no longer solely responsible for maintaining radio communication with the ground—an essential duty during the earlier days of Morse Code radio with its complicated system of dits, dots and dashes—he was now responsible for checking flight documents as well as overseeing radio telephony communication between his aircraft and Radio ZUR in Johannesburg. He also had to ensure that passenger and cargo manifests were correct. It was his job to provide the base station in Johannesburg with vital in-transit information such as his aircraft's departure and arrival times and for sending details of the aircraft's position as determined by the navigator. The Flight Traffic Officer continued to obtain meteorological reports from en-route weather stations as requested by the pilots and navigator but in actual fact, the jets heralded the end of the road for this position on the flight crew. Ease of communication by voice between pilots and ground stations and advanced equipment and technologies simply made the job redundant.

Conversely, a host of other jobs were created with the arrival of the 707s. A building known as 'Cabin Services' located between the main terminal and the control tower at Jan Smuts Airport was enlarged to cater to the increased passenger needs and additional cabin crew members of the big jets. Comprising three stories, one of the levels was devoted entirely to pantries, refrigerated areas and kitchens for preparing in-flight meals and for packaging snacks, as well as for washing and sterilizing trays, utensils, crockery, glasses and plastic serving items. The second floor was occupied by facilities for storing alcoholic drinks and liquid refreshments, as well as sections for laundering first class table cloths, napkins and pillows as well as blankets for both first and economy class cabins. Seat covers, children's toys, toiletry kits, magazines and writing supplies were also stored, packaged and distributed from this level. The third floor housed bathrooms, lockers, change rooms and other amenities for cabin crews, including a hairdressing salon and make-up cubicles. To add to the constant flurry of activities in this busy building, a section was set aside for training cabin crews for their roles in the first and economy class cabins. This included a mock-up of a small section of the first and economy class sections on board the Boeing 707. Tuition in deportment and taking care of passengers' needs—especially in emergency situations—were also based

Technicians work on JT4 engine of Boeing 707 in the technical division of the airline at Jan Smuts Airport

here. In the meantime, extra facilities for flight crews were created in the technical area near the hangars where pilots and flight crews were briefed prior to a flight or where they could take a shower and change or simply relax and go over reams of paperwork, weather forecasts and technical manuals before boarding their allotted airplanes. A new safety training section for cabin crew devoted to rapid evacuation procedures, inflating life rafts at sea and general survival techniques was opened in the technical and maintenance area.

The unforeseen and unpredicted were a constant presence back in those days, just as they are today. On October 29, 1960, Boeing 707 ZS-CKC underwent a serious mishap while trying to land at Nairobi Airport. This was the first involving SAA's new 707s. The aircraft was operating flight SA 218 from Johannesburg to London. After stopping at Salisbury, Nairobi was its second port of call along the way. Don Smith was the engineer on the flight. These are his recollections of what happened. "I had spent most of my time training other engineers on the 707 in Johannesburg and they were all familiar with the route but I hadn't personally been on it myself yet. Finally the day came for me to be Flight Engineer to Captain Chris Rosslee and First Officer Robert Brian Bird to do a 707 flight to London. Jack Tindall, also an SAA pilot, was flying in the back as a passenger, as was J.N.R 'Bushy' del la Rey, a flight engineer. The first leg was from Johannesburg to Salisbury. We took off from there with an ETA (estimated time of arrival) in Nairobi at about midnight. As we approached Nairobi we were told that the weather had fouled up. Clouds had descended, visibility was poor and it was suggested that we divert to Entebbe in Uganda. But we old-timers all knew the conditions in East Africa pretty well and were familiar with Nairobi weather. In our previous years of experience low clouds often used to drift across the runway, completely covering it, but then the clouds would pass and things became perfectly clear again. That night we heard that two other aeroplanes had landed there safely so Captain Chris Rosslee decided to go in and have a look rather than divert to Entebbe. We got to Nairobi and did a very low approach in order to check things out as best we could, but the weather was grim. There were no landing aids in those days, no ILS (Instrument Landing System,) no glide slope indicators, nothing. We did a long approach towards Nairobi and then started a slow let-down procedure. Eventually, during the descent, I heard Jack Tindall cheerily call out 'Runway in sight!' I looked up and saw the runway but it seemed peculiarly short and flat. That meant only one thing. We were already way too low. We were at the same height as the runway and yet we were still a couple of away miles from it. We were going to hit the ground. At that very second we smacked the deck with a tremendous bang. I felt the aircraft shudder and buckle beneath me. Fortunately, Captain Rosslee anticipated what was going to happen so he had fully opened the throttles just before we hit but we still hit the ground before gaining altitude again. We could all have been killed yet miraculously we were back in the thick clouds again. The blow on impact was so hard that all the instruments had stopped working. Warning lights were coming on all over the place. Number three engine seemed to be in trouble. The only instrument that seemed to be operating normally was the turn-and-bank indicator. Thank heavens for that. We now had a moment to look around and take stock of things and I said to Captain Bird, 'Can you see number three engine, because all indications here on my panel is that it's gone.' All the instruments were dead but warning lights were flashing for number three. Praise heaven, the engine might still be running. Circuit breakers had popped out by the hundreds. We pushed them all back in again but they immediately popped out because there was a colossal electrical short circuit somewhere. But where? None of us had any way of telling.

"Although very shaken by what had happened Captain Rosslee announced that he thought we should head for Entebbe. The weather and visibility at Nairobi were just too awful to attempt another landing. So we started to climb and straight away I found out that I could not pressurize the cabin. I guessed that there must be a breach in the fuselage somewhere from which the pressurized atmosphere was escaping. Also, as soon as the landing gear was raised we discovered that there was no hydraulic fluid left. It had all gone. Where the leak was we had no idea. I told the Captain that we couldn't go on to Entebbe because that would require a climb to 40,000 feet and then a descent down to the airfield and we simply didn't have enough fuel left for that kind of manoeuvre. Breathing a deep sigh Captain Rosslee said that we had no option in that case. We'd have to land at Nairobi. So, we started to do a wide circuit above the Nairobi Airport area. Meantime, I decided to go and take a look at the condition of the aircraft and determine what, if anything, was mechanically damaged. Beneath the flight deck is a small compartment that you can climb down into. We used to refer to it as 'Area 41.' I lifted the hatch in the cockpit floor and squeezed down into it. I was shocked when I could see the lights of Nairobi directly beneath us. That whole section of the forward fuselage had been torn open when the nose wheel had hit the ground. And that breach in the hull was why I could not pressurize the interior of the aircraft. It had a gaping hole in it! The nose wheel assembly had been bent backwards, pushing the whole nose wheel box up into the floor of the cockpit, pinching or severing all electrical wiring and cables. That is what had caused the circuit breakers to pop out everywhere. The whole lower 41 area was also filled with a mist of hydraulic fluid because the hydraulic pipes there had been ruptured. That meant that we couldn't lower the landing gear. We could have tried winching the undercarriage down manually but once the gear was down there was no way you could retract it. Based on what I'd seen we now knew the nose wheel was severely damaged, but we didn't know what might be wrong with the main undercarriage further aft beneath the wings. We decided that we couldn't risk having the heavy drag of the landing gear down while we were trying to find the runway in those terrible weather conditions, especially with less instruments than we normally had, so the Captain decided to land with all the gear up; in short, a belly landing—no wheels.

"We were trained for all kinds of emergency situations but I have to admit that my palms were becoming sweaty and perspiration began streaming down my forehead. All I could think of were all those people in the back. Their safety was of paramount importance to us. We flew a long circuit and then did a slow let down and broke cloud with the runway about a quarter mile to the left. We had an ADF (automatic direction finder) but because of the electrical problems it wasn't reliable and was swivelling around a lot. The only compass we had now was an ordinary standby magnetic one. That also swung around and, in any case, it wasn't gyro stabilized. To line up on a runway in terrible weather with only those instruments was practically impossible. We missed the runway by about a quarter of a mile and so we throttled up and started to do another very long circuit. Meanwhile, at this low altitude the engines were using a tremendous amount of fuel. I said to the Captain that this circuit would have to be our last. We didn't have enough fuel for another go-around and that, believe me, was a very nasty thought. We might have to try to land in the blackness of night in the middle of the Nairobi National Wildlife Park, which was not far from the airport. Imagine that. It was a terrible thought. We would come down into the midst of herds of wild animals, including lions and elephants. So we did our long circuit and made another attempt at landing. But we were off-track to the runway, way too far to the right. It was our very last chance so Captain Rosslee miraculously brought us in through a little break in the clouds and suddenly there we were, right on the centre line of the runway. But half of it was already behind us! We had overshot most of it! We were going to land too far along its length. But good old Rosslee had his wits about him. He put us down right on the center line. The experience was one of a very soft cushioning effect at first because we had no landing gear. We landed on our belly. The wings were so close to the ground that the air beneath them made for a surprisingly soft landing. But that was no reason for complacency. Then there came metal directly on asphalt, with no rubber tires in between. Suddenly everything was vibrating and the noise was absolutely awful. We were shooting along what little was left of the runway at breakneck speed. The end of the runway was coming up fast and we could do absolutely nothing about it. Captain Rosslee turned to me and shouted, 'Don, how the devil am I going to stop this thing?' I said there was nothing that could be done. We had no wheel brakes, no air brakes, no spoilers, no reverse engine thrust, nothing. So there we were, just tearing along, sliding on our belly, sparks flying like fireworks outside. We shut down everything electrical and pulled all the firewall handles and made sure everything was as safe as we could. If all went well it wasn't going to be too dangerous because we didn't have much fuel on board to start a fire. Towards the end of the runway the aircraft started veering off to the left. There was no way we could control it or steer it and suddenly we slid off the runway and ploughed into a big bank of soil and grass, coming to a violent stop. With that a huge pile of dinner trays that the steward had stashed in the galley behind us came crashing into the cockpit. They cluttered and tumbled all around us. Then we discovered that the emergency lighting didn't work. Emergency cabin lights were supposed to come on when we switched all the power off, but they didn't because of all the shattered electrical circuits. In the pitch darkness we heard the steward behind us screaming that the number two engine was on fire, so I grabbed the fire extinguisher which was on my right hand side and felt my way to the door as fast as I could. Somehow I managed to get it open and I let myself down to the ground. Brian Bird came with me. It wasn't too far to the ground because there was no landing gear so we weren't very high off the surface. We just hung onto the door and dropped down the small distance. I ran to the number two engine and gave it one squirt with the fire extinguisher and the flames went out immediately. The fire was caused by oil from the accessory drive case at the bottom of the engine nacelle which had been ruptured on the tarmac of the runway and the oil had started to burn. The engine itself had been ripped halfway off its pylon. Fuel was running out of broken pipes. It could have caught alight but thankfully it didn't. I ran around to the other inboard engine, number three and, sure enough, it was also burning. I gave it one puff from the extinguisher and out it went. Everything now seemed OK but then I heard Captain Rosslee yelling, 'Hey Don, come back up here! Fast!'

"I had recently gone through the emergency engineering training course at Boeing in Seattle and I knew a little more about the emergency evacuation systems on board the airplane than the rest of the crew did. They pulled me back up into the aircraft, all in pitch darkness, and I felt my way around to find the handles for the emergency escape chute. This was before the days that it was stowed in a compartment beneath the doorway. At that time it was located in a special housing in the ceiling. I reached up, found the handles and then, with a great whoosh, the escape chute came down. I tossed the end of the chute out of the door, reached back up to the ceiling and pulled a cord which was supposed to inflate it. But even in the darkness I could see that the slide hadn't gone all the way out of the aircraft. It was only halfway out the door so when I pulled the inflation cord it ballooned inwards, blocking the whole door. Things had become chaotic and I have to admit that I couldn't help laughing because one of the poor navigator's legs had become jammed against the wall with the chute pressing up into his crotch. I pulled out my pocket-knife and was just about to slash a hole in the chute to let the air out when it mysteriously unravelled and dropped all the way down to the ground. I found out afterwards that flight engineer J.N.R 'Bushy' del la Rey who was travelling in the back as a passenger had come forward to see what was happening and managed to partly deflate the chute, causing it to fold outwards from the door. Meanwhile, passengers were bailing out on other chutes in the main cabin. Then the fire trucks and emergency vehicles started arriving. We were blinded by spotlights as they surrounded us and smothered the whole aircraft in fire-retardant foam. Of course, there was no actual fire but what had frightened the pants off the emergency teams was that as we went skidding down the runway we had thrown up such a tremendous shower of sparks that they were sure we were going to burst into flames.

"The biggest miracle of all that night was that there weren't any fatalities or injuries. A few passengers sustained minor grazes or bruises but nothing serious. Once we got to the airport buildings by ambulance, fire truck or one of many other vehicles that had been sent to pick us up the first thing I wanted to do was phone my wife in South Africa because I knew she would soon hear about the crash and think it was fatal. So I managed to get through and tell her that there had been an accident and that we were all OK. After that initial low approach that had caused the damage in the first place Captain Rosslee had redeemed himself by going on to save us all with his wonderful airmanship skills. The following day the Kenyan Civil Aviation Board wanted statements from all of us. We gave them our reports as to what happened and then they told us later there would be a civil inquiry about the incident. In the meantime, we were sent back to South Africa.

"About a month later we were flown back to Nairobi for the official inquiry. The questions the Board asked were complicated and filled with criticism so the proceedings were very tense and intimidating. I can remember Captain Brian Bird in the dock being angrily questioned by the Queen's Council for the Crown and having a very hard time answering everything. Eventually the QC thought that he had better take the tension out of things by asking something a little more light-hearted so he asked Bird,

'Captain, what were your exact words as you hit the ground two full miles short of the runway?' Everyone in the court chuckled, including the judge, expecting some sort of crude or rude expletive to come out of Bird's mouth, but good old Brian remained calm and professional as he thought what to say and then answered, 'What did I say, your honor? What do you *think* I said? It certainly wasn't Oops!, that much I can assure you!' The result of the inquiry was that the incident was due to pilot error but even though poor old Captain Rosslee had done such a wonderful job of getting us down safely he was hauled over the carpet, both in Kenya and back home in South Africa. But what can you do? None of us are perfect, especially when the weather isn't cooperating. Fortunately for Rosslee, it didn't spell the end of his flying career."

As for the damaged aircraft lying on its belly at the end of the runway the first thing that had to be done was to have its tail removed. At a height of 38 feet, it was a dangerous obstacle to other traffic using the runway. An emergency repair team was flown out from Seattle and the heavy Boeing was lifted off the ground by having inflatable airbags placed under its wings. Then it was manoeuvred onto heavy-duty trailers and towed to the hangar and maintenance area. After a couple of months of hard work by the Boeing team and technicians flown up from South Africa, the fuselage was beautifully patched up, the undercarriage repaired and the aircraft was as good as new. On January 10, 1961, a successful test flight was undertaken at Nairobi and the aircraft was then flown back to Jan Smuts Airport. Within days it was back in service again. But the luckless airliner was soon to experience another unfortunate incident. On January 31, 1961, with Captain de Villiers Rademan at the controls, it aquaplaned while landing during a severe rainstorm and over-ran a very slippery and ice-encrusted runway at Zurich's Kloten Airport in Switzerland. The nose wheel suffered damage when the Boeing overshot the end of the runway and ran into a ditch. In those days it was difficult to avoid incidents like that in adverse weather conditions. Repairs were carried out and on February 19, 1961, the airplane was flown to Seattle via London and Montreal where it was fitted with the same sort of leading edge flaps that had been built into ZS-CKE. On March 31, 1961, ZS-CKD was also sent to Seattle for modification with the leading edge flaps. During its ferry flight back to South Africa it stopped off in London and then, with Captains 'Pi' Pienaar and Bob Truter as pilots, it was flown back to Johannesburg, shattering the non-stop run to a record 10 hours and 45 minutes. With the leading edge flap modifications completed all three Boeing 707s had now been brought up to the highest standards for operating in and out of Johannesburg's hot and high conditions. As for dealing with wet and icy runways in Europe that had caused the nosewheel incident with ZS-CKC, airplane tire manufacturers soon modified their tread designs to minimize the risks of aquaplaning.

On September 13, 1960, another new jetliner arrived at Jan Smuts Airport. UAT French Airlines introduced a daylight service between Paris and Johannesburg, becoming the first airline serving South Africa to operate the Douglas DC-8, main competitor to the Boeing 707. On November 7, Alitalia Airlines of Italy also introduced Douglas DC-8 services, replacing Douglas DC-6 aircraft on their Rome to Johannesburg route. On October 1, SAA opened an office in New York. On the same day a quadripartite arrangement came into effect which extended the pool partnership between SAA, BOAC and Central African Airways (CAA) to include East African Airways (EAA.)

Aviation was now alive and well in Africa but in other respects those were uncertain and dramatic times. After a month-long visit to British colonies throughout the continent, British Prime Minister Harold MacMillan paid a call to South Africa. He delivered an historic address to cabinet ministers and members of Parliament in Cape Town on February 3, 1960. The gist of his speech was all about the upwelling spirit of nationalism that was sweeping Africa. He predicted a rapid end to colonial rule and announced that Britain itself would now start granting independence to all of its remaining colonies, protectorates and possessions.

"The wind of change is blowing through this continent," he warned. "Whether we like it or not, this growth of national consciousness is a political fact."

What has now gone down in history as the 'Winds of Change' speech was not welcomed by the South African government at all. Clearly, Macmillan was implying that the country should give up its racist policies, dispense with segregation and incorporate its indigenous people into the nation's political and economic processes. But nothing was further from the mindset of the ruling National Party. To further rile the South African government, the rest of the European powers who had possessions in Africa also began murmuring about granting autonomy to their dependencies. As Macmillan had accurately predicted, the winds of change were blowing. And if they were not properly addressed by the powers-that-be, those winds would become a gale and eventually be fanned into an unstoppable hurricane.

One of the many European nations that decided to relinquish its hold on its single African possession was Belgium. In response to growing civil unrest and pressure for self-rule, independence was officially granted to the Belgian Congo on June 30, 1960, with Patrice Lumumba as Prime Minister. But competing factions, a multitude of 60 different political parties, long-simmering anti-white sentiment and brooding influences caused by the Cold War and its American and Soviet cronies in the Congo had turned members of the new black government against one another. This made things inflammatory. Like an ignited powder keg, the new Democratic Republic of the Congo exploded into chaos. Reflecting the most disturbing elements of Joseph Conrad's 1899 novel, *Heart of Darkness*, political rivalry and violence on an unprecedented scale erupted throughout the country. Many expatriates were trapped in a vicious civil war that followed a revolt by the army. Widespread looting, raping, maiming and murdering quickly followed. European and foreign citizens frantically crossed the Congo River from the city of Leopoldville to Brazzaville in French territory on the other side of the river and, in response to desperate pleas from the Belgian and French governments, SAA's fleet of Douglas DC-4s were despatched to evacuate expatriates—mainly women, children, the elderly and the infirm—and flew them to safety in Northern Rhodesia, Southern Rhodesia and South Africa. These mercy missions saved scores of lives. Large groups of South Africans were also stationed in the Congo and an SAA DC-7B was sent to Leopoldville to rescue them. In the resource-rich southern province of Katanga—where its leader Moise Tshombe wanted to secede from the rest of the Congo and declare itself a separate independent nation, backed by Belgian and American commercial and mining interests—more South Africans were trapped. They had been stationed there to help run copper, iron ore, manganese, cobalt, uranium, diamond and other mining operations. A couple of SAA DC-4s were sent to Katanga's largest city, Elisabethville, where they remained on standby to ferry people out of harm's way while United Nations peacekeeping troops patrolled the city's streets to try to restore order.

For security reasons, on July 16, 1960, Leopoldville was dropped as a stopover on the regular Springbok Service from Johannesburg to London. It was replaced by Luanda, largest city in Angola, the vast oil and diamond-rich Portuguese-held territory along the Congo's flank on the west coast. Unlike other European powers, Portugal stubbornly held on to its African colonies—or 'provinces' as it called them—of Angola, Mozambique, Guinea and the island groups of Cape Verde and Sao Tome off the West African coast. As opposed to a growing number of African states, at Lisbon's behest those territories maintained cordial relations with South Africa. But intensifying militancy against the Union because of its apartheid policies was gaining ground in many parts of Africa.

By now the United Nations had joined the rhetoric following a tragic incident on March 21, 1960, at a place called Sharpeville near the town of Vereeniging when police had opened fire on a crowd of blacks demonstrating against apartheid and the enforced carrying of identity documents. Racist laws required all blacks to carry identity cards or 'passes.' If they did not have legal permission to be in a specific area they were liable for immediate arrest or deportation to their native tribal region or place of birth. Sharpeville resulted in the killing of 69 people and serious injuries to hundreds more. On April 1, 1960, the Security Council of the U.N. adopted Resolution 134 virulently condemning the South African government. Animosity against South Africa was building.

Despite the worsening image of South Africa in the eyes of the rest of the world and the difficulty of trying to retain a clean public relations image for itself, SAA's mandate was clear. It was an airline. It had a job to do. Even though it was wholly owned and controlled by the South African government, its purpose was to provide safe, reliable air services to the traveling public, both domestic and foreign, whether white, black, brown, yellow or otherwise, transporting them to, from and within the country without prejudice. If it became a target of criticism in the intensifying political conflagration, it would be due to no fault of its own. But some critics—in Africa and abroad—could not resist emphasizing its links with prevailing South African government policies, even going so far as openly labelling it the 'apartheid airline.'

It should be remembered that South Africa was a member of the prestigious British Commonwealth of Nations in 1960. Most of its members—some of which were colonies only recently liberated from British rule—continued to turn up the anti-apartheid rhetoric. Prime Minister Hendrik Verwoerd felt that "This is because few understand my party's reasoning behind our policies."

He stated that the country was being unfairly singled out in a continent now rife with political upheaval. In his opinion it was probably time for South Africa to go it alone by no longer remaining subservient to the British Crown and to declare itself a republic. This was not only because members of the British Parliament were becoming some of the country's most vociferous critics but also because Verwoerd saw the move as a convenient final severing of the strings that attached South Africa to Britain as a result of losing the Boer War decades earlier. Verwoerd did, however, hope that this could be accomplished while still remaining a member of the British Commonwealth. On October 5, 1960, a national referendum was held and the majority of the all-white electorate chose the path for becoming a republic. But only just. Fifty-two per cent of the electorate—mainly members of the Afrikaner-dominated National Party—voted in favor of it. The overwhelming majority of English-speakers expressed an unequivocal no. But the road to becoming a republic was now a *fait accompli.* While Verwoerd had hoped that the Commonwealth would accept the result of the referendum, most member countries were not prepared to allow South Africa to retain its membership if it declared itself a republic, especially if it did not immediately forego its divisive racist policies. On May 15, 1961, at a meeting of Commonwealth heads of state in London, Verwoerd was further criticized for his nation's policies. In an attempt to resist humiliation, he politely withdrew from the meeting, announcing that he would not even bother seeking renewal of Commonwealth membership. South Africa would take its own independent path, he bellowed to the world. So, on May 31, 1961, the Union of South Africa ceased to be and the Republic of South Africa was born.

International criticism and a sense of isolationism within the country intensified. Around this time, various anti-apartheid black groups had ratcheted up campaigns within the country to try to coerce the government to end apartheid, but to little avail. One man in particular had a special role to play in these efforts. On August 5, 1962, a 46-year-old lawyer and amateur boxer was arrested for a second time for what were claimed by the prosecution to be 'subversive activities endangering the state.' On June 12, 1964, together with a group of others belonging to a banned organization called the African National Congress (ANC), he was sentenced to life imprisonment. But, 27 years later, the man whose name was Nelson Mandela would be released from prison, rise to become one of the greatest statesmen in history and lead the country to a democracy with the most tolerant and liberal constitution of any nation on earth.

Back in the sixties, SAA was trying to be as unaffected as it could by all the wrangling that were tainting the political landscape. The Flying Springbok continued to criss-cross African skies. By the end of 1960, the number of Boeing 707 frequencies to Europe were increased to five per week. Three services operated the east coast route via Nairobi and two along the west coast via either Luanda or Brazzaville. Earlier that year, on September 14, 1960, another special flight had been arranged from Johannesburg, this time using SAA's Douglas DC-7B, ZS-DKF, to fly all the competitors in the South African Olympic team to London. From there, they were flown onwards to Rome where the summer games were held. Little did anyone know it at the time but it was to be the last occasion that South Africa would compete in the Olympic Games for the next 32 years, another result of international abhorrence of the government's apartheid policies. That was an especially bitter blow to the people of South Africa—of all colors and all ethnicities—as sport was always regarded with utmost importance, even in the tiniest white country *dorp* (small town) or dustiest makeshift football field in the poorest black rural *kraal* (village settlement).

The regularly scheduled SAA service to Europe was now the exclusive preserve of the Boeing 707. In March, 1962, a non-stop service was introduced between Johannesburg and Athens. Bypassing all intermediate stops the Boeing streaked through the stratosphere straight across Africa in under ten hours. The first flight, on March 3, with Captains J.A. 'Bert' Rademan and Colin Beattie at the controls, was accomplished in an astonishing nine hours and 31 minutes. On that same date, frequencies on the Springbok Service were increased to six flights per week. On May 14, 1962, Germany's Lufthansa airlines introduced Boeing 720s—a slightly smaller but longer-range version of the 707—on its new Frankfurt to Johannesburg service.

Seven more Boeing 707s—in two variants, the model 344B and the 344C—would enter service with SAA during the next eight years. These airplanes were equipped with more powerful Pratt & Whitney JT3D-7W fan-jet engines. Each power plant delivered an unprecedented 19,000 lbs. of take-off thrust. They were also equipped with revolutionary water injection capabilities, giving added impetus to the engine's thrust. Incredibly, when water injection was employed, almost two tons of water passed through the engines in less than two minutes during take-off, using three times as much water than fuel. This was a huge boon to performance in the dry, hot conditions at airports such as Jan Smuts. The newer engines were not only more powerful but a lot quieter than the early 'organ pipe' models, making them far more neighbourhood-friendly. But it was their economic advantages that made them so much better for general operations. Larger and improved flaps on the Boeing 707 B and C models, together with the increased take-off thrust, resulted in significantly increased take-off weights, shorter take-off runs and lower take-off speeds. The flaps also improved landing performance, with speeds reduced by approximately 10 knots (12 mph.) This also shortened landing distances. The aerodynamic improvements on the B and C models, together with the improved economy of the fan-jet engine, brought about a fuel saving of almost twenty percent. This gave the later variants at least thirty to forty percent more range than the earlier A models while carrying similar or even heavier payloads. As these were also larger aircraft compared to the original A variants passenger capacity was increased to accommodate 178 people.

Boeing 707-344B, ZS-SAE, in flight. The more powerful water-injection engines made an enormous difference to the performance of this later model of the 707

SAA Boeing 707-344B. The later generation Pratt & Whitney JT3D-7W engines can be clearly seen

With the additional airplanes in the fleet, a Boeing 707 flight simulator was eventually installed in SAA's technical facilities at Jan Smuts Airport. It had no visual display capabilities and no pitch or yaw movement unlike the super-sophisticated hydraulically mounted simulators of today, but it provided sterling duties for training new pilots, for keeping them *au courant* on the airplane and for simulating emergencies such as stalls, engine flame-outs and other situations that could arise in the real world.

Boeing 707 flight simulator in the SAA training division at Jan Smuts Airport

During the sixties, SAA sales offices were opened in Hamburg, Dusseldorf, Milan and Geneva. That decade a decision was made to extend the Boeing's orange-tail livery to all other aircraft in the fleet, creating uniformity of branding and identity. In contrast to those who expressed doubts about the new look just a couple of years earlier, many exclaimed what a fine sight it was to see all those different aircraft types—Boeing 707s, Douglas DC-7Bs, Vickers Viscounts, Lockheed Constellations, Douglas DC-4 Skymasters, Douglas DC-3 Dakotas—lined up on the flight line outside the terminal building at Jan Smuts Airport sporting their striking orange tails and modern color schemes.

Douglas DC-3 in new livery

Douglas DC-4 in new livery

Douglas DC-7B in new livery

**Vickers Viscount in new livery. The aircraft is seen with one of the
fully steerable antennae of Radio ZUR in the background**

The Flying Springbok was happily aloft, plying the African skies
and proudly flying the South African flag. It seemed that little
could thwart its progress. But then came 1963. And with it came
a challenge of such magnitude that it would threaten the very
survival of the airline.

Chapter 10

The Great Detour

1963 got underway with SAA's route network continually expanding. Additional or increased services were operating to neighboring territories Mozambique, Swaziland, Basutoland, Bechuanaland, Southern Rhodesia, Nyasaland and South-West Africa. Internal domestic services using Vickers Viscounts, Douglas DC-4s and Dakotas were usually filled to capacity. International services to Europe, the Middle East and Australia were also carrying full passenger loads and on April 27, Qantas — equally popular with the traveling public — replaced their Lockheed L1049 Super Constellations with turboprop Lockheed 188 Electra aircraft on the Sydney to Johannesburg route.

But there was another side to this rosy picture.

As more African nations gained their independence, anti-South African attitudes intensified. Even though for the most part criticism of South Africa's policies was well meant and intended to help bridge the ruthless racial divide in the country, it was also becoming quite fashionable to hop on board the anti-apartheid bandwagon. Never mind that racial segregation was still alive and well in many other places around the world. In the United States, for example, the Civil Rights movement was still in its infancy. 1963 was the year when incoming Alabama governor called for 'Segregation now, segregation tomorrow, segregation forever.' It was also the year that Martin Luther King gave his famous 'I Have a Dream' speech. But the world's eyes were narrowly and scrupulously focusing on South Africa.

If newly independent African countries really wanted to inflict harm on the country the easiest way to do that would be to target something soft and vulnerable. What better example than the national airline? Things could get nasty. And dangerous. What if

SAA aircraft were impounded when they landed? What if some countries threatened to inflict damage on airplanes by pointing guns at them? How could passengers' safety be assured? How to prepare for the worst? Behind closed doors at government offices in Pretoria and at SAR & H and SAA headquarters in Johannesburg, these were questions that were being seriously discussed in an emergency project code-named in Afrikaans 'Operasie Ompad' ('Operation Detour'). A solution had to be found to maintain the regular Springbok Service to Europe without jeopardizing the safety and security of any aircraft or its passengers and crew. Because of the foresight of people like Mike Vialls of SAA's technical division, Chief Navigator Mick Mackin, Flight Technical Manager 'Duke' Davidson and L.C. du Toit of the Division of Civil Aviation, contingency plans were already underway.

A year earlier—on December 10, 1962—with Captain Mathew McFarlane in command and without any passengers on board, an SAA Douglas DC-7B had taken off from Jan Smuts Airport on a secret mission. Its purpose was to survey the west coast of Africa to seek out an alternative route to London and other destinations in Europe. Stops were made at three Portuguese-controlled territories, Luanda in Angola and the islands of Sao Tome´ and Ilha do Sal. Four days later, McFarlane returned with his report about the airport facilities at those destinations. Should the need arise, Luanda might just be adequate enough to handle a Boeing 707 aircraft but the other two airfields fell far short of safety and technical requirements. However, the lighting at Luanda's longest runway was insufficient, restricting flights to daylight operations only. It would need a completely upgraded lighting system. There was a shorter runway with better lighting but it was not long enough for the big jets. Ground support equipment at the airport was also below par. Much of it was fine for servicing the smaller types of aircraft that SAA was already operating there but certainly nowhere near what was required

for coping with a Boeing 707. Another problem was the terminal
building. It was way too small for dealing with large groups of
passengers. There was no restaurant. Restroom facilities were
insufficient and in need of repair. Clearly, if Luanda airport
would ever have to serve as an alternative stopover on the
Springbok Service it would need a lot of work and attention.

Fortunately, a new runway designed to accommodate large
jetliners was under construction at the Aeropuerto de Gran
Canaria (Gran Canaria Airport) on the Spanish island of Las
Palmas in the Atlantic Ocean, 124 miles off the coast of Morocco.
If the worst came SAA Boeing 707s might be able to land there,
avoiding a large proportion of African airspace by bypassing
the central and eastern parts of the continent altogether. London
and Europe were well within reach from Las Palmas. The trouble
was that SAA had no regularly scheduled services to the island
so no ground support facilities for handling its aircraft existed
there.

In May 1963, the inevitable happened. Africa began pulling
a grass curtain across its skies. Under the chairmanship of
Emperor Halie Salassie of Ethiopia, leaders of 32 nations met
in Addis Ababa to create an organization intended to give them
a united voice in all political matters relating to the continent.
Known as the Organization of African Unity (OAU), the new
body was also intended to help leaders of independent African
nations work towards the process of 'dismantling colonialism'
in the few remaining white-ruled areas of Africa. As far as the
OAU was concerned that meant Southern Rhodesia, Angola,
Mozambique and South Africa. In its manifesto, the OAU
declared to do whatever it could to support 'freedom fighters'
in those countries. It would also finance and create training
bases to help indigenous populations in their aspirations to free
themselves from white domination and to provide arms and
assistance wherever needed. In addition, it would encourage
member nations to cloister their airspace against any aircraft

registered in white-ruled countries. On May 25, 1963—the day the conference ended—Algeria and Egypt announced that with immediate effect aircraft from South Africa would no longer be allowed to overfly their territories. It would only be a matter of time before other nations followed suit. SAA needed to act. Fast.

It is important to remember that one of the essentials in the world of commercial aviation is that every airline captain has to be 'familiarized' with a route before he can take charge of a flight operating that route. He has to know about all the prevailing conditions at an airport long before he flies into or out of it with passengers. He needs to be *au fait* with local air traffic control regulations, radio communication formalities, the topography around the airport, weather patterns, instrument landing systems, runway conditions, procedures for taxiing, for approaching the terminal building and for parking his aircraft. He also needs to be fully acquainted with ground support and maintenance facilities and, of course, refuelling operations.

Because SAA now urgently needed an alternative to flying directly over Africa, two pilots were selected to familiarize themselves with the route from Johannesburg to Las Palmas and then onwards to Europe. They were Senior Captains J. de Villiers Rademan—the airline's Overseas Fleet Captain at the time—and Salomon 'Pi' Pienaar. Accompanied by Traffic Manager Doug Kirkwood and Head of Technical Operations Trevor Philips, in June 1963, they visited Madrid, Lisbon and Las Palmas for an exploratory survey. Arrangements were made for Pienaar to sit in as an observer on the flight deck of a Trans World Airlines (TWA) Boeing 707 flight from Rome to Madrid and Lisbon on June 12, just in case Spain and Portugal might one day have to serve as technical stop-overs for SAA. Then, on June 16, he flew as an observer on an Iberian Airlines Lockheed L1049 Super Constellation flight from Lisbon to Madrid. On June 17, he sat in the cockpit jump seat of in an Iberian Caravelle jet flight from Madrid to Las Palmas, returning to Madrid the following day. In the exploratory group's opinion, Lisbon and Madrid were very well equipped to handle big jets but Las Palmas was not quite up to standard yet. That would change as soon as the new runway under construction there was completed. In the meantime, if push came to shove, the existing runway would have to suffice. Having gained some first-hand experience flying into the Aeropuerto de Gran Canaria at Las Palmas, Rademan and Pienaar were now ready to train other pilots on familiarization flights into it, if and when, the time arose. To ensure that one of them was always available to do this, they were stationed at opposite ends of the Springbok route, with 'Pi' Pienaar in London and de Villiers Rademan in Johannesburg. Hastily drawn up rosters made certain that if one of them was in the air the other would be on the ground, ready to board a flight at any time to coach a crew unacquainted with the route.

Captain 'Pi' Pienaar. Stationed in London he helped pioneer the southbound 'round-the-bulge' route

As another precautionary measure, at the end of June, an SAA Douglas DC-4 Skymaster left Johannesburg for Luanda loaded with a variety of Boeing 707 spares, engine parts and ground support equipment. Also on board were SAA's Traffic Operations

**Captain de Villiers Rademan. Stationed in Johannesburg, he helped
pioneer the northbound 'round-the-bulge' route**

Manager Doug Kirkwood, Flight Operations Planner Jack Mowat,
Commercial Officer Jeff Scott and Captain de Villiers Rademan.
Their mission was categorized as 'top secret' by SAA as well
as by the South African government and by the Portuguese
authorities in Angola, who were being very cooperative about the
whole affair. As no Boeing 707 had ever landed at Luanda, a vast
number of technical problems needed to be resolved. In addition
to the runway lighting and terminal deficiencies, arrangements
had to be made to address matters regarding jet fuel availability,
ground support services, crew slipping accommodation, on-
board catering supplies, the taking on of fresh drinking water,
aircraft toilet evacuation and cleaning services, the training of
ground staff, the storage of emergency aircraft spares, assisting
the Portuguese to expand existing customs and immigration
facilities and to help upgrade the airport's emergency rescue
and fire brigade facilities. These and a host of other items that
go hand-in-hand with the operation of a big transcontinental jet
airliner service were crucial.

When the DC-4 returned to Johannesburg, Jeff Scott remained
in Luanda and was appointed Station Manager there. He had
been fully briefed about what might happen if the 707s had to
suddenly divert from their normal route and go through Luanda.
In that event he had to plan for the most taxing of scenarios. Exact
arrival times of aircraft would be unpredictable. What sort of

chaos might ensue when the first of the big jets landed was hard to imagine. Even though Scott had taken an apartment in the city, he decided to set up a small office with a bed and cooking facilities at the airport so that he could be on-site at all times, just in case the route change-over was implemented at short notice. In the meantime, temporary permission was obtained from the Spanish civil aviation authorities in Madrid for SAA to use the airport at Las Palmas as a refuelling stop-over. Of course, no one knew if and when the two alternative airports might be needed.

And then the decisive blow fell.

On August 21, 1963, Libya announced an immediate overflight ban of any South African-registered aircraft. As if this weren't enough, Prime Minister Mahmud al-Muntasir threatened that if an SAA airliner violated the ban and flew through Libyan airspace, it would be intercepted and shot down. This completely sealed off all North African airspace. Now there was no way that an SAA aircraft could approach the northern latitudes of the continent from either the north or the south. The grass curtain had become a solid, unbridgeable brick wall. At 3.30 p.m. the following day, the airline's Chief Executive Johan G. Grove announced to a hastily gathered group of senior SAA staff that the Libyan ban was in effect. However, he was adamant that the Springbok Service should not be cancelled. Acting on direct instructions from the Minister of Transport, he stated that, come what may, everything had to be done to keep the service operating. Flights would be diverted to the new route around the west coast of Africa that very night.

There was only one problem. And it was a big one. With one country after another announcing that they would follow the actions of Libya, Algeria and Egypt, SAA could not fly a direct vector from Johannesburg to Las Palmas. The reason was because following a straight line between those two points meant flying over the so-called 'Bulge of Africa.' That bulge—where the continent extends westwards into the Atlantic Ocean from Cameroon on the Gulf of Guinea to Libya on the Mediterranean Sea—is a gargantuan geographic feature. It is nearly 4,000,000 square miles in area and includes a vast swathe of the Western Sahara desert plus countries such as Nigeria, Ghana, Liberia, Senegal, Mauritania, Morocco, Algeria, Mali, Niger, Chad and about a dozen others, all of them now openly hostile towards South Africa. The airspace above these countries was now out of bounds to SAA. There was no option but for SAA aircraft to make a wide detour around the entire bulge of the continent, remaining far out over Atlantic Ocean and maintaining a safe distance away from the African mainland.

Tremendous technical challenges now existed. The detour added over two thousand extra miles to the route, not to mention the three or four more hours that would be spent in the air. Extra fuel would have to be carried, adding a great deal of weight to the airplane. This would reduce passenger and freight capacity. It would also tax the aircrew's skills because their airplane would have to fly at the most optimum altitude to reduce fuel consumption while also trying to avoid the notorious headwinds in the area. Headwinds not only slowed down an aircraft's speed but increased fuel consumption. It was all a delicate balancing act that would challenge the most experienced of pilots. Fortunately, SAA's Radio ZUR station at Jan Smuts Airport would help the situation by monitoring the flight's progress and ensure direct voice communication between headquarters and the aircraft at all times. The challenges were enormous but there was no turning back. The show had to go on. But could it really be pulled off?

At midnight on August 21, an SAA Douglas DC-4 Skymaster freighter secretly left Johannesburg for Luanda. On board were Lee Swartz, the airline's technical support officer, a few other members of the engineering staff, and Eric Bradford, a representative of Mobil Oil, the company that had been contracted to supply SAA with Jet A-1 fuel. Also on board was a ground electrical power unit for the Boeing 707. Custom-built by engineers and apprentices of SAA's technical workshops at Jan Smuts Airport, it was smaller than the normal unit used to provide power to the aircraft while it was stationary but it would do the job. A hastily-built compact mechanical runway sweeper was on board too, plus a drinking water purifying unit. Tucked in among all this equipment were banks of auxiliary battery-operated lighting fixtures for Luanda's main runway.

Everything was perfectly calm and relaxed at Jan Smuts Airport when passengers checked in for the Brazzaville and London-bound flight SA 224 on the evening of August 22, 1963. Nobody—including counter clerks, check-in personnel, ground crew or passengers—were vaguely aware of the extraordinary tension and high drama that was going on behind the scenes. In command of flight 224 was Captain de Villiers Rademan. As he had already flown into the Gran Canaria Airport at Las Palmas, he would provide familiarization training to two other senior pilots accompanying him on the flight deck that night. They were Captains Theo Purchase and Ken Jones. Travelling as passengers in the rear were Chief Airways Manager, Colonel 'Japie' Louw, who was going to London to make arrangements at Heathrow for accommodating the change in routing and Traffic Manager Doug Kirkwood who was headed for Las Palmas to finalize permanent landing rights there. As soon as the flight was airborne, Rademan made an announcement over the public address system. Offering sincere apologies to the passengers on behalf of the airline, he said that the trip to London would take a little longer than originally scheduled. The flight would land at Brazzavile, as scheduled, but would then go on to Las Palmas in the Canary Islands before continuing on to London. Trying to make it all sound pretty simple and straightforward, he said that it would be the first time that an SAA airliner would stop at Las Palmas. He did not mention anything about the great detour the aircraft would take around the bulge of Africa but their journey, he told his passengers, would be an historic one.

What very few people knew—including those within the airline itself—was that on the previous night, two other SAA flights had been exposed to extremely dangerous situations because of the newly imposed ban. A northbound flight under the command of Captain Harry Launder was heading for Athens via Nairobi. No banning order had yet been received from Libya but senior SAA management knew it was imminent. Launder was contacted by radio and told that if a banning order was issued whilst his flight was en route he was to ignore it and maintain radio silence until he entered the Athens air traffic control area. Needless to say, he was to do whatever he could to remain undetected. Rising to the demands of the unexpected and the difficult, which are two of the hallmarks of any good pilot, that is exactly what Launder did when news of the overflight ban came through on Radio-ZUR. The next morning his aircraft landed safely at Athens. It was the last of any SAA flight to operate a direct northerly vector directly across the continent for many years to come.

That same night, southbound flight SA 217, commanded by Captain Frank Retief had left Athens for Johannesburg before he was able to be informed about the upcoming ban. Shortly after take-off, he received an urgent message from the air traffic controller at Athens telling him that his intended flight path over North Africa was forbidden. Under no circumstances should he enter Libyan airspace. If he did, his aircraft would be attacked and shot down. By the time he was contacted by Radio ZUR from Johannesburg a few minutes later to tell him about the prohibition, he had already taken the initiative by deciding to divert to Rome. Once there he had planned to contact SAA headquarters for an assessment of the situation and to await instructions as to what he should do next. To avoid wasting any more time, Radio ZUR immediately patched him into a voice link with Captain de Villiers Rademan who advised him to proceed to Rome, refuel his aircraft, pretend that all was well, then take off, ignore the ban and fly directly over North Africa at maximum height and speed to Johannesburg. He was to maintain radio silence until he entered friendly skies. As explained to Retief by Rademan, there was not enough time for him to go around the bulge as his airplane was urgently needed to operate the next northbound round-the-bulge flight from Johannesburg the following evening. Like many pilots, Retief relished a challenge and was also enamoured with the prospect of high speed so he was only too happy to oblige. Taking off from Rome he piloted his Boeing 707 to maximum altitude above the Mediterranean, then turned south, thrust the throttles all the way forward and streaked over Africa at full speed, making a direct beeline for Johannesburg. Fortunately, because of the aircraft's extreme altitude and velocity it was neither detected nor intercepted as it dashed over Libya, Chad and the Central African Republic before overflying the Congo, Northern Rhodesia, Southern Rhodesia and Bechuanaland to South Africa. It landed safely at Jan Smuts Airport the following morning with the passengers none the wiser about their close brush with fate except for being somewhat surprised at having arrived so much ahead of schedule.

The following night, on August 22, the first officially planned round-the-bulge northbound flight, SAA 224 with de Villiers Rademan at the controls, landed at Gran Canaria Airport in Las Palmas from Brazzaville and Johannesburg. Ground crew, Spanish immigration personnel and members of Iberia Airlines' ground staff gave the aircraft a very warm welcome. However, the airport manager was more reserved. He had not yet received the official directive about the flight from the Civil Aviation authorities on the Spanish mainland. As far as he was concerned, flight SA 224 was accepted purely on the basis of an emergency refuelling stopover. When told by Doug Kirkwood that other SAA flights might follow, he expressed grave doubt whether landing rights would be granted. This was not good news for Kirkwood. Obviously, there was a very serious lack of communication between the Civil Aviation authorities in Spain and the airport manager. The matter had to be sorted out before the first southbound SAA flight arrived. When SA 224 departed for London, Doug Kirkwood was not on board. He stayed behind to continue conducting feverish negotiations with the recalcitrant manager who—to complicate matters—spoke no English. Fortunately, a friendly travel agent in Las Palmas was located and turned out to be an excellent interpreter and go-between. After lengthy discussions, the airport manager reluctantly agreed to allow the expected southbound flight to land but, he insisted, if government clearance from Madrid had not come through by the following day no more SAA aircraft would be permitted to use the airport. Kirkwood was at a loss for answers. Desperately worried he could only stand by and wait, his pulse racing.

A couple of hours later, an SAA flight that originated in Rome came in from the north. At the controls were Captains Doug Meaker and Hylton Inggs. Neither of them had ever flown the route before so 'Pi' Pienaar had travelled from London to Rome to join their flight and familiarize them with the Las Palmas airport approach procedures. In the meantime, crew rosters were frantically rearranged at SAA's home base in Johannesburg where it was decided that Meaker would leave the southbound flight at Brazzaville and then wait for the next northbound flight, hop aboard and guide that aircrew through their route familiarization process.

Luanda in Angola remained an alternative stop-over in this unfolding drama. But things were not progressing as smoothly as hoped. A Portuguese engineer in charge of teams installing the additional new lighting along the airport's long runway was turning out to be disinterested and unmotivated, behaving like an archetypal bored European civil servant in the tropics. An incoming jet may be imminent at any moment but the runway was littered with mounds of earth, cables, rubble and construction equipment. Despite every coercive effort by Lee Swartz to speed things up, the work proceeded at a snail's pace. Swartz had no recourse but to plead to the highest diplomatic levels in town for help. Once Lisbon was informed about the issue, local authorities whipped into action, bearing down on the engineer and getting him to speed up his work. Within hours the runway and taxiways were cleared of all obstacles. SAA technicians who had flown in on the DC-4 moved in, using their makeshift runway sweeper to rid the runway surface of any remaining dirt and debris that might be ingested by a Boeing's jet engines. Then they laid down wide strips of light-reflecting Scotchguard tape along both sides of the runway, clearly marking it for any potential incoming flight. Visibility was enhanced by staggering batteries of lights along the perimeter to illuminate the tape. Swartz also arranged for the city's fire brigade to be on standby to supplement the inadequate fire-fighting facilities at the airport in case of an emergency. By nightfall everything was in order. Luanda was ready to land a Boeing 707.

But that would not become necessary. At least, not yet. Springbok Service flights would only start coming through Luanda a few weeks later. Station Manager Jeff Scott recalled that he couldn't leave his post at the airport throughout that uncertain period. "I ate, slept and lived at the airport. We never knew when one of our aircraft might be diverted to Luanda and suddenly come flying out of the blue with very little warning. I had to be ready for that eventuality at all times. It was nerve-wracking. I don't think I got any sleep for weeks." When Boeing 707 flights did start coming through Luanda SAA opened an office in the city in September, 1963, making it an official destination on the airline's route network.

As for Las Palmas, nothing had been resolved when the first

two flights were routed through it. Following his frustrating experience with the airport manager, Doug Kirkwood was on the verge of hysteria. Would any more SAA aircraft be given permission to land? Finally, on his third day of waiting Kirkwood heard that diplomatic clearances from Madrid had duly been issued. But his jubilation was short-lived. As far as the airport manager was concerned no confirmation had yet been received by him. The fourth day was equally exasperating. Not hiding his irritation, the airport manager issued a directive that no more SAA flights could land at Gran Canaria. Period. Kirkwood did not know what to do. He was only too aware of the fact that more Boeing jetliners were heading towards Las Palmas at close to the speed of sound from both the north and the south but now they wouldn't be allowed to use the airport.

Kirkwood had little choice but to resort to subtle psychological tactics. The airport manager was of an older generation, often chatting about the grand old days when he was young and when Junkers Ju52s were in service in Spain. He did not hide the fact that the Ju52 was an airplane especially dear to his heart. Kirkwood seized his chance. Pulling up a chair in the manager's office, he painted a detailed verbal picture of how reliably the trusty old Ju52s had served SAA. He stressed that for many years they were wonderful, dependable and loveable airplanes and that no one in South Africa missed them more than he did. His story worked. It struck a sensitive chord with the manager. Now the two men had something in common. Now they could mourn the past and pine for the good old days. The manager's attitude softened even further when conversation drifted to the subject of headwinds and their infamous severity around the bulge of Africa. It was a topic of great concern to him. Kirkwood had found another tender spot within the man so he asked whether SAA aircraft could land for refuelling purpose only if the headwinds had been particularly strong. The airport chief thought it over very carefully and then agreed that, yes, that would certainly be a valid reason for landing. If SAA needed the airport in another emergency, it could land. And just in time too. Within hours of the conversation an aircraft swooped in from the south.

But Kirkwood's troubles weren't yet over. As the Boeing landed it burst a tire. Because SAA had no access to spare parts in Las Palmas he now had to engage in skilful negotiations with the local customs authorities, begging them to instruct the ground engineering staff to provide a replacement tire from the airport's locked spares warehouse. Eventually it was agreed that a new tire would be made available if the damaged one was handed over in exchange to the Spanish customs authorities. It seemed like an absurd trade but Kirkwood had to keep his cool and play along with local rules. After an hour of wrangling, the tire was changed and the Boeing departed for London. Despite all the petty glitches and irritations that Kirkwood had to endure, within another day landing clearances finally arrived from Madrid and the necessary documents were handed over to the airport manager. Things were officially rubber-stamped and legal. All was well. Las Palmas would now become a regular stopover on the Springbok Service.

Meantime, one by one, countries all over central and eastern Africa had also begun shutting their airspace to South African aircraft. After many years of serving Kenya, SAA was denied landing rights in Nairobi in September, 1963. With that development came the termination of the quadripartite pool agreement between SAA, BOAC, Central African Airways and East African Airways. On May 11 the following year, Brazzaville shut its doors and its airspace. When Northern Rhodesia became the independent Republic of Zambia in October 1964, it too denied South Africa any further traffic or overflight rights. Luanda now became a crucial west coast stop-over as SAA aircraft began using it as a springboard to head out over the Atlantic, bypass the entire African continent and follow a course around the bulge to Europe. In addition to landing at Las Palmas, with the cooperation of Portuguese authorities, regular landing facilities were also acquired for Lisbon. So, in times to come, whether bound for London or Rome or even as far east as Tel Aviv, SAA paved a regular aerial pathway to all its northerly destinations via the great bulge of Africa.

The lengthy 'Round-the-Bulge' route to Europe, the Mediterranean and the Middle East from South Africa. SAA was compelled to avoid African airspace after the 'grass curtain' came down. This map dates to the early eighties and includes Abidjan in the Ivory Coast as a technical stop-over, but the great detour that SAA had to fly around the entire continent went into effect in 1963 and lasted for nearly three decades

There are very few people who were with the airline during those turbulent years who do not have intense personal memories about how the round-the-bulge service came about. Bill Poyser, SAA's station manager at Heathrow at the time, recalled that when flight 224 arrived in London on the morning of August 23, 1963, he simply entered a note in his diary: 'SA 224 diverted via Las Palmas.' "But," Poyser commented, "although it was such a tiny note in my diary those few words tell a tremendous story. The organization and behind-the-scenes work that were required to change our route pattern overnight without the cancellation of a single service was an amazing achievement. It's hard to believe that we did it. But we did."

James Adam, who became Chief Executive of the airline ten years after the inauguration of the round-the-bulge service, went on record saying that the establishment of the circuitous route around Africa was probably SAA's 'finest hour.'

Many would agree. In the face of enormous adversity, the Springbok Service was pulled from the brink of catastrophe. The financial ramifications of its demise would have been disastrous, possibly threatening SAA's very survival as an international carrier. But that is not what happened. Flights both north and south were smoothly maintained, not only ensuring unbroken passenger and freight operations without a single cancelled service, but allowing the airline to eventually spread its wings to many new destinations throughout Europe.

The demands of the round-the-bulge route would even generate valuable technical spin-offs. Working in close consultation with manufacturers abroad, SAA's needs would spur the development of innovative ideas and equipment to improve the long-distance range, payloads and fuel efficiency of future aircraft and engines. Other carriers around the world would benefit from those advancements. And it all came from an unlikely and unexpected chain of events back in 1963 when the orange-tailed jets were expelled from African skies and forced to fly a wide detour around the vast, hulking western mass of the continent. That trail, difficult and exceptionally costly though it was, would be operated without incident or mishap for the next 28 years.

Chapter 11

Triumph and Tragedy

On February 1, 1964, champagne corks popped and festivities were in the air. It was SAA's 30th anniversary. There was much to celebrate. Although it was still not fully covering its operating costs, traffic was healthy. Load factors were good. The airline's safety record was untarnished. The African closed-sky crisis had been overcome and the round-the-bulge route had become routine. The Boeing 707 fleet continued to be expanded and the Springbok Service was in full operation without a glitch.

Lisbon was now added as a regular port of call. During the ensuing year new sales offices were opened in many cities throughout Europe as well as in the United States. On the domestic and regional front things were going well too. In May, an order was placed for five Boeing 727 three-engine medium-range jet aircraft. Their arrival the following year would significantly improve local services. The new planes would slice huge chunks of time off routes between Johannesburg, Durban, Cape Town, Port Elizabeth, Kimberley and Bloemfontein, as well as to Salisbury and Bulawayo in neighboring Southern Rhodesia and to Blantyre in Malawi.

But with all these developments came moments of sadness and nostalgia. On October 10, 1964, SAA's four much-loved Lockheed L749A Constellation 'Gold Plate' aircraft were sold to Aviation Charter Enterprises in the U.K. Also, after many years of stalwart service, Douglas DC-3 Dakotas were withdrawn from routes between Johannesburg and Cape Town. In April 1965, flights to Victoria West and Beaufort West were permanently cancelled. These two towns in the vast semiarid plateau region of South Africa known as the Karroo had featured prominently during the early days of commercial aviation and now their airfields lay silent, used only by the occasional charter flight or by local flying clubs on weekends.

As Portugal's Transportes Aéreos Portugueses (TAP) airline had commenced operations to Johannesburg from Lisbon a pool partnership agreement between it and SAA came into effect on April 1, 1965. Meanwhile, SAA's pool partnership with BOAC was as strong as ever, with BOAC now operating British-made Vickers VC10 aircraft on the London to Johannesburg route. These beautiful airplanes, with four Rolls-Royce engines located in a pair of pods at the rear end of the fuselage, were not subject to the Organization of African Unity's (OAU) closed-sky policy because they carried United Kingdom registrations and not South African. The VC10s served London and Johannesburg via Nairobi, making the journey between Heathrow and Jan Smuts a few hours faster than flights operated by SAA on the more circuitous route around the bulge of Africa. On May 7, 1965, SAA increased its flights to Perth, Australia from a bi-weekly to a weekly service using Douglas DC-7B aircraft. For a while these airplanes alternated with a specially chartered Lockheed Constellation Starliner L1649A in a new revenue pool partnership with Qantas. The Constellation was leased from Trek Airways, a small, privately owned South African company that operated low cost flights from Johannesburg to Dusseldorf, Germany and to Luxembourg. SAA contracted Trek Airways to do ten flights to Perth, mainly due to the fact that many SAA aircrews were temporarily unavailable because of their conversion training in preparation for the arrival of the eagerly awaited new Boeing 727 aircraft. However, SAA navigators accompanied Trek Airways pilots and flight engineers during the contract period. The Trek Constellation was used until September 28, 1965, after which all flights were once again resumed with SAA DC-7Bs.

SAA Constellation on the main apron at Jan Smuts Airport. These beautiful airliners were withdrawn from service in 1964

An interesting sidebar to this episode is that while SAA normally operated their DC-7Bs at altitudes around 20,000 feet, the Trek Constellation was operated at a height of between 12,000 and 14,000 feet. Trek Airways believed that flying at lower altitudes saved engine life by not using the high-altitude superchargers on the Constellation's engines. The Wallaby Service from South Africa to Australia was exclusively operated by either piston-engine or turboprop aircraft by both SAA and Qantas until runway extensions at Perth Airport could accommodate jets.

On June 24, 1965, the first of the new Boeing 727 trijets arrived from the United States. ZS-DYM *Tugela* (the name of the longest river that flows through Zululand and Natal) was flown to Johannesburg under the command of Captains 'Pi' Pienaar and Albertus Geldenhuis 'Bert' Rademan—brother of renowned pilot Captain de Villiers Rademan—accompanied by flight engineer Malcolm McKendrick and navigator Owen Richard 'Mick' Mackin. Also on board was a Boeing technician and a navigator. In addition, traveling along for fun as an informal guest of SAA was the famous South African championship professional golfer, Gary Player. According to the logbooks of Pienaar and Mackin the aircraft left Boeing Field at Renton, Seattle at 3 p.m. on June 21, bound for Montreal,

Canada. The flying time was exactly four hours. The following day the aircraft departed Montreal at 1 p.m. and landed at Gander, Newfoundland two hours later. After a brief 25-minute refuelling stop, the jet departed Gander at 3.25 p.m., landing at Santa Maria in the Azores at 6.40 p.m. After refuelling, it left Santa Maria at 7.10 p.m., arriving at Las Palmas at 9.00 p.m. The crew then spent a rest day at Las Palmas, not to mention frequenting their favorite piano bar a couple of blocks away from their hotel. Over the years this little dive became a long-time favorite of SAA aircrews. The barman behind the counter eventually picked up quite a good smattering of Afrikaans. Just after midnight on June 24, the Boeing 727 departed for the Portuguese island of Ilha do Sal, landing at 2.35 a.m. Refueled once again, the airplane left for Portuguese Sao Tomé at 3.20 a.m. Four hours and 35 minutes later, it landed there. Were it not for the Portuguese islands the delivery flight would not have been possible because the aircraft—carrying a South African registration—was not permitted to overfly or land at any airport on the African mainland due to the OAU ban. Departure from Sao Tomé was at 9.05 a.m., arriving at Luanda, Angola an hour and 40 minutes later. Taking on fuel again, the 727 left Luanda at 11.20 a.m. and touched down at Jan Smuts Airport two hours and 55 minutes later at 2.15 p.m. on June 24.

The decor of the main cabin of the Boeing 727 matched that of SAA's Boeing 707s, depicting subtle graphics of South African flora and fauna on the walls and bulkheads. A Boeing 727 flight simulator arrived shortly after the first aircraft was delivered. This one was slightly more sophisticated than the Boeing 707 simulator already in use for aircrew training. Nevertheless, crews gained most of their required 50-hour flying training on actual aircraft as soon as the rest of the 727s were delivered. These training flights invariably took place from Jan Smuts Airport in the very early hours of the morning before the airplanes were needed for normal daily passenger flights.

Boeing 727-100, 1965

Boeing 727 at D.F. Malan Airport, Cape Town

A line-up of three Boeing 727s outside the domestic terminal at Jan
Smuts Airport

SAA's Boeing 727-100 aircraft had a wingspan of 108 ft, a length of 133 ft 2 ins and a height of 34 ft. Its empty weight was 80,602 lbs and its maximum all-up weight 170,000 lbs. Its greatest speed—or VMO in aviation parlance—was 632 mph or Mach 0.88. (Mach 1 is equivalent to the speed of sound so this means that the aircraft was certified for safe operation at 88 percent of the speed of sound). Cruising speed was 570 mph at a height of 30,000 feet. Maximum operating height was 40,000 feet. Fully laden the jet's maximum range was 1,420 miles. The 727 was equipped with three Pratt & Whitney JT8D-7 engines situated at the rear end of the fuselage, two on either side of the body and one at the base of the rudder assembly. The engines had ducted turbofans developing 14,000 lbs (6,227 kN) of thrust each. Crew consisted of two pilots and a flight engineer with a minimum of three cabin attendants taking care of passengers' needs. In its first configuration the 727 carried 98 passengers in five-abreast seating but this was later altered to 119 passengers in a six-abreast arrangement.

The mid to late sixties was a time of economic prosperity in South Africa. Cities such as Johannesburg constantly echoed to the rattle of pneumatic drills, earth pounders and the grinding cacophony of cement mixers as new skyscrapers soared skyward. Industries of all sorts were thriving. Because the government's strict apartheid policy and draconian 'job reservation' laws prevented blacks from seeking employment in many sectors of the economy, there was a vacuum in the labor market for skilled workers. This resulted in an inflow of white immigrants from Europe. Demand for skilled workers was so great that on August 11, 1965, SAA and UAT French Airlines introduced a special low-cost fare of R150 (South African rands) for immigrants and their families traveling from Paris or Nice to Johannesburg. During the sixties white immigrants streamed into the country, coming mainly from places as diverse as the United Kingdom, Germany, France, Portugal, Italy, Holland and Greece. Because of the Suppression of Communism Act—passed by Parliament in 1950—visitors or immigrants from any Soviet bloc country were prohibited from entering South Africa.

More nostalgia was experienced by many SAA employees, members of the travel industry and the public at large when the venerable Douglas DC-4 Skymasters operated the last scheduled passenger service for SAA on September 30, 1965. The final flight, SA 605, was from Windhoek to Upington, Kimberley, Bloemfontein and Johannesburg. At the controls were Captain 'Topper' van der Spuy and co-pilot Gus Ferguson. The aircraft was ZS-AUA *Tafelberg*. This was the very first DC-4 to be delivered to SAA from the Douglas plant in California in 1946 and the first DC-4 to operate a scheduled passenger service from Johannesburg to Cape Town on May 1 of that year. It was also the first aircraft to have landed at Jan Smuts Airport on April 17, 1952. Seeing *Tafelberg* end her career with the airline was a deeply emotional and upsetting experience for a lot of the older generation of SAA's staff. Fortunately, *Tafelberg* was not destined to disappear into oblivion. On January 17, 1966, it was sold to the South African Air Force (SAAF) and allocated military tail registration number 6901. With this identity, it saw sterling service as a transporter with 44 Squadron until it was purchased by Portland, Oregon-based international airplane broker and sales agent Aero Air in August 1995. Registered ZS-NUR, the aircraft was flown to Antwerp, Belgium and then sold to the Flying Dutchman Foundation in January 1996. Once in Holland it was again re-registered, this time as PH-DDS. On April 15, 2003, the aircraft was leased to a South African company, Springbok Classic Air, and was once more registered ZS-AUA. The man behind Springbok Classic Air, Captain 'Flippie' Vermeulen, was a pilot for SAA from 1970 to 2011. His love of adventure, aviation and wildlife encouraged him to found a company offering aerial safaris in which tourists were transported around the wilds of Africa in authentic vintage aircraft. As a result of his efforts *Tafelberg*—still in the colors of the Flying Dutchman Foundation—came back to the country. After some time it was taken out of service and now rests quietly among the fine collection of historic aircraft on display at the South African Airways Museum Society at Rand Airport. At the time of this writing, its ultimate fate was unknown as discussions were underway to bring it up to airworthy condition and fly it back to Europe. So, for the moment, this noble Queen of the Sky—with her long and unblemished history—is frequently visited, admired and photographed by aviation enthusiasts and DC-4 aficionados from all over the world.

From October 1, 1965, Vickers Viscounts replaced the retired Douglas DC-4 Skymasters on routes to Windhoek. Those other old reliable workhorses of the sky, the Douglas DC-3 Dakotas, began operating connecting—or 'feeder'—services between Windhoek, Alexander Bay and Cape Town. At the same time a bi-weekly Douglas DC-3 Dakota service was introduced between Kimberly and Windhoek, with stops at the important town and agricultural center of Upington in the arid Northern Cape province and at Keetmanshoop in the Kalahari Desert of South-West Africa. Because the new fleet of Boeing 727 jets began operating the domestic routes between South Africa's major cities the Vickers Viscounts were released for other duties, including offering low-cost 'Skycoach' services between Johannesburg, Durban and Cape Town and to Windhoek via Kimberley and Bloemfontein.

In November 1965, Windhoek was included as a regular stopover on Boeing 707 flights from Johannesburg to Frankfurt and London. That same month all services to Lourenco Marques in neighboring Mozambique were taken over by Vickers

Viscounts. By December 1965, passenger demand on domestic services was so great that an additional two Boeing 727s were ordered. When all of the Boeing 727s eventually entered service, two of the Douglas DC-7B aircraft became redundant so ZS-DKD and ZS-DKG were sold to Transair of Sweden.

1965 was also the year when major political upheavals north of the Limpopo River generated repercussions within South Africa that would significantly affect regional air services. The Limpopo River is the border between South Africa and what was then known as the British colony of Southern Rhodesia. Once part of a short-lived federation that included the colonies of Northern Rhodesia and Nyasaland, the territory sought independence from Britain when the federation was disbanded in 1963. Under the leadership of Prime Minister Ian Smith and his all-white government, Southern Rhodesia campaigned for independent rule, the same that had been granted to Northern Rhodesia and Nyasaland in 1964. Independence in those two ex-colonies had created the black-ruled republics of Zambia and Malawi. The sticking point was that Ian Smith and his government refused to relinquish political control to Rhodesia's black majority population which would have been in keeping with the spirit of independent rule that had changed the entire political landscape of the rest of the continent. Britain's Prime Minister Harold Wilson would hear none of Smith's pleas. Wilson and his Labour Party-led government insisted on what they referred to as 'NIBMAR,' an acronym that stood for 'No Independence Before Majority Rule.' But Smith was adamant. If Britain did not grant self-rule to Rhodesia, the colony would seize its independence. Not only was this highly irregular and controversial but also illegal by all standards of international law. Endless to-ing and fro-ing by Rhodesian and British delegations between London and Rhodesia's capital, Salisbury, produced no results that would satisfy either side. So, on November 11, 1965, Rhodesia announced UDI—a unilateral declaration of independence—and proclaimed itself free of British rule, with Ian Smith as prime minister presiding over an all-white Cabinet. Naturally, this incensed black political leaders within Rhodesia itself because they were hoping to gain their freedom under a majority black government. Their anger and frustration at continuing to be subjugated to white dominance triggered a liberation struggle that became dubbed the 'Bush War.' It was to become a violent conflict between black and white that would rage for the next 15 years with an estimated death toll of more than 30,000. The war would only end in 1980 when Rhodesia was reborn as the Republic of Zimbabwe with a black government under the leadership of President Robert Mugabe who, as history would show, turned out to be a ruler far more tyrannical and destructive to the country than Ian Smith could ever be. But, in 1965, UDI unleashed the wrath and ire of the entire world. Led by Britain and the majority of members of the United Nations, Rhodesia was turned into a scorned and isolated pariah state with boycotts imposed upon it by the international community. But South Africa's Nationalist-led white government was sympathetic to Ian Smith's cause, so the country's only air links to the outside world were provided by SAA. Rhodesia's very survival relied heavily upon assistance from South Africa. It supplied the landlocked country with fuel and other essential supplies, allowing it to survive the stringent international trade boycott against it. While Air Rhodesia—the national carrier born of the now-defunct Central African Airways—continued to fly internal services and to serve routes linking Rhodesia with South Africa, SAA was instructed by South Africa's Minister of Transport to continue regular air services to Bulawayo and Salisbury and to route some of its Springbok Services to London and Europe via Salisbury.

In April 1966, pool partnership arrangements came into effect between SAA and the Italian airline, Alitalia, as well as with Germany's Lufthansa. That month SAA's frequencies on routes between South Africa, Europe and the United Kingdom increased to nine per week. In addition to orders for long-range Boeing 707-344C jet airplanes already discussed in chapter nine, in July 1966, the airline ordered two short-range, twin-engine Boeing 737s to help cope with ever-increasing traffic on the domestic route network. That same month frequencies on the Rhodesian service were increased to ten per week.

With the development of the internal and regional services serious attention was now given to streamlining the overseas service to Europe. Because of the ever-growing popularity of the London flights, officials at SAA headquarters deemed that the time had come for a more expedient one-stop service between Jan Smuts Airport and Heathrow. That story shifts our focus to a tiny Portuguese-controlled island called Ilha do Sal (Island of Salt) situated 375 miles off the west coast of the bulge of Africa. Parallel to Senegal and Mauretania, it is only 83 square miles in size. With a length of 18 miles and a width of 7.5 miles, it is part of an archipelago of ten islands and eight islets known as Cabo Verde (Cape Verde). Warm and temperate, the archipelago is blessed with abundant sunshine. In 1966, Ilha do Sal had a population of about 5,000. Its economy depended on fishing and on the export of salt from a natural lake in an extinct volcano near the small town of Pedra Lume. Salt had been extracted there for centuries. During the heyday of European expansion and exploration ships often called at Ilha do Sal so that sailors could slaughter turtles that were once abundant on the island's powdery white beaches. The salt was used for preserving their flesh for consumption by ships' crews during long voyages at sea.

Sal island is almost a thousand miles nearer to Johannesburg than Las Palmas in the Canary Islands, the normal stop-over for flights operating the round-the-bulge route to Europe. Sal's location was perfect as an alternative and closer refueling stop. As fate would have it, a runway had already been built there by the

Portuguese. Facilities were fairly primitive but the runway was paved and durable enough to accommodate a fully-laden Boeing 707. Other than the runway, there was little else besides a service hut and an antiquated radio transceiver station. Negotiations took place between representatives of the governments of South Africa and Portugal and permission was obtained for a weekly SAA service to stop over at Ilha do Sal. With the aid of South African funding, a fuel storage facility was hastily constructed, the radio system was upgraded, landing lights were installed along the runway and, on July 3, 1966, SAA Boeing 707-344B ZS-DYL was the first South African jetliner to touch down there, officially beginning an express Springbok Service to London. The flight heralded the start of a long relationship between SAA and the island. In November, a second service routed through Ilha do Sal. In the years to come this little pinprick of geography jutting out of the shimmering waters of the Atlantic Ocean would feature very prominently in the airline's expanding overseas service.

1966 was also the year that SAA introduced a weekly Douglas DC-3 Dakota service between Johannesburg and Gaborone, Bechuanaland. Flights commenced on September 1, just four weeks before the territory gained its independence from Britain and was renamed the Republic of Botswana. Unlike the majority of other independent African nations Botswana maintained a very cordial relationship with South Africa, primarily because its economy was so closely tied to that of South Africa's. Soon after air services started SAA entered into a pool partnership with Botswana National Airways. At the same time a similar arrangement came into effect between SAA and the Angolan airline, DTA (Divisão dos Transportes Aéreos) later renamed TAAG (Transportes Aéreos de Angola).

But everything was not only about all work and no play. As SAA's engineering section at Jan Smuts Airport continually expanded employees decided to pool their personal resources together and begin their own flying club. In October 1966, the Flying Springbok Aero Club was formed. A vintage de Havilland DH.82A Tiger Moth ZS-BYM was the first aircraft to be purchased and lovingly restored by members during their spare time. Once it was all spick and span and airworthy it was used for weekend instructional and recreational flying.

The following year a dark cloud suddenly descended upon the airline. Despite a long period of incident-free operations tragedy struck on March 13, 1967. Vickers Viscount ZS-CVA *Rietbok*—the Viscount originally owned by Cubana airlines and purchased from it as part of SAA's fleet modernization program a few years earlier—was operating flight SA 406 from Port Elizabeth to Johannesburg via East London and Bloemfontein. The aircraft was under the command of 48-year-old Captain Gordon Benjamin Lipawsky with 31-year-old First Officer Brian Albert Richard Trenworth as co-pilot. Other members of the crew were Senior Flight Steward P.L. Bezuidenhout, Air Hostess A.P. van der Poel and Flight Steward Z.C. de Beer. There were 20 passengers on board. Although the airframe had accumulated 9,134 hours of flying since it was first rolled out of the Vickers factory in 1958, it was meticulously maintained and in excellent condition. However, two unusual incidents had occurred earlier that day. When the Viscount took off from Jan Smuts Airport on the outbound journey from Johannesburg to Port Elizabeth, Captain Lipawsky noted a red light on the instrument panel indicating that the nose landing gear had failed to retract. He immediately turned back, landed and ground engineers swiftly rectified the problem. It turned out that the glitch was due to a minor electro-mechanical fault. Then, after taking off from East London bound for Port Elizabeth, the Viscount struck a bird. This did not affect the airplane's performance so Lipawsky proceeded on to Port Elizabeth where ground engineers carefully examined the engines, turboprop blades and the entire exterior of the aircraft without finding any signs of damage.

Before taking off for East London for the return journey to Johannesburg, the crew was informed by meteorologists that weather conditions at East London were very poor. After discussing the issue with his co-pilot Lipawsky decided to take on 2,000 lbs. of extra fuel in case he had to avoid East London and proceed onwards to Bloemfontein. But if conditions did improve and the plane could land, the pilots decided to fly a vector via East London. Perhaps they might still be able to stop over there. Before the airplane took off two passengers who were booked on that sector of the flight were informed that due to bad weather they may not be able disembark at East London and that they might have to remain on board until the Viscount reached Bloemfontein. One of the passengers, Mr. Max Melmed, elected to take his chances, remain on board and hopefully reach East London if the aircraft did not divert. The second East London-bound passenger, a woman, decided not to fly and opted to take a train instead. She was the lucky one. Of the original 20 passengers when the *Rietbok* took off on its course for East London she was the only one to survive.

After leaving Port Elizabeth, the aircraft reached a cruising altitude of 9,000 feet. The distance to East London was only 148 miles so it was not necessary to fly higher than that. Shortly after take-off, the *Rietbok* was handed over to East London Air Traffic Control. Captain Lipawsky was informed that weather conditions had improved considerably and that runway 10 had been approved for landing. Approach should be made over the ocean on a north-easterly heading. At 5.09 p.m., when it was approximately 17 miles out to sea, the aircraft was cleared for descent. The crew confirmed the instruction and stated that the Viscount was approaching over the ocean at a height of 2,000 feet. A couple of minutes later it reported that the coastline was in sight. All was well.

But that was the last message ever received from the *Rietbok*. Seconds later it smashed into the sea at high speed. The impact site was not far from Kayser's Beach. There were no survivors. No bodies were ever found and other than a bag of mail that washed ashore there was very little wreckage. All these facts contributed to the perplexing mystery of what might have happened. A subsequent Board of Enquiry investigation concluded that in eliminating all possible causes of the accident the likelihood that the captain had suffered a heart attack could not be excluded. Medical records indicated that he had once been treated for a mild heart condition. If that was the case the first officer might not have been able to take over control of the aircraft fast enough before it hit the water. But that was all speculation and guesswork. No one has ever determined the exact reason for the disaster. Ironically, the *Rietbok* met its fate just off the very same beach where Major Allister Macintosh Miller—the pioneer of Union Airways that eventually became SAA—crashed in his bright yellow Fokker Super Universal airplane on December 31, 1931. The mystery of the *Rietbok* has lingered for decades, taxing the imagination and comprehension of all who have pondered its fate. In 1971, renowned South African author Geoffrey Jenkins used the accident as the core of his adventure novel, *Scend of the Sea* (U.S. title: *The Hollow Sea*). But the riddle prevails. We may never know what happened.

Two weeks after the Viscount accident a sombre mood still lingering within the airline was replaced by a celebratory atmosphere when the last Douglas DC-7B operated a scheduled flight on the Wallaby Service to Australia. The reason was because of the introduction of Boeing 707 jetliners on that route. By then the DC-7Bs had flown a total of 3,622,000 miles and had carried 23,160 passengers over the Indian Ocean between Africa and Australasia. SAA flights were now extended from Perth all the way to Sydney. Jeff Scott—previously Station Manager at Luanda in Angola—was responsible for opening the airline's first sales office on Elizabeth Street in the central business district of Sydney. Because of the long-range capabilities of the jets, the

Cocos Island was dropped as a stopover between Mauritius and Perth. At the same time Qantas replaced their Lockheed Electra turboprops with Boeing 707s on the same service. On May 17, SAA's Boeing 707-344B ZS-EKV *Windhoek* established a record for the sector between Mauritius and Perth by covering the 3,740 miles distance in only five hours 32 minutes. With the introduction of the jets to and from Australia the last of SAA's Douglas DC-7Bs were sold to buyers abroad. Fast and comfortable though they were, few in the engineering section were sorry to see them go because of their consistently troublesome engines. The end of the DC-7B service made the last remaining Douglas DC-4 Skymaster, ZS-AUB *Outeniqua*, redundant. Now it was no longer needed to ferry spares and replacement engines to distant destinations wherever a DC-7B was stranded because of engine problems. That particular DC-4 had been fitted with eight long-range fuel tanks especially for the task. The end of DC-7B flights signified the end of piston-engine aircraft on SAA's overseas route network, a fact that kindled strong feelings of nostalgia among older aircrew and members of the administration staff. Aviation people love their airplanes and when an era comes to an end it always engenders an abiding emotional reaction.

On October 6, 1967, a weekly return service between Johannesburg and Maseru in neighboring Lesotho was inaugurated with Douglas DC-3 Dakota aircraft. Lush and green in summer and clad in snow during the winter months, Lesotho is a small yet stunningly beautiful mountain kingdom completely surrounded by South Africa. The new air service came into effect as a result of a pool partnership agreement between SAA and Air Lesotho. That same month a sprawling new SAA cargo center was opened at Jan Smuts Airport. On October 31, 1967, SAA introduced a weekly freight service between Johannesburg and Paris in conjunction with UTA French airlines, operated by UTA Douglas DC-8F jet freighter aircraft. Formerly known as UAT (Union Aéromaritime de Transport) UTA (Union des

Transports Aériens) was born in 1963 when UAT merged with another French airline, Transports Aériens Intercontinentaux. From November 1, 1967, SAA Viscount Skycoach services between Johannesburg and Windhoek began calling at Upington in the hot and arid district of the Northern Cape province. That same month services between Johannesburg and Salisbury in Rhodesia were increased to seven per week using three Boeing 707s which stopped over en route to Europe, plus three Boeing 727s and one Vickers Viscount.

On December 5, 1967, a combined South African government and SAA delegation flew to Washington DC to discuss a proposed new SAA service from Johannesburg to New York. After long deliberations and despite the United States' openly anti-apartheid stance permission was eventually granted for flights to commence in 1969. On December 29, 1967, an order was placed with the Boeing Company for an additional twin-engine Boeing 737. But it was not enough. Because of the continuing growth of local traffic on February 4 of the following year, three more Boeing 737s were ordered. That same month the airline opened an office in Florence, Italy. On April 1, 1968, frequencies on the Springbok Service to Europe were increased to eleven per week. At the same time a pool partnership agreement between SAA and Swissair came into operation with the introduction of a weekly Swissair Douglas DC-8 service between Zurich and Johannesburg. Soon after, another pool agreement came into effect between SAA and Spain's Iberia for flights between Madrid and Johannesburg. On April 5, an SAA sales and reservations office was opened in Stuttgart, Germany.

Fifteen days later, catastrophe struck like a lightning bolt from nowhere.

Boeing 707-344C ZS-EUW *Pretoria* was a brand new addition to the fleet. It was less than six weeks old, having only arrived at Jan Smuts Airport after its delivery flight from Seattle on March

1, 1968. As a 'C' model with long-range fuel tanks and a specially reinforced floor, it was Boeing's latest intercontinental offering with all the latest instrumentation, engines and flight control surfaces. It was designed with maximum versatility in mind. Because of its strengthened floor, it could serve as a passenger aircraft or as a freighter carrying heavy cargo pallets or even as a combination of the two configurations. Its first revenue service was carried out on April 12 when it operated flight SA 214 from Johannesburg to London. Eight days later, on April 20, it was in an all-passenger configuration and was assigned to operate flight SA 228 from Johannesburg to Windhoek, Luanda, Las Palmas, Frankfurt and London. The crew consisted of Captain Eric Smith, First Officer Johnny Halliday, Flight Engineer Phillip Andrew 'Kokkie' Minaar, Navigator Harry Charles Howe and in-flight Relief Pilot Richard Armstrong. The Flight Traffic Officer was A.G. Manson. Attending to passengers in the cabin were Chief Steward J.A. Erasmus, Senior Flight Stewards H.S. Louw, R.J. Bester and J.W. Jesson, and Air Hostesses E. Janse van Rensburg and M. Nortier.

With 83 passengers on board, the afternoon flight from Johannesburg to Windhoek was smooth and uneventful. At Windhoek a small amount of cargo was off-loaded while other freight was taken aboard. Also joining the flight were 46 additional passengers, Frankfurt or London-bound. At precisely 8.46 p.m. local time under a moonless sky the aircraft's brakes were released and, with its four powerful Pratt & Whitney JT3D-7 turbofan engines gently whining, the new Boeing with all its windows ablaze with light departed from the apron outside the main terminal building and headed towards runway 08. Two minutes later it lined up on the runway and Captain Smith called for full power. The engines spooled up to a roar and the Boeing thundered down the runway. At 8.49 p.m. it reached 'rotate' velocity—or take-off speed—and left the ground. The night was so black that observers on the ground described the sight as 'a string of glowing lights disappearing into a dark hole.' The aircraft rapidly climbed to an altitude of 650 feet, then leveled off and 30 seconds later suddenly started to descend. After another twenty seconds, it plowed into the ground at a speed of 312 mph, some 17,400 feet beyond the end of the runway. The four engines hit first, gouging out four long furrows in the rocky soil before the fuselage broke up. Because the aircraft was fully fueled fires immediately broke out as tanks ruptured and ignited. As the night was so dense and the terrain so rough it took emergency fire-fighting and rescue vehicles more than half-an-hour to reach the crash site. Wreckage was strewn over an area 4,594 feet long and 656 feet wide.

123 passengers and the entire crew perished. There were only six survivors. Nine passengers seated in the first class section of the fuselage initially survived but two died before they could be taken to a hospital. Another succumbed to burns and injuries a couple of days later. On May 15, one of the remaining six, Dr. J.H. van der Wath, Chairman of the South African Wool Board, also passed away. The remaining five survivors were UK citizens William Rooke and Alfred Derbyshire, US citizen Thomas Taylor who was a courier for the United States Embassy in Pretoria, and South Africans Brian Arntzen and Peter Williams. Williams was the only passenger seated in the coach (economy) class section of the cabin to have survived. Taylor suffered multiple bruises and cuts and was in shock but all the others were treated at the Windhoek State Hospital for far more serious injuries.

Eventually recovering from his condition, Peter Williams recalled the horrifying experience. "I sat in the first row of economy class seats on the right hand side of the cabin. My wife Alma sat next to me at the window and a gentleman sat on the aisle seat on my other side. Both he and my wife were killed. I remembered nothing about the crash for about three months. When they found me in the wreckage I was still strapped into my seat. I was unconscious and in critical condition. The only clothes

I had on was my collar and my tie. Everything else was gone. My left shoe was still on but the sock was missing. I was still wearing a sock on my right foot but the shoe there was missing. I only regained consciousness about 26 days later. At first I couldn't remember who I was. There was no identification on me and so I became known as the 'Unknown Survivor.' Immediately after the crash my parents in South Africa received a telegram from my wife Alma's parents stating that both Alma and I had died in the crash. But 36 hours after the accident a former colleague of mine who was living in Windhoek identified me by a tattoo on my left arm and by my right index finger which had been amputated some years earlier. On June 3, 1968 I was flown to Johannesburg in an SAA Viscount and then taken by ambulance to the Princess Nursing Home in Hillbrow, Johannesburg. There I slowly recovered and was eventually allowed to return home."

The crash of the *Pretoria* was by far the worst accident suffered by SAA up to that time. What could possibly have gone wrong? Why would a brand new aircraft smash into the ground like that? What overcame the seasoned, experienced and highly respected aircrew? Studies of the aircraft's flight data recorder or 'black box' and lengthy analytical discourse by a Board of Enquiry showed that the aircraft had no mechanical defects. Examination of its maintenance records revealed nothing that might have prompted the crash. The Boeing had been correctly loaded. Freight and weight distribution within the hold was well within prescribed manufacturer's safety limits. Clearly—as proven by the flight data recorder—human error was to blame.

Immediately after take-off, Captain Eric Smith acted as if he believed the aircraft was climbing. The landing gear was retracted and the flaps were returned to their normal position for flight. Then the engines were throttled back from take-off power to climb mode. The stabiliser trim was altered to maintain the aircraft in that attitude. But it was a catastrophic mistake.

Contrary to Captain Smith's beliefs that the airplane was still climbing, it was actually beginning to descend. Co-pilot John Halliday must have failed to monitor the flight instruments. If he did he would have seen that the aircraft was rapidly losing altitude. The Board determined that these errors were probably due to the intense darkness outside. There were no visual reference points below for the pilots to see that the aircraft was descending. What made matters worse is that neither of them were paying sufficient attention to their instruments. They were probably too preoccupied with post take-off checks. While they must have believed that all was in order, their airplane was in fact headed towards disaster.

Senior Captain Salomon 'Pi' Pienaar later described the incident as a classic case of what he called 'spinning gyros,' in which pilots believe one thing while something completely different was happening. Wartime flying had taught him that often a pilot 'felt' how his airplane was behaving. A sense of 'up,' 'down,' or sideways movement is generated by a complex sensorimotor system in the human body that depends on information supplied by the eyes, vestibular organs in the inner ear and on joints and muscles. But in the pitch black darkness of night, with no exterior points of reference, that kind of instinct could not be trusted. The only way to really know what is going on is to scrupulously monitor an airplane's instrumentation. It was an error that often caught pilots off guard. In the case of the *Pretoria* and flight SA 228 on the night of April 20, 1968, it cost the pilots their lives, as well as those of 10 other crew members and 123 passengers. It was a lesson well learned, not only for SAA but by airlines around the world. After that dreadful accident cockpit procedures and instrument monitoring requirements became far more stringent and even more rigidly enforced. In addition, the Boeing Company began fitting a ground proximity warning system into all of their airplanes.

The rest of 1968 saw many developments for SAA. A

sales office was opened in Melbourne, Australia, as well as in Los Angeles, California and in Toronto, Canada. A weekly return service between Johannesburg, Durban and Matsapa in neighboring Swaziland commenced using Douglas DC-3s. Vickers Viscounts began operating flights between Johannesburg and Blantyre in Malawi. Additional flights went into operation from Johannesburg to Francistown and Gaborone in Botswana. Greece's Olympic Airways inaugurated a twice-weekly pool partnership service with SAA between Athens and Johannesburg.

That year the first two Boeing 737-100 twinjets, ZS-EUY and ZS-EUZ, arrived after their long delivery flights from the factory in the United States. Travelling together from Seattle via Montreal, Las Palmas, Ilha do Sal, Sao Tomé and Windhoek to Johannesburg, ZS-EUY was under the command of Captain Salomon 'Pi' Pienaar with Jacobus Frederick van Aswegen as navigator. ZS-EUZ was under the control of Captain Albertus de Wet. The two aircraft accomplished the flight in four days with a total flying time of 26 hours and 30 minutes. Because these were short-range airliners, they were both fitted with synthetic rubber-style 'bladder' fuel tanks tied down on palettes attached to the floor inside the main cabin. Each 'bladder' contained an additional 11,000 lbs. of fuel, allowing the airplanes to fly further and longer than their standard on-board tanks allowed.

In future years the Boeing 737 would go on to become the best-selling jet airliner in aviation history. In accordance with operators' demands, it would be enlarged, re-engined, stretched and developed into many new variants. SAA's first models were of the dash-100 series. At the time of this writing the 737 was being offered in models up to the dash-900 and 737 'Max' series. Continuously manufactured by Boeing's commercial airplane division at its plant in Renton south of Seattle since 1967, by early 2020 10,500 of the aircraft had been delivered to operators worldwide with 4,500 still on the order books. By then it was said that a Boeing 737 was landing or taking off somewhere in the world every 4.5 seconds. In the course of time, SAA would operate 53 of the type in different variants, including two all-freight models.

Boeing 737-200, 1968

SAA's Boeing 737-200s had a wingspan of 93 ft, a length of 100 ft 2 ins and a height of 37 ft 1 in. The aircraft's empty weight was 61,630 lbs and its maximum weight 107,000 lbs. Its cruising speed was 575 mph and it had a range of 2,136 miles. It could fly at a maximum altitude of 35,000 feet. Power was provided by two Pratt & Whitney JT8D-9 engines, each delivering 15,500 lbs (68.95 kN) of thrust. It carried a flight crew of two and could accommodate 93 passengers in a five-abreast seating arrangement or 117 in six-abreast seating.

During the latter part of 1968, SAA began re-registering its entire fleet. The first Boeing 707, for example, ZS-CKC became registered as ZS-SAA. Boeing 727 ZS-DYM became ZS-SBA, and so on. Among the reasons for the change was a plan to group the different types of airplanes into registrations that would easily identify their type. Once the change-over took place all future new aircraft would be registered under the new system prior to their delivery. As the end of the year approached the airline reached an historic milestone by exceeding the one million-passenger mark. By December 1968, it had carried a total of 1,055,381 people.

By far the most significant event of 1968 was a decision taken on May 1 to purchase a brand new type of airplane. This was an unusual occurrence for SAA because the prototype of the aircraft had not even been flown by the factory yet. The order was for a machine so radically new, so different and so important that it would bring about another quantum leap in the way humans moved around the world. The acquisition was for three airplanes that generated enormous public interest and that the international press and aviation industry jovially dubbed the 'Jumbo Jet,' simply because of its sheer size and capacity. It was, of course, the Boeing 747.

SAA's 747s were intended for operating the overseas routes. Preparations were immediately made for accommodating and servicing the gigantic new airplanes at Jan Smuts Airport, and also for landing and handling them at other major airports around the country should the need arise. New hangars, maintenance facilities and a building for housing a flight simulator and other crew training activities went into construction at the airline's base. Dr. Alex Conradie, Chief Executive of SAA at the time of the 747 purchase, recalls the high degree of nervousness that pervaded the administrative, technical and operational sectors once the order was placed with the Boeing Company. "We viewed the coming of these aeroplanes with considerable apprehension. Of course, we needed them because of ever-increasing passenger demands on our overseas services but we had heard some rather scary stories put out not only by other airlines who had also bought them but even by the manufacturer, Boeing. The very size of these things scared us. We were told that they were almost as big as a rugby field and that the tail stood as high as a five-storey building. It was frightening, especially when we considered the vast array of service equipment, specialized vehicles and customized systems that would be necessary to handle them. I can honestly tell you that for the next two years we were in a state of panic as we desperately tried to make sure that we were absolutely ready to properly handle and operate these incredible new planes once they arrived. We worked around the clock to build and assemble all the facilities that we needed. Just about everything had to be upgraded, including our baggage handling system. With the introduction of the 747 all baggage and cargo would have to be containerized, unlike the old system where items were loaded and unloaded individually. It was all a whole new world and a completely new way of doing things for us."

As local engineering contracting firm Dorman Long and other private companies began constructing new hangars and all the other structures required for the 747s Jan Smuts Airport began to look like a child's giant *Erector* building set. But, in the meantime, the day-to-day business of running the airline had to go on. On January 1, 1969, an SAA sales office was opened in Copenhagen, Denmark, the very first in a Scandinavian country. Not long after that another office opened its doors in Rio de Janeiro, Brazil. But the most important agenda on the new year calendar was the commencement of services to New York City. The plan was to route the flight from Johannesburg across the South Atlantic to Rio de Janeiro and then to continue northwards from there to New York. But, at the time, all the airline's Boeing 707s had not yet been delivered from the factory. As the distance by air from Jan Smuts Airport to Rio de Janeiro's Galeão–Antonio Carlos Jobim International Airport is 4,431 miles—most of it over a vast stretch of the South Atlantic—the route had to be operated by the latest variant of the 707 equipped with the most efficient engines and with long-range fuel tanks. Permission to fly the route had been approved by both the Brazilian and United States governments but SAA lacked enough of the equipment to fly it. So, what to do? Fortunately, locally-based private low-cost carrier Trek Airways had placed an order with Boeing for one long-range Boeing 707-350C for its services to Europe. That aircraft was already on the assembly line in Seattle and would be delivered long before SAA received its own new 707 airplanes. Would Trek perhaps agree to making a swap and allow SAA to take over its order? Franz Swartz, SAA's Commercial Director at the time, approached the management of Trek Airways and pleaded with them. If they would assist SAA by letting them take over their 707-350C when it came out of the factory, SAA would make one of its shorter range Boeing 707-344A models available to Trek for their European operations. Fortunately, friendship and cordiality between Trek and its much larger cousin prevailed. The proposal was agreed to.

Once the deal went through, SAA requested that Boeing make some small modifications to the Trek airplane, transforming it from a 707-350C to a 707-344C, bringing it into accordance with SAA's exact requirements and specifications. While the new aircraft was awaited, a proving flight to New York was planned using one of SAA's other 707s. Because it would not be carrying a full load of passengers, it had the range to cross the Atlantic with ample fuel reserves. So, under the command of Captain Salomon 'Pi' Pienaar with Captain Johannes Albertus Geldenhuis 'Bert' Rademan as co-pilot and Alf Heale as navigator Boeing 707 ZS-SAD *Bloemfontein* departed Jan Smuts Airport on February 4, 1969. The Atlantic was crossed in a flying time of eight hours 55 minutes. The next day, the aircraft set out northwards on its proving flight to J.F. Kennedy Airport in New York, covering the 4,808 miles in nine hours and 50 minutes. The return sectors were flown on February 8 and 9. Fourteen days later, scheduled passenger services began under the designation flight SA 201 using one of the airline's Boeing 707-344Bs. A relief crew had earlier been positioned in Rio de Janeiro to take over from the pilots and crew who had flown the sector from Johannesburg. Initially, flights were operated on a weekly basis. With the inception of the Rio de Janeiro and New York flights the Flying Springbok was now a familiar sight on six continents. On April 23, 1969, Boeing 707-344C ZS-SAG—the one originally intended for Trek Airways—arrived from the factory and began operating the Johannesburg to Rio de Janeiro and New York service. Because of SAA's long pool partnership association with the British carrier BOAC SAA's aircraft shared BOAC's gate and check-in facilities at Kennedy Airport.

On May 30, 1969, the Boeing 707-344A ZS-CKE that SAA had agreed to make available to Trek Airways in exchange for their 707-344C was officially handed over. The aircraft had been freshly painted in Trek's livery at SAA's maintenance facilities at Jan Smuts Airport and operated its first flight for that airline on June 1. As part of the exchange agreement, SAA was now responsible for maintaining the craft for Trek. Trek later had the Boeing registered in Luxembourg as LX-LGW and it was repainted in the colors of Luxair. This gave the operator the right to overfly Africa, previously not possible while the airplane carried a South African registration. Luxair now became the official carrier between Luxembourg and South Africa, offering higher capacity low-cost travel between Johannesburg and Europe. From July 19, the same aircraft was chartered by SAA to operate flights between Johannesburg and Athens, flying a route from Johannesburg via Libreville, Gabon, once again without problem or hindrance because of its Luxembourg registration.

On June 14, 1969, the number of frequencies on the Springbok Service between South Africa and Europe was increased to thirteen per week. Two weeks later, SAA opened an office in Buenos Aires, Argentina and shortly thereafter in Sao Paulo, Brazil. In September, yet another was opened in Auckland, New Zealand. Passenger load factors were so good on the international, regional and domestic services that on November 1 a 'Fly Now-Pay Later' scheme was introduced for those traveling in either first or coach (economy) class. Also in November, the Vickers Viscount service to Blantyre, Malawi was replaced by Boeing 737s. At the same time flights to Rome were extended to Vienna, Austria. On November 18, 1969, a weekly return service was introduced from Johannesburg and Durban to Tananarive, Madagascar, and then extended on to Mauritius. Equipment used on the route was a Boeing 737 leased from Air Madagascar. SAA became responsible for servicing and maintaining the aircraft at Jan Smuts Airport. In December, an order was placed for three more Boeing 727 aircraft. These were of the QC variant, the designation representing 'quick change.' The airplanes could be converted from an all-passenger to all-freight configuration in thirty minutes. By the end of the sixties the SAA fleet comprised 29 aircraft made up of eight Boeing 707s, seven Boeing 727s, three Boeing 737s, seven Vickers Viscounts and four Douglas DC-3 Dakotas. On the order books were the two Boeing 727 QCs, three Boeing 737s and the three big Boeing 747s.

In January 1970, a Boeing 707 all-cargo service operated by Lufthansa in pool partnership with SAA began flying between Frankfurt and Johannesburg. On February 1, SAA started operating a service between Cape Town and London, bringing the number of weekly services to Europe to fourteen. In April that was extended to sixteen. In May, the Vickers Viscount aircraft were withdrawn from domestic routes. However, they continued to operate flights on routes to and from South-West Africa and neighbouring countries until more Boeing 737 aircraft became available. Because of soaring demand, that same month BOAC introduced a weekly Boeing 707 all-cargo service between London and Johannesburg in pool partnership with SAA. At the same time a Hawker Siddeley HS 748 twin-engine turboprop was leased from the Hawker Siddeley factory in the United Kingdom and began operating flights from Johannesburg to Botswana, Lesotho and Swaziland, replacing the aging Douglas

DC-3 Dakotas that had previously flown those routes.

Because the Pratt & Whitney engines on the awaited Boeing 747s were so large a decision was taken to build a bigger and more specialized facility to test them at Jan Smuts Airport. In mid-May, local company Roberts Construction was awarded the contract to erect an enormous new and completely soundproof test center where the gigantic engines could be mounted on a rig and run at full power so that their performance could be regularly monitored. Building began on this at SAA's technical overhaul complex in late May 1970.

Large engine test chamber at SAA's technical and maintenance facility, Jan Smuts Airport, 1970

On June 21, Varig Airlines of Brazil began services to Johannesburg from Rio de Janeiro using Boeing 707 aircraft and, that same month, SAA opened an office in Chicago. The leased Hawker Siddeley 748 proved so popular on routes to neighboring states that in August 1970, a contract was signed for the purchase of three new models from the Hawker Siddeley plant at Woodford in the United Kingdom. The aircraft were pre-registered ZS-SBU, ZS-SBV and ZS-SBW. The Hawker Siddeley HS 748 was a perfect machine for operating the low-density routes to neighboring countries. It had STOL (short take-off and landing) capabilities and, if need be, it could operate from unpaved dirt runways.

Hawker Siddeley 748, 1970

SAA's Hawker Siddeleys were of the HS 748 Series 2 variant. The aircraft had a wingspan of 98 ft 6 ins, a length of 67 ft and a height of 24 ft 10 ins. Its empty weight was 26,678 lbs and its maximum weight 46,500 lbs. Maximum speed was 293 mph and its cruising speed 118 mph. Service ceiling was 25,000 feet. With maximum fuel load its range was 1,987 miles and with maximum payload that dropped down to 530 miles. Power was supplied by two Rolls-Royce Dart RDA7 535 turboprop engines developing 2,280 horsepower driving four-blade Dowty-Rotol propellers. The HS 748 had a crew of three and could carry 40 passengers.

On September 28, 1970, another sad yet very significant milestone was reached. After 24 years of loyal and trustworthy service, the Douglas DC-3 Dakota ZS-DJB *Simonbsberg* (Simon's Mountain) operated the last scheduled piston-engine flight for SAA from Francistown, Botswana to Johannesburg. The aircraft—originally taken into service with SAA in 1954 after an eleven-year military career—had a checkered history after that. On February 12, 1971, it was sold to the South African Air Force (SAAF) and allocated tail number 6889. For the next two years it was operated by 44 Transport Squadron out of Swartkop Air Force Base in Pretoria until—on February 21, 1973—it was sold to the Rhodesian Air Force. Under tail number 7312, it flew with 3 Squadron in action during that country's prolonged 'Bush War.' After Rhodesia became the Republic of Zimbabwe in 1980, it was reassigned tail number R 7312 and flew for the new Zimbabwe Air Force. Unfortunately, the aircraft crashed on take-off from Chimoio, Mozambique on July 10, 1986, killing all 17 occupants. It was completely destroyed after having accumulated a total flying time of 20,036 hours over a period of 43 years.

With an eye to eventually commencing services from South Africa to Texas in the years to come, on September 14, 1970, SAA opened an office in Houston. From November 1, Brussels was included in the Springbok Service network, bringing the total number of frequencies to Europe to seventeen per week, all operated by Boeing 707s. With the commencement of flights to Brussels a pool partnership agreement came into effect between SAA and the Belgian national carrier, Sabena.

At the same time a pool agreement with Dutch airline KLM also came into operation.

In November 1970, a distinctive new-look Flying Springbok

The penultimate version of the Flying Springbok logo for the airline. The design was introduced in 1970, prior to the arrival of SAA's first Boeing 747 widebody aircraft

**The new iteration of the Flying Springbok symbol. This is the
emblem that graced the bright orange rudder (tail) of all SAA
aircraft until 1996**

logo was announced by SAA. Designed by Johannesburg graphic
artist Rex Linaker for the introduction of the Boeing 747 jumbo
jetliners, the emblem was sleeker and more contemporary than
the designs that had preceded it. Its first major public appearance
would be on the tails of the eagerly awaited new 747s.

On November 6, a red warning light flashed on the instrument
panel of Boeing 727 ZS-SBF *Komati* (the name of a river the
flows from South Africa through Swaziland to Mozambique).
After taking off from Johannesburg bound for Cape Town on
flight SA 307, the flaps were retracted and the undercarriage
stowed but the red warning light meant that the nose wheel
had a problem. It could not be lowered for landing. Captain
Doug Barker, First Officer Tony Snelgar and Flight Engineer
Nick Classe were prompted into taking urgent action. Captain
Barker decided to return to Jan Smuts Airport right away. After
trying to extend the nose wheel gear by hand-crank without any
degree of success he gave the order to dump fuel. The purpose
was to ensure a less hazardous emergency landing. Not only
was the fully-fueled aircraft too heavy to land but getting rid
of as much fuel as possible minimized the risk of fire. Barker

called the Jan Smuts tower and requested preparations for an emergency landing. As the 727 made wide circles overhead for the next two hours pumping out its load of fuel which quickly evaporated in the thin atmosphere, all other traffic into and out of the airport was halted. At the same time fire trucks sprayed the main runway with anti-inflammable foam. Exhibiting every skill as the sharply-honed professional pilot that he was, Captain Barker brought the aircraft in at a rate just above stalling speed, gently touched down on the main landing gear, applied full reverse thrust, held the nose up for as long as possible and then gradually let it down. Plowing through the thick retardant foam for about 30 seconds the aircraft came to a stop. None of the 32 passengers or five crew members were injured. Such minimal damage was done to the aircraft's nose during its contact with the foam-covered tarmac that it was fully repaired and back in service the following afternoon. Investigations revealed that the nose gear actuator lock had fractured. When the aircraft took off the following day, Doug Barker was once again at the controls, assisted by the same crew members. During the ensuing days, SAA was inundated with letters from passengers and the general public praising the crew for preventing what could have been a major calamity. Receiving all the congratulatory accolades, Barker's modest response was: "What the dickens is all the fuss about? I only did what I'd been trained to do. I'm no blinking hero. Now please, if no one minds, just let me get on with my job."

On November 30, 1970, a pool partnership agreement was entered into between El Al Israel Airlines and SAA, with El Al increasing its frequency to two flights per week between Johannesburg and Tel Aviv. One day later, SAA opened an office in Barcelona, Spain. This was a period of rapid expansion for SAA. The arrival of more Boeing 727s and additional Hawker Siddeley aircraft as well as the introduction of Boeing 747s the following year put a great deal of pressure on the air crew training section at the flight operations center. Pilots and flight engineers had to be trained and converted for duties on all the new aircraft types that were being incorporated into the fleet. As the Vickers Viscounts were nearing the end of their service life, crews were spending a great deal of time in the simulators as well as in actual flight converting to other aircraft. On January 8 and 9, 1971, the airline's reservations system was upgraded to a more automated and streamlined all-electronic operation making the existing SAAFARI—SAA Fully Automated Reservation System—even more powerful, with direct links to all of its satellite terminals domestically and abroad.

On February 12, 1971, Douglas DC-3 ZS-DJB finally left the technical area and was flown to Swartkop Air Force base near Pretoria, giving her the distinction of being the very last piston-engine aircraft ever operated by an SAA crew. There were few dry eyes as the 'Dak' lifted off from runway 03L/21R that summer morning and droned mournfully away into the indigo sky.

April 1, 1971, saw many changes to SAA's scheduled services. An additional flight was added to the Springbok Service bringing the frequency to eighteen per week and the service to Australia was increased to two flights per week. On the regional services, the Johannesburg to Maseru, Lesotho service went up to three Hawker Siddeley HS 748 flights per week and services to Bulawayo, Rhodesia were also increased to three, using one Boeing 727, one Vickers Viscount and one Hawker Siddeley HS 748 aircraft. Because of the growth in international traffic an order was placed for two more Boeing 747-244 aircraft.

But the pinnacle event of 1971 took place in the mid-morning of November 6. On that date a dark, shimmering, mirage-like shape in the western sky slowly materialized into something more distinct and discernible. As it approached it increased in size into a thing of awesome magnitude never witnessed in Southern African skies before. Bearing the registration ZS-SAN, the name *Lebombo* on its nose and sporting the flashy new Flying

Springbok design set against the blazing orange background of its enormous tail, the aircraft descended from the heavens and made a low pass above enthralled crowds at Jan Smuts Airport. Under its left wing was a temporary fifth pod that carried a spare JT9D engine. Swooping around the airfield in a wide circle the airplane lined up on the runway and made a perfect touchdown, all 18 of its wheels meeting African soil for the first time.

The mighty Boeing 747 had finally arrived.

Chapter 12

Jumbos and Pirates

When the Boeing 747-200 Super B ZS-SAN *Lebombo* touched down at Jan Smuts Airport on the late spring morning of November 6, 1971, it was more than anyone had been expecting. It was impressive. It was beautiful to look at. And it was huge. As Senior Captain Salomon 'Pi' Pienaar swung the giant off runway 03L/21R and slowly taxied towards the main terminal area onlookers—SAA staff and members of the general public—gaped in awe. None of the prior press coverage had done the aircraft justice. It was bigger than anyone had imagined. The only thing that made it look slightly ungainly was the fifth pod that had been attached under the left wing close to the fuselage. That was a temporary installation from which hung a spare Pratt & Whitney JT9D-7 engine. The power plant was too large to be carried in the aircraft's hold so Boeing engineers had located it outside the airplane. When asked later if this arrangement had caused any problems with the aircraft's aerodynamics or flying characteristics during the long ferry flight from Seattle to

Boeing 747-200 Super B, ZS-SAN, Lebombo, arrives at Jan Smuts Airport after her long delivery flight from Seattle, November 6, 1971. Note the spare Pratt & Whitney JT9D-7 engine slung in a pod beneath the left wing. The engine was too large to be accommodated as freight within the aircraft itself

Johannesburg, Captain Pienaar clucked briefly and then, in his typically underplayed and modest manner, simply replied "Oh no, not at all. She behaved as sweet as can be."

With Pienaar on the flight that morning were Captains John Trotter, Bob Truter and Bill van Reenen and Flight Engineers Chris Vorster, Vernon 'Froggy' du Toit and Don Smith. Ordered by SAA on July 17, 1968, and registered to the airline in July 1971, the aircraft was rolled out of Boeing's 747 assembly plant at Everett—at that time the largest single building by volume and floor space in the world—30 miles north of Seattle on August 24, 1971. The airplane's first flight took place on September 30. Official handover to SAA was on October 22. The delivery flight left Seattle on November 4. With full fuel tanks and the awkward-looking fifth engine attachment under its port wing, the 747 flew non-stop to Stansted Airport, London in nine hours 20 minutes. After taking on a tightly packed stack of cabin seating that was specially made for the aircraft by a third party supplier in England the 747 took off for a short 20-minute hop to Heathrow Airport. The next day, November 5, it left London for Lisbon, completing the leg in three hours 10 minutes. Later that day, it departed for South Africa, flying the round-the-bulge route to Johannesburg in 11 hours five minutes, landing at Jan Smuts Airport the following morning, on November 6. Total time spent in the air was 23 hours 55 minutes.

The Boeing Company had bet big on its 747. Led by Pan American Airways, 26 airlines ordered the plane before the prototype even flew. The first of the enormous jets was rolled out of the factory on September 30, 1968. Its maiden flight took place on February 9, 1969, with pilots Jack Waddell and Brian Wygle at the controls and Jess Wallick as Flight Engineer. Despite some minor teething problems Boeing exhibited its new jetliner at the Paris Air Show in 1969 where it captured the imagination and attention of the world's press as well as representatives of the international aviation industry. Airworthiness certification for commercial service was awarded by the Federal Aviation Administration (FAA) of the United States in December 1969.

The traveling public took to the new airliner with fervor. In a one-class configuration the 747 could seat a maximum of 500 passengers but most airlines opted for far less than that in a first class and coach (tourist) class layout. On its upper deck, a large area with six windows aft of the cockpit could be used as a first class lounge, cocktail bar or dining room with its own dedicated galley. Some United States-based carriers introduced the 747 with a piano bar upstairs—with live music performed in-flight—while American Airlines added an extra indulgent touch by even including a piano bar at the rear end of the coach class section downstairs too. Referred to in the industry as a 'widebody,' the 747 was the first airplane to have twin aisles separating three blocks of seating. But in those early days of high density air travel all that space was not merely intended to squeeze in customers like sardines in a tin can but to make life as pleasant, spacious and comfortable as possible in the air. There was ample legroom, space to move around, room to breathe, stretch out and enjoy a flight—even in coach class—unlike the miseries endured by passengers who pay the lowest fares to travel on board the jam-packed airliners of today. The 747 introduced a completely new experience for the traveling public. Not only did it introduce cheaper fares but it made flying fun, and on an unprecedented scale.

Boeing 747-200 Super B, ZS-SAN, Lebombo, in flight

SAA's 747 *Lebombo* operated the first official SAA Boeing 747 flight of the Springbok Service on December 10, 1971. The sectors were from Johannesburg to Luanda and then around the bulge to London. The 747 brought new flair in the air with a multi-channel audio entertainment system piped via acoustic tubing to all seats. It featured movies in Super 8mm cassettes that were

---

SAA's Boeing 747-200 Super B had a length of 229 ft and an unprecedented cabin of width of 20 ft. Its wingspan stretched a breathtaking 195 ft 6 ins, 75 ft longer than the entire distance covered during the first flight of the Wright brothers. The airplane's tail towered 64 ft. Its maximum gross weight was 778,673 lbs. Maximum payload was 125,663 lbs. Fuel capacity was 51,038 gallons which allowed the plane to fly at an altitude of 45,000 feet for a range of 7,825 miles. Each of its four Pratt & Whitney JT9D-7FW engines produced 46,300 lbs (209 kN) of thrust—nearly *ten times* more powerful than the original de Havilland Ghost engines that had powered the Comet Mk.1 jetliner twenty years earlier. The 747 flew at a maximum speed of 670 mph or Mach 0.905—just over 90 percent of the speed of sound. The flight deck was manned by a crew of three comprising two pilots and a flight engineer, although an extra pilot and flight engineer were sometimes included on long-haul journeys. SAA's first 747s were configured to carry 34 first class and 307 economy class passengers. They were looked after by a cabin crew of 16. A crew rest area with two full-length bunks was included behind the flight deck where pilots and engineers could take turns grabbing some shut eye on long haul routes. Another rest area containing six bunks for cabin crew was located at the rear of the main passenger cabin.

---

projected onto screens on bulkheads in three compartments of the coach class cabin and one in first class. Passengers seated in the first class cabin in the forward (nose) section of the aircraft were especially pampered. On entering the aircraft their hats, coats and jackets were politely taken away by a Senior Cabin Steward who neatly hung the articles in a cloakroom-style closet and then, as the passengers made their way to their seats, they were greeted by a magnificent arrangement of freshly-picked proteas — South Africa's national flower — displayed in a vase secured to a low table at the foot of the circular staircase that led to the upstairs bar.

A Boeing 747 flight engineer's station

Boeing 747 and 707 alongside one another. The 747 sports the new design of the Flying Springbok emblem in comparison to the previous version on the 707. 1971

As SAA's pool partner in the Springbok Service, BOAC also introduced Boeing 747s on the same date that *Lebombo* departed for London. Three days later, on December 14, SAA's second Boeing 747, ZS-SAM *Drakensberg* (Dragon's Mountain)—the name of an escarpment along a great plateau that stretches all the way from the Cape province through the Orange Free State and Lesotho into Natal—arrived from Seattle. The third 747, ZS-SAL *Tafelberg* (Table Mountain), arrived on January 29, 1972. So that flight and cabin crews could get as much in-service training as possible for long international flights, the 747s also initially operated a number of domestic services between Johannesburg, Durban and Cape Town. The aircraft's sheer size with its two decks, twin aisles, multiple galleys and extensive passenger seating required new skills and techniques compared to inflight cabin services aboard previous aircraft. In the years to come SAA would operate a total of 28 Boeing 747 airplanes in different models and derivatives—some much larger than the Series 200 Super B and some considerably smaller—establishing the airline as one of the Boeing Company's most valued widebody customers. In fact—as will be seen later—SAA would be instrumental in promoting the development of new Boeing 747 models as well as assisting in the design of new power plants with engine manufacturers.

Coinciding with the arrival of the original Boeing 747-200s came a flight simulator that was housed in a specially built new five-storey flight operations building at Jan Smuts Airport. A cavernous space extended from the ground floor up into the first level of the building in which a huge, highly detailed miniaturized three dimensional model of Jan Smuts Airport and its environs was constructed out of wood, plastic and metal and painted right down to the tiniest detail. Mounted on its side this landscape was affixed to one of the walls, extending up through the two levels of the building. If any features in the real world changed—a new shopping center, a roadway, a housing estate, an office complex, a single new home or even if a tree was cut down or a new power line erected—the model was altered to match it exactly. Those were the days before computers and digitized animation were integrated into flight simulator technology so a color television camera mounted on a complex boom 'flew' over the model, relaying images to television screens mounted in front of the windshield of the simulator, allowing crews to practice 'flying' into and out of the airport. It was complicated. It was innovative. But it worked. Later on, of course, this cumbersome system was replaced by computerized graphics, providing a whole new level of realism to the flight simulation experience.

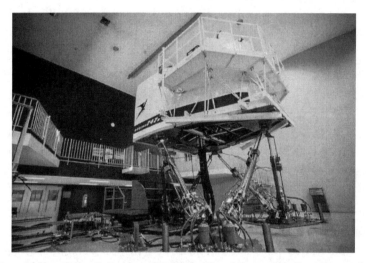

One of the airline's Boeing 747 flight simulators. A full-scale mock-up of the flight deck was installed in the enclosed cabin atop the hydraulic jacks. The rig was moveable in many directions and helped simulate movement including banking, yaw, turns, pitch, aircraft angle, trim, landings, take-offs, braking and even crashes!

In April 1972, four Boeing 707 'Combi'—mixed passenger and freight—services carrying up to 105 economy class passengers in the forward main cabin and three palettes of freight in the rear of the fuselage began flights to European destinations. Another event that month was the renaming of the first and coach class sections on board international flights. First class was christened *Blue Diamond* while coach class was re-branded as *Gold Medallion*. A second Boeing 707 flight between Johannesburg and Rio de Janeiro was implemented on Wednesday April 5. The following month—on May 15—passengers travelling on Boeing 747 and 707 intercontinental services were given the choice of being seated in either smoking or non-smoking areas of the cabin.

Ten days later an unprecedented event made riveting headlines in South Africa and quickly spread throughout the world.

On Wednesday May 25, 1972, Boeing 727 ZS-SBE *Letaba* (the name of a river in what was then known as the eastern Transvaal province) was operating flight SA 029 from Salisbury, Rhodesia to Johannesburg. It was the noon hour on a beautifully clear autumn day. At the controls were Captain Blake Flemington and First Officer Archie Schultz. The Flight Engineer was Bert Cheetham. Attending to the 76 passengers on board were Chief Steward Dirkie Nel, assisted by Flight Attendants Lance Gwyther, Thea van Rensburg and Telana Nel.

Just prior to commencing descent into Johannesburg Captain Flemington was making the usual requisite pre-arrival announcement to passengers over the public address system when suddenly the flight deck door burst open and a very rattled flight attendant, Thea van Rensburg, rushed into the cockpit. Verging on tears, she told the captain that two men were behaving very belligerently in the back and that they had told her to order him to turn around and fly to Khartoum in the Sudan.

"If we land in South Africa," she wailed, "they said they'd blow up the plane."

Completely caught off guard, Flemington responded with "Why? Who are they?"

"I don't know," van Rensburg replied, fighting off tears. "But they're foreign."

Flemington immediately contacted Johannesburg Air Traffic Control and SAA's Radio ZUR, informing them of the situation while hoping that the whole thing was little more than a practical joke.

But it wasn't.

As Flemington throttled back to continue the descent into the Johannesburg area, cabin attendant Lance Gwyther abruptly appeared on the flight deck and blurted out that the two men were holding what appeared to be explosives. One of them was yelling that no attempt should be made to land. Flemington immediately restored power, pulled back on the stick and began to climb again.

Looking over his shoulder at Gwyther he shouted "Send one of them in here."

Less than a minute later a mid-forties-year-old, dark haired, olive-complexioned man of medium build entered the cockpit. He was obviously angry but also slightly nervous. His eyes darted about the flight deck, taking it all in. By Flemington's assessment, he had never been in an airliner cockpit before.

"Who are you?" Flemington asked, not waiting for the man to issue any demands or requests.

"You can call me Captain Z," the man replied.

"There's only one captain on board this aircraft," Flemington retorted. "And that's me. Now what do you want?"

The hijacker thought for a moment, then said, "Well captain, then you can just call me Z."

The two men glared at one another. Flemington waited to hear what demands 'Z' was going to make.

"Turn around and fly us to Khartoum," hissed the hijacker.

"We can't. We don't have enough fuel to reach that destination."

Now 'Z' was caught off-guard. This was not what he was

expecting to hear. After quickly reassessing the information he said: "If you land in Johannesburg we'll destroy your aircraft. And everyone in it."

Flemington glanced at his co-pilot, both of them trying to remain calm.

"What do you want from us?" Flemington asked.

"I told you," the hijacker said. "Fly us to Khartoum."

This triggered a feverish altercation that lasted for the next five or six minutes during which Flemington and First Officer Schultz tried to explain that the Boeing 727 was only a medium-range airliner that did not have enough fuel to reach the Sudan. When 'Z' finally comprehended the message, he insisted on being taken to a destination anywhere outside South Africa. On Flemington's instructions, Flight Engineer Cheetham hastily made some calculations. After a minute or so he informed his captain that the aircraft might just have enough fuel left to return to Salisbury.

"Fine," 'Z' cut into the conversation. "But only to refuel. From there you fly us somewhere else."

Obviously, the man knew that if he attempted to actually disembark at Salisbury, he and his accomplice would be arrested immediately. Meanwhile, Flemington had no choice. He turned the aircraft around and headed back for Salisbury. Thus began the long and dramatic saga of the first and only hijacking in SAA's history.

The two men who had commandeered the Boeing 727 were 46-year-old Fouad Hussain Abu Kamil—or 'Captain Z'—and his slightly younger accomplice Ajaj Jorge Yaghi. Both men had been born in Lebanon. Kamil was married to a South African medical doctor named Melanie. The couple made their home in Johannesburg. He was a former employee of the country's giant multi-national gold mining company, Anglo American Corporation, and its diamond mining and marketing subsidiary, De Beers. Working in the security division of De Beers, his job had been to act as an undercover 'diamond trap,' posing to offer uncut diamonds—illicitly—to black market purchasers worldwide. The purpose was to pass on information about illegal diamond buying to the illicit diamond buying division (IDB) of the South African Police so that, with the help of Interpol—the International Criminal Police Organization—international illegal diamond buying syndicates and individuals could be exposed, arrested and brought to trial. The worldwide IDB trade was difficult to curtail. De Beers and its affiliates were losing fortunes from IDB activities, not to mention the loss of tax revenue due by the legitimate diamond industry to governments in countries as diverse as Holland, Belgium, Israel and the United States, the world's major diamond cutting centers. Exposing an IDB scam was very lucrative to a 'diamond trap.' According to Kamil's testimony at his trail months after the hijacking, fifty percent of the value of all uncut diamonds retrieved from illegal buyers was paid by De Beers as a reward to a 'trap.' During the trial Kamil claimed that he had exposed a mammoth IDB scheme worth at least $10 million being conducted by certain 'very high ranking senior South African government officials' who were exporting stones to Uruguay for cutting there. After exposing the carefully concealed scam, Kamil said that he was owed $5 million by De Beers. But the money was never paid. Or so he claimed.

Furious at being let down by his employer, Kamil had personally contacted the Chairman of the Anglo American Corporation and De Beers, Sir Harry Oppenheimer. When nothing was forthcoming, Kamil resigned from the company and began to lay threats against members of the Oppenheimer family. As one of the world's wealthiest families, they took the threats very seriously. Oppenheimer's wife Bridget and their two children, Nicholas and Mary, were seen to be especially vulnerable. Oppenheimer was not only a very rich man whose personal wealth could be counted in the hundreds of millions of dollars but he was also an ardent critic and opponent of apartheid. He never found favour in the eyes of South Africa's conservative Nationalist government and their racist policies. But why was Kamil threatening him and his family? Was the South African government behind the hijacking? Surely not. Then was it something far more sinister, such as a foreign or locally brewed terrorist plot? At that point no one could tell.

Unbeknown to everyone, Kamil had set his sights on someone outside of the Oppenheimer family's immediate inner circle. In 1965, Mary had married famed British rugby player, Gordon Waddell. The marriage only lasted six years but, by 1971, Waddell was still on excellent terms with his ex-father-in-law and was an esteemed and valued member of the board of directors of several of Oppenheimer's companies, including the multi-billion dollar Anglo American Corporation. So, it was Waddell who became the target of Kamil's attentions. Over a period of months, he began to hatch his plans. If Waddell could be captured, a very hefty ransom fee could be demanded for his release. Yaghi, an acquaintance of Kamil and a policeman in Beirut, Lebanon, fell in with Kamil's plans, becoming a willing accomplice in the hijacking attempt. The two men had secretly acquired information that Waddell would be on a South African-bound airliner from London to Johannesburg on May 25, 1972 and that the aircraft was due to stop over in Salisbury en route to Johannesburg. There was just one problem. They did not realize that two SAA aircraft would be departing from Salisbury to Johannesburg on the same day. One was stopping over on its way from London, the other was operating a regional flight originating in Salisbury. After laying low in Salisbury for a few days, they purchased their tickets for flight SA 029. But that was not the flight that Waddell would be on.

In the absence of airport security checks during those laid back and lenient pre-9/11 days, Kamil and Yaghi smuggled sticks of dynamite in briefcases on board the aircraft and stowed them in the overhead racks. Those were before the days of overhead bins in the Boeing 727. Open racks extended above the seating along the length of the cabin. Shortly after take-off, it became evident to the two men that they were not on board the international flight that had originated in London. Kamil cornered Cabin Attendant Lance Gwyther and demanded to know whether Gordon Waddell was on board. When Gwyther checked the passenger manifest and told Kamil that he was not, Kamil became furious. It was then that Cabin Attendant Thea van Rensburg had burst into the cockpit with news of the hijacking.

As the Boeing began heading back towards Salisbury feverish plans were launched in the background. Johannesburg ATC and Radio ZUR alerted the Rhodesian authorities of what was happening. Salisbury airport was placed on full alert and made ready to receive the hijacked aircraft. But when the head of South Africa's BOSS—the Bureau of State Security—General Johan van den Bergh was informed of what was going on in the air, he immediately contacted Prime Minister Balthazar Johannes Vorster. Whatever happened, the two men decided, no negotiations would be entered into with the hijackers. As far as they were concerned South African airliners do not get hijacked. It would be a disgrace to give in to the brigands' demands. The most appropriate action would be to shoot the aircraft down. A request to do so was relayed from military headquarters in Pretoria to the Rhodesian military authorities in Salisbury.When the call went through it said: "Shoot to kill."

Because Rhodesia and its military forces relied so heavily on South African support for its efforts in the 'Bush War' against black freedom fighters, two Royal Rhodesian Air Force (RRAF) Canberra jet bombers were scrambled and ordered to trail the Boeing as soon as it entered Rhodesian airspace. (It should be noted that despite UDI and self-proclaimed independence Rhodesia still predicated an affiliation with Britain and maintained the prefix 'Royal' in the title of its air force.) Within minutes the Canberras were in the air and in close but unseen formation behind the 727. On being told about the grave situation developing in its skies, the Rhodesian Prime Minister Ian Smith was appalled. Defying his loyal and supportive South African benefactors in his efforts to win the Bush War Smith was adamant.

"Under no circumstances will I allow a civilian airliner to be shot down in our air space," he declared, "No matter *who* requests it."

And just as well. Minutes later the SAA Boeing 727 touched down at Salisbury airport, its fuel tanks virtually empty. Once it was on the ground the Canberras were told to land at a nearby RRAF airfield and to stand by for further instructions.

Now came the tricky part. More than anything else Captain Blake Flemington wanted to assure the safety of his crew and passengers. Kamil insisted that the aircraft be refuelled as quickly as possible and that as soon as that task was completed the Boeing should take off again. But to where? If Khartoum was beyond its range where could it go? Where would he and Yaghi seek asylum or safe haven? In the meantime, Flemington spoke via radio to the Rhodesian civil aviation authorities. He explained that the lives of everyone on board his aircraft were in dire danger and that the explosives that had been smuggled on board might be detonated if it was not fully refuelled and allowed to take off again. The Boeing was parked at the end of the main runway and not at the terminal building so tanker trucks soon pulled up alongside the jet and ground personnel began pumping fuel into it.

Flemington then began pleading with Kamil. If he could be allowed to disembark the passengers the aircraft would be much lighter and would fly a lot further. But Kamil wasn't buying it. Flemington began trying every ploy at his disposal to release at least some of his passengers. He begged Kamil to allow the women and children to leave. Their presence on board would only be a hindrance to a successful hijack, he said. Surely, he argued, having only able-bodied men on board as hostages would make things a lot easier for Kamil and his colleague. Kamil went back into the main cabin to discuss things with Yaghi. And that is when First Officer Archie Schultz seized his opportunity. He called up Radio ZUR in Johannesburg once again and asked them for suggestions as to what to do next. The advice given to them by SAA's Chief Navigator Mick Mackin was to fly to either Blantyre in Malawi or to the British-ruled islands of the Seychelles just off the East African coast. At least those countries were friendly towards South Africa. Who could tell what would happen if the plane landed in a hostile country? Never mind the explosives on board; it may get shot out of the sky before it even landed. Quick as lightning, Flight Engineer Bert Cheetham assisted Schultz to scribble down details of a flight plan for going to either Blantyre or the Seychelles that was dictated over the radio to them from Johannesburg. By the time Kamil returned to the flight deck, they had all the coordinates they needed for setting a vector to either destination.

Amazingly, and to Flemington's relief, Kamil announced that he and Yaghi had agreed that most of the passengers could be released, provided of course that the Boeing had as much fuel as possible in its tanks. The two hijackers then went from passenger to passenger, examining everyone's passports. Apart from five men, everyone else on board was told that they would be allowed to leave. As soon as refueling was complete, Flemington instructed Chief Steward Dirkie Nel that he could lower the hydraulic air stairs located in the rear of the aircraft and disembark everyone except the five male passengers. Kamil even allowed the two female cabin attendants to leave. Once the 71 passengers and the two flight attendants were safely outside the airplane two buses escorted by armed Rhodesian soldiers in military Land Rovers arrived to pick them up. Minutes later, the rear airstairs were closed again and the Boeing was ready to depart. The only persons on board now were the flight crew, Chief Steward Nel, Flight Attendant Gwyther, the five male hostages and Kamil and Yaghi.

But there was still no agreement as to where the aircraft should go. Flemington, Schultz and Kamil became locked in more bargaining and arguing. Although Kamil had his heart set on flying directly to Khartoum, Flemington carefully explained to him that, even with full fuel tanks, that was still too far away for the 727's limited range. Besides, he explained, if they attempted to overfly or land at any destination in Africa that was not friendly towards South Africa, they risked being shot down because of the OAU ban on South African-registered aircraft. Flemington subtly tried to coerce Kamil to agree to fly to the Seychelles. The premise of his argument was that as it was still under British rule they would be in no danger when they landed there and, once on the ground, negotiations could take place between the local British authorities and Sudanese diplomatic representatives to allow the Boeing to refuel and then proceed to Khartoum. Slowly, bit by bit, talking point by talking point, Kamil began to come around to agreeing to the plan.

By sundown, the Boeing was back in the air. Unseen and close behind it once more were the two RRAF Canberra bombers. It was now that the Canberras made radio contact with the Boeing, informing the crew that they were being followed. Up until then neither Flemington nor Schultz were even aware that they were there. As soon as Kamil got to hear of this, he became enraged, threatening to blow up the Boeing there and then unless the Canberras showed themselves and then left them alone. Flemington duly informed the RRAF pilots about this threat and the Canberras accelerated, flew alongside the Boeing for a minute or two, then peeled away and made a wide turn back to base.

What Kamil and Yaghi did not know was that with its reduced passenger load and its full tanks, the Boeing actually had enough fuel on board to reach a destination as far away as Khartoum. What they also did not know was that the crew had set a flight vector for Blantyre, Malawi and not the Seychelles. As night fell, the Boeing roared through the African sky with features on the ground below becoming less discernible every minute. As it approached Malawian airspace Flemington called Kamil to the flight deck and told him that with the intensifying darkness it was becoming very dangerous to attempt an ocean crossing to the Seychelles, especially to an unfamiliar airport without the necessary navigational equipment on board. The 727 was not equipped to undertake a night flight like that, he lied. It would be far safer to land at Blantyre's Chileka Airport and wait it out there until dawn, then take off and carry on to the Seychelles during daylight. As SAA regularly served Blantyre from Johannesburg, he and his crew were familiar with the airport. Kamil mulled it over briefly and then reluctantly agreed.

It was ten o'clock and very dark by the time the Boeing overflew Blantyre's Chileka Airport. The plane's crew had now been on duty for more than fifteen hours, but this fact elicited no sympathy from Kamil. Of course, the airport authorities had been expecting the hijacked flight and gave it permission to land. Airport Operations Manager, Ralph Casey, took charge of all radio communication between the airport and the aircraft. After touchdown, it was directed to the end of the runway where it was ordered to stop and shut down its engines. As soon as it was stationary, Yaghi opened the briefcases in the overhead racks, removed the sticks of dynamite, connected a fuse cord to them and strung them all along the racks on both sides of the cabin. To all intents and purposes, the Boeing was now a time bomb, waiting to be detonated.

It was then that Kamil made his demands known to the crew. He provided full details about his IDB work for De Beers, how the company had failed to compensate him for exposing one of the biggest IDB scams in its history, how South African cabinet ministers were implicated and why Harry Oppenheimer personally owed him $5 million. But, he continued, if he and Yaghi made it safely to Khartoum and left the aircraft without hindrance, he would drop all threats against Oppenheimer and his family as well against De Beers and the Anglo American Corporation, provided that Oppenheimer himself personally fly to Khartoum, meet him face to face and make the necessary arrangements to pay him the $5 million that he was due.

As the night wore on Malawian military authorities got involved in the hijacking. On army instructions, Air Malawi ground staff quietly surrounded the jet and, working as deftly as possible, disconnected the nose wheel steering mechanism and deflated the airplane's tires. The South African government and SAA were informed of this and, at midnight, an SAA Boeing 737 secretly landed on Chileka's secondary runway and surreptitiously taxied towards the technical area where it shut down its engines. On board was a contingent of South African Railways police and SAA technical staff. The Railways police worked exclusively for the South African Railways & Harbors Administration. It was their duty to ensure security at railroad stations, harbour facilities and airports in South Africa but, despite the fact that they had been sent to Chileka Airport to supposedly take control of the hijacking situation they were completely out of their depth. An airplane hijacking was way beyond anything they had ever experienced. Besides, they were inept at aviation radio procedures, knew nothing of the Chileka Airport environment and were simply not capable of being of any use to defuse the deadly situation that confronted them. After botched attempts by them to negotiate with the hijackers, all further communication between Captain Blake Flemington and the outside world became the responsibility of Chileka Airport Operations Manager, Ralph Casey.

Meanwhile, using electrical power generated by the 727's on-board auxiliary power unit (APU), Flight Engineer Bert

Cheetham turned up the aircraft's interior cabin temperature to an uncomfortably high level in an effort to tire out and subdue the hijackers. With the system sucking in air from Blantyre's humid subtropical atmosphere, the heat on board soon became unbearable. When Kamil complained about it, Flemington and Cheetham merely said that it was beyond their control and that lowering the temperature would require starting the engines and wasting precious fuel. To alleviate the heat, the hijackers were persuaded to allow the crew to open the cockpit windows and the main cabin door. But by then a side effect of the excessive heat was that the sticks of dynamite had begun sweating toxic fumes. Because both Kamil and Yaghi had spent time carefully arranging the sticks in the overhead racks, they had developed splitting headaches, a direct effect of handling nitro-glycerine. While Cabin Attendant Lance Gwyther administered cups of water and aspirin to the two men, the flight crew meandered into the main cabin and quietly briefed the five male passenger hostages on the use of the aircraft's emergency over-wing exit hatches and main door escape slide, just in case a rapid escape might become possible.

Shortly after midnight, with pressure, frustration and discomfort mounting, Yaghi started shouting and arguing loudly with Kamil in Lebanese. He had become delirious from the nitro-glycerine and suddenly pulled out a length of fuse cord from his pocket and ignited it. In the tumult and flurry of smoke and flickering blue flames, Captain Blake Flemington shouted out the order to evacuate the aircraft. Unfortunately, by this late hour Chief Steward Dirkie Nel had been quietly helping himself to one too many of the bar's miniature bottles of scotch and brandy and had fallen asleep in the forward left row of seats next to the main cabin door. When the hostages ran forward to try to make their escape, the hijackers pursued them, trying to stop them and yelling abusive threats. The noisy chaos quickly awoke the sleeping steward who, on seeing some of the passengers attempting to deploy the escape chute and life raft, jumped out of his seat. A scuffle ensued and, with a great whooshing sound, the life raft inflated, completely jamming the doorway. This left only the two cockpit sliding windows on the flight deck open as a possible means of escape. Anticipating this eventuality, Flemington, First Officer Schultz and Flight Engineer Cheetham had already deployed escape ropes through the cockpit windows and tossed them outside so that they reached the ground below. The crew immediately ran to the flight deck and seconds later they were followed by two of the passengers. The five of them squeezed through the windows, slid down the ropes and ran as fast as they could along the runway to a safe distance from the airplane.

When it became apparent to Flemington in the dim moonlight that no one else had managed to get out of the aircraft, he decided to return to his airplane. He ordered Schultz to guide the escaped passengers to the terminal buildings and to provide a full report of what had happened. Flemington, accompanied by Flight Engineer Cheetham, then carefully crept back to the aircraft. At this point Kamil and Yaghi were once again in firm control of things, saw Flemington and Cheetham approaching and forced the quickly-sobering Chief Steward Nel to use the aircraft's loudhailer to call out to them. As Flemington stood under the nose of the Boeing, Kamil leaned out and threatened to kill the remaining hostages unless he re-boarded the aircraft at once. Flemington shouted up to Kamil, asking him to please allow Chief Steward Nel to lower the aft stairwell so that he could come back on board. This was agreed to and, after ordering Cheetham to run away to the airport buildings, Flemington re-entered his aircraft. As soon as he was inside the cabin Yaghi lunged at him, threatening him with physical violence. It seemed to Flemington that Yaghi had gone insane from the nitro-glycerine poisoning as he was yelling and gesticulating uncontrollably. Then Kamil intervened. He calmed down his accomplice and persuaded Flemington to return to the flight deck and re-establish communication with the ground.

Negotiations now proceeded at a snail's pace with Kamil demanding money and Airport Manager Ralph Casey doing his best to ameliorate what was becoming an increasingly unpredictable situation. At around three in the morning Chief Steward Nel—now cold sober once again and sitting in the First Officer's seat in the cockpit—quietly slipped out of the side window and slid down the escape rope. This left only Captain Blake Flemington and the three remaining hostages on board with the hijackers. When Kamil and Yaghi discovered that Nel had eluded them, they demanded that all hatches and windows be closed and locked, despite the still-excessive heat on board.

As dawn approached a breakthrough occurred. Kamil agreed to allow a South African embassy official to come aboard and negotiate directly with him. As the sun crested the horizon, the diplomat arrived, boarded the aircraft and spoke to Kamil, learning nothing new from him but agreeing to do what he could to request a personal meeting with Harry Oppenheimer. Unbeknown to Kamil, the embassy official was really a BOSS State Security agent. While aboard he carefully assessed the situation and formulated a plan of action. After he disembarked, negotiations continued and, whilst assuring Kamil that Oppenheimer was being contacted, arrangements were made to send up a metal trunk that would contain $5 million in cash in US currency. It was also agreed that a Britten Norman Islander aircraft would be made available to the hijackers for a flight to Mogadishu, capital of the Somali Democratic Republic in the Horn of Africa. The hijackers were told that, if they spared the life of Captain Flemington, he would personally be allowed to pilot the getaway aircraft. Of course, what the hijackers did not know was that a commercial airline pilot is only certified to fly one type of aircraft at a time. The truth is that Flemington had no knowledge or previous experience of flying a Britten Norman

Islander which was a small, short-range, twin piston-engine aircraft. The real plan was for members of the Malawi armed forces' sharpshooters to pick off the hijackers as soon as they disembarked from the Boeing. Flight Engineer Bert Cheetham was stationed with them to help identify Captain Flemington, the two crew members and the three hostages so that they would not be caught in the line of fire.

At ten in the morning of Thursday, May 26, a military steel trunk was delivered to the stranded 727. The rear airstairs were lowered and while Yaghi sat in the flight engineer's seat to prevent any further escapes from the cockpit, Kamil went down the stairs, grabbed a handle of the trunk and dragged it up the stairs into the cabin. As he began opening it, Yaghi left the flight deck and ran through the cabin to see what was inside the trunk, but not before warning Flemington not try anything he might regret. However, as soon as Yaghi passed through the galley area Flemington sprang out of his seat and threw open the two cockpit windows. The escape ropes were still attached and he yelled out to the remaining three hostages to join him. They immediately rushed towards the flight deck, made a beeline for the open windows and slid down the ropes to the ground. There they were met by SAA maintenance engineer Pev Peverelli who bundled them into a waiting vehicle.

At this point, Flight Engineer Bert Cheetham was rushed out to the aircraft where he opened the exterior emergency control panel of the APU and shut it down. The hijackers were now trapped without air or lighting inside the aircraft. But they would not give up. Using the airplane's loudhailer, they continued to try to negotiate their freedom during the rest of the day. This only ended when the loudhailer's batteries ran out. The Boeing 727 had now become Kamil and Yaghi's holdout. And they weren't budging.

Keeping a safe distance in case the explosives on board were detonated, members of the Malawian military and their commanding officers, the contingent of South African Railways Police, SAA technicians and Air Malawi ground crew surrounded the aircraft. For hours the clock ticked and nothing happened. By nightfall the stand-off simply dragged on without any sign of Kamil and Yaghi's capitulation. The deadlock may have continued for days were it not for the fact that Malawi's President Hastings Kamuzu Banda was scheduled to board a BOAC aircraft for a conference in London on Friday evening, May 27. That morning a stern directive came through from the President's office.

"Do not obstruct the President's plans. Clear the runway. End the hijacking. NOW."

As the Malawian military unit was not aware of the fact that Kamil and Yaghi were Muslims, a priest from a nearby church was summoned to the airport to administer the last rites to them. The soldiers were intent on killing them. They lined up on the port side of the Boeing and readied their automatic weapons. As soon as the priest arrived, the order was given to commence firing. An ear-splitting din erupted as firearms sprayed the aircraft with bullets. The clang and rattle of metal repeatedly hitting metal was terrifying. In the midst of the turmoil Kamil and Yaghi came running down the rear airstairs with their hands raised. A command was shouted to cease firing. Smoke and the acrid smell of gunpowder wafted around the Boeing as security forces rushed forward to handcuff the hijackers. Amazingly, their only injury was a bullet that was imbedded in Yaghi's left foot. The two men were shoved into a military vehicle and driven off to prison, there to await trial.

The Boeing had not come out of the skirmish as lightly as the hijackers. It had been hit 150 times. Most of the strikes along the fuselage were just below the window line, but the number one engine had also been struck several times. Various hydraulic lines had been punctured. Miraculously fuel lines and tanks had not been ruptured. A tug soon arrived and towed the stricken airliner off the runway to an open area on the far end of the airport where explosive experts boarded the craft and defused the sticks of dynamite in the cabin's overhead baggage racks. The explosives were then removed.

Later that day, a scheduled BOAC VC-10 airliner touched down after a flight from London and that evening President Banda boarded it and took off to attend his conference in the U.K. The only sign that a hijacking had ever taken place were the hundreds of empty shell cases that littered the grass on the side of the main runway. A few days later, Malawi security forces took the explosives that the hijackers had stashed on board the Boeing to the perimeter of the airfield and detonated them. They underestimated the size of the blast and, although no one was injured, a number of windows in the terminal building were blown out. Of course, the metal trunk of banknotes given to Kamil and Yaghi was retrieved from the airliner. It was found to contain not $5 million in U.S. currency but 10,000 single bills of Kwatchas, the official Malawian currency. Mysteriously, less than half of it was finally recovered by the police. No one ever found out what happened to the rest of it but rumor has it that all the bills at the local military officers' club in town were fully paid by an undisclosed source that month.

At Kamil and Yaghi's trial in Blantyre in September 1972, the two men were each sentenced to eleven years in prison, the maximum allowed by Malawian law. They were sent to the main detention center at Zomba where they served only eight months before being released for reasons never fully explained by the Malawian judicial authorities. Yaghi returned to Lebanon and subsequently disappeared without trace. But Kamil was another matter. He continued to make appearances from time to time until 1982, at hotels in Madrid and Lisbon where SAA slip crews were accommodated during layovers on the Springbok Service. Then, out of the blue, on August 11, 2009, a Facebook page carried a statement posted by him. In it he offered an apology to SAA, to the crew members and passengers of flight SA 029 and 'to all South Africans' for the hijacking 37 years earlier. The statement said that he was now 83 years of age, residing in Brazil, that he did not know how much longer he might live and that he wanted to clear his conscience about the hijacking. He begged forgiveness for his actions from the victims of the incident all those years ago, confessing deep regret for what he did. Following the Facebook statement he was never heard from nor seen again.

As for the fate of Boeing 727 ZS-SBE *Letaba*, a group of mechanics and ground technicians arrived in Blantyre on a special SAA Boeing 707 flight from Johannesburg on May 3, 1972. For the next month, they toiled to patch up the damaged airplane, doing what they could to make it airworthy for a ferry flight back to Jan Smuts Airport where it would undergo extensive repairs and refurbishing. At 6.00 a.m. on the morning of Saturday, June 3, it took off under the command of Chief Training Captain Francois 'Doc' Malan, Captain Mike Kemp and Flight Engineer Louis Smuts. Because of all the breaches in the hull made by the bullets, it could not be pressurized, so it flew at low altitude on its two operative engines. Travelling via Salisbury, it landed at Johannesburg later that afternoon. Two-and-a-half months afterwards, on August 17, 1972, it was as good as new and a test flight was undertaken. Within a few days it was returned to service, none the worse for a moment in history that could have gone horribly wrong and that could have seen it blown clear out of the sky. It continued to provide unblemished service for another eleven years before it was finally retired and sold to a buyer in the United States.

In September 1972, the world's first spacious vanity rooms for airline passengers were installed in the five Boeing 747 Super Bs. Each aircraft was equipped with three of these facilities in the coach class cabin at the rear of the fuselage. Equipped with large mirrors, bright lighting, hot and cold water, a comfortable collapsible seat, soap, towels and a generous supply of basic cosmetics, the vanity rooms were a boon for women travelling on long intercontinental flights. Also in September, the engines of all the airline's Boeing 727 and 737 aircraft were fitted with non-smoke combustion chambers, making them virtually smoke-free. In November, an ultra-modern new international arrivals and departure terminal complex was officially opened at Jan Smuts Airport. That month, SAA increased its services to Buenos Aires and signed a pool partnership agreement with Aerolineas Argentina. The rest of the year saw services expanded to many destinations, including Mauritius, Lisbon, Rome, Manzini and Blantyre.

On January 6, 1973, services began from Johannesburg to Hong Kong, SAA's first destination in Asia. Operated in conjunction with BOAC, the flights were routed via the Seychelles islands. By April of that year, the Springbok Service was operating 16 flights per week to Europe using nine Boeing 747s, five Boeing 707 Combis and two all-passenger Boeing 707 aircraft. In July, a new in-flight magazine for passengers called *The Flying Springbok* was introduced on all domestic, regional and international routes. On August 22, an unusually happy event was celebrated on board an SAA flight between Johannesburg and Durban. Mrs. Molly Chetty was sure that her baby would not be born prematurely when she boarded Boeing 737 ZS-SBL *Pongola* at Jan Smuts Airport. Despite the apprehension of check-in personnel she convinced them to allow her to fly as she wanted to have her baby under the watchful eye of her mother in Durban. But nature had other plans. The baby arrived before the aircraft was halfway to its destination. As there were no doctors or medical personnel among the passengers, cabin attendant Martjie de Beer acted as midwife. As the baby's first cry was heard behind the curtained-off area at the rear of the cabin, all fifty passengers broke out in cheers and loud clapping. Captain Maynhardt Slabbert left the flight deck and came aft to offer his congratulations too. He suggested the name Aerolene for the child. The name stuck. And so Aerolene Chetty had the proud distinction of being the first baby born on board an SAA flight.

By September, Springbok Services were increased to 17 per week and, for the very first time, a non-stop flight began between Johannesburg and London. Considering the wide detour required to route the flight around the bulge of Africa this was a major milestone in SAA's history. Two months later, an additional flight was introduced between Johannesburg and New York, the first to the United States to be routed via the island of Ilha do Sal. This reduced the flying time to New York by three hours 15 minutes compared to the route flown via Rio de Janeiro.

But 1973 was the year when other events cut deeply into the jugular veins of the world's aviation industry.

Chapter 13

Beating the Odds

Aviation is an industry that responds to world events in the same way that mercury in a barometer reacts to temperature changes in a room. It rises and falls, depending on the atmosphere, conditions and circumstances around it. And that is how it was in 1973.

October of that year was another hot, dry month in the wedge-shaped Sinai Peninsula that juts into the Gulf of Suez, the Red Sea and the Gulf of Aqaba. 236 miles to the north of the blistering Sinai desert, the mountainous Golan Heights marked a fragile separation between Israel, Syria and Lebanon. Sinai and the Golan had been won and occupied by Israel in the so-called 'Six Day War' of 1967, when the invading forces of Egypt, Syria and Jordan had been swiftly repelled during yet another bitter chapter in the on-going conflict between Israel and its Arab neighbors. October 6, 1973, was not just another hot, dreary, ordinary day in the region. It was the eighth day of the Muslim holy month of Ramadan. It was also Yom Kippur—the Day of Atonement—the most solemn and sacred event in the Hebrew calendar year. Most of Israel's armed forces were on stand-down in observance of the day. For President Anwar Sadat of Egypt, President Hafez al-Assad of Syria and King Hussein bin Talal of Jordan, it was an ideal opportunity to strike without warning and reclaim territories lost to Israel in the war six years earlier. On no other day would Israel be more vulnerable.

Thus began what has generally gone down in the pages of western history as the Yom Kippur War, though many refer to it as the 1973 Arab-Israeli War. In Arab nations and text books, it is also called the Ramadan War, the October War or the Fourth Arab-Israeli War. Because Israel was caught totally off-guard and was unprepared to deal with the sudden invasion, the campaign dragged on for three weeks, embroiling the then-Soviet Union to supply arms and assistance to its Arab allies and the United States to support its ally, Israel. When the opposing forces were eventually halted and the dust settled, the ramifications for the world at large were enormous. Led by Arab nations who were furious about the United States' support for Israel, the Organization of Petroleum Exporting Countries (OPEC) decided to cut crude oil production and slapped an oil embargo on all nations that either supported Israel or that maintained cordial relations with it. This included the United States, many countries in Western Europe and — of direct pertinence to our story — South Africa and its national airline.

Gasoline pumps quickly dried up around the world. Long lines of vehicles queued up for hours — sometimes for days or more — outside gas stations with drivers hoping for at least a few drops of fuel to keep them going. In South Africa, stringent fuel rationing was implemented. Without a government-issued pink form stipulating precisely how much petroleum a driver could purchase over a strictly-controlled and limited period of time vehicles of all types — trucks, buses, taxis, private cars, tractors — simply waited their turn or lay idle along the roadside. It was devastating. People's lives were turned upside down. The nation's economy took a nosedive. Much of the rest of the world went into a downward economic spiral too. Needless to say, one of the hardest hit industries was aviation. Many European and American carriers found themselves in dire straits, their finances shattered or on very shaky ground. As for SAA, it had no choice but to push up air fares and slash the fuel-intensive round-the-bulge Springbok Service to Europe down to only 13 flights per week.

Fortunately for South Africa a lifeline of fuel still trickled in. While other OPEC countries completely turned off the taps, Iran continued to supply 75 percent of South Africa's needs. The fact is that the two countries enjoyed a very special relationship at that time. The reasons go back to Iran's old royal dynasty. Previously known as Persia, Iran had a monarchy that stretched back some 4,700 years. Reza Shah Pahlavi—also known as Reza Khan the Great—was the reigning head of state from 1925 until 1941. During World War II, he was forced by the Allies to abdicate after his nation was invaded by British, Commonwealth and Soviet forces. Though Iran was neutral during the war and although Reza Shah consistently denied it, he was secretly sympathetic towards Germany and the Axis powers. The invading forces wanted to take over his country's rich oil fields in their efforts to defeat Germany on the Eastern Front. British Prime Minister Winston Churchill personally consented to allow the Shah's descendants to remain in power provided that the Shah himself agree to leave the country and live in exile abroad. After his abdication, his place was taken by his son, Mohammed Reza Shah Pahlavi. The new Shah formed a friendly relationship with the West and has subsequently become known to history as The Last Shah of Iran. His reign only came to an end when the exiled revolutionary political and religious leader Ayatollah Ruhollah Moosavi Khomeini returned to Iran from Paris in 1979, thereby ending the monarchy and creating the modern Islamic Republic of Iran. But what of the Shah's father, Reza Shah Pahlavi, or Reza Khan the Great? In accordance with British directives after he abdicated so that his son could take the throne, he sought refuge elsewhere. After a short and unhappy spell in India and then Mauritius he decided to settle in Johannesburg. There he was warmly welcomed by the government and the people of South Africa and was provided with everything that he needed. He lived in comfort but in slowly declining health at his home in Johannesburg until his death on July 25, 1944.

Before the Ayatollah Khomeini's return to Tehran in 1979, the government and people of Iran had not forgotten South Africa's hospitality toward their late Reza Shah and so, despite the OPEC oil embargo and the United Nations sanctions that were in place against South Africa, oil continued to flow to the country from Iran. Without it, South Africa would have been brought to its knees. Much of the oil was pumped into huge underground chambers in very deep unused or abandoned old gold mine shafts—some of them plunging two miles beneath the earth's surface—there to be stored in case it was needed if and when all oil imports from abroad were entirely halted. Under the apartheid-regime's cloak-and-dagger plans to try to ensure that the country survive increasingly hostile international actions against it because of its racist policies, enormous underground storage tanks were also constructed in isolated areas along the western coast and in the hinterland. These great subterranean vats of liquid black gold were held in reserve for many years, just in case the oil was needed for the country's rapidly developing military machine to help repel possible invasion from independent black nations to the north. In addition, the government held another trump card up its sleeve. Because South Africa had no natural sources of oil but abundant reserves of very high grade seams of coal an enterprise known as the Suid Afrikaanse Steenkool Olie en Gas Korporasie (South African Coal, Oil and Gas Corporation)—or SASOL—had been established in the early fifties. This venture produced large refineries in which oil was extracted from coal in a complex process on a massive, highly industrialized scale. No other similar enterprise of its kind existed anywhere else in the world. So, with the help of SASOL, covert supplies from Iran and small supplies from one or two Western-owned Middle Eastern oilfields, South Africa rode the oil embargo storm better than many other countries. But the cost, effort and strain were tremendous. Not only was fuel tightly rationed but also extremely expensive. Once again, SAA became a victim of circumstances far beyond its own doing. Its fuel bill soared. But, survive it did.

By the end of 1973, air freight services had grown so much that a new cargo handling terminal was opened in the north-western sector of Jan Smuts Airport. At the beginning of 1974, the airline could boast that it had carried a total of 2,405,953 passengers, a figure far exceeding all expectations, particularly during those fragile times when most world economies were in deep recession. There were now 7,486 staff on the airline's payroll, of which 354 were pilots. By April of that year, the number of Springbok Services to European destinations was returned to 16 frequencies per week, using 11 Boeing 747s, three Boeing 707 Combis and two regular Boeing 707s. In July, an order was placed for three ultra-long range Boeing 747SP (Special Performance) aircraft for delivery two years later. In July, Springbok Services were increased to 17 per week and Boeing 747s began operating to Athens and Amsterdam. The routes were not profitable. But in the wake of the ever-growing anti-apartheid movement, it was expedient for the South African flag on a South African aircraft to be seen at those airports. Also in July, new, enlarged freight terminals were opened at airports in Cape Town, Durban and Port Elizabeth.

On September 14, 1974, Boeing 727 ZS-SBD *Orange* (the name of South Africa's longest river) suffered a nose gear that failed to extend during its approach into Jan Smuts Airport. Captain Topper van der Spuy and his crew were unable to extend the gear by normal, mechanical or manual means so fuel was dumped and the aircraft landed on a runway that had been sprayed with fire-retardant foam. There were no injuries to the crew or the 69 passengers on board, and very little damage was sustained by the aircraft. It was repaired and returned to service a couple of weeks later.

On October 1, 1974, an agreement was reached between SAA and local airfreight company Safair for the leasing of two Lockheed L100 aircraft—the civil version of the military C-130 Hercules—to be used as freighters on certain high density domestic routes. The payload of the Lockheed was 21 tons, releasing some of SAA's hard-working Boeing 727s from cargo services. The airline's Boeing 727 and 737 aircraft were now reconfigured from five to six-abreast seating, thereby increasing passenger capacity on the 727 from 97 to 119 and on the 737 from 93 to 111. In October, Boeing 747s began calling at Paris. Domestic airfares were increased once again in November as international oil prices kept rising. At the same time, five daily Boeing 707 services were added to the existing Boeing 727 and 737 schedules between Johannesburg and Cape Town.

As 1975 got underway, cyclones at Mauritius forced SAA's Boeing 707s to temporarily bypass the island and operate a non-stop service between Johannesburg and Perth, a distance of 5,160 miles. In February, a new twice-weekly service was inaugurated between Johannesburg and the Victoria Falls utilizing Hawker Siddeley HS 748 aircraft. In April 1975, a luxurious new first-class lounge was opened at Jan Smuts Airport for the exclusive use of Blue Diamond (First Class) passengers.

An undeniable fact is that airlines are not impervious to the undulating tides and rhythms of world affairs. Remote and unrelated though it may seem, political events in faraway Portugal would soon reach out and touch SAA in unexpected ways. When authoritarian fascist dictator António de Oliveira Salazar suffered a brain hemorrhage while stepping from his bathtub in his palatial home in Lisbon in 1968, Portugal entered a new era of conservative, heavy-handed rule. Salazar was replaced by Marcello José das Neves Alves Caetano who became the new Prime Minister. Unlike the heads of other European nations, both Salazar and Caetano were ardently against granting independence to Portugal's overseas possessions, the two largest of which were Angola and Mozambique in Africa. In fact, Salazar had been a friend and staunch ally of Rhodesian Prime Minister Ian Smith. When Smith rebelled against Britain and declared UDI in 1965, Salazar ensured that neighboring Mozambique maintain an open transit line for the export and import of essential commodities between Rhodesia and the outside world through Mozambique's ports at Beira and Lourenco Marques.

But things were neither peaceful nor placid in Mozambique and Angola. Because Lisbon refused to grant the territories independence, black resistance fighters had taken up arms against their Portuguese masters. Fierce guerrilla fighting and acts of sabotage became the order of the day in both territories. Railway lines were sabotaged, bridges were blown up, families were murdered on their farms, crops were set alight, tourists were killed in hotels on some of the remote beaches that stretched up and down the coastline. Portuguese troops—aided by locally trained soldiers and police—tried to quell the rebellion but it was only a matter of time before the freedom fighters would succeed in their quest. That day came on April 25, 1974, when a military coup in Portugal itself toppled the Caetano regime. The people had had enough of fascism and dictatorship. It was time for a freely elected democratic government. Besides, the cost of holding on to the African colonies was proving to be far too costly, in both financial terms and in human lives. With the toppling of the Caetano-led government, Portugal let go of its overseas possessions. The result was a surge in black political movements for control of Mozambique from which white Portuguese residents fled in terror en masse.

In oil and diamond-rich Angola, three black nationalist groups, the Popular Movement for the Liberation of Angola (MPLA), the National Union for the Total Independence of Angola (UNITA) and the Frente Nacional de a Libertação de Angola (National Front for the Liberation of Angola, or FNLA) formed an uneasy transitional government. But within a year the coalition collapsed and a full scale civil war broke out. The three groups became pawns in the Cold War, with the United States, the Soviet Union, Cuba and even South Africa getting involved by throwing their weight and military muscle into the fray. By

1975, 25,000 Cuban troops were based in Angola in support of the pro-Marxist MPLA movement, while UNITA and the FNLA became proxy agents of the United States, backed also by South Africa.

Despite the conflict Luanda—the largest city in Angola—remained an important technical and refueling stopover for some SAA flights to Europe. But the place was becoming increasingly dangerous. No one knew if and when some trigger-happy group would strike out against South Africa and its interests, especially its airline. On Monday, April 7, 1975, Boeing 747 ZS-SAP *Swartberg* (Black Mountain) was operating flight SA224 from Johannesburg via Salisbury and Luanda to London. On the flight deck were Captain Guy Paterson, First Officer Chris Hickson and Flight Engineer Thomas Rautenbach, with In-Flight Relief Pilot Iain Maricich in the jump seat. The flight was smooth, uneventful and going according to plan until 9.50 pm when it began descending into Luanda for an approach to runway 24. At only 500 feet above the ground, all hell broke loose. Tracers began streaking past the windows. Then the fuselage began echoing to the impact of heavy fire from the ground. The crew immediately deduced that they were under attack by .303mm or .5mm rifle fire as well as by a weapon such as a bazooka-type anti-tank rocket launcher because bright puffs of orange explosions began detonating outside. As there was no means of assessing any damage done to the aircraft, Captain Paterson opted to land immediately instead of aborting and diverting to Windhoek in South West-Africa, some 988 miles away.

After touchdown, the local air traffic control officer requested the Boeing to clear the runway and hold on the taxiway with all its lights turned off. Fire trucks raced out to the aircraft but, fortunately, there were no signs of flames. Seconds later a military vehicle arrived and escorted the stricken Boeing to a military base located at the far end of the airport. Confusion reigned on board the 747 as it pulled up at the military sector of the airport, with the cabin crew doing everything possible to pacify the passengers. Once the relief crew that was supposed to have flown the aircraft onwards to Europe arrived, they walked around the airplane in disbelief. A number of bullet holes were clearly visible. Captain George Dodson, who was not only earmarked to take over command of the aircraft from Guy Paterson but was also head of the South African Airways Pilots Association, immediately resolved that the airplane was in no condition to safely go on to London. Locally-based SAA ground crew and technical personnel thoroughly inspected the craft while passengers disembarked and huddled in a cluster of Quonset huts nearby. It was unanimously agreed that the airplane was airworthy but that it could not be pressurized and should be flown at a lower than normal altitude to a safe destination outside Angola. Surrounded by soldiers, it was refuelled and then, at 1.00 am, the relief crew boarded, the previous crew took up seats in the main passenger cabin and, with Captain George Dodson in command, the Boeing took off. Avoiding the slum housing areas that surrounded Luanda, it set a vector directly for Johannesburg. Flying at an unpressurized height of 11,500 feet, it reached Jan Smuts Airport and landed at 4.45 am on the morning of April 8, 1975. Detailed inspection revealed three bullet holes in the wings, one in the main body door, one in the bulk cargo door, six in the fuselage and one in the vertical stabilizer. Over the ensuing weeks, the damage was repaired and the airplane returned to service, none the worse for its ordeal. After many years of hosting SAA flights—especially during the critical period when the round-the-bulge route first came into operation in the mid-sixties—Luanda was now dropped from the airline's route network. While the Angolan civil war raged it was simply too unpredictable and dangerous to land there.

From June 1975, the first of SAA's original Boeing 747-200 Super B models began returning to the Boeing factory in Seattle for major modifications. The main purpose was to upgrade the 46,300 lbs. thrust (2,060 kN) of the Pratt & Whitney JT9D-7 engines to 53,000 lbs. (2,357 kN,) thereby converting the powerplants into JT9D-7Q variants. The new engines provided much improved fuel consumption, saving money and improving range, speed and payload capacity. The engines were the products of close cooperation between members of SAA's engineering staff and designers at the Pratt & Whitney plant in the United States. In a television interview in 1983, Robert E. Rosati, then Senior Vice President of the Pratt & Whitney Group, recalled how it came about. "In a trip to South Africa on a delivery flight during the seventies a number of Boeing representatives, SAA's Chief Executive Eddie Smuts, Technical Directors Viv Lewis and Duke Davidson and ourselves got together over coffee, pulled out our notepads and, on paper, we drew up specifications for what became the JT9D–7Q engine. Since then the 7Q's operational record has been exceptional and we have sold the engine to operators around the world but it was essentially a South African concept and design."

As the effects of the oil crisis and the international economic slump continued, but with air traffic to South Africa steadily on the rise, three long-range Boeing 747SP (Special Performance) aircraft were ordered from Boeing in August, 1975. At the same time, the start of a long relationship with the new European-based Airbus Group began with the placing of an order for four Airbus A300 widebody aircraft for the domestic route network. August 1975 also saw the opening of SAA's new Cabin Services building a mile north of the main terminal complex at Jan Smuts Airport. A large, airy, multi-storey facility with a warren of hallways and passages it contained dressing rooms, hairdressing facilities, bathrooms and rest areas for cabin crew, plus an inflight-training center that included detailed full-scale mock-ups of sections of passenger cabins of all aircraft used by the airline. On the ground floor of the new building an immense area was devoted to freezers and kitchens for preparing in-flight meals. Another section was set aside for the mechanical conveyor belt-style washing and preparation of trays, cups, plates, glasses and utensils for use on board aircraft. A test kitchen for trying out new meals and menus occupied another area while subdivisions were devoted to the creation and packaging of special meals such as vegetarian, vegan, Hindu, kosher, halal, low-sodium, low-sugar, non-dairy and gluten-free food. For a comparatively small airline operating out of the southern hemisphere of Africa, it was all pretty ambitious yet in keeping with similar services offered by much larger carriers abroad. The Cabin Services facility was also responsible for the design and development of cabin crew uniforms. In November 1975, female attendants were introduced to new outfits comprising a chequered, tailored blazer, a medium-length skirt or slacks, a sleeveless jacket, two body shirts—one short sleeved, one long—a turtle-neck sweater and a heavy coat for winter, all neatly finished off with a jockey-style cape. In addition, newly designed tuxedos for male Flight Service Officers and royal blue jackets for Chief Flight Stewards serving in Blue Diamond—the first class section—of international Boeing 747 flights made their debut.

In March 1976, SAA took delivery of its first Boeing 747SP airliner. The fuselage was 47 ft shorter than the standard 747 model, giving the aircraft phenomenal new capabilities, hence the suffix 'SP' which stood for 'Special Performance.' Because of its shorter length and reduced weight, it could fly higher, faster and for longer distances than any of its predecessors. Boeing designed the plane to fill a much-needed niche between the capacity of its giant wide-bodied 747 and the narrow-bodied 707, both of which were still in production at the time. The genesis of the 747SP lay in an original request by Pan American airlines for an aircraft capable of flying a non-stop service between New York over the North Pole to the carrier's key destinations in Asia, especially Tokyo. But Boeing's chief designer, Joseph

F. 'Joe' Sutter, was also deeply aware of the growing needs of one of the company's most loyal other customers, SAA. Generally regarded by the aviation industry as the 'Father of the 747,' Sutter had many meetings with executives from Pan Am and SAA—especially Abercrombie 'Duke' Davidson, SAA's Technical Director of Engineering—carefully weighing up SAA's requirements and aspirations. While Pan Am would eventually go on to operate 11 of the aircraft and, in later years, United Airlines a total of 22, the needs of SAA with its 'hot and high' conditions at Johannesburg and its extremely demanding round-the-bulge of Africa flight path to Europe were factored into the design and development of the airplane.

Boeing 747 SP, ZS-SPA, Matroosberg, arrives in Johannesburg after its delivery flight from Seattle. This was a world record-breaking non-stop delivery flight of 10,290 miles. March, 1976

The first of the new 747SP airliners to arrive from the United States was ZS-SPA *Matroosberg* (the name of a mountain range north of Cape Town). Not only was it a brand new aircraft to African skies but it garnered the distinction of shattering the world's long distance record during its delivery flight. The airplane was specially prepared for the attempt by the Boeing Company. Extra fuel was carried in tanks fitted in the hold and the fuel that was pumped into the wing tanks was chilled by refrigeration to lower its specific gravity, thereby making

The Boeing 747SP had an overall length of 184 ft 9 ins, a wingspan of 195 ft 8 ins and an overall height of 65 ft 10 ins. For aerodynamic reasons due to its shorter fuselage its vertical stabilizer or tail was 2 ft 5 ins taller than the 747-200 Super B models. Its empty weight was 336,870 lbs and its maximum weight 696,000 lbs, if it was not carrying deionized water for injecting into the engine intakes on take-off for extra thrust, or 700,409 lbs if it was. It had a cruising speed of 581 mph, a maximum speed of 606 mph and it could fly at an altitude of 45,100 feet. Its maximum range was 7,650 miles. In its SAA configuration, it carried a crew of three pilots and two flight engineers plus a cabin crew of 14. It could seat 24 passengers in first class and 240 in economy class. It had four Pratt & Whitney JT9D-7RFW engines rated at 50,000 lbs thrust each. They were ten times more brawny than the engines that powered the Comet in 1952. When all four engines were running at full power, the Boeing 747SP could generate a staggering 200,000 lbs of thrust.

it more dense or virtually 'shrinking' the liquid. Departing Seattle's Paine Field at 9.28 am local time on March 23, 1976, with Captains Lynedoch Graham (Bill) van Reenen, Gus Britton and Willem Steytler on the flight deck and Chief Flight Engineer Vernon (Froggy) du Toit and Chief Training Flight Engineer Charlie Hibberd manning the flight engineer's station, the aircraft covered a distance of 10,290 miles between Seattle and Cape Town in a non-stop flying time of 17 hours 22 minutes. Following what is known as the Great Circle Route from Seattle to New York via Bermuda over the Atlantic to Johannesburg, the crew decided to skip landing at Jan Smuts Airport and continue on to Cape Town because there was a lot of fuel still remaining on board. When it landed, there were still 37,400 lbs. of Avjet in the main tanks. The airplane's first revenue-earning flight took place on May 1 when it operated a passenger-carrying service from Johannesburg to Lisbon, Rome and Athens. By the time it would reach the end of its service life in 2001, the aircraft would accumulate a total flying time of 74,410 hours 53 minutes with 15,527 take-offs and landings recorded in its log book.

Interior First Class cabin of a Boeing 747 SP. The array of fresh proteas and other indigenous South African flowers was a traditional feature on board all 747 First Class cabins. In the background is the stairway leading to the aircraft's upper deck where more First Class seating was situated

Meal time in the First Class cabin of a Boeing 747 SP

Forward section of First Class cabin aboard a Boeing 747 SP

In April 1976, the latest generation Redifon flight simulator arrived for installation in the airline's Flight Training Center at Jan Smuts Airport. Exactly replicating an Airbus A300 flight deck, its purpose was to familiarize pilots and flight engineers with the new Airbus A300 B2K airplanes that had been ordered from Europe. The simulator was equipped with full motion control as well as a Novoview computer-generated imaging system. In April, Hawker Siddeley HS748 flights to the Victoria Falls were replaced with Boeing 737s and, also that month, the second Boeing 747SP, ZS-SPB, arrived from the factory. On May 28, 1976, that airplane was used for the first time on a scheduled flight from Johannesburg to New York. A day later the return flight—under the command of Captain Lynedoch Graham (Bill) van Reenen with Laurie Lourens as co-pilot—operated the first non-stop flight from New York to Johannesburg, covering the 7,976 mile distance in 13 hours 42 minutes.

While most of Africa's airspace remained closed to SAA traffic, one independent nation temporarily broke rank with the rest of the continent. Sandwiched in between Ghana and Liberia in the bulge of Africa, the Republique de Cote d'Ivoire (Republic of the Ivory Coast), under the leadership of its president, Félix Houphouët-Boigny, decided to allow a limited number of SAA flights to land at his nation's capital, Abidjan. As a result, from May 5, 1976, Abidjan became a stopover for SAA flights SA220 and SA229 between Johannesburg and Athens. The service was operated by Boeing 747SPs. Despite this act of friendship by President Houphouët-Boigny and the Ivory Coast towards South Africa, interminable fights for political power and freedom continued to rage in other parts of the continent. One of them was right on South Africa's doorstep. It may be recalled that during WWI South Africa was given a mandate to administer the once-German territory of South West-Africa. Following WWII it was supposed to become a United Nations Trust territory but, by then, the South African government refused to relinquish control over it. After all, South-West Africa was rich in alluvial diamonds and other natural resources. South Africa had ruled the place with an iron fist, even going so far as treating it as an undeclared extension of the Republic of South Africa itself. Despite international condemnation, South Africa illegally hung on very tightly to its 'possession.' In 1966, a United Nations resolution finally terminated South Africa's mandate. But what difference did that make? The Pretoria-based Nationalist Afrikaner government simply refused to let go. By the 1970s, its reason for maintaining control was more than simply the abundant revenue it earned from taxes, diamonds, mineral mining, karakul pelt farming, livestock and fishing from the territory but because South-West Africa sat as a convenient buffer zone between the Republic of South Africa and the ex-Portuguese, unstable, war-torn, Cuban-influenced, quasi-independent nation of Angola. But freedom fighters campaigning within South-West Africa itself for independence now also posed an increasing headache to the white-led South African government. Black nationalist groups—primarily the South West Africa People's Organization or SWAPO—stepped up their activities, embarking on widespread guerilla campaigns to terrorize white residents and to force the South African government to grant the territory independence. But quite the opposite happened.

Emboldened and bolstered by its strong domestic armaments industry—most significantly the government-controlled and operated South African Armaments Corporation (ARMSCOR)— South Africa began to develop a potent array of weapons to take on the 'terrorists.' In a concerted effort to counteract the UN-led international arms embargo against it, artillery, long range cannons, howitzers, automatic and semi-automatic guns, small arms, grenades, bombs, a wide range of ammunition, armored vehicles, all-terrain personnel carriers, rockets, guided missiles, anti-aircraft radar systems, land mines and a variety of other locally-designed and developed equipment were by now being produced at plants throughout South Africa and were already in the arsenal of the South African Defense Force. And so began an outright campaign intended to eliminate SWAPO. But members of SWAPO quickly went into hiding or found safe haven north of the Kunene River, the border between South-West Africa and Angola. From there, they launched covert attacks deep into South-West African territory. Although conscription for young, white, able-bodied males over the age of 17 began in South Africa in the early sixties, by 1976, compulsory two-year military training went into effect. Many conscripts—drafted straight out of high school or prior to starting a college education—were being sent 'to the border' to assist members of the Permanent Forces in the spiraling fight against SWAPO, as well as against guerilla fighters and Cuban troops stationed in Angola. It was not a pretty picture, and none of it bode well for the airline.

What made matters especially difficult was the fact that Johannesburg's hot and high conditions would prevent airliners from taking off with full passenger and fuel loads if they could not use Angolan airspace for the round-the- bulge route to Europe. As SAA did its best to provide regular services to neighboring countries and to destinations abroad, the raging conflict in South West Africa and Angola posed great dangers to it. What if Angola banned it from its airspace? What if Soviet-built MIG-21 fighters—flown by Cuban pilots—were to be placed on standby to shoot down any South African airliners if they flew a direct vector from Johannesburg over Angola to the Atlantic? Even worse, what if SWAPO captured Windhoek in South West Africa and banned SAA from using it as a technical and refueling stopover? Things did not augur well for SAA during those troubled and uncertain times. But, come what may, the show had to go on. No matter what happened, schedules had to be maintained with no interruption of services. But how? It did not take long to find a solution.

Upington is a small 'Wild West' type of town on the banks of the Orange River in the Northern Cape province of South Africa. Hot, remote and surrounded by parched savannah, its primary claims to fame were illicit diamond smugglers, cattle rustlers, gun runners and British missionaries intent on bringing the words of the Gospel to indigenous inhabitants during the last decades of the 19th century. In later years, it became known to a very close-knit group—including the CIA—because of its proximity to a top-secret military facility known as 'Vastrap.' In English the word means 'to hold fast', or 'traction.' In 1976, Vastrap was intended to become a test facility for atomic weapons that were under development by South Africa's fledgling nuclear armaments program. Fortunately, the base was never used for that purpose. Although South Africa eventually did manufacture six nuclear bombs at its Pelindaba Atomic Energy facility near Pretoria, they were all placed in storage and later dismantled under the supervision of the International Atomic Energy Agency after the fall of apartheid in the early 1990's. But, as they say, that is another story.

During the 1970s—and even now—few towns could be more remote than Upington. But it had an airport. And it was only 2,740 ft above sea level. That meant that it was perfect as an alternative launching platform for long distance flights to destinations abroad. Its altitude was half that of Johannesburg's so it did not have the limiting hot and high characteristics of Jan Smuts Airport. In order for Boeing 747s to take off with a full load of fuel and passengers, all it needed was a longer runway—a much longer one—than it already had. Wasting no time, contractors quickly moved in and extended the existing runway to a wide, heavy duty, paved runway with a length of 16,000 ft, making it one of the longest in the world. Remarkably, it was constructed in just under seven months. Some Springbok Service flights were immediately routed via the new airfield. Boeing 747-200 Super Bs—equipped with special high speed tires—left Jan Smuts Airport, landed at Upington, had their fuel tanks fully topped up and, hurtling down the runway at faster than normal take-off speed, took to the air. From there, they flew westward to the Atlantic Ocean, made a tight right turn and continued northwards to Europe around the bulge of Africa, solving the problem of what do if South West African or Angolan airspace was ever closed to SAA traffic. After a short trial period, the Upington stopover was terminated, but at least it had been proved that it could be pressed into service in case it was ever needed. An interesting sidebar to this tale is that when the United States' National Aeronautics and Space Administration (NASA) began operating the Space Shuttle program in 1981, Upington Airport was chosen as an alternative landing site for the shuttle spacecraft in the event of an aborted launch or for some other type of emergency. Thankfully, it was never required for that purpose.

In August 1976, three SAA Boeing 747 Super B flights originating in Europe—Frankfurt, Madrid and Paris—began a non-stop service around the bulge to Johannesburg. Flights to the Americas also changed that month. The Thursday Boeing 707 service operating flight SA209 between Johannesburg and New York via Ilha do Sal was replaced by a Boeing 747SP, and the Friday Boeing 707 operating flight SA207 to New York was

replaced by a Boeing 747 Super B. Sunday's Boeing 707 flight
SA205 via Rio de Janeiro to New York was discontinued. It
was replaced by a Boeing 707 Combi flight terminating in Rio,
making that an exclusively Brazilian service.

On November 25, 1976, the airline's first twin-engine wide-
body jet aircraft arrived on its delivery flight from Toulouse,
France. The Airbus A300 B2K-3C, ZS-SDA, *Blesbok* (the name
of a large antelope indigenous to South Africa) left the Airbus
Industrie plant in Toulouse, France on November 23, with SAA
pilots Johan Lambrecht, Hugh Pharoah, Gus Fergusson, Hennie
Pieterse, Francois 'Doc' Malan and Franklyn Barrett on board.
Airbus Chief Test Pilot Jacques Grangette accompanied them.
The Flight Engineer was Ben Hattingh. Departing Toulouse on
November 23, 1976, the aircraft reached Ilha do Sal after flying
via Las Palmas in six hours 30 minutes. The next morning it
flew via Abidjan to Windhoek in eight hours 55 minutes. After
refuelling it continued on to Johannesburg, arriving at Jan Smuts
Airport two hours 25 minutes later. Total time spent in the air
was 17 hours 50 minutes.

The Airbus was an all-new type of aircraft. Unlike Boeing,
Douglas, Lockheed, Vickers, de Havilland or airplanes from other
manufacturers, it was not the product of one single company
based in one geographic location. Because of the size and
complexity of the program to build the wide-bodied airliner—
not least of which was the splitting of the financial burden to
help develop and pay for it—Airbus Industrie was made up of a
consortium of companies based in France, the United Kingdom,
Spain, Germany and the Netherlands. The Airbus A300 can be
likened to something put together from a giant, modern day
kids' Lego-style construction kit. The nose section, flight deck,
lower center fuselage and the engine pod pylons were made by
the Aerospatiale company of France. The forward fuselage—the
passenger section in front of the main wing root—and the wing
leading and trailing edges and flaps were the product of Vereinigte

Flugtechnische Werke-Fokker or VFW-Fokker of Germany. The upper center fuselage, rear fuselage, tail cone, vertical stabilizer, rudder (or tail assembly) and the underwing flap track fairings were made by Messerschmitt-Bolkow-Blohm of Germany. The main wing assembly came from Hawker-Siddeley in the United Kingdom. The horizontal stabilizers or tailplane assembly was manufactured by Construcciones Aeronáuticas SA or CASA of Spain. The wheels and landing gear were made by Messier of France.

A choice of two engine types were offered by Airbus for the new plane, one made by Rolls Royce of Britain and the other by General Electric of the United States. SAA opted for the General Electric CF6-50 engine which was also a product of multi-national cooperation. Thirty-five percent of the engine's components came from European manufacturers with the rest supplied by General Electric in the U.S. All the parts for the aircraft were shipped to the Airbus assembly facility in Toulouse, France where everything came together to produce the A300. It was the first aircraft offered by then-new Airbus company. SAA was one of the earliest launch customers for the airplane, including the first in Africa, the first in the southern hemisphere and the first based in a country not associated with any of the factories that manufactured parts for the aircraft. Roger Beteille, Executive Vice President and General Manager of Airbus Industrie at the time, referred to SAA as the 'breakthrough airline' for its belief in his company and its products. Because of Johannesburg's unique hot and high location, SAA's engineering heads 'Duke' Davidson and Viv Lewis convinced Airbus to include what is known as a Krüger flap on the aircraft. This is basically an in-board leading edge flap on the wing root, ostensibly extending the airplane's leading edge flaps from wingtip to fuselage, helping it to cope with low speed take-offs and landings in Jan Smuts Airport's notoriously hot, thin atmospheric conditions. Because of SAA's requirement, Airbus made the decision to standardize the

Krüger flap and incorporate it on all future production models of the airliner for other operators worldwide. Intended to serve the domestic route network, the Airbuses replaced Boeing 707 services on the high-density services between Johannesburg, Durban and Cape Town.

Airbus A 300 B2K. November, 1976

SAA's Airbus A3400 B2KJ — the 'K' standing for the Krüger flaps — had a wingspan of 147 ft 8 ins. Its overall length was 175 ft 9 ins and its height 54 ft 4 ins. Its maximum take-off weight was 313,053 lbs and its operational weight 189,845 lbs. Its cruising speed was 530 mph and its maximum speed 628 mph. It could fly at an altitude of 40,300 feet and had a range of 2,690 miles. Each of its powerful General Electric CF6-50C2R high bypass engines delivered 52,000 lbs (23,353 kN) of thrust. The flight crew consisted of two pilots and a flight engineer. There was accommodation on board for 270 passengers, 35 in first class and 235 in the coach class cabin.

The purchase of the new airliners was the beginning of a very long and lucrative relationship between SAA and the European Airbus company. In years to come, SAA would operate many different short-haul and long-range airliners made by Airbus and, in time, SAA would fly far more of their aircraft than those made by Boeing. But 1976 was still an early date in that story. While most carriers around the world waited to see whether the new products from Toulouse were safe, reliable and suitable for a variety of different types of operation SAA willingly committed to the company. They did not look back. Airbus exceeded all expectations predicted by aviation and economic pundits. Today there are only two major players in the large, long-range aircraft construction business, Boeing and Airbus. The other two major American manufacturers, McDonnell-Douglas and Lockheed, have long since ceased making intercontinental airliners.

On December 31, 1976, the last two remaining Boeing 707 model A airplanes that had made up the original fleet of SAA's long haul jets in 1960, were withdrawn from service. They had been operating the domestic route between Johannesburg and Cape Town but were now replaced by the new Airbuses. A week later Boeing 747SP aircraft replaced Boeing 707s on the Australian Service. On January 28, 1977, the three first Boeing 747SP aircraft taken into service were returned to the factory in Seattle for modifications that would bring them up to the standard of the last three SPs that had been ordered. This included the removal of a spiral staircase to the upper deck and the installation of a straight staircase. Modifications were also made to the cabin floor and sidewalls to improve decompression stresses. The landing gear was strengthened to allow for higher loads. Most importantly, a water injection system was fitted to the Pratt & Whitney engines. Spraying water into the engine intake increased power during take-off and landing at high altitudes and temperatures, such as the conditions experienced in Johannesburg. Each of the SPs were out of service for a month while the modifications were made. In due course, all six of SAA's 747SPs were upgraded to seat 16 first class passengers on the upper deck, 24 in the first class section on the lower deck, and 225 in the main economy class cabin.

On February 1, 1977, Boeing 707 passenger services to Europe were withdrawn. Spiffy new cabin crew uniforms were introduced that month. Direct services to London from Cape Town were introduced in April, using Boeing 747SP equipment. In June, Boeing 727 jet services began calling at the town of George on the attractive 'Garden Route' along the south-eastern seaboard of South Africa as part of the expanding domestic route network. In July, Boeing 747SP aircraft were introduced on flights between Johannesburg and Hong Kong. That month, the original two Boeing 707-344A airplanes, ZS-SAA and ZS-SAB, bade their final farewells when they were sold to British Midland Airways. By then, ZS-SAA had accumulated a total flying time of 44,277 hours and ZS-SAB 44,229 hours. In August, rising international anti-South African sentiment due to the government's apartheid policies caused Qantas to operate its final flight between Sydney and Johannesburg, terminating its participation in the 'Wallaby Service.'

As the calendar changed to the year 1978, Springbok Services to Europe were increased to 18 per week. A new weekly service by Boeing 747SP aircraft began operating on Sundays between Johannesburg and Madrid via Lisbon. Nine weekly Boeing 747-200 Super B services now terminated in London and two in Frankfurt. Eight Boeing 747SP flights served Amsterdam, Paris, Rome, Athens, Brussels, Frankfurt, Zurich, Madrid, Vienna and Tel Aviv. Few of these routes carried full passenger loads or were profitable but, in accordance with South African government policy, it was felt important to maintain a South African 'presence' at these destinations as international anti-apartheid vitriol continued to spread. An additional Boeing 747 service was now operated between Cape Town and London. Because of unexpectedly high demand, weekly Boeing 707 flights from Johannesburg to Buenos Aires were replaced by Boeing 747SPs. Taking up the slack left by the cancellation of Qantas flights to Australia, in June, SAA began operating two weekly flights from Johannesburg to Perth and Sydney using Boeing 747-200 Super B aircraft. To cope with passenger demand, later that year two more Boeing 747s were ordered from Boeing. These aircraft would be of the latest 747-200 Super B 'Combi' — combined passenger and freight — variant.

By April 1979, the number of weekly flights on the Springbok Service was increased to 19 but by then London-bound flights via Salisbury had been withdrawn. However, eight weekly regional service flights were now operated between Johannesburg and Salisbury using Boeing 707 and 737 aircraft, and seven weekly Boeing 737 flights served Bulawayo. An additional weekly Boeing 737 service now connected Salisbury with Durban. Three weekly Boeing 747SP flights were now operating between Johannesburg and New York. In May, another Airbus A300 was ordered as well as 13 Boeing 737 Advanced airplanes intended to eventually replace the Boeing 727s on the regional and domestic networks. As passenger demand rose, the 747SP aircraft that were serving New York were replaced by higher capacity Boeing 747-200 Super Bs. By the end of the year, weekly frequencies to New York were increased to four. At the end of the decade, SAA had a fleet of 36 aircraft, consisting of five Boeing 747 Super Bs, six Boeing 747SPs, nine Boeing 727s, three Boeing 707s, six Boeing 737s, four Airbus A300s and three Hawker Siddeley 748s. Sixteen aircraft were on the order books — 13 Boeing 737 Advanced models, two Boeing 747 Combis and one Airbus A300.

As the eighties dawned, it looked like growth could not be curtailed. Although the financial state of the airline was still in fairly reasonable shape, SAA was now heavily committed to paying for the all those new airliners that it had ordered. Besides, the scary monster of increasing world fuel costs still lurked in the shadowy background. When the seventies began, SAA's fuel bill represented eleven percent of its total operating costs. Now that figure had grown to a staggering 36 percent. And fuel prices around the globe were still spiralling upwards. Other costs were also on the rise. Because many countries were in deep recession as a result of the high oil prices, landing fees were increasing at major foreign destinations. Just a couple of years earlier, SAA was reeling under what it called the 'exorbitant fee of $1,000' to land a 747 at London's Heathrow Airport. Now that fee had risen ten-fold. The moment a 747's wheels touched the ground at Heathrow it was eligible for a peak-hour landing fee of $10,000. Some airlines stopped flying there. But London was by far SAA's most important, popular and prestige international destination and no services were halted.

Fortunately, the South African economy as a whole was still very strong. It experienced a growth rate of eight per cent during the previous year. Because of high gold prices it was doing better than most other countries and was now the 15th most important trading nation in the world. But inflation was steadily edging up. By 1980, it had reached 14.6 per cent. Tight reins would have to be kept on SAA to keep it healthily airborne.

And then, without warning, the heavens opened and nature struck a blow that would not only cost millions of dollars in damages but put a third of the fleet out of commission. Bad weather in the form of thunderstorms have always been a hazard to aircraft in the air or on the ground. Johannesburg is especially susceptible to them, particularly during the summer months. On January 15, 1980, an unusually strong thunderstorm dropped hailstones the size of golf balls on Jan Smuts Airport. When the storm passed, it looked as though everything was covered in snow, but the white coating was really a deep layer of icy stones that had shattered windows, torn through roofs and battered everything in sight. Aircraft waiting on the apron outside the terminal buildings were pummelled. Ailerons, flaps, empennages and wings were beaten and broken. Hundreds of passengers who were huddled in the terminals picked their way across a carpet of shimmering ice that had crashed through skylights or been blown in from outside. But they were not the only victims. Thousands of people around the country had their flights cancelled or suffered indefinite delays. In SAA's maintenance section at Jan Smuts Airport, aircraft that were undergoing servicing or repairs were also severely damaged as the hailstones smashed their way through the roofs of hangars. Fourteen aircraft were put out of action that day. These included four of eleven Boeing 747s, four of six Boeing 737s, two of three Boeing 707s, one of nine Boeing 727s, one of four Airbus A300s and all three Hawker Siddeley HS 748s. The airline was so overwhelmed by the devastation that it called for emergency assistance from the Boeing Company. Fortunately, several of the damaged aircraft were soon returned to service by using components held in the airline's stores and also by cannibalizing parts from planes that were undergoing major maintenance. But the financial cost had been enormous. It would take years for the airline to recover from the blow.

Chapter 14

Contraction and Expansion

As the decade of the eighties began, the political mosaic of sub-Saharan Africa was undergoing constant metamorphosis. The quavering rhythm of relationships between one place and another was perpetually altering, shifting, drifting. As nations, tribes and ethnic groups clamored to assert themselves or kindle new identities on the landscape of Capricorn Africa—that vast stretch of territory between the equator and the southern tip of the continent—flags, maps and names were changing with the regularity of a sunrise. South Africa was no exception.

Of the ten tribal homelands or 'Bantustans' that had been set up as autonomous states within South Africa under the apartheid blueprint, three had already been declared 'independent.' They had their own presidents, coats-of-arms and national anthems. As South Africa's official carrier, SAA was obliged to serve these synthetically created nations. That was well and good but the dark humor of it all was that flights to and from them were categorized—by government decree—as 'international.' Passengers flying out of or into the homelands from South Africa were required to go through passport, immigration and customs control. As can be imagined, the cost and inconvenience to the airline was considerable. Nevertheless, on February 2, 1980, SAA began serving Umtata—capital of Transkei, the first of the traditional tribal homelands to accept the autonomy foisted upon them by Pretoria—with a daily Hawker Siddeley HS748 flight from Johannesburg. This was an extension of flights to Transkei that had originally begun three years earlier using Beechcraft King Air 100 ten-seat aircraft. Services to the other two pseudo-independent states—Bophuthatswana and Venda—were served by small, independent carriers. However, SAA would begin serving the 'republic' of Ciskei after it gained its autonomy and be set adrift from South Africa in 1981.

But other pivotal events were taking place north of South Africa across the Limpopo River. The fierce 'Bush War' that had been fought for control of Rhodesia had mercilessly pummeled that country and left its soil stained with blood. The result was that in 1979, peace talks finally took place in London. For a short period, Rhodesia was once again brought under British supervision. A new constitution was drawn up and blacks were assured equal power-sharing with whites. Despite on-going squabbling and disagreements among rival political factions, the fighting slowly ended and, in April 1980, the Republic of Zimbabwe was born. Things looked promising. SAA maintained uninterrupted services to Salisbury and Bulawayo while Air Rhodesia changed its name to Air Zimbabwe and continued its own domestic and cross-border services, flying routes to Johannesburg and Durban.

Even though the OAU ban on South African-registered aircraft remained in force, Zambia—the country directly to the north of Zimbabwe—opened its door a tiny crack to SAA on March 9, 1980. This was a relief to many, particularly in the mining and financial worlds. Zambia was home to some of the richest and most productive copper mines on earth and there was a need for a regular air service between Johannesburg—the unquestioned financial powerhouse of the continent—and Lusaka, Zambia's capital city. On March 9, 1980, a weekly Boeing 737 service began linking the two centers. Interestingly, that was exactly 43 years since the first passenger-carrying flights between the two countries commenced in 1937, when an SAA Junkers Ju52 took off from Rand Airport bound for Lusaka.

In March 1980, SAA introduced luxurious new 'Stratosleeper' seating in the first class cabins of its intercontinental Boeing 747 fleet. Boeing 747-200 Super Bs now offered 20 of the comfortable, reclining new seats in the 'Blue Diamond' section on its main deck and eight in what used to be the upper deck lounge and bar area. Passengers travelling in 'Blue Diamond' on board Boeing 747SPs were accommodated in 16 of the seats on the main deck and 12 upstairs. On June 30, an order was placed for a sixth Airbus A300 aircraft, due for delivery in the second half of 1982. This was for an A300-C4-203 variant, the only 'Combi' version of the A300 to be ordered by the airline. July 4, 1980, saw the introduction of a weekly return service between Johannesburg and Victoria Falls using Boeing 737 aircraft. Flights took place in conjunction with Air Zimbabwe which operated Vickers Viscounts on the route. In September, flights from Johannesburg to Hong Kong were no longer routed via the Seychelles Islands. Instead, stopovers were now made at Mauritius. Another Mauritian stopover came into effect on November 3, when a new SAA flight was inaugurated between Johannesburg and Taipei, Taiwan.

A brand new aircraft joined the fleet on November 7, 1980, when the first Boeing 747-244 Combi arrived at Jan Smuts Airport from the factory. Sporting a radically redesigned livery and a sleek new Flying Springbok emblem on its tail, ZS-SAR *Waterberg* (a scenic mountain range in the north of South Africa) touched down after a 19-hour flight from Seattle via Ilha do Sal. The delivery crew consisted of Captains Cyril Rodgers, Alan Dros and Hinton Bradfield Horsecroft, aided by flight engineers Ben Hattingh and Andre Gouws. Similar to the Boeing 707s before it, the 747 Combi model was constructed with a large fuselage side cargo door to allow for the loading of seven large freight pallets. The rear third of the fuselage could serve as a passenger cabin or as a cargo hold. In the latter configuration, a safety net and moveable bulkhead separated the passenger section from the freight area. The design was such that passengers were none the wiser that cargo was being carried right behind them. Of course, additional freight and passengers' baggage were still carried in the lower main hold, similar to other 747 models. The second 747 Combi that had been ordered, ZS-SAS *Helderberg*, (a mountain range in the Western Cape) arrived on November 24, 1980. The two aircraft entered service in December on routes linking Johannesburg with Windhoek, Las Palmas, Frankfurt, Madrid, Paris and Brussels. Later that month they began operating the Johannesburg to New York route, bumping up services from Jan Smuts Airport to Kennedy Airport to five per week.

With the introduction of the Boeing 747 Combis another milestone in the airline's history was reached, this time with sad intonations. On December 26, 1980, SAA's last scheduled Boeing 707 service was flown when ZS-SAH travelled from Paris to Johannesburg. It was a solemn day indeed for many people in the airline, in the travel industry and indeed among the public at large. The Boeing 707 was a much-revered airplane. It had brought widespread and affordable jet travel not only to South Africa but to the entire world. 707s had pioneered many routes to distant destinations for SAA. To finally see the handsome, multi-windowed airliner with its swept-back wings and raked tail tipped with a forward-pointing needle-like high frequency (HF) radio antenna take a final bow was like witnessing the bringing down of a curtain on the past, the severing of a link with a time that could not be brought back again. It was the ending of something beloved but now finite and over. Unlike with most other aircraft, many people—layman and expert alike—could recognize a 707. It had shrunk the map for SAA. It had even found its way into everyday culture. There was a time in the late 1950s when South African breakfast cereal manufacturers included coupons on the backs of their packages of popped rice and cornflakes for kids to purchase little cheap build-it-yourself plastic model kits of the 707. Those were the days when just about every schoolboy owned a toy Boeing 707 made of plastic, balsa wood, tin or die-cast metal. Even in the financially depressed black townships, little barefoot boys in tattered shorts and T-shirts fashioned 707s out of twisted wire, mounted soda-pop bottle tops on them for wheels, attached a long stick to their rickety creations and raced them down muddy and rutted lanes. For many people, merely seeing the 707's four vapour trails and orange tail streaking across the sky was like witnessing a swiftly-moving link to a vast, distant, outside world, far from the confining restraints and depressions of apartheid, sanctions, racial tensions and censorship. And now it was gone.

The rest of SAA's fleet was also undergoing a facelift at this time. As each aircraft was brought in for periodic maintenance at Jan Smuts Airport, it was taken into the paint shop and decked out in the smart new, cleaner livery first seen on the 747 Combis.

Last redesign of the Flying Springbok emblem and aircraft livery. In addition to a larger and more prominent modern version of the Flying Springbok that was first introduced on the Boeing 747s in 1971, now the entire fuselage sported a fresh, new look with a redesigned cheat line along the windows from nose to tail. 1980

On April 3, 1981, a three-class layout was introduced on all international flights. In addition to the first class 'Blue Diamond' service, a business class cabin called 'Gold Class' was implemented right behind the first class section and a much-improved economy class was re-branded 'Silver Class.' The new business class service quickly caught on and became enormously popular. With the introduction of 'Gold Class'—which offered services and amenities similar to the old first class—'Diamond Class' was elevated to an even higher level of luxury. A wide range of French, German and Italian wines was added to the already extensive variety of South African wines on offer. The

South African wine industry had long enjoyed an excellent reputation, both locally and abroad. SAA became a showcase for some of its finest products. In addition to outstanding red, white and sparkling wines, 'Blue Diamond' also offered the best of South African brandies and liqueurs. A typical dinner in first class on a long-haul international flight was made up of traditional South African dishes as well as French-style cuisine and foods often representative of the departure or destination country. The following example of a dinner menu is taken from flight SA270 flying between Johannesburg, Madrid and Paris in 1981:

Canapés
Roquefort cheese and celery on croutons
Smoked salmon triangles
Rollmop herring with cream cheese
Baluga Malossol caviar with garnish and Russian Blini
pancakes
Paté de Foie-Gras
Melba toast
Westphalia Pumpernickel

Clear vegetable soup
Asparagus cream soup
Mushroom cream soup
Variety of breads

Apple and celery salad
Seasonal salad with lemon
Variety of salad dressings

Fillet of Sole Mossel Bay with stuffing and pan gravy
Grilled king prawns with parsley butter
Sosaties Malay style

Roast loin of pork and apple sauce Langkloof
Prima baron of beef Northern Transvaal with horseradish
sauce
Breast of turkey Delmas

Green beans with almonds
Baked pumpkin
Baby marrows with potato shreds
Green peas
Glazed carrots
Rice with raisins
Baked potatoes

Cassata ice-cream
Ice bombe Mona Lisa
Black Forest gateau
Baked Alaska with wafers

Assorted cheese and crackers

Fresh fruit

Coffee
Tea

Cognac
Liqueurs

Chocolate mints

The preparation of in-flight meals was still the responsibility
of SAA's cabin services department. Because that fell under
the jurisdiction of the South African Railways & Harbors
Administration (SAR & H) it was ostensibly a division—or

perhaps extension is a better word—of the catering service of the South African Railways. The staff were all civil servants. At first, for some people in the travel trade this state of affairs was viewed with a wry sense of humor. How could lowly civil servants create dishes that were worthy of an international airline, especially for fussy passengers travelling in first class? Critics pointed out that food on board South Africa's long distance sleeper trains was notoriously mediocre, at best. The exceptions were meals served on the world famous Blue Train that operated a luxury service between Pretoria and Cape Town. It boasted a dining car and a menu comparable to that of the Orient Express in Europe. The Orange Express—another luxury service that connected Durban and Cape Town—also offered superlative meals on board. But the average run-of-the-mill sleeper service—even for passengers travelling in first class—left a lot to be desired. Yet here was this enormous kitchen at Jan Smuts Airport, staffed entirely by members of the Railways' catering division, turning out meals for SAA's domestic, regional and international flights. Contrary to expectation, they proved all the cynics wrong. Time and again, they showed that they could create gourmet, world-class meals, especially for first class on the international routes. It is to their credit that SAA consistently received high praise by the world's travel and food press for its in-flight catering. First class passengers are a finicky lot. And rightly so. For the high fares they pay they have every reason to be. Yet, flight after flight to or from Europe, Asia, Australia, the Middle East, the United States or South America, SAA seldom disappointed the well-heeled lover of fine food.

Now that the two Boeing 747 Combis had joined the fleet, a new state-of-the-art flight training simulator containing every bell and whistle imaginable was installed in the Flight Operations building at Jan Smuts Airport. In addition, the original Boeing 747 simulators were upgraded and fitted with computer-generated visual display systems. By 1981, the Springbok Service to Europe had gone up to 21 frequencies per week. Of these, eight were operated by Boeing 747-200 Super B aircraft with seven flights terminating in London and one in Amsterdam. Boeing 747SPs operated nine of the services. They terminated in Zurich, Vienna, Tel Aviv, Frankfurt, Athens and London. Boeing 747 Combi aircraft operated four services, terminating in Frankfurt, Brussels, Paris and Amsterdam. On June 4, an order was placed with Boeing in Seattle for two of the company's latest generation airliners, the Boeing 747-300. At the same time, a fifth Airbus A300, ZS-SDE was delivered from the factory in Toulouse.

In July, 1981, SAA carried a very special VIP passenger from New York to Johannesburg. The relevance of this occasion can only be appreciated when viewed against the political backdrop of the time. It is important to remember that in July of that year, three of the ten black homelands or Bantustans had received their 'independence' from Pretoria and one was about to do so. Of the three, Bophuthatswana was comprised of no less than eight separate areas, none of them even touching one another. One of these fragmented pieces was located on the doorstep of the platinum-mining city of Rustenburg, barely 86 miles from Johannesburg. Just 25 miles beyond that lay a verdant valley snuggling against the Pilanesberg mountain range and game reserve. It was a perfect spot for a lavish playground for the white man. Under the strict, conservative laws of Nationalist Party-controlled South Africa, gambling was strictly forbidden in all four provinces. Entertainment was tightly regulated. Movies were heavily censored; no inter-racial mixing on screen; no nudity; no blasphemy. Films like *In the Heat of the Night*, *Guess Who's Coming to Dinner*, *The Exorcist* and *A Clockwork Orange* were banned outright. Musicals like *Godspell* and *Jesus Christ Superstar* that had taken Broadway and the West End by storm were also banned. Sexuality was whitewashed, sterilized and kept under lock and key. But not so in Bophuthatswana. Although Pretoria and the Afrikaner policy-makers who bequeathed independence unto the black homelands frowned down upon the trend, little could be done to halt the sort of liberal thinking and behaviour that was taking root in those territories. After all—according to Pretoria—they were independent. They could do whatever they liked after they were set adrift from South Africa. And South Africa could certainly not be seen to be interfering in their internal affairs and policies. To do so would be to make a mockery of the type of 'independence' that the South African government was trying to sell to the outside world in an effort to paint a rosy, legitimate, acceptable picture of the entire concept of apartheid. So, liberalism quickly overtook conservatism in the quasi-independent homelands. It would seek out many outlets and take on many forms. But none more so than in Bophuthatswana.

A brilliant 45-year-old South African hotelier and entrepreneur by the name of Sol Kerzner decided to take full advantage of the situation. Not only would he create a vast entertainment complex in Bophuthatswana for whites from 'across the border' in nearby Pretoria, Johannesburg and the string of cities that make up the wealthy, industrialized Witwatersrand mining complex, but he would inject millions of dollars into the infrastructure of the Bophuthatswana economy and open up a bewildering array of employment opportunities for its people. And so the dazzling resort that the world now knows as Sun City came into being.

In 1981, Kerzner enlarged the facilities of his enormous gambling and golf-course center by constructing a 6,000-seat theater-style stadium there called the 'Superbowl.' In addition to swinging golf clubs on a magnificent course designed by famed South African golfing champion Gary Player or exploring artificial lakes, watching uncensored X-rated movies, enjoying the offerings of multi-racial restaurants, night clubs and supper clubs, consuming alcohol at all hours, browsing the offerings of well-stocked shopping arcades or watching wildlife in the nearby Pilanesberg Game Reserve, guests would now be able to see some of the top entertainers from abroad perform in the new stadium.

But, many wondered, was that even possible? Would they come? After all, international artistes, singers, dancers, musicians and sports figures now shunned South Africa because of the UN-led performing arts and sporting boycott that was in force as a form of protest against apartheid. South Africans were desperately hungry for talent from abroad. The sports ban was especially painful to bear. South Africa was barred from the Olympic Games. The country's top players could not compete abroad and nobody came to play against them. A feeling of isolation and desolation permeated the very fabric of the performing arts and sporting fields. And then Sol Kerzner issued a stunning statement. He had signed Frank Sinatra to be the opening attraction at the new Superbowl. He would give performances there between July 24 and August 2, 1981. Bophuthatswanans rejoiced and celebrated. South Africans were amazed and elated. The world was shocked and horrified. But—for a fee of $2 million for ten concerts—Ol' Blue Eyes was coming.

Before agreeing to Kerzner's offer Sinatra had sent his attorney Mickey Rudin to Sun City from the U.S. to ensure that there would be no racial divisions in the audience. "I wouldn't have any part of racial segregation," Sinatra said. "The deal with Kerzner is that I play to everyone, regardless of race, color or creed. Also," he mused, "I don't care if they're drunk. The only proviso is that I play it sober."

Because of the steep ticket prices the audience—many of whom would travel to Sun City by road from Johannesburg—would overwhelmingly be white. But Sinatra need not have feared. South African-styled apartheid did not exist in Bophuthatswana or in any of the 'independent' homelands.

SAA was chosen as the carrier to bring Sinatra and his entourage to South Africa from New York. As one of the world's most celebrated and popular entertainers, he was given treatment normally accorded only to royalty. The entire upper deck of the Boeing 747-200 Super B was turned into a luxurious, private penthouse for him and his wife, Barbara. Special arrangements were made in 'Blue Diamond' class on the main deck to accommodate his long-time friend and sidekick Jilly Rizzo as well as his musical director and 33 New York-based musicians. SAA also laid on security personnel to accompany the flight. When the aircraft landed at Jan Smuts Airport, Sinatra and Barbara were immediately whisked off to a waiting executive jet and flown directly to Sun City. Not only was this more convenient for them but it also allowed them to avoid the stigma of having to go through South African immigration formalities. The idea was that if they did not deal with the South African authorities, they were technically not in South Africa itself and therefore not acknowledging apartheid. Three other chartered private aircraft followed Sinatra's jet, ferrying his musicians for the 25-minute flight to Sun City. As for the scintillating new Superbowl venue, Sinatra would by no means be the last to play there. Despite the international performing arts boycott, Liza Minnelli, Shirley Bassey, Rod Stewart, Elton John, Julio Iglesias and many others followed, and SAA was invariably the carrier that brought them to that shimmering resort under the African sun in a 'republic' that did not really even exist.

Another passenger requiring special attention on SAA some years earlier was King Goodwill Zwelithini kaBhekuzulu, reigning monarch of the Zulu nation. Shortly after succeeding his late father King Cyprian Bhekuzulu kaSolomon as head of South Africa's largest ethnic group, he undertook a trip abroad to the United States. The role of deceased ancestors figures prominently in the rites and rituals of Africa. So it is with the Zulu, a people directly descended from the legendary Shaka who trained and unified the young warriors of his tribe during the early years of the 19th century to help forge one of the mightiest and most powerful empires on the continent. As a symbol of his regal position and in deference to his forefathers, King Zwelithini always had to have a somewhat unusual object near his person—the *izinyongo*, the dried-out gall bladder of a goat. Brownish in color and looking like a brittle, inflated balloon the size of a goose's egg, this totem has much meaning and is an integral component of tribal culture. Its significance is so rich in complexity that it far exceeds the scope of this book. Suffice it to say that the gall bladder was presented to the king by a Zulu *sangoma* or shaman when the king completed an important initiatory rite of passage when he ascended to the throne. From that moment onwards, he could never be without it. On those occasions when he wore full tribal regalia, it would be strung around his neck, tied to his wrist or knotted into his hair. When he wore western style dress, he would not have it on him but it always had to be nearby. It hung above his bed at night. It dangled from the rear-view mirror of any automobile in which he travelled. And when he flew abroad it had to be there too. So, when King Goodwill Zwelithini sat in the first class cabin of an SAA airliner on its way to New York, flight attendants carefully attached the *izinyongo* to the overhead lighting console above his seat, ensuring that his ancestral spirits were with him throughout the flight and that he was fully protected by their powerful supernatural energy.

In 1981, the fiftieth anniversary of the founding of the airline was less than three years away. Much thought was being given to the best way of celebrating the event. This brings us back to one of the most important airplanes that figured in SAA's history, the much-loved Junkers Ju52. The type first began flying for SAA way back in 1934 and provided outstanding service until the outbreak of WWII. During that period, Ju52s pioneered many routes throughout Africa. So, the question was asked, why not bring one back for the 50th anniversary in 1984? Many in the airline thought that a splendid idea. If one could be found, repainted in an original thirties' vintage SAA livery and flown as a crowd-pleasing attraction to celebrate the Golden Anniversary, it would be wonderful publicity for the airline. But there was only one catch. Where to find one, especially a Ju52 that was still airworthy?

In the late 1970s, one of SAA's senior technical managers, Johann Prozesky, had already begun searching for what many lovingly referred to as a *Tante Ju*, (pronounced 'you'). This is a wordplay on the letters JU for Junkers and is a term that comes from the German where it means 'Aunt Ju,' simply because so many aircraft historians regarded the Ju52 as the quintessential Grande Dame of the Sky. As Prozesky conducted his quest, it quickly became evident that no Ju52s were available anywhere. The remains of a few could still be found in Southern Africa in places like Mozambique and even near the village of Figtree in Zimbabwe, but none were fit for restoration to flying condition. Then a few derelict airframes were found at an air force base at Alverca in Portugal but they too were in a very poor state. However, good news came from Spain. After WWII, the Spanish had been building Ju52s under license from the German Junkers company. Designated in Spanish as the CASA 352L, these airplanes were exact replicas of the original Ju52/3m aeroplanes that saw passenger service with SAA in the 1930s. After many years with the Spanish Air Force, they began to be retired in the early seventies. British aircraft collector and dealer Doug Arnold bought a number of them for his famous collection, 'Warbirds of Great Britain,' based at Blackbushe Airport in Camberley, Surrey. After acquiring British registrations for them, five were put up for sale by Arnold. One, G-BFHE, was not only airworthy but still in fairly good condition. Originally built in 1954, it was one of the last of its type to be made and was equipped with ENMA Beta B4 engines, produced by Empresa Nacional de Motores de Aviación S.A. of Spain. These were license-built versions of the original German BMW 132 power plants.

When Prozesky heard about this, he travelled to Camberley to inspect the machine and, on carefully looking it over, he estimated that it would not take too much money, work and effort to make it look very much like one of the original Ju52/3ms that had served SAA so many years ago. When he told SAA's Technical Director Abercrombie 'Duke' Davidson about the availability of the machine, the two men approached Airbus Industrie for financial support. Because Airbus was only too happy to more closely cement the company's relationship with SAA, the funds were duly provided and, on May 12, 1981, CASA 352L, G-BFHE, took off from Blackbushe airfield southwest of London on the first leg of its delivery to South Africa. The aircraft was flown across the English Channel to Lemwerder, near Bremen, Germany. There it was disassembled by a team from SAA's Apprentice Training School in Johannesburg, under the supervision of Johann Prozesky, Dave Ackerman, Karel Gronum and John Ikking. The wings, wheels, engines and fuselage of the CASA were crated for the next stage of the journey by ferry up the Wesser River to Bremerhaven. There the parts were loaded aboard the Le Havre-registered 'ro-ro' cargo ship *Ronsard* for the ocean voyage to Durban. The crates were offloaded in Durban on July 6, 1981. Packed onto flat-bed trucks they arrived at Jan Smuts Airport a week later. Once there everyone began referring to the dismantled aircraft as 'Tante Ju.'

Over the course of the next couple of years the parts would come together. Extensive maintenance, rebuilding and refurbishing would take place, and CASA 352L would slowly find its reincarnation as a fully restored replica of an original 1934-vintage SAA Junkers Ju52 in preparation for the upcoming 50th anniversary celebrations.

On August 23, 1981, the first of thirteen Boeing 737 Advanced passenger aircraft, ZS-SIA, arrived at Jan Smuts Airport on its delivery flight from Seattle. In November, Boeing 727s replaced Hawker Siddeley HS 748s on what many in the airline referred to as the 'Milk Run' between Johannesburg, Kimberley, Upington, Keetmanshoop and Windhoek. As the new Boeing 737 Advanced fleet increased, from April 1, 1982, they began replacing Boeing

The refurbished CASA 352L, restored to look like one of SAA's original Junkers Ju-52 aircraft for the airline's 50th anniversary. This machine is lovingly referred to as Tante Ju, German for 'Auntie Ju.'

727s on the Johannesburg to Windhoek run, the Cape Town to Windhoek route and on Johannesburg to Cape Town services that were not being operated by the larger Airbus A300 wide-body aircraft. The new 737s also replaced 727s on the Johannesburg to Maputo route. (With the coming of independence in Mozambique in the seventies, the country's capital city Lourenco Marques had been renamed Maputo after a river that marks the southern border of Mozambique with South Africa.) The new Boeing 737s also replaced 727s on some regional routes, including between Johannesburg and Lusaka and Johannesburg and Blantyre.

From May 6, 1982, the weekly Boeing 747SP service between Johannesburg and Rio de Janeiro was combined with the weekly service between Cape Town and Buenos Aires. The new flight operated the sectors Johannesburg to Cape Town, Rio de Janeiro and Buenos Aires. This was due to a major cost-cutting program that was being implemented in the airline at that time. As had been the case for many years, not all routes were proving profitable. For quite some time the senior management of SAA were recognizing the fact that, in accordance with directives issued to them by the SAR & H and the Department of Transport, many routes were being flown primarily to show off the

South African flag. They were more politically motivated than profitable. As far as the Nationalist government was concerned, it was becoming increasingly expedient for it to have SAA play a public relations role on its behalf.

Saving money was becoming a prerogative of other airlines too. On June 7, 1982, TAP Airlines of Portugal replaced their Boeing 747 service from Lisbon to Johannesburg with Lockheed L1011 Tristar aircraft. Because the Tristar had three engines as opposed to four on the 747, a considerable saving in fuel was made possible. That month also witnessed the end of SAA's Boeing 727 operations. After 17 years of loyal and dependable service, the popular trijet had come to the end of its days in Southern African skies. On June 24, flight SA 308, operated by Boeing 727 ZS-SBC *Vaal* (the name of the largest tributary of the Orange River), flew from Cape Town via George to Johannesburg. Prior to landing at Jan Smuts Airport, it did a flypast over the airport in formation with five Mirage F1 interceptor-fighter jets of the South African Air Force, to the delight of crowds and the press gathered below.

The first SAA jet airliner—as opposed to piston-engine aircraft or turboprops—to land at Mbabane in neighboring Swaziland was Boeing 737 ZS-SBL on September 6, 1982. It was a VIP flight carrying President Marais Viljoen, Foreign Minister Roelof Frederik 'Pik' Botha and Minister of Home Affairs Chris Heunis. Together with 13 other passengers, they were in the country to attend the official funeral of the Swazi head of state, King Sobhuza II. As the gleaming jet taxied to a stop where a red carpet awaited the VIPs, few were aware of the fact that Swaziland was where the SAA story had really begun. After all, it was there in the green and khaki folds of its rolling mountains that Allister Macintosh Miller was born, played as a boy, then reached up and grasped for the sky, becoming the father of commercial aviation in Southern Africa nearly six decades earlier.

As Qantas flights from Australia to South Africa had stopped operating in protest against apartheid, it introduced a weekly service from Sydney and Perth to Harare in neighboring Zimbabwe. Under the government of President Robert Mugabe, the capital city Salisbury had been renamed Harare in April, 1982. The name was taken from a tribal chief who had ruled over Central Africa during the 19th century. Most passengers using the Qantas service were not destined for Zimbabwe at all but for South Africa so in November, SAA introduced a high-capacity Airbus A300 wide-body service from Johannesburg to connect with the Qantas flight. It is interesting to note that with the cessation of Qantas operations to Johannesburg SAA's own flights to Australia peaked. In 1982, a total of 68,000 passengers had been carried on the 'Wallaby Service.' In December, one of SAA's flights to New York was rerouted to a new destination, Houston, Texas. The Lone Star State now offered passengers a regular alternative gateway to North America from Johannesburg. The introductory flight, SA 211, was operated by Boeing 747SP, ZS-SPC *Maluti* (a mountain range in the Orange Free State), landing at Houston International Airport on December 9 after an 18-hour flight via Ilha do Sal.

Meanwhile, work on the Ju52 'Tante Ju' project proceeded at a steady pace in the apprentice workshops at Jan Smuts Airport. But it was not only apprentice mechanics who were involved. Only too enthusiastic to work on the historic craft, pilots and flight engineers willingly rolled up their sleeves and contributed to the restoration on their days off. As the program moved along, it became obvious that the Enzalda Beta B4 engines that came with the airplane were not in prime condition. They would need a lot of work. But ever since Douglas DC-3s had been retired from the airline back in February 1971, no one had worked on piston engines. All aircraft in the SAA fleet—or those serviced in Johannesburg for other airlines—were now either pure jet or turboprops. Nevertheless, the team plunged into the task with enthusiasm. Then it was discovered that the Swiss Air Force still had three original Ju52 aircraft in their collection. They were approached for help and, only too happy to assist, Swiss Air Force instructor pilot Georg Schilling flew out to South Africa to acquaint pilots with the airplane in preparation for training flights. 1983 soon arrived and everyone hoped that, by February the following year—the actual date of the Golden Anniversary—Tante Ju would once again take to the skies and become the focus of the 50th anniversary celebrations.

In February 1983, a major break in tradition took place at the airline's catering division at Jan Smuts Airport. It was decided that the preparation of meals would no longer be undertaken by members of SAA or Railways staff. The US-owned Marriott Corporation was awarded the contract to provide all meals and refreshments on board SAA airliners and so the company took over operations at the Flight Meal Center in the Cabin Services building. Menus were now under the supervision of Executive Chef, Gilbert Palma. The privatization move was also a result of austerity and cost-cutting measures. On April 1, Las Palmas was dropped from the airline's route network. From then onwards all flights to North America and to many destinations on the Springbok Service would use the island of Ilha do Sal instead. By then, significant improvements had been made to Sal's airport and terminal facilities, most of it paid for by the South African government. The termination of Las Palmas services ended an association with that island that had begun in April 1963, when SAA was forced to start using the round-the-bulge route. The problem was that passenger demand for seats to and from the island was very limited. To save costs the airline had no option but to stop flying there.

Meanwhile, at the Ilha do Sal airport flight crews, cabin attendants and passengers who regularly stopped over there fell in love with an unusual little creature. It was a mixed breed brown dog the size of a fox terrier that was lovingly named 'Springbok.' Owned by a ground staff crew worker at the airport, there was one very distinguishing feature about the little animal that endeared it to everyone. It was lame in both back legs. Every time an SAA airliner landed at the airport—always in the dead of night—en route to some remote destination in Europe or North America or on a return trip to Johannesburg, little Springbok would wait at the edge of the apron in front of the terminal building and then drag itself to the foot of the stairs as soon as the aircraft doors were opened, there to wag its tail and pant a welcoming greeting to everyone alighting from the airplane. For longer than anyone could remember, Springbok was a common sight at Sal.

On April 16, 1983, the first of the two new Boeing 747-300 airliners that had been ordered arrived at Jan Smuts Airport on its delivery flight from Seattle. The crew were Captains Cyril Rodgers and Hugh Pharoah with Flight Engineers Andre Higgs, Theo Stein and Danie Burger. With its distinctive extended upper deck, the Series 300 could carry 40 more passengers than the Series 200, giving it a total capacity of 376 passengers in three classes. Equipped with the latest Pratt &Whitney JT9D-7R4G2 engines that provided 56,000 lb. of thrust each, the new airplanes boasted decreased fuel consumption and significantly increased take-off power, making regular non-stop services between Johannesburg and Europe a viable proposition. In time, SAA would re-engine all the older Boeing 747-200 aircraft in the fleet with the 7R4G2 engines. The first of these would be modified at the factory in Seattle but the rest of the work would be done in Johannesburg. The transformation would also include the removal of the old water-injection feature used on previous engines. This was no longer required with the powerful new 7R4G2s.

Because of rising international condemnation of apartheid on May 1, 1983, the Australian government issued a directive to SAA to reduce its services from Johannesburg to Sydney to only one flight per week. More essentially needed cost-cutting within the airline resulted in a decision to dispose of the three

Hawker Siddeley HS 748 aircraft. This impending move caused the cancellation of regional services to the neighboring countries of Botswana, Lesotho and Swaziland. On May 26, a new hangar was opened at Jan Smuts Airport. Divided into two sections of 656 ft by 500 ft 'Hangar 8' could accommodate a total of six Boeing 747s, making it one of the largest commercial aircraft hangars in the world at that time.

On June 2, 1983, six of the seven Boeing 747-200 Super B services that operated the Springbok Service to London were replaced with the new Boeing 747-300 airliners. Two northbound and most southbound services operated non-stop instead of via Ilha do Sal. In July, one of the two weekly Boeing 737 Advanced flights to Blantyre was extended to the city of Moroni in the Comores Islands in the Mozambique Channel just off the east coast of Africa. From October, Boeing 747-200 Super B aircraft with their greater passenger and freight capacity replaced Boeing 747SPs on the Johannesburg, Mauritius and Hong Kong service. On November 1, flights to Malawi started serving the capital city of Lilongwe instead of Blantyre. Also in November, two of SAA's retired Hawker Siddeley HS748 aircraft, ZS-SBU and ZS-SBV, were delivered to their new owners, Austin Airways of Canada. The third one, ZS-SBW, departed for the same buyer on December 2. The Hawker Siddeley HS748s were the last turboprop aircraft operated by SAA. From now on, it would become an all-jet airline.

1983 was the year when an unusually high number of live animals were transported on Boeing 747 Combi services to and from New York. These included bulls and horses on southbound flights and elephants, wildebeest, lions and even two rhinoceroses bound for the north. All the animals were conveyed in special cages in the fully pressurized and air-conditioned main deck cargo area directly behind the passenger cabin. As 1983 drew to a close, the latest statistics about the airline were reported. With the cost-cutting measures that had been implemented the stats were impressive. SAA had carried a total of four million passengers and there were now 11,500 people on its staff. Only one ambition remained unfulfilled. The Ju52 Tante Ju had not yet flown. Then, in December, the tall sliding doors of hangar five in the technical section at Jan Smuts Airport were pushed open to the sound of a high-pitched metallic squeal. As sunlight filled the hangar there she was, resplendent, polished and proudly wearing the 1934 livery of an SAA airliner. Tante Ju was ready. The venerable Junkers Ju52 had been resurrected.

As cameras clicked and mechanics and technical personnel swarmed around to witness the historic event, the grand old lady was pushed outside, accompanied by members of the Apprentice School who beamed with pride. The aircraft's fuel tanks were filled to capacity to test for leaks. Electrical systems were checked out. A few days later the three engines were fired up. Spluttering smoke and flame their throaty cough recalled a bygone era and soon the props were spinning in the warm summer air. After more tweaking and testing over the next couple of weeks, on the morning of January 14, 1984, Swiss Air Force pilot Georg Schilling climbed into the aircraft and strapped in to the left-hand seat of the cockpit. Captain John Tainton took the right-hand seat and Steve Morrison manned the flight engineer's station.

At 11.40 a.m. the engines were started. With its corrugated skin shuddering, its nose in the air and its tail wheel rolling over the tarmac, Tante Ju taxied out to the runway, past the line-up of Boeing, Lockheed and Douglas jets in the liveries of SAA and a dozen other foreign carriers. Onlookers were amazed and puzzled to see this magnificent relic of times long past rumble by. Minutes later it was gone, a distant drone in the dazzling sky.

Tante Ju's first test flight lasted 55 minutes. All went well and then it returned to its cradle. Surrounded by technicians and mechanics wielding wrenches and oil cans and the accoutrements of their trade like a group of doctors and nurses fussing over a new-born infant, the aircraft was soon released once again and it took off for an afternoon test flight. Things could not have gone better.

The next day Georg Schilling began overseeing familiarization flights with SAA pilots and flight engineers. But getting the aircraft ready for the airline's 50th anniversary—now only a few weeks away—was not without drama. During subsequent engine run-ups, number one engine failed completely and could not be repaired. What now? Flight Engineer Steve Morrison quickly came forward with information about a contact he had made with another airworthy CASA 352 owner and operator, Keith May, of Rochester, Kent in England. Engineer Johan Prozesky immediately called him at his home to ask for assistance. May was ecstatic to hear about the restoration of Tante Ju, was only too eager to help and, because his own aircraft was laid up for the winter, he offered his number one engine to SAA provided that it was returned to him in time for his heavily booked air show schedule in the summer. Senior SAA mechanic Dave Ackerman and a crew from the apprentice school departed for England that night on board an SAA Boeing 747. As soon as they arrived in London, they drove out to Kent and, in freezing weather, set about the task of removing the number one engine from Keith May's airplane. By that night, the engine was at Heathrow and loaded into the hold of an SAA Boeing 747. Next morning, the team installed it on Tante Ju.

That afternoon test runs were made. The engine performed beautifully. And then, without warning, the number three engine failed. Slightly embarrassed, once more Prozesky called May in England. But once more the response was the same. They could have another engine provided he got it back for his summer show schedule. Once again a team left for England and once again an engine from May's CASA 352L was secured and flown back to Johannesburg. The next morning, it was installed on Tante Ju.

On January 31, a test flight was flown and everything worked perfectly.

And just as well. The fiftieth anniversary—the Golden Year— was the very next day.

Chapter 15

A Golden Year

Ambitious plans were in place for Tante Ju for the Golden Anniversary. To celebrate the founding of SAA on February 1, 1934, the restored CASA 352L airplane was not only meticulously painted in the livery of a vintage SAA Junkers Ju52/3m, it also carried the registration number ZS-AFA and proudly sported the name *Jan van Riebeeck* on its nose. This made the craft virtually indistinguishable from the very first Ju52 taken into service by SAA fifty years earlier. Arrangements called for it to fly a batch of first day issue mail covers from Durban—home base of the airline in 1934—to Rand Airport, SAA's center of operations from 1935. As Durban's old Stamford Hill Airport was no longer in use, Tante Ju would take off from Louis Botha Airport. Rand Airport near Johannesburg was still a very lively and fully functioning airport so Tante Ju would land there with the mail bags. Rand Airport was also chosen as the site for the main 50th anniversary celebrations that day. VIPs and specially invited guests would be gathered there to welcome Tante Ju's arrival.

There was only one glitch. No one counted on the presence of hurricane *Demonia* that raged just off the coast northeast of Durban on the morning of February 1, 1984. Weather conditions were too unpredictable for the old aircraft to undertake the flight so Tante Ju remain grounded at Jan Smuts Airport. Other arrangements were hastily made to fly the mailbags to Johannesburg. Nothing was going to thwart the festivities planned for that day. It was decided that a regularly scheduled SAA Airbus A300 flight operating a service from Cape Town to Port Elizabeth and then on to Durban and Johannesburg would pick up the bags. The A300 flight was already earmarked to fly dignitaries from those cities to the celebratory events. It was perfect as a replacement for carrying the first day covers.

As the sun slowly rose casting long shadows on the tarmac of Cape Town's D.F. Malan Airport on February 1, 1984, the Minister of Transport, Hendrik Schoeman, the General manager of SA Transport Services Dr. E.L. Bart Grové, the Chief Executive of SAA, Gert van der Veer, the Mayor of Cape Town, other VIP guests and their wives boarded flight SA600 on Airbus A300 ZS-SDE *Springbok* under the command of Captain Lynne Viljoen and took off to begin a day filled with fun and merry-making. Calling at Port Elizabeth—the original home of Major Allister Miller's Union Airways, the forerunner of SAA—the flight picked up the city's mayor, his wife and more VIPs and then proceeded on to Durban. On arrival there additional VIPs boarded the flight, including the city's mayor and his wife and one of the pioneers of South African aviation, Captain Reinhold Ferdinand 'Caspar' Caspareuthus. 'Caspar,' now 85 years old, had been a pilot for the country's first experimental airmail service way back in 1925 and had flown solo down the length of Africa in 1930, before joining Allister Miller's fledgling Union Airways. He was one of the last of the legendary figures who had helped develop commercial air travel on the continent.

From Durban, flight SA600 took off for the final sector to Johannesburg. Jan Smuts Airport was thronged with VIPs and specially invited guests when the Airbus touched down. Dressed in their fineries, dignitaries from Bloemfontein, East London, Kimberley and Windhoek were already there, waiting to board a fleet of luxury coaches to take them to Rand Airport in Germiston, some 15 miles away. VIPs from Upington, George and Keetmanshoop—all destinations served by SAA—had been flown in the previous day and were already on their way to the venue. Government officials, senior personnel from South African Transport Services, SAA executives and mayors of cities and towns across the Witwatersrand were traveling independently by limousine and by car to the party. Meanwhile, the mailbags with the first day covers were transferred from the Airbus to Tante Ju. The grand old lady would fly them on the last leg to Rand Airport.

At historic Rand Airport, the VIP crowd had swelled. It was an enormous gathering of people. Old friends were reacquainted after decades of having last seen one another. Politicians and pilots rubbed shoulders and told jokes. Executives and engineers picked at hors de-oeuvres and remembered old times. After a few hours of speeches, hand-shaking and back-slapping—fueled by an excellent buffet-style lunch, bottles of French champagne and the best South African wines—the crowd emerged from the cool shade of large striped marquee tents on a grassy field next to the main terminal building. By now everyone was ready for the climax of the day. They were not to be disappointed. A distant drone came out of the east. At first visible only as a grey smudge against the perfect summer sky, Tante Ju slowly metamorphosed into the magnificent flying machine that she was. With engines roaring, she did a few low circuits over the airfield before landing gracefully and taxiing up to the cheering crowds. Time had been turned back. The mailbags had been delivered. The Ju52 was revived. *Jan van Riebeeck* was flying again.

But more was to come. To the delight of the guests, SAA's latest acquisition, Boeing 747-300 ZS-SAU *Johannesburg*, swept in from the north and with a whispering rumble from her powerful Pratt & Whitney engines did a majestic low-level pass over the airfield. There were few dry eyes after the huge Boeing had soared her way in salute over Tante Ju sitting quietly on the grass. The contrast in technologies that had given birth to both machines could not have been more stark. It was a display of the extremities of old and new, of yesterday and today. As the VIPs and guests bade their farewells and filtered back to the long line of coaches, limousines and sedans Tante Ju's engines were fired up and the noble machine took to the air, homeward bound to its roost back at Jan Smuts Airport. It had been a memorable day. But the celebration of the SAA's 50th anniversary was by no means over. The events of February 1, 1984, would be eclipsed by an even larger party planned for Friday, November 23, when the world would come to celebrate the founding of the airline. The message of the golden anniversary would also be carried aloft to every destination served by SAA in the form of a large 50th anniversary celebratory decal affixed to each side of the forward section of the fuselage on every aircraft in the fleet. The design of the special Golden Anniversary Springbok logo on the decal was the result of a competition that was won by 25-year-old industrial design lecturer at Johannesburg's Witwatersrand Technikon, Michael Aylmer. It depicted a streamlined Flying Springbok within the numerals 50. It was a striking reminder of how long the winged antelope had been aloft in African skies and, as the symbol of the airline, how far they had both come.

As for Tante Ju, the two engines that had been loaned to it by Keith May in England were eventually returned. Tante Ju's own remaining ENMA Beta B4engine was also removed, fully overhauled and presented to May as a gift. Over the next few months, it was further restored by members of the SAA Apprentice School and was then fitted with three Pratt & Whitney R-1340 Wasp engines that had been salvaged from North American T-6 Harvard training aircraft that had been retired from the SAAF. Ju52-style window panels, period interior fittings, luggage racks and passenger seats were installed. By 1986, Tante Ju would start flying the air show circuit and begin carrying paying passengers on nostalgia flights around the country. Acquisition of the remarkable old aircraft would also be the catalyst behind a mission to collect other vintage aircraft that had served the airline.

In July 1984, ten of the Boeing 747s in the airline's fleet received licenses to operate worldwide in what is known in the industry as Category III or 'CAT III' ratings. This allowed landings in fog at airports with visibility as low as 650 feet. The Boeing 747SPs were the first to gain their CAT III grades, followed by the two Boeing 747 Combis and the two new B747-300 aircraft. To be eligible for the license, they were each fitted with three separate autopilots. The five older Boeing 747-200 Super B aircraft were already fitted with dual autopilots but the expensive upgrade to three of them would not have been cost effective at that time.

On September 19, 1984, Boeing 737 ZS-SBP *Nossob* (the name of a dry river bed in the Namib Desert) had an unfortunate encounter with one of the country's national birds on a flight between Kimberley and Bloemfontein. *Anthropoides paradisia* is more commonly known as the Blue Crane. Standing over three-feet (120 cm) tall with an impressive wingspan of six feet, the bird normally weighs between eight and thirteen lbs. The captain of the aircraft, Terry Jones, was new to the route and was undergoing route training by veteran pilot Klaus Bonow. After taking off from Kimberley at noon, the airliner was climbing through 12,000 feet when two large Blue Cranes were seen flying ahead of and above the flight path. This was most unusual. The Blue Crane does not normally fly at that altitude. Bonow immediately called out "Watch out! Don't hit those birds!"

But it was too late. One of the big birds suddenly dived directly in front of the Boeing. A split-second later there was a deafening bang as the aircraft slammed into it. The impact point was the plane's fibreglass dome on the nose. The dome protected a radar dish that searched for other aircraft and bounced signals off meteorological formations such as clouds and thunderstorms as part of the 737's weather avoidance system. Because of the size of the bird and the speed of the aircraft, the Blue Crane was shredded into tiny pieces. Many of these penetrated the metal wall between the radar bay and the cockpit. Body parts then hit the back of the cockpit's instrument panel, dislodging instruments and causing a mixture of blood, bones, flesh, feathers, glass, metal and pieces of cable to splatter all over the walls, floor and roof of the cockpit. So great was the impact that the cockpit door was flung open, sending grisly fragments of flesh hurtling down the aisle of the passenger cabin. Passengers were horrified but, of course, they had no idea of what had happened. Cabin crew quickly informed them that the pilots were fine and that the little pieces of flesh were from a bird that had been struck. What they were not told was that things could have been much worse. If the bird had been ingested by one of the jet engines, the aircraft would have been in serious trouble.

The hole in the Boeing's nose caused an immediate reduction in the internal pressurization of the aircraft, but this was not a major issue as the jet was still only at flight level 120, or 12,000 feet. What was far more serious was the fact that the roaring sound of wind rushing in from the cavity in the nose made speech impossible in the cockpit. Using sign language to communicate with one another, the two pilots decided to turn back to Kimberley. Radio messages were sent to Kimberley ATC but neither of the pilots could hear the response. The noise level was just too high. Passengers were notified of the pilots' intention to land as soon as possible. Amazingly, despite the roar of the wind and the mess that littered the carpet of the main cabin or the fleshy clumps that had hit the first couple of rows of passengers in the chest, there was a surprising lack of panic on board. Conditions were a little more tense on the flight deck, however. Visibility was seriously impaired by the amount of blood on the windshield. But there were small clear patches here and there so, with Terry Jones at the controls, the jet began its descent. As communication with the ground was impossible the pilots kept sending messages to Kimberley's tower and ATC, hoping that their flight path would be kept clear of other traffic.

Ten minutes later, the damaged Boeing pulled up outside the terminal buildings, its nose looking like the bloodied olfactory organ of a badly punched-up prize fighter. As passengers disembarked, they were shown into the airport's restaurant and handed complimentary beverages. Many were in a delayed state of shock and it was only then that they realized the full extent of the high drama that had just befallen them. No longer calm, they broke out into a loud cacophony of nervous chatter. A few days later, the Boeing 737 was fitted with a replacement nose dome and flown back to Johannesburg for repairs.

In the meantime, SAA soldiered on in the face of ever-increasing international hostility towards it and towards the entire country. No matter what the odds, the executives of the airline and the entire South African cabinet wanted to keep the orange tail and the Flying Springbok in the air. By 1984, its route network covered all six of the world's inhabited continents.

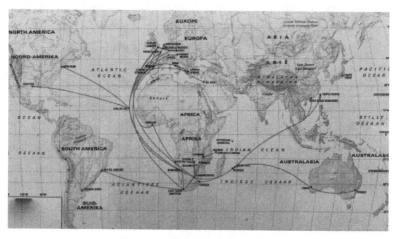

SAA's route network in 1984

As part of the airline's on-going cost-cutting program, from October 30, 1984, flight SA170 was rescheduled to terminate at Lilongwe, Malawi instead of at Moroni in the Comores islands. To ensure continuation of services to the Comores, an agreement was signed with Air Comores in which an SAA Boeing 737, ZS-SIB, was leased to the airline. The aircraft was painted in Air Comores colors at Jan Smuts Airport and then re-registered D6-CAJ, with SAA continuing to maintain it. The first Air Comores service between Moroni and Johannesburg was operated on

November 4, 1984. At the same time, Air Mauritius also signed an agreement with SAA for leasing Boeing 747SP ZS-SPC. The aircraft was painted in Air Mauritius livery and re-registered as 3B-NAG. Once again, SAA continued to technically maintain the airliner for its new operator.

November 1984 also saw the introduction of Gold Class (Business Class) on all of SAA's Boeing 737 aircraft. This brought in much-needed additional revenue on the domestic and regional service. Gold Class would be extended to Airbus airplanes the following year. Domestic business class offered passengers wider seats, extra leg-room, better meal options, special check-in counters with shorter check-in times and at all destinations Gold Class baggage was offloaded first. That month, some of the Boeing 747 Combi flights to Germany were rescheduled to operate from Johannesburg to Windhoek, Ilha do Sal and then terminate at Frankfurt. The stop at Windhoek would ensure that more passengers and freight could be carried. Boeing 747SP services flying from Cape Town to London no longer called at Sal Island and operated the route non-stop. Also in November, new uniforms were introduced for female ground staff including check-in personnel, secretaries, clerks and office workers, both locally and abroad.

But the highlight of the year took place on November 23, 1984. Under the astute supervision of Senior Public Relations Officer Marie-Hélène Maguire, a gala ball was held in the cavernous Hangar 8 at Jan Smuts Airport to celebrate the airline's 50th anniversary. Everyone who was anyone in the world of international aerospace was invited to attend the black tie event. Emptied of all aircraft, vehicles, maintenance stands, scissors lifts, compressors, cranes, machinery and the numerous tools and paraphernalia normally scattered everywhere for maintaining Boeing 747s, the hangar was swept spotlessly clean and transformed into another world, a vast dining area and ballroom arranged in a horse-shoe shape fronting a gigantic lilac-white stage. Dimly lit and surrounded by cascades of indigenous South African flowers, the venue looked like something out of a fairy tale. Crisp white table cloths, silverware, porcelain and crystal glassware sparkled beneath candles placed in the center of every table. 3,500 guests came from the farthest corners of the globe bedecked in ball gowns, glittering evening wear, black ties and tuxedos, deposited by limousines and luxury cars at the red carpeted entryway. The list of attendees read like a Who's Who of the major figures in aviation, space flight, engineering, avionics, aircraft manufacture, the travel industry, the international travel press, the diplomatic corps and the local political scene. Guest of honor was Colonel Edwin 'Buzz' Aldrin, USAF-NASA, the second man to set foot on the surface of the moon.

At 9.30 p.m. the entertainment began. The lights dimmed, white-jacketed waiters disappeared, the conversation and the laughter dwindled to a whisper and a spotlight illuminated the stage. Nobody was expecting what they were about to see. Following a lively performance of traditional Afrikaans songs by a troupe of 'Cape Colored Coons'—a disparaging and politically incorrect term but still acceptable at that time for members of the peripheral group of mixed-blooded people forced to live on the fringe of society in the Cape province—the show became a razzle-dazzle spectacle that could have been staged on Broadway. At around midnight the vast stage, its backing and proscenium silently split into two halves, glided apart into the shadows and then, from the darkness beyond the towering doors of the hangar, a gleaming giant appeared, flooded in light. It was SAA's Boeing 747-300, ZS-SAU, *Cape Town*. Gently nudged through the doorways by a motorized tug, the huge aircraft slowly made its entrance, coming to a stop when its nose towered high above the first three rows of tables. Music rose to a crescendo and the crowd cheered, silenced only when the four over-the wing emergency exits popped open, disgorging two dozen beautifully costumed young ladies. In sync with the pulsating music and flashing strobe lights, the girls danced their way to the edges of the wings, carefully avoiding flaps and ailerons. Then, emerging from the fuselage, an array of uniformed SAA flight crew and cabin attendants appeared, followed by the evening's guest-of-honor, astronaut Buzz Aldrin. He was attired in full white United States Air Force mess dress bearing all his medals. It was a show-stopper.

The numerous black VIPs and faces in the crowd at the Golden Anniversary Gala spoke clearly of the fact that apartheid—though still enshrined within the legal and political rule books of the country—was beginning to wane. The system was starting to crack. In large cities around the country, mixed racial groups were now being allowed to attend live performances together, no longer separated by walls and barriers. Theatrical audiences had become multi-racial. Many restaurants—provided they had sought legal reclassification to do so—were now serving whites and blacks together. Hotels were now taking in guests of all colors and ethnicities. To the surprise of many hardliners, particularly in rural areas, the country was not falling apart at the seams because of this relaxed trend in the cities. But the core of the system stubbornly prevailed. While Indians and Coloreds were being allowed to vote for their own representatives to serve on newly-created side benches in the all-white parliament blacks were still being denied the general franchise. To elect their own representatives, they could only do so in their own Bantustans or homelands. No blacks could yet serve in parliament. And so, the struggle continued. The world looked on in disgust.

By 1985, the financial doldrums that were continuing to plague SAA began to bite deeper into its operations. This was the seventh year in a row that it had posted a financial loss. During the previous year it was R637 million (South African rands) in the red. Due to low load factors and to save money, in February, flights to Buenos Aires from Cape Town were suspended. A number of other flights—including those on the Springbok

Service to Europe—were reduced. The biggest culprit was the high cost of fuel which was making some international routes very unprofitable. If at least fifty per cent of the seats were not occupied on a flight, it was losing money.

With reduced flights and a trimmed timetable, SAA was now beginning to find itself with an excess number of aircraft so in March 1985, Boeing 747SP ZS-SPD was leased to Royal Air Maroc of Morocco. In April, Boeing 747SP ZS-SPB was leased to Air Malawi. Also because of low passenger demand, on June 19, the last SAA flight departed Johannesburg for Houston. When Boeing 747SP ZS-SPF left Houston for South Africa the following day, all further services to Texas were cancelled. Due to the wobbly financial situation that the airline industry in general was going through, there was a lot of to'ing and fro'ing between carriers. From September 10, Air Comores discontinued its Boeing 737 service between Moroni and Johannesburg, so SAA reintroduced flight SA170 to the Comores Islands via Lilongwe, Malawi. The Boeing 737 that been leased to Air Comores was returned on October 30. Soon, two more SAA Boeing 737s were leased to foreign airlines. In November, ZS-SIA went to VASP airlines in Brazil and in December ZS-SIA to Lan (Línea Aérea Nacional) of Chile.

January 2, 1986, was a milestone date in the airline's history. After years of requesting it, permission was finally granted by the government for it to begin hiring staff of all races. While limited numbers of non-white cabin crew were already being employed on some flights to the Far East, this new development began making it possible for SAA to start interviewing black candidates for many categories within the airline. There was one exception: air crews. Pilots and flight engineers would remain white. At least for now. But cabin crew, ground staff, mechanics, check-in personnel, office clerks and a range of other jobs would now be open to black and colored applicants. The first of these to be employed in the maintenance section at Jan Smuts Airport was Dawie Daniels who was offered a position in the plastics molding division. However, the sad fact is that he was in the minority. It would still take years before non-white personnel began appearing in any significant numbers in the technical positions now open to them.

From April 7 to 13, 1986, special flights were operated in Johannesburg, Cape Town, Durban and Port Elizabeth to enable the public to view Halley's Comet which was making its once-every-76-years appearance. Unfortunately, viewing was disappointing, but there was no shortage of passengers for the short one-hour flips to nowhere far beyond the glare of city lights. As 1986 wore on, further financial pruning remained a top priority. On June 1, SAA's Melbourne and Auckland offices were closed. In July flight crew members began being hired out to serve with foreign carriers. Sixteen pilots and flight engineers were sub-contracted out to Parc Aviation of Dublin, Ireland. In August, three Airbus A300 wide-body aircraft were leased to Wardair airlines of Canada. In September the Boeing 747SP that had been leased to Royal Air Maroc was sold outright to that carrier.

Growing political dissent and public opinion abroad about South Africa's racist policies began to bite ever more deeply into the airline's affairs. Its sales office at Oxford Circus in London was vandalized and daubed with red paint. Demonstrators carried placards outside its sales office on Elizabeth Street in Sydney. Less than a year earlier, nine anti-apartheid demonstrators in New York had seized its offices on Fifth Avenue and barricaded themselves inside for three hours before being arrested by police.

Then a really bitter blow fell. On October 2, 1986, the United States Congress announced that it would impose more stringent sanctions on South Africa to try to coerce the government to get rid of apartheid through what was called the U.S. Comprehensive Anti-Apartheid Act. This would include the termination of all commercial air links between the two countries. Republican President Ronald Reagan was very reluctant to enforce such drastic measures but most members of Congress were determined to do whatever was necessary to bring apartheid to its knees. Acting on an overwhelming vote in both the Senate and the House of Representatives, the U.S. Department of Transport revoked SAA's landing rights, effective November 14. Representatives from the South African government immediately asked the U.S. Supreme Court to block the ban, stating that the Department of Trade's decision violated a 1947 treaty between the two countries that required a twelve-month notification period to halt air links. At the same time SAA's Chief Executive, Gert van der Veer, issued an affidavit stating that the revocation of flights to and from the U.S. would cost the airline "immediate and significant financial losses." He estimated the value of that loss at around $29.1 million annually and that it would also inflict "severe harm and irreparable injury to the airline's worldwide image and reputation." But U.S. Chief Justice William H. Renquist rejected the pleas. The order would stay. The ban would take effect on November 16, 1986, as planned. The last SAA flight to Johannesburg departed New York's J.F. Kennedy Airport on November 9, terminating air services to and from the United States. Halting SAA flights was only one of a number of steps called for by the U.S. Congress and, despite his opposition, the measures were signed into law by President Reagan. This included the banning of imports of South African agricultural products, manufactured items, textiles, steel, coal and uranium. It also prohibited U.S. bank loans to the South African government and stopped any new investments by U.S. companies who were already doing business in South Africa. Computer companies such as IBM and Apple withdrew their products and closed their retail outlets. US-owned Marriott Corporation gave up its in-flight catering and cabin services operation at Jan Smuts Airport. The facility was taken over by locally-owned Air Chefs Limited.

While all this was going on, on October 30, the Australian Government in Canberra issued the South African government a one-year notice to terminate all flights to Australia. In November, Iberia Airlines of Spain ceased operations between Madrid and Johannesburg. That same month SAA's offices in Belgium and Canada were closed. Operationally and financially the skies were becoming decidedly more turbulent and hostile towards the airline. With an even greater number of excess aircraft in its fleet SAA had little option but to lease Boeing 747SP ZS-SPA to Air Mauritius on April 1, 1987. On April 11, Boeing 747-200 Super B ZS-SAM was leased to Varig Airlines of Brazil. On May 10, Airbus A300 ZS-SDH was leased to Philippine Airlines. On October 27, the last flight was operated to Australia when the air services agreement between the Australian and South African governments was terminated. With the departure of the last SAA flight from Sydney's Charles Kingsford-Smith Airport to Johannesburg, the 'Wallaby Service' came to an end, bringing the curtain down on 30 years of aviation links between the two countries. By then, SAA had carried 665,000 passengers and flown some 32 million miles on what had been one of the world's most well-patronized routes.

But with SAA's rising travails all was not bleak. A frequent flyer program known as *Voyager* was introduced in July 1987. It immediately became very popular with domestic passengers and stimulated growth. Because of an increase in passenger and freight demand, on November 2, a second weekly flight was introduced between Johannesburg and Taipei, Taiwan. Operating via Mauritius, this brought weekly services between South Africa and the Far East to three per week, the third one terminating in Hong Kong. And then, just three weeks after the commencement of the new service the worst disaster in SAA's entire history occurred on one of the Asian flights.

On November 28, Boeing 747 Combi ZS-SAS *Helderberg* was operating flight SA295 out of Taipei, bound for Mauritius and

Johannesburg. There were 159 people on board, consisting of 140 passengers, a flight crew of five and 14 cabin crew. The captain was Dawid Jacobus Uys (49 years old,) assisted by First Officers David Hamilton Attwell (36) and Geoffrey Birchall (37.) The Flight Engineers were Guiseppe 'Joe' Michele Bellagarda (45) and Alan George Daniel (34.) The cabin crew consisted of Herman Burger, Peter Cramb, Manuel de Almeida, Andries Kellerman, Martha Kruger, Sandra Lourens, Jo Anne McEwan, Louise O'Brien, Andre Schalekamp, Estelle Schalekamp, Fleur Strydom, Ettienne van der Westhuizen, Nicolas van Skalkwyk and Johannes van Zyl.

As the aircraft was a Combi version of the Boeing 747-200 model, the forward two-thirds of the main deck carried passengers while the rear third—separated from the passengers by a safety web and a solid bulkhead—was loaded with six high-capacity cargo pallets. Both sections shared the same pressurized atmosphere and air conditioning. There was a total of 95,294 lbs. of cargo and baggage on board. Most of the freight was on the pallets in the cargo section while all passenger baggage was stowed in containers beneath the main deck.

The flight departed Taipei's Chiang Kai-Shek Airport at 23 minutes after midnight, local time. The flying time to Mauritius's Plaisance Airport was estimated to be 10 hours and 14 minutes. One hour and 32 minutes after take-off a routine call was made from the cockpit to the airline's Radio ZUR at Jan Smuts Airport in Johannesburg. The operator on duty at ZUR, Gavin Dick, was informed that all was well and that the aircraft was at cruise level 'FL 310,' (31,000 feet). The ETA at Plaisance Airport was 4:35 a.m. Mauritius time. Dick acknowledged this information and requested another routine call at 18:00 UTC (8.00 p.m. South African time). As the flight proceeded over the Indian Ocean radio contact was made from SA295 with Hong Kong radar and then, at regular intervals, position reports were sent to flight information centres (FICs) at Hong Kong, Bangkok, Kuala

Lumpur, Colombo and the Cocos Islands. The flight could not have been proceeding more smoothly.

And then something went catastrophically wrong.

Several hours into the journey Captain Dawie Uys contacted Plaisance Airport on high frequency (HF) radio stating that there was a 'smoke problem' on board. He requested permission to descend to flight level 140 (14,000 feet). The following transcript is taken from a recording that was made in the tower at Plaisance Airport. It provides a chilling insight into what was happening on board the *Helderberg*. 'Springbok Two Niner Five' was the aircraft's call sign. The times indicated are for local time Mauritius.

23:48:51:
Aircraft (SA295) :   "Eh, Mauritius, Mauritius, Springbok Two Niner Five."

23:49:00
Mauritius (MRU):   "Springbok Two Niner Five, eh, Mauritius, eh, good morning, eh, go ahead."

23:49:07:
SA295:   "Eh, good morning, we have, eh, a smoke , eh, eh, problem and we're doing emergency descent to level one five, eh, one four zero."

23:49:18:
MRU: "Confirm. You wish to descend to flight level one four zero."

23:49:20
SA295:   "Yeah, we have already commenced, eh, due to a smoke problem in the aeroplane."

23:49:25:
MRU: "Eh, roger, you are clear to descend immediately to flight level one four zero."

23:49:30:

SA295:   "Roger, we will appreciate if you can alert, eh, fire, eh."

23:49:40:

MRU: "Do you wish to, eh, do you request a full emergency?"

23:49:48:

SA295:   "Okay Joe, can you (garbled)... for us." (Spoken in Afrikaans.)

23:49:51:

MRU: "Springbok Two Nine Five, Plaisance."

23:49:54:

SA295:   "Sorry, go ahead."

23:49:56:

MRU: "Do you, eh, request a full emergency, please? A full emergency?"

23:50:00:

SA295:   "Affirmative, that's Charlie, Charlie."

23:50:02:

MRU: "Roger, I declare a full emergency, roger."

23:50:04:

MRU: "Thank you."

23:50:40:

MRU: "Springbok Two Nine Five, Plaisance."

23:50:44:

SA295:   "Eh, go ahead."

23:50:46:

MRU: "Request your actual position, please, and your DME distance."

('DME' stands for 'distance monitoring equipment', used by aircraft to determine their exact distance from fixed transponders on the ground.)

23:50:51:

SA295:   "Eh, we haven't got the DME yet."

23:50:55:
MRU: "Eh, roger and your actual position please."

23:51:00:
SA295:   "Eh, say again."

23:51:02:
MRU: "Your actual position."

23:51:08:
SA295:   "Now we've lost a lot of electrics. We haven't got anything on the aircraft now."

23:51:12:
MRU: "Eh roger, I'll declare a full emergency immediately."

23:51:15:
SA295:   "Affirmative."

23:51:18:
MRU: "Roger."

23:52:19:
MRU: "Eh, Springbok Two Nine Five, do you have an Echo Tango Alfa, Plaisance, please."

('Echo Tango Alfa' means ETA or estimated time of arrival.)

23:52:30:
MRU: "Springbok Two Nine Five, Plaisance."

23:52:32:
SA295:   "Yeah, Plaisance."

23:52:33:
MRU: "Do you have an Echo Tango Alfa, Plaisance, please."

23:52:36:
SA295:   "Yeah, eh, zero zero, eh, eh, eh, three zero."

23:52:40:
MRU: "Roger, zero zero three zero, thank you."

23:52:50:
SA295:   "Hey Joe, shut down the oxygen left."

23:52:52:	
MRU:	"Sorry, say again please."
00:01:34:	
SA295:	"Eh Plaisance, Springbok Two Nine Five, we've opened the door to see if we can (garbled)...We should be okay."
00:01:36:	
SA295:	"Look there!" (Exclamation by somebody else is said over the last part of the previous sentence)
00:01:45:	
SA295:	"Close the bloody door!" (Shouted in Afrikaans.)
00:01:57:	
SA295:	"Joe, switch up quickly, then close the hole on your side!"
00:02:10:	
SA295:	"Pressure? Twelve thousand."
00:02:14:	
SA295:	"Is enough (garbled)... otherwise our flight could come to grief!" (Spoken in Afrikaans.)
00:02:25:	
SA295:	High pitched carrier wave humming sound only. (No voice.)
00:02:38:	
SA295:	"Eh Plaisance, Springbok Two Nine Five, did you copy?"
00:02:41:	
MRU:	"Eh negative, Two Nine Five. Say again, please. Say again."
00:02:43:	
SA295:	"We're now sixty five miles."
00:02:45:	

MRU:	"Confirm, sixty five miles."
00:02:47:	
SA295:	"Yeah, affirmative. Charlie, Charlie."
00:02:50:	
MRU:	"Eh, Roger, Springbok, eh, Two Nine Five, eh, you're recleared flight level five zero. Recleared flight level five zero."
00:02:58:	
SA295:	"Roger, five zero."
00:03:00	
MRU:	"Springbok Two Nine Five, copy. Actual weather Plaisance. Copy actual weather Plaisance. The wind one one zero degrees, zero five knots. The visibility above one zero kilometres. And we have a precipitation in sight to the north. Clouds, five octas one six zero zero, one octa five thousand feet. Temperature twenty two, two, two. And the QNH one zero one eight hectopascals. One zero one eight. Over."

('QNH' refers to barometric pressure and is a measurement expressed in 'hectopascals.')

00:03:28:	
SA295:	"Roger, one zero one eight."
00:03:31:	
MRU:	"Affirmative, eh, and both runways available if you wish. And two nine five, I request pilot's intention."
00:03:46:	
SA295:	"Eh, we'd like to track in eh, on eh, one three."
00:03:51:	
MRU:	"Confirm, runway one four."
00:03:54:	

SA295: 00:03:56:	"Charlie, Charlie."
MRU:	"Affirmative, and you're cleared, eh, direct to Foxtrot Foxtrot. You report approaching five zero."
00:04:02:	
SA295: 00:08:00:	"Kay."
MRU: 00:08:11	"Two Nine Five, Plaisance."
MRU: 00:08:35	"Springbok Two Nine Five. Plaisance."
MRU:	"Springbok Two Nine Five. Plaisance."

Full emergency services were on standby at the airport after the airplane was cleared to descend to flight level 50 (5,000 feet). But there were no further responses from SA295. The last transmission from the aircraft was at 00:04:02. At precisely 00:04:07, the big jet had plummeted at very high velocity into the Indian Ocean. Its position was 154 miles northeast of Mauritius, on compass coordinates 19°10'30"S and 59°38'0"E.

Before the radio operator and his colleagues at Plaisance airport knew about the deadly accident, the silence from SA295 was baffling. No one had the slightest inkling of what had gone wrong. Other than the mention of smoke during the pilot's transmissions and the indication that something was seriously amiss based on the recorded conversation of the flight crew, the reason for the silence was a mystery. But when no further responses were forthcoming from SA295, it was obvious. The aircraft had gone down. A massive search and rescue operation immediately got underway.

Participating in the effort were the Mauritius National Coast Guard, the Mauritius Marine Authority, the helicopter division of the Mauritius Police, Air Mauritius, the South African Air

Force, the South African Navy, Safair (an air cargo operator based at Jan Smuts Airport in Johannesburg), the French Air Force and Navy based on the island of Reunion, the United States Navy based at Diego Garcia, the Perth-based Rescue and Coordination Center of Australia, private fishing boats, a couple of private operators of light aircraft based at Plaisance Airport and the Toulouse office of the International Satellite Search and Rescue System (SARSAT) in France.

Within hours, SAAF Transall C-160 military transport aircraft were despatched from Waterkloof Air Force Base in Pretoria to Mauritius carrying disassembled SAAF Aérospatiale SA 330 Puma military helicopters. Hastily reassembled at Plaisance Airport, the helicopters joined the Transalls to search the area where it was thought SA295 last reported its position. Then, at 12:47 p.m. on November 28, the crew of a privately-owned twin-engine Beech 18 aircraft observed two oil slicks, pieces of wreckage and bodies floating on the ocean close to the actual impact point. Once the word was out a flotilla of vessels and other aircraft—including a French Air Force Transall C-160 transporter, a United States Air Force P3 Orion maritime patrol aircraft and an Air Mauritius airliner—headed for the area.

At 3.20 p.m., the Mauritius Search and Rescue Center (SARC) broadcast an alert that an empty dinghy, some debris including an escape chute and a few pieces of passenger luggage were seen drifting at sea. The broadcast went on to say that ships were on the way, with an estimated time of arrival of 9.00 p.m. that night. It also stated that one of the South African helicopters had dropped an emergency locator beacon in the water to mark the site. As night fell, the air search was temporarily called off. But ships and boats were converging on the area. By sunrise the next morning, it was clear that there would be no survivors when body parts began being pulled from the water. Floating debris was spread over a large expanse. The *Helderberg* had either broken up on impact or, because of the two separate oil slicks, it may already have been in pieces when it hit the water. After anxious deliberations among the many rescue parties, at 7.30 a.m., it was unanimously decided to terminate the search for survivors. The focus now concentrated on the recovery of bodies and wreckage. Many fragments of human remains were retrieved but, after a long search, only eight bodies were in a condition that allowed for detailed post-mortem examination. All remains were taken to Mauritius and then flown to Johannesburg for autopsy and pathological study.

The victims of the accident were of many nationalities. One was from Denmark, one from Germany, one from South Korea, one from the Netherlands, one from the United Kingdom, two from Australia, two from Hong Kong, two from Mauritius, 30 from Taiwan, 47 from Japan and 52 from South Africa. On December 5, a memorial service for the dead was held in Port Louis, the capital city of Mauritius. SAA arranged special flights to transport close members of the victims' families from Johannesburg to the service. But people wanted closure. There was a desperate need to know exactly how and why family members and loved ones on the flight had perished.

And so, the search continued. A coordinated effort involving all craft and personnel was placed under the supervision of Rennie van Zyl, Director of Aviation Safety of the South African Directorate of Civil Aviation (DCA). It is a credit to all the foreign organizations involved — especially the U.S. and French air forces and navies — that proceedings went ahead as smoothly as they did. Overnight the stigma of apartheid disappeared and all barriers fell away as the multi-national search operation intensified. Floating debris, including passengers' personal effects, were retrieved and taken to Mauritius where it was sorted and stowed in a hangar at Plaisance Airport before being transferred to Johannesburg.

On December 11, ships began a search for possible 'pings' from the aircraft's 'black boxes.' The term 'black box,' however, is a misnomer. These recording devices—sealed in heavy-duty watertight steel containers—are painted bright orange so that they can be easily spotted underwater, in ice fields, snow, thick vegetation, deserts or in piles of rubble. They are designed to withstand heat, water and severe impact. The Boeing 747 Combi carried three of them. A Penny & Giles 'quick access' recorder (QAR) logged basic flight data. Not considered essential to understanding the reasons for a traumatic accident, it was mounted in the main equipment bay just forward of the lower cargo hold. Of far more importance to unlocking the secrets of what may have happened in an accident, a Lockheed model 209F digital flight data recorder (DFDR) fitted with a Dukane underwater locator beacon had been mounted on top of a stowage facility in the left-hand rear side of the main deck cargo compartment. This was deemed to be a less vulnerable location in the event of a crash. If found, the DFDR could provide valuable information regarding the aircraft's operational behavior. It could tell a lot about what the engines, electrics, electronics and mechanical systems were doing prior to an accident.

A Collins type 642 C-1 cockpit voice recorder (CVR) fitted with a Dukane underwater locator beacon had been mounted next to the DFDR. The CVR recorded the voices of the flight crew. Based on a looped tape system, it preserved everything that was said in the cockpit for a period of 30 minutes prior to an accident. The latter two data recorders were the ones designed to emit pinging sounds. They had now become the prized objects of the search. Each was equipped with batteries designed to last at least a month. The batteries are what powered the 'pinging' locator beacons.

To help locate the recorders, a German-registered oceanographic research vessel, the *R.V. Sonne* and the Singapore-registered *M.V. Omega* were contracted to undertake a sea bed survey and to map the ocean floor at the crash site. Under the supervision of Rennie van Zyl, with representatives from the

DCA, the South African Council for Scientific and Industrial Research (CSIR,) the U.S. Federal Aviation Administration (FAA,) the U.S. National Transportation Safety Board (NTSB) and the Boeing company on board the vessels, a contour map of the ocean floor was created. But no one counted on how deep the waters were. The bottom was all of 16,000 feet beneath the surface, equal to a staggering 3.3 miles. This was far deeper than the depth at which the *Titanic* was found by Robert Ballard in the North Atlantic two years earlier. No one in the history of salvage operations anywhere in the world had ever attempted to plumb such immense depths before. It was going to be an unprecedented task to find anything, let alone actually retrieve wreckage from down there. Incredible atmospheric pressures made it impossible for humans to work so deep and, besides, sunlight could not penetrate that far. It was pitch black at the bottom. Any underwater cameras lowered required the accompaniment of powerful lighting units.

In mid-December, the 2,918 ton South African-built deep sea tug, *Wolraad Woltemade*, based in Cape Town, arrived to join the search. It was soon followed by its sister ship, the *John Ross*. Within days another South African vessel, the 2,471-ton fisheries research vessel *RS Africana*—equipped with a hull-mounted sonar—arrived and also began listening for any pinging sounds. Then—without warning—at the end of December, the *Wolraad Woltemade* picked up a weak signal. That was quickly confirmed by the *Africana*. Could it be coming from one of *Helderberg's* black boxes? It was a month to the day since the aircraft went down. And then the signal faded. But hope was not lost. The search teams were convinced they were in the right place. And so began *Operation Resolve*, an all-out attempt to employ every means possible to try to find the wreckage, retrieve the black boxes and, ultimately, to bring up whatever was possible from the sea floor, no matter how difficult.

By now, autopsies of bodies in Johannesburg had indicated

the presence of soot in the tracheas of passengers aboard the flight. Pathological examination of other human remains showed that soot, carbon dioxide and carbon monoxide had been inhaled. Death might actually have been caused by smoke inhalation and asphyxiation long before the crash occurred. To find out more, a full-scale mock-up was created of the cargo hold and rear passenger cabin of a Boeing 747 Combi in a hangar at Jan Smuts Airport. This included a replica of the fire alarm system on board the *Helderberg*. Investigators wanted to know how a fire in the cargo section might have spread, how smoke and noxious fumes might have reached the passenger area and even the flight deck and whether a fire could have been extinguished on board. The Combi had a fire and smoke warning system in the cargo area but no sprinklers or firefighting equipment to douse the flames. At that time, the installation of automated firefighting systems was not standard practice on commercial airliners. If a fire had started and was detected the cabin crew would have had to don masks, break through to the rear cargo section from the passenger cabin and personally fight the flames with hand-held fire extinguishers.

Researchers duplicated the sizes of the cargo consignments on the pallets carried aboard the *Helderberg* and covered them with the same sort of plastic tarpaulins and packing material. Then a fire was set in the cargo hold mock-up. It took 40 minutes before the smoke detection system sensed the flames and set off alarms on the flight deck. Using ducted fans to force flames and smoke into the passenger section, it was clear that a fire in that part of the aircraft could not be extinguished fast enough without it spreading uncontrollably forward. More importantly, the size of the pallets and their cargo made it virtually impossible for crew to enter the cargo area, move around in it and fight the blaze. There simply was not enough room for people to maneuver freely in such confined space, especially while carrying heavy fire extinguishers. As these efforts continued, telltale evidence of severe fire damage and soot were being found on pieces of floating wreckage and personal items that had been pulled from the ocean. There was little doubt that *Helderberg* had suffered a very lethal fire on board.

On January 29 1988, a large debris field was located on the ocean floor by the research vessel, *M.V. Omega*. According to sonar signals the bottom was strewn with fragments of the big Boeing. The 3,375-ton Swedish-registered oceanographic research and salvage vessel, *Stena Workhorse*, was contracted to join the task force in the Indian Ocean. Equipped with a side-scan sonar, heavy-duty cranes and a variety of ancillary equipment, it also carried the deep water American-built remotely operated underwater vehicle (ROV) called *Gemini* owned and operated by Eastport International Salvage Inc. of the U.S.A. The *Stena Workhorse* and *Gemini* had participated in the quest for wreckage of NASA's space shuttle *Challenger* off the Florida coast of the U.S. earlier that year.

A four-mile length of cable carrying electrical and fiber optic lines was specially manufactured in the United States for *Gemini* and—after endless technical problems that included snapped cables and ferocious battles with storm-tossed seas—over the next few months 3,940 color photographs and 806 hours of video recordings were made of the *Helderberg* debris field. A number of high-tensile cables were constructed and attached to 'lift baskets' and hooks designed to bring up items from the depths. Twenty-five targets were selected for retrieval. *Gemini* was equipped with mechanical manipulators or 'pincers' for grabbing the items and depositing them in the lift baskets or attaching them to the hooks, after which they would be hauled up to the surface by cranes on board the *Stena Workhorse*. Considering the depth of the ocean and the incredible length of the cables many observers and critics in the engineering and maritime worlds said that it was a futile task, that it was a job that could not be accomplished. But they were wrong. The salvage crews were daringly tenacious, determined and dedicated, and they pulled off a miracle.

With superhuman effort and at enormous expense, one by one the pieces of the *Helderberg* were gradually brought to the surface from the ocean floor. These included sections of the main fuselage, parts of the floor and roof of the rear cargo compartment, sections of the tailplane assembly, remnants of cargo and, of primary importance, the cockpit voice recorder or CVR. The reason it had not transmitted regular pinging sounds was glaringly, frighteningly obvious. Its battery compartment had been completely melted by intense heat. The flight data recorder or DFDR was never found but what was on the CVR tape would be revelatory. But getting to the tape was no simple task.

After recovery and while it was still underwater, the CVR was transferred to a special container. The seawater was then replaced with de-ionized water and ice to maintain a temperature below 53 ºF. The CVR was flown to SAA's maintenance division at Jan Smuts Airport. In a laboratory there, the temperature of the liquid was allowed to stabilize at room temperature at approximately 69.8ºF. Then the CVR was opened. The tape was carefully transferred to a reel and cleaned in the de-ionized water. It was then dried in a vacuum chamber over a period of 24 hours. After that the tape was packaged and carried by hand— bypassing all magnetic security checks along the way—to the NTSB flight recorder laboratory in Washington D.C. There, it was copied and transcribed. What was learned during playback was that after 28 minutes of idle personal chatter between the pilots and the flight engineer, the following conversation and events occurred. Some of the dialogue is in Afrikaans. The time on the thirty-minute recording appears to the left of the transcript.

28:31:   Fire alarm bell ringing loudly (but stopped very quickly by the crew.)
28:35:   Intercom chime.

28:36:	Flight engineer: "What's going on now?"
28:37:	Unknown: "Huh?"
28:40:	Flight engineer: "Cargo?"
28:42:	Flight engineer: "It came on now, afterwards."
28:45:	Strong click sound.
28:45:	Unknown: "And where is that?"
28:46:	More clicking sounds.
28:48:	Possibly flight engineer: "Just to the right."
28:49:	Unknown: "Say again."
28:52:	Flight engineer: "Main deck cargo."
28:57:	Flight engineer: "The other one came on as well. I've got two."
29:01:	Flight engineer: "Shall I (get/push) the (bottle/button) over there?"
29:02:	Unknown: "Ja. (Yes.)"
29:05:	Captain: "Lees vir ons die check list daar, hoor." ("Listen, read us the check list over there.")
29:07:	Double clicking sound.
29:08:	Unknown: "The breaker fell out as well."
29:09:	Unknown: "Huh?"
29:10:	Two click sounds.
29:11:	Unknown: "We'll check the breaker panel, as well."
29:12:	Captain: "Ja. (Yes.)" Sounds of movement can be heard with clicks and clunks.
29:33:	Captain: "Fok, dis die feit dat altwee aangekom het. Dit steur mens." ("Fuck, it's a fact that both came on together. That is troubling.") Intercom chime (while captain is speaking.)
29:38:	Unknown: "Ag, shit." ("Oh, shit.")
29:40:	Very loud 800 Hz test tone commences.
29:41:	Captain: "Wat die donder gaan nou aan?" ("What the hell is going on now?")
29:44:	Sudden very loud sound.

29:46:   Large and rapid changes in amplitude of test tone.
29:51:   End of test signal, very irregular near end.
29:52:   End of recording.

From the CVR tape, it was evident that a fire had indeed broken out and that its location was the main deck cargo compartment at the rear of the fuselage. The erratic test tones on the tape indicated that the recording was interrupted, possibly by wiring being melted by fire.

A large hangar at Jan Smuts Airport had been designated a debris center. An outline of a Boeing 747 Combi was painted on the hangar floor and any debris from the *Helderberg* that had been found or brought up from the sea bed was placed inside the outline, corresponding to its actual position on the real aircraft. An entire wall of the hangar was dedicated to displaying photographs that had been sent back from the wreckage site. A large section was dedicated to the storage of baggage and personal items from those who perished. But it was the wreckage that was beginning to tell the horrific story of what had happened. Parts of the fuselage structure had been melted by intense heat. Temperatures had reached at least 1,832ºF. Soot was found in many places. The fire had started on one of the six pallets in the cargo section. It had broken out on pallet 'PR,' situated in the forward right hand side of the fuselage. Lengthy forensic investigation revealed that the aircraft's smoke alarm system was fully functioning but, based on experiments in the mock-up, fire alarms were probably triggered too late. The flames were so intense that the fire was completely out of control and spreading rapidly.

There was only one unanswered question. And it was by far and away the biggest single question of them all. What had caused the fire? Could it have been triggered by some form of extremely flammable or explosive substance that was being carried on the front right cargo pallet? An intense investigation

then began into the exact nature of all freight items that had
been carried aboard flight SA295.

SAA's cargo manager at Taipei stated that he had not been
informed of any toxic or inflammable items that made up the
cargo manifest. Six consignments of computers and electronic
equipment were discovered to contain small lithium battery cells
that were fitted to circuit boards but these were not considered
dangerous. Taiwan's Commissioner for Customs informed
investigators that a random sampling of the cargo on the flight
had been undertaken prior to the flight but this revealed that all
consignments exactly matched the waybill documentation.

Between August 15 and 25, 1989—two years after the crash—a
special Board of Inquiry was held in Johannesburg to investigate
the crash of flight SA295. Under the chairmanship of South
African judge Cecil Margo, seven other members made up the
Board. They were from the United States, the United Kingdom,
Mauritius, Japan, Taiwan and South Africa. Their deliberations
were held in public and included the testimonies of witnesses
from organizations and groups as diverse as the FAA in the U.S.
and the Boeing company, as well as many others from South
Africa, Taiwan and Mauritius. Their findings were presented in
a report to the Minister of Transport and made public on May
14, 1990.

Distilled down from its highly detailed 264-paged report, the
findings of the Margo Board of Enquiry were that the aircraft
was serviceable and defect-free on take-off. The flight had
proceeded normally until an intense fire had developed in the
right hand forward pallet on the main deck. The substances
involved in the combustion included plastic and cardboard
packing materials, but the actual source of ignition could not
be determined. The fire generated considerable smoke, carbon
monoxide and carbon dioxide which penetrated the passenger
cabin and possibly even the cockpit. The aircraft was out of
control when it smashed into the sea. Sabotage was ruled out.

The Board stated that two possible causes lay behind the actual crash. Firstly, pilot incapacity from carbon monoxide and carbon dioxide poisoning and smoke inhalation, or disorientation due to smoke in the cockpit and hence reduced visibility or pilot distraction. Secondly, damage to the structure and to the control systems of the aircraft directly or indirectly caused by the fire. It went on to say that there was a strong possibility that the quantity of carbon monoxide and carbon dioxide released by the fire caused loss of consciousness or the death of some, if not all, of the occupants before the aircraft hit the sea. The report emphasized that no individual person or agency could be blamed, including the crew, South African Airways or the Boeing Company. However, repeated references were made to the main deck cargo compartment of the Boeing 747-200 Combi aircraft. It was felt that its fire and smoke detection systems were inadequate. As a result, it believed the fire was not discovered early enough to prevent it from spreading. The report stated that speculation and controversy continued to exist regarding the type of cargo that was carried. How and why the fire began could therefore not be determined.

As families grieved loved ones who had been lost in the crash and as the years went by there was no closure, no solution, no end to the mystery of flight SA295. But theories proliferated. Many believers in conspiracy theories and in the idea of government cover-ups conjured up an array of speculations about what might have happened. Most of these were centered on the idea that the South African government—unbeknown to SAA—was using the airline to transport substances into the country that were banned under the international anti-apartheid sanctions in place at that time. Some alleged that the National Party government had been using the airline to also smuggle weapons into the country. There were theorists who argued that an oxidant known as Ammonium Perchlorate (APC) was on board and that this was intended for use as rocket fuel as part of the government's nuclear armaments program. But such theories did not hold up. APC had been produced in South Africa for many years and, as far as weapons were concerned, the country's state-owned Armscor division was already producing sufficient quantities of armaments to fight its border wars, protect itself from foreign invasion and maintain its iron-fisted hold on the apartheid system.

In later years, during the well-publicized Truth and Reconciliation Commission (TRC) hearings that began in post-apartheid South Africa in 1996, the *Helderberg* disaster was once again drawn into the spotlight. Many claimed that the Margo Commission of 1989 had covered up the real facts. A number of testifiers said that Justice Margo and his investigatory board members deliberately withheld or distorted the facts. Many were adamant that the *Helderberg* was carrying dangerous, illicit and contraband materials. A number of people said that SAA was frequently used by the apartheid government to ship weapons into and out of the country. One journalist investigating the crash suggested that South Africa could not produce sufficient amounts of solid rocket fuel for its military operations in Angola in the 1980s and that lethal substances had been shipped from the United States via Taiwan and clandestinely loaded on board the *Helderberg*. Some claimed to have information that there was a fire on board the aircraft shortly after take-off but that the captain thought the flames could be contained. He did not return to the airport to avoid having the real nature of his cargo discovered. A lot of people believed that the airline's senior management and pilots on the international service were fully aware of the practice of shipping armaments and dangerous fuels and other substances into the country. More than one person even went as far as saying that once it was known that there was a fire on board the *Helderberg*, the South African government instructed the air force to shoot down the aircraft so that no evidence could ever be found about what it was actually carrying. Countless numbers of people were convinced that the terrible accident that took the lives of 159 people that dark November night high over the Indian Ocean was merely a result of the cunning deeds of a government acting illegally in the face of international condemnation of its racist policies and its warmongering across the borders of neighboring countries. But the TRC found no evidence of falsification of records, of unlabelled dangerous substances on board or of any information that could refute the findings of the Margo Commission. An open invitation was made to current or retired SAA staff to step up to the TRC witness stand and provide evidence—without fear of retribution—that the airline's management and senior pilots were fully aware of the fact that dangerous substances were often carried on board international flights. But no one ever came forward.

What did come out of the horrific crash was that the FAA and the NTSB in the United States issued a directive on May 16, 1988, to all operators of Boeing 747 Combi aircraft to install additional smoke alarm systems in the cargo compartment and to implement amended new fire-fighting measures. The directive stated that the Combi cargo compartment must have sufficient access to enable a cabin crew member to effectively reach any part of the compartment while in flight. Separate smoke or fire detectors needed to be installed to alert flight crew members at their stations about smoke or fire within the compartment as soon as it began and that immediate measures were to be taken to prevent smoke from the cargo area entering the passenger cabin. Class B cargo compartments—the type such as that on board the Combi—had to comply with standards allowing crew members to leave their normal stations, don protective equipment, enter the cargo compartment without hinderance, locate Halon fire extinguishers, attach extension nozzles to them and point them at a fire within five minutes of the flames being detected. It was further directed that all cargo carried in the rear of passenger aircraft be carried only in fire resistant containers.

Subsequently, the Boeing company itself took remedial action by redesigning and upgrading the alarm system and the safety features of all future Combi and freighter aircraft. After the crash, SAA reconfigured its other Boeing 747 Combi to carry passengers only. No more freight was ever loaded into the rear end of a fuselage in which passengers were seated.

Painful memories, a thousand probabilities and untold uncertainties continued to haunt many about the *Helderberg* for years after the tragedy. Retired SAA pilot Ray Pike recalled how he first felt when he was shown into the hangar at Jan Smuts Airport where wreckage from the aircraft was stored and reassembled about two years after the accident. Prior to retiring in 1986, his last flight was on the *Helderberg*. Confronted by large sections of the broken and bent fuselage with pock-marked and peeling cheat lines of orange, white and blue paint—including a grotesquely dented panel with a section of the Flying Springbok still visible—Pike admitted to experiencing a debilitating and very eerie feeling. He used to fly that plane, he wailed. He spent hundreds of hours piloting it from one corner of the globe to the other. He had crossed all the world's great oceans in it. And now it lay before him, a twisted carcass of its former self. It was overwhelming enough to witness the hulk of what was once the pride of the fleet but when he saw a torn piece of the sponge mattress that had once lined one of the bunks in the small crew rest area behind the cockpit, he was overcome with emotion.

"I cannot recall how many times I dozed on that very mattress during long haul flights," he said in an interview before his death. "The last people to use it are no longer with us. They died in a terrible calamity. And I knew them all personally."

Equally poignant in the tragic drama of the *Helderberg* is a lonely, tall pyramidal-shaped stone monument that sits on the grassy outskirts of a breezy plain near Belle Mare beach in Mauritius. Sadly unkempt today and in dire need of some tender loving care, it is a memorial to the victims of the crash. A rusty bronze plaque on the monument reads: 'In memory of the 159 passengers and crew on South African Airways Boeing 747, ZS-SAS, *Helderberg*, flight SA295 who tragically lost their lives near the coast of Mauritius in the early hours of the morning of 28 November 1987.'

To this day the silent, isolated monument belies the controversy that still rages about the *Helderberg* and about what it might have been carrying. But we may never know the truth. The catastrophic crash that took place that November night in 1987 remains one of the great unsolved mysteries of international civil aviation.

Chapter 16

A New Era

Very few people knew it but far beyond the precincts of aviation
and air travel momentous events were happening in 1982 that
would profoundly affect South Africa, its political make-up, its
economy and its national airline.

On March 28, a motorized launch pulled up at the dock at
Robben Island in the chilly Atlantic waters 4.3 miles northwest
of Cape Town. The island—only 3.5 square miles in area—
was the site of the country's maximum security prison. It was
there that political prisoners—all black and usually jailed with
lifetime sentences—were locked up in solitary confinement in
tiny concrete cells. They spent their days chiseling stones in a
nearby quarry under the eyes of armed white guards. On that
March day, five handcuffed black men were marched out of the
main prison building and boarded the launch. Puttering away
towards Cape Town, the little vessel took the prisoners from
their place of incarceration to Table Bay harbor where, under
heavy guard, they boarded police vans and were relocated to
other prisons. One of the men was the political dissenter Nelson
Mandela who received a life sentence for treason at the much-
publicized Rivonia Treason Trial in June, 1964.

Mandela was transferred to Pollsmoor Prison in a suburb of
Cape Town. There he was to languish for the next six-and-a-
half years. But even though it would never be openly admitted,
his relocation was probably motivated by a sense of inevitability
by the South African government. Apartheid was unsustainable.
It could not possibly last. A handful of the senior inner circle
members of the ruling National Party were beginning to see
the writing on the wall. Their views were shared by members
of a secretive yet very powerful underground Afrikaans

society known as the Broederbond (Brotherhood). It was this organization that created the mechanism whereby Afrikaans politicians and businessmen were able to rise within the ranks of society, taking positions of leadership and dominating the political and business scene for the past forty years. It was now their view that if South Africa was to be spared a bloody civil war and if conflict between black and white was to be avoided, lines of communication had to be opened between the Afrikaner National Party and members of the African National Congress (ANC) of which Mandela was a senior player. The fact that the very name of Nelson Mandela could not be uttered in public on pain of immediate arrest spoke of how much importance the authorities were ascribing to this banned, outlawed and silenced amateur-boxer-cum-lawyer who was the head of the largest— and outlawed—black political organization in the country. In fact, showing or even seeing images of Nelson Mandela were illegal. Quoting him risked immediate arrest.

On September 11, 1985, prison doctors diagnosed 67-year-old Nelson Mandela with an enlarged prostate. He was also found to have cysts on his liver and his right kidney. Immediate surgery was prescribed and successfully carried out. Earlier that year, Mandela had rejected an offer of release from prison by the State President, Pieter W. Botha, because the terms of his freedom included renouncing violence to achieve his political aims. So, he continued to remain behind bars. But, totally unknown to the public at large or to senior members of the ANC who were living abroad or in neighboring countries, South Africa's Minister of Justice, Police and Prisons, Kobie Coetsee, visited Mandela in hospital and opened negotiations between him and the government. This new path of communication was so secretive that during the next few years Mandela was allowed out of prison on numerous occasions and was allowed to reconnect with the world at large. Years before it would actually come to pass, the die had been cast for Mandela's release back into society.

But the pathway to reconciliation was still littered with obstacles. In June 1986, the government had declared a state of emergency following nationwide outbreaks of protest and strikes. Curfews were imposed on many urban areas. Freedom of the press was severely restricted. Thousands were arrested and imprisoned without trial. At the same time, international sanctions were biting ever deeper into all levels of the economy. It was time to change. And everyone knew it.

Meanwhile, SAA's first intake of multi-racial cabin crew took place in 1987. On January 8, 1988, the new recruits began their training at D.F. Malan Airport in Cape Town. After being awarded their wings in March, five black cabin attendants, Glory Legodi, Pinkie Mashele, Cecilia Matila, Thandi Madise and Gloria Mathidi took up their duties flying on domestic routes. They were the first of many to follow. At long last, the airline was officially being allowed to change with the times. As a show of solidarity with the shifting political landscape and to proudly display the familiar symbol of the airline, on March 16, SAA's Chief Executive Gert van der Veer unveiled a statue of the Flying Springbok in front of Airways Towers, the airline's 25-storey administrative headquarters in Braamfontein, Johannesburg.

The changes in employment opportunities with the airline were not only extended to all racial groups but bridged the gender barrier as well. On June 2, 1988, SAA employed its first female pilots. Brenda Howett, Jane Trembath and Jennifer Burger began working as in-flight relief First Officers on Boeing 747s on the international service, then progressed to full First Officers on the regional and domestic Boeing 737 fleet. Following that position, they advanced to First Officers on the 747s and, eventually, to the ranks of Captain. Brenda Howett had originally joined SAA as a Boeing 747 simulator instructor on December 1, 1983.

Whilst political dissent stole the headlines during most of 1988, the airline continued to pull out all the stops to develop its reputation as an efficient and trustworthy air carrier. On June

20, 1988, it attained its highest domestic on-time departure rate with a record 99.3 per cent on-time departures, one of the highest in the world. In August that year, SAA celebrated 25 years of uninterrupted and accident-free service flying around the bulge of Africa to European and Middle Eastern destinations. 1988 was also the year that the airline decided to order two Airbus A320 aircraft for the domestic and regional routes. In September, all the Boeing 747 aircraft in the fleet were reconfigured. Boeing 747-300s were altered to carry 34 Blue Diamond (First Class) passengers, 61 in Gold Class (Business Class) and 223 in Silver Class (Coach.) The 747-200s were reconfigured for 27 Blue Diamond, 76 Gold Class and 196 Silver Class passengers. Boeing 747SPs were revamped to carry 28 in Blue Diamond, 44 in Gold Class and 159 in Silver Class while the single remaining Boeing 747 Combi was altered to accommodate 28 in Blue Diamond, 76 in Gold Class and 200 in Silver Class. These changes were made to comply with market demands on the international routes served by those aircraft.

On November 1, 1988, new international timetables came into effect. In addition to the Springbok Service to London, the airline's route structure made use of three hubs in Europe, namely Lisbon, Zurich and Frankfurt with extensions to Amsterdam, Paris, Rome, Vienna and Tel Aviv. Due to low load factors services to Brussels and Madrid were discontinued and flights to Athens also ceased because of the expense of flying there all the way around the bulge of Africa. In December 1988, a new record was set when the airline transported over 500,000 passengers in a single month.

But other things were happening that month too. On December 7, 1988, Nelson Mandela was transferred from Pollsmoor Prison to Victor Verster Prison Farm, about 50 miles outside Cape Town. There the government had built him a large, comfortable house. He was allowed frequent visitors, he swam in the pool with his wardens, his refrigerator and kitchen were stocked with his favourite foods and he made regular incognito visits far beyond the walls of his garden to Cape Town and other environs. Day by day, month by month, he was being groomed for eventual release. But when would that be? At that time, no one knew.

On July 5, 1989, the unthinkable happened. Mandela was taken to visit President Pieter W. Botha at his official residence in Cape Town where the President was recuperating from a mild stroke. The meeting was cordial and conducive, though no firm date was set for Mandela's release. Unlike some of the more liberal and enlightened members of his cabinet and the National Party caucus, Botha would not let go. He steadfastly held on to the notion that if he continued to detain Mandela—especially in the comfort and luxury of his house at Victor Verster Prison Farm—Mandela and the leadership of the ANC may still be willing to renounce violence to end apartheid. Who knows? They may even be amenable to negotiating a possible power-sharing arrangement between the ANC and the National Party. But Mandela and the ANC were not going to compromise.

Botha was also suffering the indignity of having to accept a peace accord with rebels, freedom fighters and Cuban troops in Angola which resulted from diplomatic wrangling abroad between US President Ronald Reagan and Soviet Premier Mikhail Gorbachev. The treaty that ended the Angolan war also led to South Africa being forced to comply with UN Security Council Resolution 435 in which South Africa was finally compelled to relinquish its control over South-West Africa. After decades of failed diplomacy and a costly military campaign that took countless lives, it was now possible for that vast territory to become the fully independent nation of Namibia.

On February 2, 1989, Botha resigned as leader of the National Party. In March, the party nominated the Minister of Education Frederick W. de Klerk to head it and then nominated him to replace Botha as President. But Botha clung to his position.

However, by August, he could no longer assert his role and he resigned as President. In September, de Klerk took over the position and, without delay, began to implement drastic measures to end apartheid. While claiming that his actions were never a result of a spiritual epiphany such as that experienced by the biblical apostle Paul on the road to Damascus, de Klerk was quick to realize that unless apartheid came to a swift end the country may not be able to face the consequences. Loss of South-West Africa, escalating dissent among black communities inside the country, widespread violence, crippling international sanctions and the erosive loss of friends and trading partners would bring South Africa to its knees, with no one left to help it fight the possible civil war that was undoubtedly brewing within its borders. When questioned about his actions in later years, he had no hesitation to say that his fundamental motive was to do it to 'preserve my people.' In other words, the Afrikaner nation would have been doomed to extinction if they did not accept change and unburden themselves from the scourge of apartheid. As a minority group, they would have been steamrollered into oblivion by the rising forces massing against them. And, in all likelihood, they would have taken the entire white community of South Africa down with them.

The changes in the political structure of the country heralded colossal changes for SAA. On March 3, 1989, the first non-white pilot, an Indian, Nasseem Mahomedy, joined the airline. On May 9, he was First Officer on board flight SA248 bound from Johannesburg to Frankfurt. With political dispensation slowly getting underway in South Africa, inch by inch the doors of Africa were once again creaking open. On April 1, SAA operated its first service between Johannesburg and Lubumbashi—formerly known as Elisabethville—in the southern province of Shaba of the Republic of Zaire (modern-day Congo). With international services beginning to pick up, in May, the airline announced that it was purchasing two new Boeing 747-400 aircraft, with an option for two more. The delivery dates were set for November 1990 and May 1991. On June 3, 1989, SAA operated its first Hajj pilgrimage flight for Muslims from Johannesburg to Cairo. Pilgrims were flown from Cairo to Jeddah in Saudi Arabia on other carriers. On June 6, regular SAA passenger services went into operation between Johannesburg and Cairo, the first time since flights ceased way back in 1956.

On August 1, 1989, Boeing 737 ZS-SIA was leased to Namib Air. Boeing 747SP ZS-SPF was leased to Luxair on the same date. Suddenly, SAA found itself short of equipment to operate domestic and regional services so a Boeing 737-200 registered CS-TEU was leased from Air Atlantis of Portugal. Three months later, on November 4, SAA introduced a third weekly service to Taipei from Johannesburg.

On October 15, 1989, President Frederick W. de Klerk freed four of Nelson Mandela's senior ANC colleagues from prison. Many saw this as a foreshadowing of things to come and that it would not be long before Mandela himself would be released. And yet, the aging grey-haired representative of the ANC remained a prisoner in his house within the grounds of Victor Verster Prison Farm.

By December 1989, SAA's fleet stood at forty aircraft, consisting of seventeen Boeing 737s with one leased out, thirteen Boeing 747s with three 747SPs leased out and nine Airbus A300 with one leased out. One Boeing 737 was on lease from Air Atlantis. On order were two Boeing 747-400s and seven Airbus A320 aircraft. Passenger traffic was slowly on the increase. The transportation of freight was healthy. Things were looking up. In 1990, Cyprus-based *Travel Trade* magazine gave SAA its distinguished Gold Award for the top airline in Africa and the Middle East. It was to be the first of many similar awards issued to the airline in the coming years.

As bright as things were beginning to look no one was quite expecting the earth-shattering events that took place on

February 2, 1990. On that day, the status quo of South African politics changed for all time. Delivering a speech in parliament in Cape Town, President Frederick W. de Klerk announced that he was lifting the 30-year ban on the African National Congress and other illegal political organizations. What's more, he stated, Nelson Mandela would soon be released from prison. These sweeping moves went far beyond what anyone—either at home or abroad—was expecting. In effect, the speech openly dealt a death blow to apartheid. It also meant that white rule was over. It would only be a matter of time before South Africa would become the democratic, multi-racial nation that people like Nelson Mandela had been fighting for. Nine days later, Mandela walked out of Victor Verster Prison a free man, to the jubilation of South Africans of all colors and, indeed, to the cheers of tens of millions glued to TV screens around the world. A new era had finally dawned.

On March 23, 1990, SAA operated its first regular service between Johannesburg and Manchester in the U.K. On April 1, SAA's parent organization, South African Transport Services— an incarnation of the old South African Railways and Harbors Administration, or SAR & H—was reorganized as Transnet, a quoted company in compliance with the South African Companies Act. While the South African government remained in full control at the top of the structure, SAA became a division of Transnet with a full board of directors. A few months later, South African Airways was renamed South African Airways (Proprietary) Limited, which is tantamount to the status of a private corporation but with the South African government as the sole holding company.

On April 1, Boeing 747SP ZS-SPF was leased to Namib Air, the young airline of the newly independent Republic of Namibia. On April 10, SAA began operating a weekly flight from South Africa to Brazil, routing from Johannesburg to Rio de Janeiro, Sao Paulo and back to Johannesburg. April 26 saw the launch of SAA's

African Wildlife Heritage Trust, under which SAA undertook to donate a portion of the revenue received from every international ticket sold towards preserving Africa's endangered wildlife. In September 1990, *Executive Travel Magazine* voted SAA the 'Best Carrier to Africa' for a third consecutive year. On December 1, the Flying Springbok returned to Nairobi once again when regular services were reinstated between South Africa and Kenya after a break of 27 years.

In January 1991, the first female technical apprentices were engaged at the airline's maintenance base at Jan Smuts Airport. On January 21, the first Boeing 747-400, ZS-SAV, *Durban*, arrived from the factory in Seattle. The delivery crew was Johan Dries, Alan Dros, Quentin Mouton and two Boeing training captains, Oleg Komanitsky and Dan Bourne. On February 22, it operated its first revenue-earning service from Johannesburg to London, arriving at Heathrow after a non-stop flight of 12 hours 16 minutes.

While the 747-400 looked very much like the 747-300 on the outside, on the inside it was a very different and far more advanced airplane. The only distinguishing exterior feature that separated it from the 300 series were winglets on the tips of each wing. Winglets were specifically designed to cut down wingtip vortices, swirls of air created by the difference in pressure between the upper and lower surfaces of an airplane's wing. Vortices can be very dangerous and destabilizing to other aircraft flying in the wake of the big 747-400. But winglets also dramatically reduce drag, allowing for shorter take-off distances, higher speeds in the air and significant savings in fuel. Unlike the Boeing 747-200 or 300, the 400 series was also known as an airliner with a 'glass cockpit.' This is a simplified way of saying that the flight deck was equipped with electronic or digital flight instrumentation and displays—most often in the form of large LCD touch-screens—as opposed to the older type of analog dials, gauges, instruments, buttons and switches. Sophisticated computerization did away with the need for a flight engineer so the cockpit was designed to accommodate only a two-person crew.

Boeing 747-400, 1991

SAA's Boeing 747-444 had a length of 231 ft, a wingspan of 218 ft and a height of 64 ft. Its empty weight was 396,830 lbs and its maximum take-off weight 868,621 lbs. It had a cruising speed of 564 mph and a maximum speed of 700 mph or Mach 0.92. Its operating ceiling was 45,100 feet and its maximum range 6,900 miles. The airliner was equipped with four Rolls-Royce RB.211-524GT-T-19/15 engines. Each one produced 58,000 lbs of thrust. Even though there were only two crew members on the flight deck during long-haul operations, a back-up relief crew of two pilots was carried. Eighteen cabin crew members took care of passengers.

Although SAA Technical at Jan Smuts Airport in Johannesburg remained one of the largest and best maintenance facilities in the southern hemisphere, it was not adequately equipped to handle the Rolls Royce RB-211 engines that were fitted to the new Boeing 747-400 fleet. These engines were maintained and serviced at London's Heathrow Airport. As SAA's aircraft normally spent a full day at Heathrow after a flight had arrived from South Africa, there was adequate time to sub-contract the work to either Rolls Royce or to a private maintenance operator. If an engine was due for major work or an overhaul, it was removed from the aircraft and a replacement engine was fitted in time for the evening departure back to South Africa. In the past, SAA had always overhauled and maintained its own engines but now a lot of the work was being outsourced, in keeping with industry trends around the world. In the tight financial environment of the times this method was proving to be extremely cost effective.

On April 3, 1991, a new West African service began from Johannesburg to Abidjan on the Côte d'Ivoire (Ivory Coast) and Kinshasa—the former Leopoldville—in Zaire (Congo). On June 1, a service was introduced to Milan from Johannesburg. Milan replaced Rome on the Italian service because of greater commercial opportunities in that predominantly industrial city. On June 7, flights to Europe were rerouted directly over the West African nations of Mali, Mauretania and Morocco. On September 8, Egypt and the Sudan lifted their ban on SAA overflying their territories. For the first time in 28 years, African airspace was once again open to aircraft registered in South Africa. It was a momentous development, finally bringing an end to the lengthy, tedious and costly detour of having to fly around the bulge of Africa. Once more the Flying Springbok was free to roam the skies of its home continent.

Bans and barricades were now falling everywhere. Five days before the commencement of the East African route that took SAA over the Sahara once again, China Airlines began operating a direct service between Taipei and Johannesburg. A month later, Air Austral began operating flights between Reunion Island and Johannesburg. Also in October, Athens was once again added as a destination to SAA's route network. Now SAA services could fly a non-stop, direct route to Greece without fear of being apprehended or shot down in African airspace. Suddenly, SAA was once again an integral part of the aviation community of the continent. Seemingly overnight, Africa welcomed it back into the fold.

On November 1, 1991, SAA signed an interline agreement with the Soviet airline, Aeroflot. Just a couple of years earlier such an arrangement would have been unthinkable. Then, on November 3, SAA reintroduced Boeing 747 services between Johannesburg and New York once again, flying via Ilha do Sal. Flights between South Africa and the United States had been halted by order of Congress four years earlier. As soon as the service commenced, load factors were excellent. As the only carrier flying directly between South Africa and the United States the flights were very popular with passengers as well as with companies specializing in cargo and freight.

Within the first year, over 50,000 American tourists were carried from New York to Johannesburg. The country was hot. The airline was hot. Prospects for the route exceeded all expectations.

Airbus A320, 1991

The first Airbus A320 ZS-SHA *Blue Crane* arrived in Johannesburg from the factory in Toulouse, France on November 9, 1991. Traveling from Toulouse via Casablanca in Morocco and Abidjan in the Ivory Coast, the aircraft landed at Jan Smuts Airport after a 12-hour flight. At the controls were SAA Captains John Withers, Gerhard Robberts and Grant MacAlpine.

The A320 was perfect for operating the airline's domestic and regional route network.

SAA's Airbus A320-321 had a wingspan of 112.25 ft and a length of 123.25 ft. Its maximum take-off weight was 162,038 lbs. Service ceiling was 39,000 feet. Cruising speed was 520 mph or Mach 0.82. Its range was 2,940 miles. It was equipped with two underwing International Aero (IAE) V2500-A1 turbofan engines each producing 25,000 lbs of thrust. It carried a two-person flight crew and three or four cabin attendants. A narrow-body aircraft with a single aisle, it could accommodate 25 passengers in business class and 95 in coach.

In December 1991, Kenya Airways introduced flights between Nairobi and Johannesburg and, on December 5, SAA made its first foray into the Soviet Union by flying a Boeing 747 to Moscow to pick up the cast, supporting personnel, props and wardrobe of the Moscow State Circus for their first performance in South Africa. Not only was this a major event in the history of South Africa and SAA but also for the Soviet Union. Three weeks later, on December 26, 1991, the Soviet flag came down over the Kremlin and was replaced by the flag of the Commonwealth of Independent states. Russia had been born anew. Times were changing dramatically all over the world. Communism in Eastern Europe was dead. The Berlin wall had fallen. West and East Germany had been unified. Apartheid was over. All that remained now was for a new constitution to be written for South Africa, for people of all racial groups in the country to be given the vote and for a new government to be elected.

On January 18, 1992, SAA flights between Johannesburg and Sydney, Australia were resumed. Later that month, a new corporate wardrobe was introduced for all SAA air crew and ground personnel. On January 30, SAA was voted the world's best airline serving Africa for the fourth consecutive year. In March, Singapore Airlines began operating to South Africa. That month SAA reopened its sales office in Toronto. In April, Air Tanzania signed a partnership agreement with SAA and started flying between Mombasa and Dar es Salaam to Johannesburg. Also in April, SAA signed a cooperative agreement with Czechoslovakian Airlines for services connecting Johannesburg with Prague. Eight months later, Czechoslovakia was reborn as the Czech Republic.

With the demise of apartheid, South Africa was rapidly being reaccepted into the world community. Of primary importance to sports-crazy South Africans, international sports barriers began to fall too. On April 4, SAA flew the official South African cricket team to a test match in Kingston, Jamaica. Because of his ground-breaking political actions President Frederick W. de Klerk was no longer a *persona non-grata* in the world arena. Between May 31 and June 8, 1992, he undertook a whirlwind tour to explain his motives and reasons for dismantling apartheid to national leaders and various organizations abroad. SAA's Boeing 747-200 ZS-SAO *Magaliesberg* was designated as his aerial chariot. The upper deck was converted into a private bedroom for de Klerk and his wife and, with Captains Koos Vermaak and Dave Germishuis in charge of the flight, assisted by First Officers Chris Fourie and Nick Valengoed, Flight Engineers Peter Kiely and Dennis Barry, and Flight Planner Derek Whittal, de Klerk was whisked around the globe to Moscow, St. Petersburg, Tokyo and Singapore. In the rear of the aircraft was a contingent of assistants, secretaries, security personnel and members of the press.

On June 2, 1992, SAA introduced regular services between Johannesburg and Bangkok, Thailand. Two days later it commenced weekly flights to Singapore. On June 23, a partnership agreement was signed with Abidjan-based Air

Afrique. In December,, a weekly non-stop flight was introduced between Cape Town and Miami, Florida. In February 1993 Cyprus was included as a stop-over on SAA's service between Johannesburg and Tel Aviv. On June 30, Hamburg became an additional destination on services to Germany. In September flights were resumed between Johannesburg and Lisbon. On October 21, SAA introduced a weekly flight to Dubai in the United Arab Emirates.

SAA also entered into an agreement with Ukrainian operator Antau to operate three Russian-built Ilyushin Il-76 and a couple of Antonov An-26 freighters on regional and domestic routes in South Africa. These services were initially very profitable due to the relatively low salaries paid to the Ukranian crews who flew them, but the aircraft were plagued with technical problems. SAA found that an Airbus A300 that it had converted into a freighter to haul cargo on the same routes as the Russian-made machines used fifty per cent less fuel than they did. The collaboration soon ended.

On December 10, 1993, something very special happened. On that day President Frederick W. de Klerk and Nelson Mandela jointly received the Nobel Prize for Peace at a glittering ceremony in Oslo, Norway. The world watched and applauded the two men whose efforts had brought down apartheid. That in itself was an extraordinary accomplishment. But what made it so unique and such a contradiction to what most people had been expecting was the fact that the racist system fell without the spilling of a single drop of blood. The war that most South Africans and political pundits around the globe were predicting never happened. Mandela's personality and incredible conciliatory demeanour prevented a catastrophe. He galvanized everyone—black and white—into making the transition to a free, democratic society with minimal animosity. It is to his eternal credit that the so-called 'Rainbow Nation' was born under the African sun in a spirit of peace and goodwill, devoid of bloodshed, rage and revenge.

1993 was the year when all of the country's major airports were transferred to the control of a new state-owned corporation known as the Airports Company of South Africa (ACSA). All nine major airports—Johannesburg, Cape Town, Durban, Port Elizabeth, East London, Kimberley, Bloemfontein, Upington and George—were previously under the control of the Department of Transport but now financial responsibility, operations, maintenance and future development became the task of ACSA. Its purpose was to act as a semi-independent profit-driven entity under the ownership of the state.

On January 18, 1994, SAA was once again voted 'Best Airline to Africa' by readers of the US-based *Business Traveller International* magazine. As a run-up to the eagerly anticipated general election to choose a new government the face of South Africa and many of its apartheid-era institutions began to change in a variety of ways. On April 4, 1994, Jan Smuts International Airport—the nation's primary aerial gateway named in honor of the late white Prime Minister Field Marshal Jan Christiaan Smuts—was renamed Johannesburg International Airport. It would not be long before the name was changed again to Oliver Tambo International, a much revered anti-apartheid activist who served as President of the African National Congress (ANC) from 1967 to 1991. With apartheid gone, other things were changing too.

On April 27, 1994, a brand new national flag was officially adopted by the country. Replacing the old flag with its orange, white and blue bands containing miniature versions of the British Union Jack, the Zuid-Afrikaansche Republiek 'vierkleur' ('four colors') of the old Transvaal Boer Republic and the 'Dutch tricolor' of the Boer Republic of the Orange Free State superimposed over the center white band, the colourful new flag was designed by the country's State Herald, Frederick Brownell. Incorporating a horizontal band of red on the top, one of blue on the bottom and a central green band that splits into a horizontal

'Y' shape, the colors incorporate all those from the original British and Dutch flags that preceded the formation of the Union of South Africa in 1910, plus the green, black and yellow colors of the African National Congress (ANC).

But no event—before or since—equalled the epochal significance of the days between April 26 and 29, 1994. Those were the dates when the country's first openly democratic, non-racial general election took place. Contested by no less than 28 separate political parties, the election brought out people in their millions, most of them voting for the very first time in their lives. Queues lined up for hours and, in some cases, for days in cities, towns, villages, rural areas, mines, farms and Bantustans or 'homelands' in rain, hail, dust, wind and sunshine to cast their votes at more than 9,000 polling stations, staffed by 200,000 specially trained personnel. Over 20 million people marked their ballots and indicated their choice of candidates, not only in South Africa itself but at South African embassies, legations and consular offices around the world, from Beverly Hills to Berlin. It was an election on an epic scale. When the ballot papers were collected and counted the results were not surprising. The African National Congress, the ANC—the party of Nelson Mandela—had won a landslide victory.

On May 10, 1994, in the regal amphitheatre of the Union Buildings in Pretoria —the official administrative heart of the nation—Nelson Mandela took the oath of office and was sworn in as South Africa's first black president. Three days later, on May 13, SAA reflected the new leadership and the new democratic nature of the country by switching to a different form of greeting passengers over the public address system on board all aircraft on international flights. Instead of using only English and Afrikaans as before, now a friendly multi-lingual message included the vernacular languages of Zulu and Sotho, two of the dominant black languages of South Africa.

A new day, a new beginning, a fresh start, had finally come.

Chapter 17

A New Identity

By 1994, the commercial aviation industry in South Africa had been fully deregulated. That decision had been taken in 1991. While at first it had seemed like a good idea and opened the way for more airlines to take to the southern skies of Africa as well as creating a more competitive spirit, in hindsight it may not have been the most expedient choice for SAA. What was once the exclusive preserve of the national airline was now open to all. As the next few years unfolded, deregulation would bring about major economic ramifications for SAA.

In March, SA Express Airways (SAX) was granted a license to operate domestically. SAA was a twenty per cent shareholder in the new carrier. SAX's main purpose was to act as a feeder service for SAA and to take over some of SAA's low density internal routes. Long-time low cost carrier Trek Airways decided to switch its focus from flying to Europe and also formed a new domestic airline. Three years earlier, its foreign operation, Luxavia, had been merged with newly-formed Flitestar. By 1994, it was operating a service to Europe using a Boeing 747SP that it had leased from SAA plus four Airbus A320s and two ATR 72s turboprop short-haul aircraft on domestic routes. Flitestar became SAA's main competitor on the domestic front but as the value of the South African rand fell in relation to the US dollar and as the worldwide airline industry quavered in the face of rising costs Flitestar was finding it very difficult to remain aloft. On April 11, 1994, Trek Airways shut down both Luxavia and Flitestar and the company was liquidated, leaving SAA as the dominant player on the domestic scene. But there was no room for complacency. Other domestic carriers were either waiting in the wings or already flying, ratcheting up the competition.

In May, SAA's sales and ticketing office on the corner of Oxford Street and Regent Street at Oxford Circus in London was closed and relocated to St. George's House on Conduit Street. With the closing of the Oxford Circus office—regarded for years by many industry insiders as the prime location of any airline office in London's West End—what had long been a landmark in the city came to an end. There were many who mourned the closing. Even during the virulent anti-apartheid years, passersby often stopped outside the offices to gaze longingly at posters depicting South African cities, beaches and wildlife basking in golden sunshine, always tantalizing images that beckoned amidst the busy sidewalks, heavy traffic and all-too-frequent rainfall in the city.

In July 1994, SAA received a very special honor. In order to pay tribute to the airline now that it had been freed from the bonds of apartheid and to recognize its extensive contribution to the development of aviation in Africa, it was invited to attend an international gathering of aircraft at Oshkosh, Wisconsin in the US. The annual event was known at the time as the Experimental Aircraft Association (EAA) Annual Convention and Fly-In and was a celebration of historic, modern, experimental, commercial, military, sport and home-built airplanes from around the globe. To take up the invitation, the airline reacquired one of its Douglas DC-4 Skymasters that had been sold to the South African Air Force (SAAF) in 1966. The Skymaster, ZS-BMH *Lebombo*, was repainted in original 1950s-style SAA livery and on July 19, 1994, it departed from Johannesburg for Oshkosh flying by way of Mokuti in Namibia, Abidjan, Las Palmas, the Azores and St. John in Newfoundland. On board were aviation enthusiasts from around the world who had snapped up seats for the once-in-a-lifetime trip. ZS-BMH was the very last DC-4 to have come off the Douglas Aircraft Company's production line in Santa Monica, California in July, 1947. As such, it held the ranks of being one of commercial aviation's most historic aircraft. It was originally delivered to SAA on August 9, 1947. The airplane was a huge draw at the Oshkosh show, primarily because of the pristine state to which it had been restored. In 1994, it was one of only a handful of DC-4s in the world that were still airworthy. The beautiful bird with its four Pratt & Whitney R-2000 radial engines did numerous low-level flights over Oshkosh, generating invaluable publicity and goodwill for the beloved old Skymaster as well as for SAA. The return journey from Oshkosh to Johannesburg was via Gander in Newfoundland, the Azores, Funchal in Madeira, Las Palmas, Abidjan and Windhoek.

By August 1994, it had become clear that SAA had overstretched its resources. Despite the upbeat ambience following Mandela's release it was finding it difficult to re-establish itself on the world's stage. Though acting with all honesty and with every good intention, its optimism was not paying off. Some of its new routes were not proving profitable at all so services to Milan, Hamburg and Manchester were cancelled. The Birmingham and Glasgow offices were closed. At the same time, a new service was inaugurated to Dusseldorf, Germany. In September, flights to Lisbon, Athens and Cairo were terminated due to low load factors. Later that year, a Best Traveller magazine readership survey voted SAA 'Best Airline for First Class Travel Worldwide,' not an insignificant accomplishment for a relatively small airline based at the southern end of Africa. On December 2, a new African airline, Alliance Air, was launched in Dar es Salaam, Tanzania. This was a three-way venture between SAA and the governments of Tanzania and Uganda. In February 1995, SAA placed its Boeing 747SP ZS-SPA at the disposal of the new carrier, repainting it in a livery that included a striking lion's head painted on the vertical stabilizer.

At the beginning of 1995, SAA joined forces with American Airlines in a shared Advantage/Voyager frequent flyer program. Services to Buenos Aires were cancelled due to unprofitability of that route but, at the same time, a new twice-weekly service was launched to Bombay, India, with one flight routed via Dubai. In April, SAA's cargo service was unanimously voted 'Favorite Cargo Airline Carrier to Africa' by shippers and cargo agents around the world. Two months later, the airline was voted 'Best Business Class Airline to Africa.'

Now that South Africa was once again part of the international sports community, the 1995 Rugby World Cup was held in the country. SAA was one of the sponsors of the games. Without letting anyone know about it the airline—inspired by a brilliant campaign planned by its ad agency, Sonnenberg, Murphy, Leo Burnett—decided to pull off an advertising coup by making an appearance over Ellis Park Stadium in Johannesburg on the day the final game was played. As the South African team, the Springboks, battled it out against the New Zealand team, the All Blacks—a reference to their all black jerseys, shorts and socks—on June 24, Boeing 747-200 Super B ZS-SAN *Lebombo* with Captain Laurie Kay at the controls descended from the sky and made two slow, low level passes over the stadium to the tumultuous roar of over 60,000 delighted rugby fans. The flyover was witnessed not only by those attending the final but by tens of millions of viewers watching the game on TV around the world. As the big jet passed overhead the wording 'Good Luck Bokke' (Good luck, Bucks), painted in bold black letters, was clearly visible on the underside of its wings and fuselage. Nothing could possibly have generated more potent publicity than that. And the message worked. Just before the big game ended the Springboks clinched their final goal, winning the game 15 to 12. At the end of the match, President Nelson Mandela strode out onto the field from his presidential box and donned a Springbok rugby shirt and cap presented to him by the winning team. It was another monumental gesture by that remarkable man, once again helping to bridge chasms between the country's white and black communities. Understandably, many blacks still saw rugby as a privileged white man's sport. The scene—including the flyover of the 747—was immortalized in the 2009 motion picture *Invictus* directed by Clint Eastwood and starring Matt Damon and Sidney Poitier.

On July 3, 1995, SAA launched its Cadet Pilot Training Program to provide 'historically disadvantaged individuals'— in other words, blacks—the opportunity to join the airline and to be trained as pilots for SAA at BAE Systems Flight Training College in Adelaide, Australia. And so ended the last remaining racial barrier within the airline left over from the apartheid era.

By October, there were 12 weekly flights serving London from South Africa. New first and business class lounges had been opened at various airports, including a state-of-the-art facility at Cape Town International airport, formerly known as D.F. Malan. But this was not enough. With the country presenting a completely fresh face to the world and with a black majority government in power, it was felt that the time had come for SAA to abandon its 61-year-old image. Over a period of weeks in 1995, the airline's board of directors met to investigate the possibility of reinventing the airline's corporate identity. Discussions ranged over topics to do with altering the livery of aircraft, the logo on the tail and even the design of tickets, timetables, menus and baggage tags.

The prevailing belief was that with the release of Nelson Mandela in 1994, the national airline should reflect what many were calling the 'The New South Africa.' To meet this need SAA put out a brief to 19 international and local ad and publicity agencies, inviting them to respond with a suitable proposal for rebranding the airline. This invitation created a feverish scramble among the agencies. All wanted to be assigned the prestigious and historic task. One of the agencies was Diefenbach Elkins of New York. The firm had had previously worked for major corporations such as Mastercard and Eastman Kodak. They were very anxious to secure the contract so they hired New York-based

South African Tony McKeever to advise on how to go about attaining the job. McKeever had previous strategic publicity and branding experience with AeroMexico, Mexicana Airlines, Austrian Airlines and Royal Jordanian Airlines. McKeever contacted Herd Buoys Marketing of Sandton, Johannesburg, asking them to offer indigenous South African input for the campaign. Herd Buoys had been involved in campaigns for Coca-Cola in South Africa and for the national electricity generating and supply commission, Escom. This turned out to be a fruitful alliance and the partnership beat out all the other 18 contenders.

With the contract in place Diefenbach Elkins and Herd Buoys began working on the enormous task of bringing about a new image for the airline. As Ian Bromley, senior manager for marketing communications at SAA, said at the time, "We're looking for something that gives us a break with the past and a key to the future."

Bromley likened the rebranding program to the changing of the South African flag.

"The flag is a combination of images that people have found attractive," he said. "We at SAA see ourselves as having the same potential."

Peter Vundla, managing director of Herd Buoys, added that the new identity project "must reposition the airline not only internally but externally because the world has suddenly opened up to us after so much isolation. We have just come out of a regimented, divided and polarized society. Because of apartheid we were never able to develop a common national character or a common 'South Africanism,' if you will. There just isn't a single unifying icon that all segments of the population can identify with. We need to change that."

There was truth in what he said. Many black South Africans associated the orange tail of the airline with the apartheid regime, especially because it so closely resembled the predominant hue of the old National Party's color scheme. Equally important, according to Tony McKeever who was now in charge of the project, the symbol of the Flying Springbok was no longer appropriate. The winged antelope was an image that had come from a previous time, an era relegated to the past. Perhaps it was fitting to rethink things. A research program was implemented to test four possible design directions from 2,500 different elements that had been generated from images depicting the national icons of South Africa, including its flora, fauna, landscape and flag. McKeever appointed the company Research Surveys to join the team of Diefenbach Elkins and Herd Buoys and they began questioning South African consumers, airline employees, fliers in overseas markets such as London, Frankfurt, New York and Hong Kong and even SAA'S frequent flier members to determine what kind of new livery would best suit the airline. The four possible directions were carefully tested against the liveries of British Airways, Lufthansa, Cathay Pacific, as well as the old SAA corporate identity, the Flying Springbok. In addition, a public participation process was launched in South Africa. Blank outlines of an Airbus were distributed via inserts in millions of national newspapers published by the *Sunday Times*, *Rapport* and *City Press*. Readers were asked to draw or color in design suggestions for the new SAA logo and livery. More than a half-million proposals were received from design agencies, schools, art colleges, individuals and amateur groups. Almost 98 per cent of the submissions were derivatives of the new South African flag.

As often happens when new things come along, some revered and much-loved traditions have to give way. This was the case with the Flying Springbok logo. After representing the airline for over sixty years, it was time for it to go. Behind closed doors at Diefenbach Elkins' offices in Rockefeller Plaza in New York, a new livery and color scheme gradually began to take shape on computerized drawing boards. The design that won was code-named 'Horizon Mark.' But there was still much work to be done. It was too early to show anything to the world.

By 1996, the airline employed 11,000 people and operated a fleet of 48 aircraft. With the coming of that year, a new in-flight magazine, *Flight Path*, made its first appearance on board. On January 19, Boeing 747SP ZS-SPE *Hantam* (a mountain range in the Northern Cape province) suffered severe turbulence off the Mozambique coast while operating a flight to Jeddah. A sudden downdraft caused the aircraft to drop 5,000 feet in just a few seconds. The on-board dinner service was in progress and many passengers were not wearing their seat belts. A few suffered serious injuries as they were flung from their seats and hit the overhead panels and ceiling. Fortunately, Captain Tom Bremner, First Officer Andre van Rensburg and Flight Engineer Trevor Paulses managed to return the aircraft safely to Johannesburg so that the injured could receive urgent treatment.

For the sixth year in succession, SAA was voted 'Best Airline to Africa' by *Best Travel* magazine. In January, 1996, the third intake of black cadet pilots began their training at BAE Systems Flight Training College in Adelaide, Australia. That month ticketless travel was introduced on all routes. Also in January, the readers of *Executive Travel* magazine voted SAA 'Best Airline to Africa.' In March, additional flights were added to the schedule for services to Bombay and Hong Kong. In April, a new service was introduced between Johannesburg and Accra, Ghana.

Now that South Africa was readmitted as a participant in the Olympic Games, SAA's Boeing 747-300 ZS-SAJ *Ndizani* (a Zulu word meaning 'Flying to New Heights') was painted in a riotous array of patterns and symbols based on the colors of the new flag. In June, the airliner was used to fly the entire South African Olympics team and their trainers from Johannesburg to Atlanta, Georgia for the 1996 Summer Olympics. In October, Singapore was dropped as a destination and was replaced by Bangkok as the airline's primary hub in Asia. On February 1, 1997, smoking was prohibited throughout the cabin on all flights to and from the United States. That month an alliance was formed between SAA, SA Express Airways and new local carrier, South African Airlink.

Income for 1997 climbed to R5.68 billion (South African rands) but, due to increasing competition, high fuel prices and a 35 per cent drop in the value of the rand, the airline posted a loss of R323 million ($45 million US dollars). This was a trend that would continue to bedevil the airline.

On March 22, 1997, SAA's redesigned corporate identity was officially unveiled to the press in Johannesburg. On April 3, at a gala function in New York, the modernistic red, green, black, white, blue and gold logo was shown to the U.S. press and travel industry. Following that event, the entire aircraft fleet was slowly converted from the old orange, white and blue livery to the bold new design. The vertical stabilizer or tail now depicted a completely revamped color scheme that some dubbed 'African Horizon.' It embodied all the colors of the new South African flag with the fuselage and wings painted plain white. Gone forever was any Afrikaans wording on the aircraft. Previously, the name 'South African Airways' was depicted on one side of the fuselage with the Afrikaans equivalent, 'Suid-Afrikaanse Lugdiens' on the other. Now only the English wording 'SOUTH AFRICAN' appeared in big capital lettering on both sides. But, to the mournful dismay of many old-timers, staff members, aviation buffs and loyal SAA passengers around the globe, gone too was the Flying Springbok icon.

But although no longer visible, the Flying Springbok had not become entirely extinct. The international radio call sign of all SAA flights remained 'Springbok.' Whenever the flight crew of an SAA aircraft called in to an air traffic control center (ATC) or an airport tower at home or abroad, they always announced the flight as 'Springbok Two Zero Four' or whatever the number of the flight may have been. Likewise, the reverse was also true. When ATC or a tower wanted to establish contact with an SAA

Boeing 747-400 in post-apartheid SAA livery, 1997. Eye-catching and indicative of the spirit of the new South African flag, gone forever was the much beloved Flying Springbok emblem.

flight, the outgoing message began with 'Springbok Two Zero Four' or whatever the flight number was. So, the Springbok may have been visually banished from aircraft fuselages, tails, billboards, airport buildings, passenger tickets, check-in kiosks, menus and advertising material but to the relief of all who mourned its passing it had by no means been entirely expurgated from the skies. Every flight remained a Springbok flight. But, sadly, that much-treasured antelope with its stylized outstretched wings would never be seen again.

In its new incarnation, the airline experimented with many additional international destinations. But in hindsight, there were perhaps too many new routes. Unlike the lucrative services to London, New York and Washington, not all international flights proved profitable so, one by one, they were trimmed from the schedule. Soon, a much protracted network served only destinations abroad in Australia, Germany, the United Kingdom and the United States. Over the years, Boeings were completely phased out of the international services and were replaced by an all-Airbus fleet. The introduction of Airbus A340-300 and 600 equipment would eventually prove to be an unwise decision because four-engine airliners were more expensive to operate than long-haul twin-engine equipment like the Boeing 777. By the last few months of 2019, widebody twin-engine Airbus A330 and A350 aircraft and narrow-body Boeing 737 and Airbus A320 variants were serving pruned down destinations in Africa, the Indian Ocean islands, Europe and the United States. Apart from London, Frankfurt, Washington and New York SAA had become an essentially African airline, primarily serving destinations on the continent on which it was based. This had turned out to be something of a dream fulfilled because that is what aviation pioneers like Allister Miller always had in mind—an African airline for the people of Africa. In partnership with local airlines SA Express and SA Airlink—in which SAA had investments— and with its own low cost carrier subsidiary, Mango, in 2019, SAA was serving a total of 36 destinations locally, regionally and abroad, much less than just a few years earlier.

However, with the demise of the apartheid regime and a new managerial takeover by executives selected by the ruling African National Congress (ANC), things had not always gone as smoothly as anticipated. Due to a series of poor decisions, the efficiency of the airline began to suffer. This was made worse by cases of ineptitude by members of its senior management, especially during the period of the corrupt and troubled presidency of Jacob Zuma. In the course of a decade, SAA went through no less than nine Chief Executives, all of whom were expected to try to change its worsening course but with little success. As with so many other government enterprises under Zuma, behind the scenes at SAA fingers had been pilfering the cookie jar. There were bouts of personal clashes in high places and blatant fiscal errors. The airline had steadily built up soaring debt. The last time it had shown a profit was in 2011. Since then it had accumulated losses totaling nearly two billion dollars. As in years past it began to rely even more heavily on anticipated government bailouts and on state-guaranteed debt agreements to remain operational. But by 2019, the ANC government under the new Presidency of Cyril Ramaphosa had had enough. Government aid was no longer to be forthcoming. No more taxpayers' money would be siphoned into an enterprise that simply was not functioning efficiently and was not being able pay its own way. On December 5, 2019, the Board of Directors announced that a notice of 'business rescue' proceedings had been filed with the Companies and Intellectual Properties Commission (CIPC) as per Chapter 6 of the South African Companies Act of 2008. The airline was hemorrhaging money and the only source of potential funding were government coffers which neither Parliament, the Department of Public Enterprises nor the National Treasury were prepared to commit to. The CIPC-appointed individuals in charge of trying to keep the airline flying were Les Matuson of the firm Matuson Associates and Siviwe Dongwana of the auditing and accounting firm Adamantem. Many financial pundits began predicting that the airline would not survive in its existing incarnation. Routes were slashed, most of the fleet was grounded and management and began to speak of retrenchment of the entire staff. But representatives of unions whose members were in the employ of SAA including the South African Transport and Allied Workers' Union (SATAWU), the National Union of Metalworkers of South Africa (NUMSA), the South African Cabin Crew Association (SACCA), the South African Airways Pilots' Association (SAAPA), the National Transport Movement (NTM), the Aviation Union of Southern Africa (AUASA), Solidarity and non-unionized staff flatly rejected the idea of mass lay-offs. There had to be another way. Come what may, they argued, the airline had to be kept operational and all those threatened jobs—4,700 of them, as compared to a peak of 11,000 back in 1996—had to be saved. And then came 2020.

As the year began to unfold, it brought a vicious invisible enemy that forced the entire world to its knees. The outbreak of Covid-19, the coronavirus, mercilessly swept across the planet, bringing everyday life to a standstill. With ruthless rapidity, it killed tens of thousands around the world. Equally catastrophic, it tore the entire global economy to shreds. Like many industries and enterprises, aviation suffered the worst disaster in its history. Already vulnerable, SAA could not have faced a more devastating threat to its existence. The virus heralded the possible death knell of many major carriers on all six continents. By April 2020, the writing seemed to be on the wall for SAA. It began to look like it had reached the end of the line. It cancelled all its flights, including international, regional and domestic services. While the virus held the world captive SAA's flying days were over. In trying to placate the unions and save jobs as well as a genuine desire to resurrect a dying phoenix from the ashes of the past, on May 1, 2020, Pravin Gordhan, the South African Minister of Public Enterprises, officially announced the termination of SAA in its present form and the prospective birth of an entirely new yet very much downsized version of its former self. The plan was summarized in the following statement:

Extraordinary times call for extraordinary measures. The challenges facing South African Airways has required the Leadership of all the stakeholders to rise above the crisis created by both the weaknesses within SAA and COVID 19, and agree on a long-term vision and strategy to mitigate the impact on employees, tourism, the aviation industry and become a catalyst for economic development and job creation. This requires an absolute focus on becoming internationally competitive for safety, quality, and cost. It will not be the old SAA but the beginning of a new journey to a new restructured airline, which will be a proud flagship for South Africa.

And thus it was that, after 86 years—91 if you include the five year existence of its predecessor, Union Airways—SAA came to the end of its incarnation as one of the world's great carriers and the flagship airline of the African skies. Regrettable though these developments unquestionably were, there was much for SAA to be proud of. For 23 consecutive years, it was voted Africa's leading airline by the UK-based World Travel Awards organization. Often operating against enormous odds its achievements and accomplishments had been many. Its efficiency was often the envy of many much larger carriers around the globe. Behind it lay the abiding legacy of that ubiquitous Flying Springbok, the logo that represented the carrier during its most turbulent, controversial yet successful heydays. Fortunately, today that image—the stylized Springbok with its sprouted wings—can be still be seen in the form of a variety of aircraft and other items enshrined in the South African Airways Museum Society's exhibits at Rand Airport in Germiston on the outskirts of Johannesburg. The wonderful collection of aviation memorabilia ensures a lasting tribute to the history of one of the oldest, longest surviving and, at its height, one of the world's most indisputably respected carriers.

No matter what new form the airline may take in years to come, or whether it ceases operations entirely and recedes into the annals of aviation history as so many other great airlines before it, long may the Flying Springbok be remembered.

Acknowledgements

A book like this is not the work of one person. Many contributed to it in a multitude of ways. I want to offer my gratitude to those who have directly or indirectly been part of that process. When I was fortunate enough to produce a series of documentary films to celebrate SAA's fiftieth anniversary four decades ago, my then-production secretary and researcher Esme Jacobson dug up more facts, photographs and documents and located more retired crew members from the airline's early years than I ever thought possible. I thank her for her diligence and dedication. Much of that archived material has found its way into this book. I want to acknowledge the important role played by my late friend and colleague Barney Joffe who ran the English Documentaries Department at the South African Broadcasting Corporation head office in Johannesburg. It was Barney who commissioned me to produce the television series *Springbok in the Sky* in 1983. That project provided invaluable opportunities to interview many personnel from the airline's early days. Barney also helped locate one of the last existing prints of the fascinating SAA publicity documentary *The Blue and Silver Way* that was made in the late thirties. It provided a fascinating overview of the early years of the use of Junkers Ju-52 aircraft by the airline. Marie-Helene Maguire, formerly of SAA's Public Relations Division, was an exceptional guiding light during the production of the television series and helped our team make contact with many airline retirees. She was also instrumental in putting me in touch with the late German pilot Hans Baur in Bavaria who shared his memories and photographs with me. She found, among many others, one of South Africa's first experimental airmail pilots, Rheinhold Ferdinand 'Caspar' Caspareuthus. He was a font of information going back to the pioneering days of Allister Miller and Union Airways, the small airline that eventually became SAA. I am very thankful to John Austin-Williams of the South African Airways Museum Society for the very fruitful interactions we had during the planning phases of this book. I also want to add my very deep admiration to him for being so active in establishing the wonderful South African Airways Museum Society at Rand Airport in Germiston. John connected me with his colleagues Karel Zaayman and the late Steve Morrison who deserves very much credit. As a long-time flight engineer on many different aircraft types with SAA, Steve shared a wealth of interviews, transcripts, stories and anecdotes with me and devoted his undivided attention to reading the evolving manuscript. He was scrupulous about technical detail and provided enormously helpful corrections and suggestions. I am forever indebted to the Transnet Heritage Library for most of the illustrations used in the book. Johanness Haarhoff of Transnet went way beyond the call of duty to root out photographs no matter how obscure or difficult to find in response to my requests and then spent much time checking the manuscript for accuracy and offering insightful advice. I am extremely grateful to Transnet librarian Yolanda Meyer for the tedious months she spent locating and scanning images and transferring them over to me here in California. Without these two people, the book would not be what it is. As doubt and insecurity often clouded my vision as to whether there would be enough international interest in a book about an African airline, I owe thanks to my late friend Fred Silton in Los Angeles for his persistent nagging. He compelled me to tell this story. A special tribute is due to my dear friends Paul and Sharon Boorstin. As exceptionally accomplished writers, their constant encouragement kept me going and helped me finally get the book to my publishers. I want to thank my good friend Wolfgang Schlink for his help in translating some of my collection of German material pertaining to Hitler's personal pilot, Hans Baur. My wife Diana has been an unending source of strength and inspiration. Knowing how much personal history and passion I have vested in the subject, she was an immeasurable source of heartfelt reassurance. I could not have finished the project without her. It would be impossible to list everyone consulted and interviewed during the years it has taken to complete the work, be they pilots, flight engineers, radio operators, navigators, cabin crew and attendants, passengers, ground staff, air traffic controllers, station managers, maintenance technicians, operations staff, airport workers, administrative personnel, equipment suppliers, airplane and engine manufacturers and representatives, subcontractors, public relations consultants, travel agents, military personnel, historians, hobbyists and aviation enthusiasts. This is therefore an expression of very deep gratitude to everyone who so generously and graciously gave of their time and helped bring the project to fruition. The book is above all a tribute to those who contributed to the genesis, development and growth of aviation in Southern Africa and especially to those who were an integral part of South African Airways itself. I salute you all. I thank you for opening your scrapbooks, your memories, your lives and your personal histories to me. Finally, I want to acknowledge the enduring influence and inspiration on my life generated by that wonderful orange tail emblazoned with the much-beloved logo of the springbok with sprouted wings. It will forever remain aloft in my dreams.

Lionel Friedberg
Los Angeles
May, 2020

CHRONOS
BOOKS

HISTORY

Chronos Books is an historical non-fiction imprint. Chronos publishes real history for real people; bringing to life people, places and events in an imaginative, easy-to-digest and accessible way - histories that pass on their stories to a generation of new readers.
If you have enjoyed this book, why not tell other readers by posting a review on your preferred book site.

Recent bestsellers from Chronos Books are:

Lady Katherine Knollys
The Unacknowledged Daughter of King Henry VIII
Sarah-Beth Watkins
A comprehensive account of Katherine Knollys' questionable
paternity, her previously unexplored life in the Tudor court
and her intriguing relationship with Elizabeth I.
Paperback: 978-1-78279-585-8 ebook: 978-1-78279-584-1

Cromwell was Framed
Ireland 1649
Tom Reilly
Revealed: The definitive research that proves the Irish nation
owes Oliver Cromwell a huge posthumous apology for
wrongly convicting him of civilian atrocities in 1649.
Paperback: 978-1-78279-516-2 ebook: 978-1-78279-515-5

Why The CIA Killed JFK and Malcolm X
The Secret Drug Trade in Laos
John Koerner
A new groundbreaking work presenting evidence that the CIA
silenced JFK to protect its secret drug trade in Laos.
Paperback: 978-1-78279-701-2 ebook: 978-1-78279-700-5

The Disappearing Ninth Legion
A Popular History
Mark Olly
The Disappearing Ninth Legion examines hard evidence for the
foundation, development, mysterious disappearance, or possi-
ble continuation of Rome's lost Legion.
Paperback: 978-1-84694-559-5 ebook: 978-1-84694-931-9

Beaten But Not Defeated
Siegfried Moos - A German anti-Nazi who settled in Britain
Merilyn Moos
Siegi Moos, an anti-Nazi and active member of the German
Communist Party, escaped Germany in 1933 and, exiled in
Britain, sought another route to the transformation
of capitalism.
Paperback: 978-1-78279-677-0 ebook: 978-1-78279-676-3

A Schoolboy's Wartime Letters
An evacuee's life in WWII — A Personal Memoir
Geoffrey Iley
A boy writes home during WWII, revealing his own fascinating
story, full of zest for life, information and humour.
Paperback: 978-1-78279-504-9 ebook: 978-1-78279-503-2

The Life & Times of the Real Robyn Hoode
Mark Olly
A journey of discovery. The chronicles of the genuine historical
character, Robyn Hoode, and how he became one of England's
greatest legends.
Paperback: 978-1-78535-059-7 ebook: 978-1-78535-060-3

Readers of ebooks can buy or view any of these bestsellers by clicking on the live link in the title. Most titles are published in paperback and as an ebook. Paperbacks are available in traditional bookshops. Both print and ebook formats are available online.

Find more titles and sign up to our readers' newsletter at
http://www.johnhuntpublishing.com/history-home

Follow us on Facebook at
https://www.facebook.com/ChronosBooks

and Twitter at https://twitter.com/ChronosBooks

Printed and bound by CPI Group (UK) Ltd, Croydon, CR0 4YY

29/01/2025

01827999-0003